So Sweet

Story and Art by
Amu Meguro

Contents

Story Thus Far

Soon after starting high school, the fearsome-looking Onise asks Nao to be his girlfriend. At first Nao is afraid, but once she discovers that Onise is actually a gentle soul, Nao asks him out and their blissful relationship begins.

In the middle of the sports festival, Onise's friend Futami tells Nao he's fallen for her. Nao's love for Onise never wavers, and Futami and Nao remain friends. ♥

Later, everyone discovers that Yashiro has a boyfriend in college who cheats on her, which causes Misaki and Yashiro to get into an argument. When Misaki comes to apologize, he ends up confessing his feelings to her! And he tells off her boyfriend.

After listening to Misaki, Yashiro comes to terms with her true feelings about the situation and breaks up with her boyfriend. But is everything settled?!

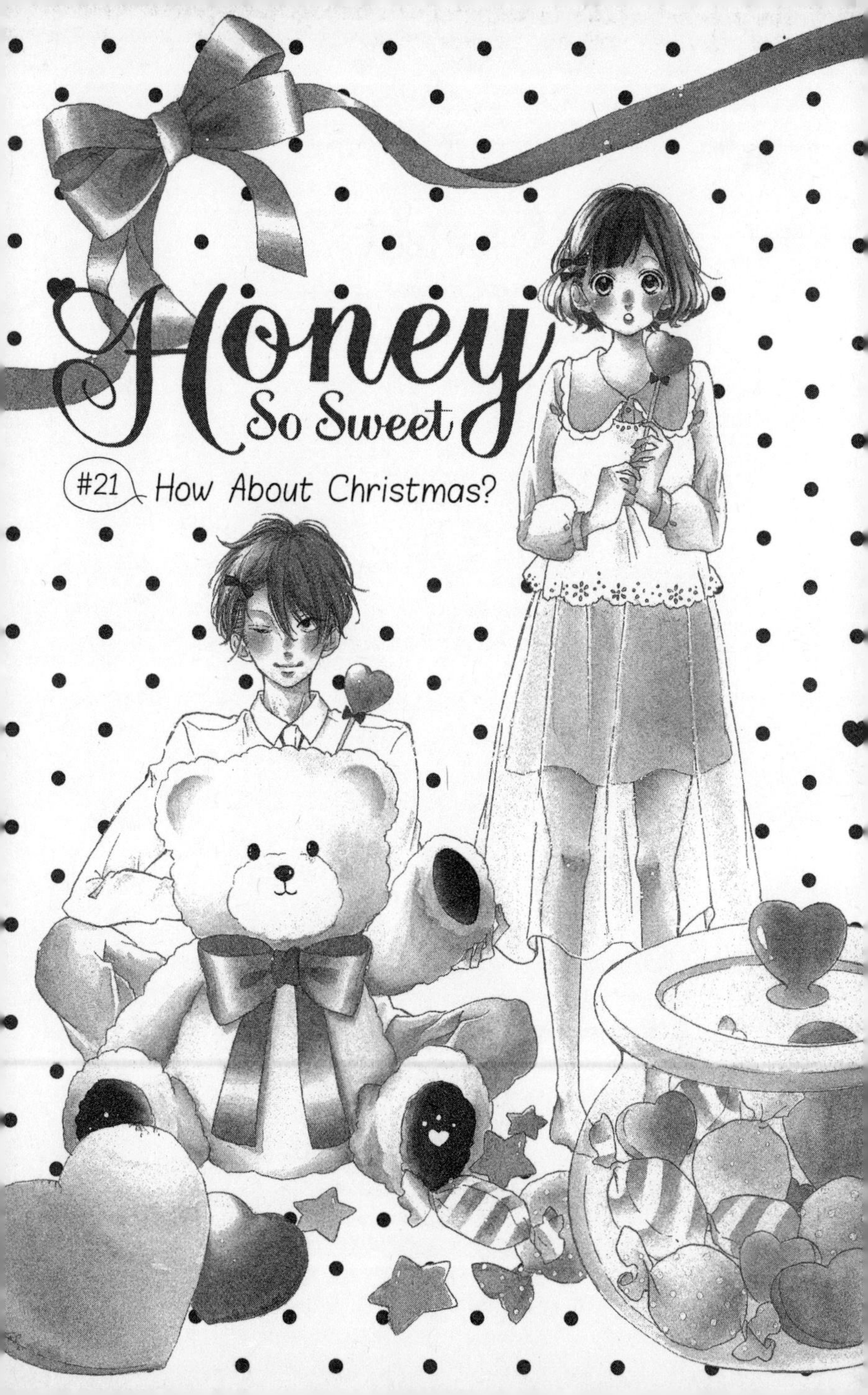
Honey So Sweet
#21 How About Christmas?

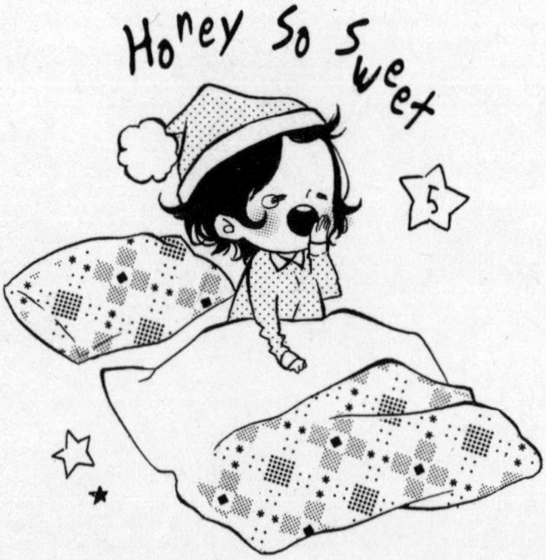
Honey So Sweet
5

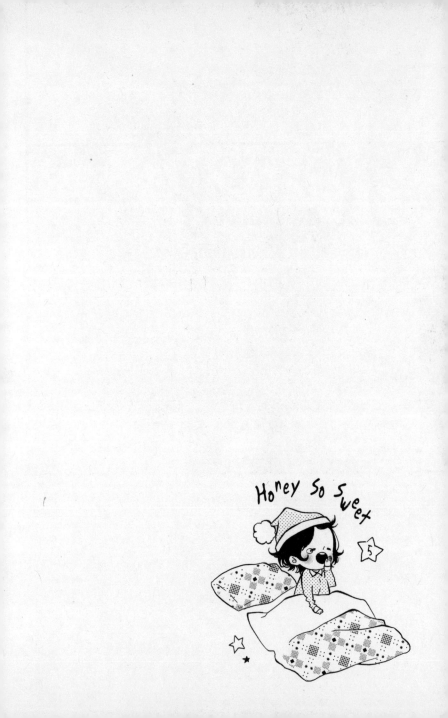

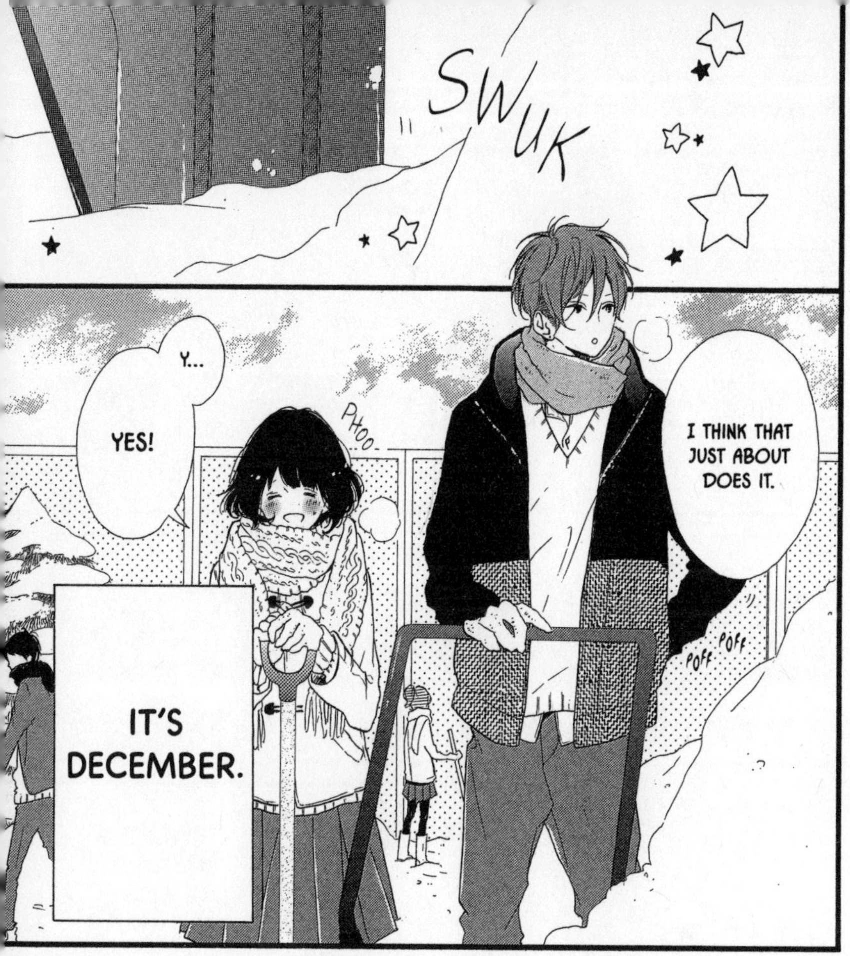
SWUK
I THINK THAT JUST ABOUT DOES IT.
POFF POFF
PHOO
Y...
YES!
IT'S DECEMBER.

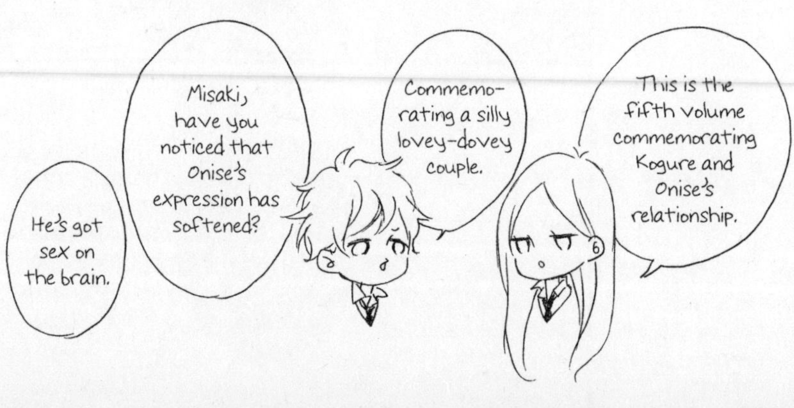
This is the fifth volume commemorating Kogure and Onise's relationship.
Commemorating a silly lovey-dovey couple.
Misaki, have you noticed that Onise's expression has softened?
He's got sex on the brain.

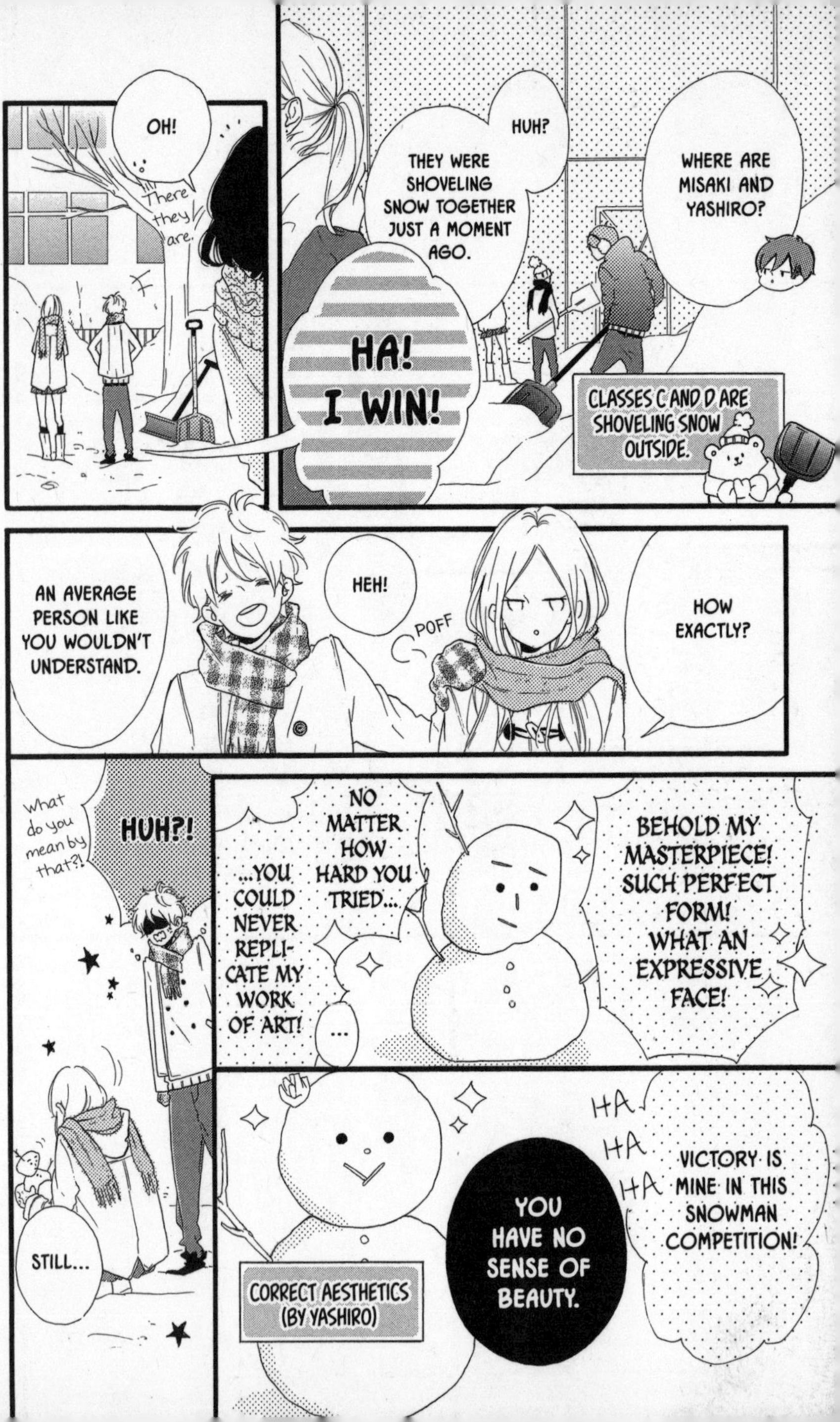
WHERE ARE MISAKI AND YASHIRO?
HUH?
THEY WERE SHOVELING SNOW TOGETHER JUST A MOMENT AGO.
CLASSES C AND D ARE SHOVELING SNOW OUTSIDE.
OH!
There they are.
HA! I WIN!
HOW EXACTLY?
POFF
HEH!
AN AVERAGE PERSON LIKE YOU WOULDN'T UNDERSTAND.
BEHOLD MY MASTERPIECE! SUCH PERFECT FORM! WHAT AN EXPRESSIVE FACE!
NO MATTER HOW HARD YOU TRIED...
...YOU COULD NEVER REPLICATE MY WORK OF ART!
...
VICTORY IS MINE IN THIS SNOWMAN COMPETITION!
HA HA HA
YOU HAVE NO SENSE OF BEAUTY.
CORRECT AESTHETICS (BY YASHIRO)
HUH?!
What do you mean by that?!
STILL...

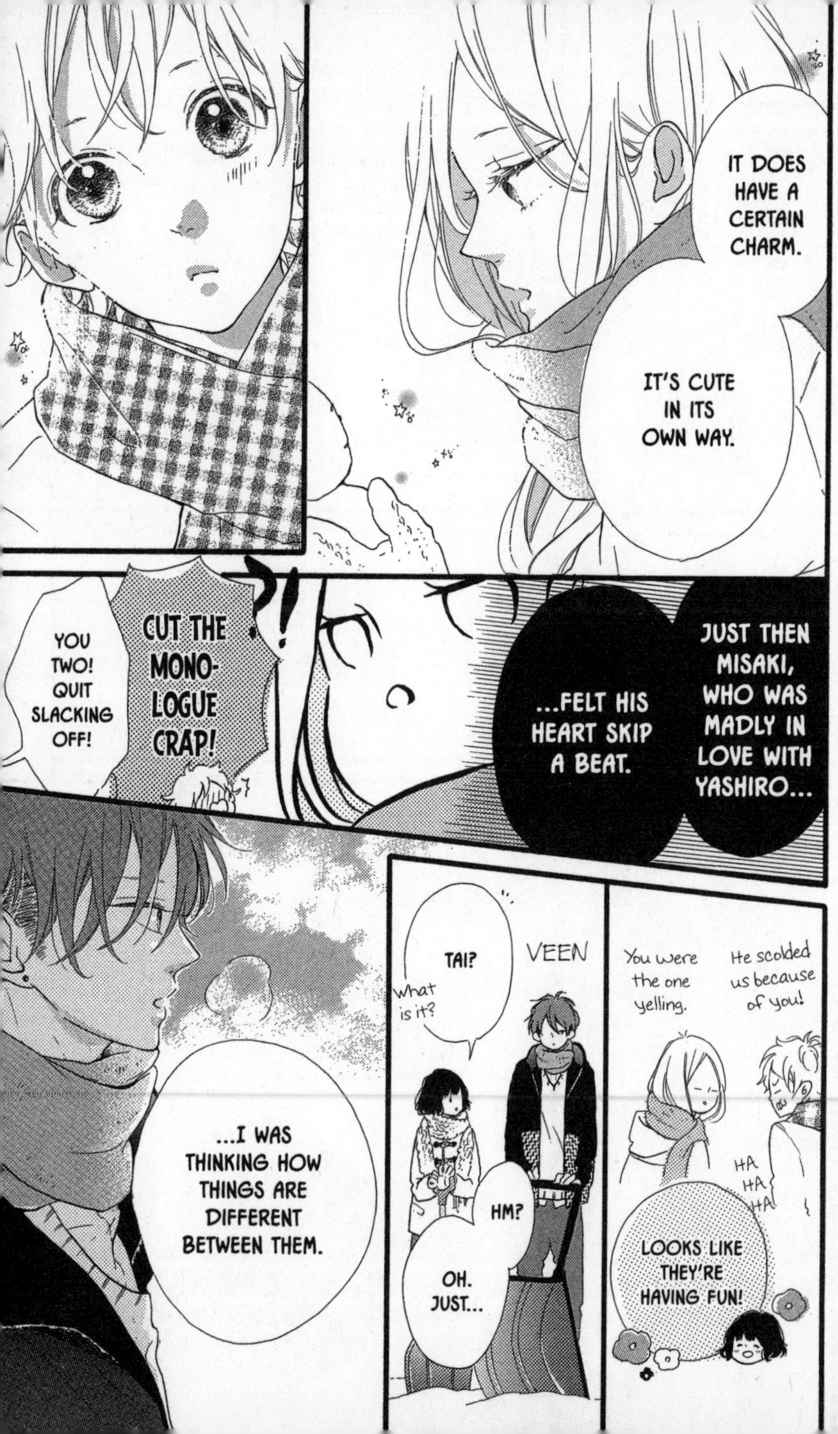
IT DOES HAVE A CERTAIN CHARM.
IT'S CUTE IN ITS OWN WAY.
JUST THEN MISAKI, WHO WAS MADLY IN LOVE WITH YASHIRO...
...FELT HIS HEART SKIP A BEAT.
?!
CUT THE MONO-LOGUE CRAP!
YOU TWO! QUIT SLACKING OFF!
He scolded us because of you!
You were the one yelling.
HA HA HA
LOOKS LIKE THEY'RE HAVING FUN!
VEEN
TAI?
What is it?
HM?
OH. JUST...
...I WAS THINKING HOW THINGS ARE DIFFERENT BETWEEN THEM.

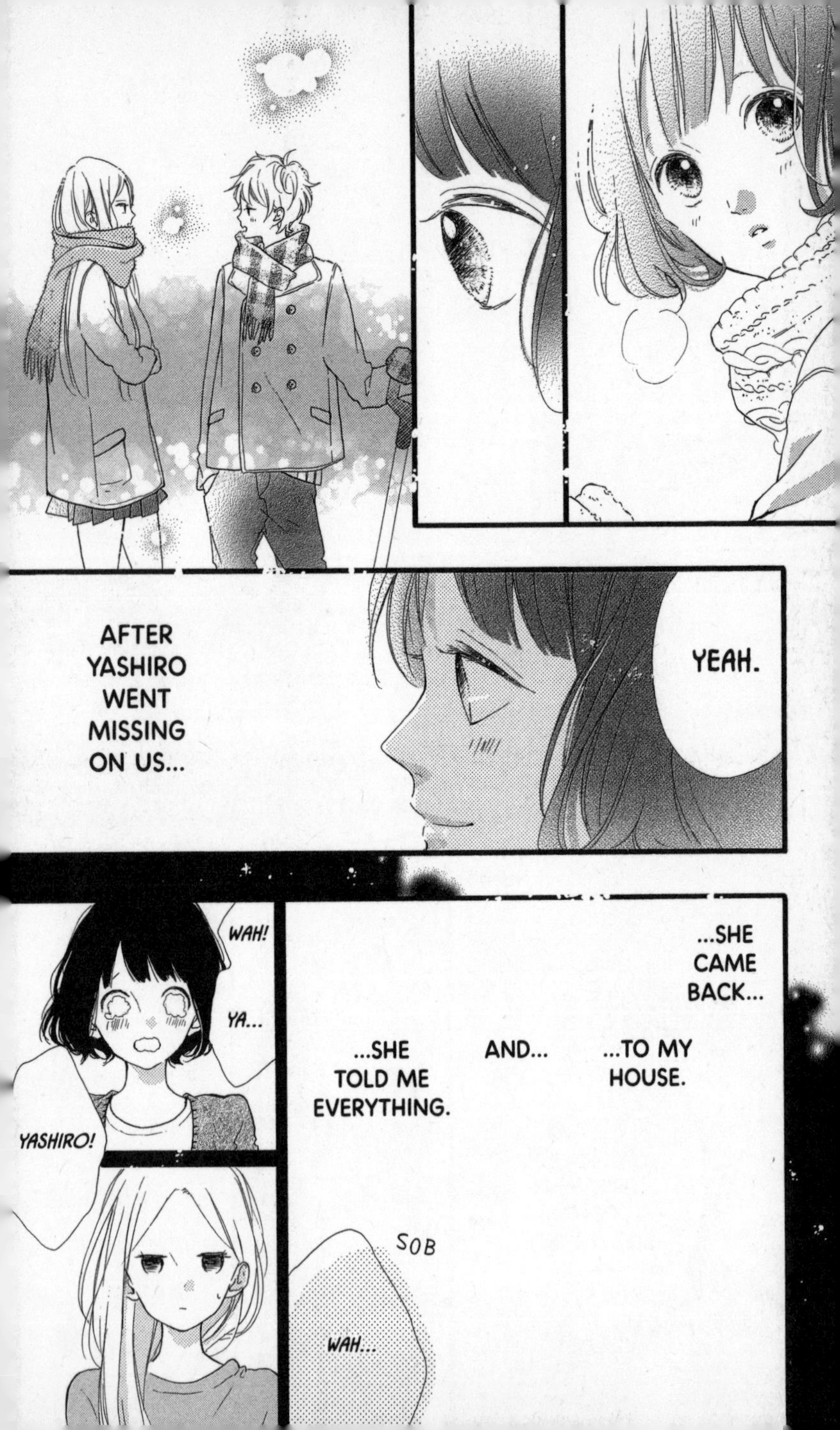

AFTER YASHIRO WENT MISSING ON US...
YEAH.
...SHE CAME BACK...
...TO MY HOUSE.
AND...
...SHE TOLD ME EVERYTHING.
SOB
WAH...
WAH!
YA...
YASHIRO!

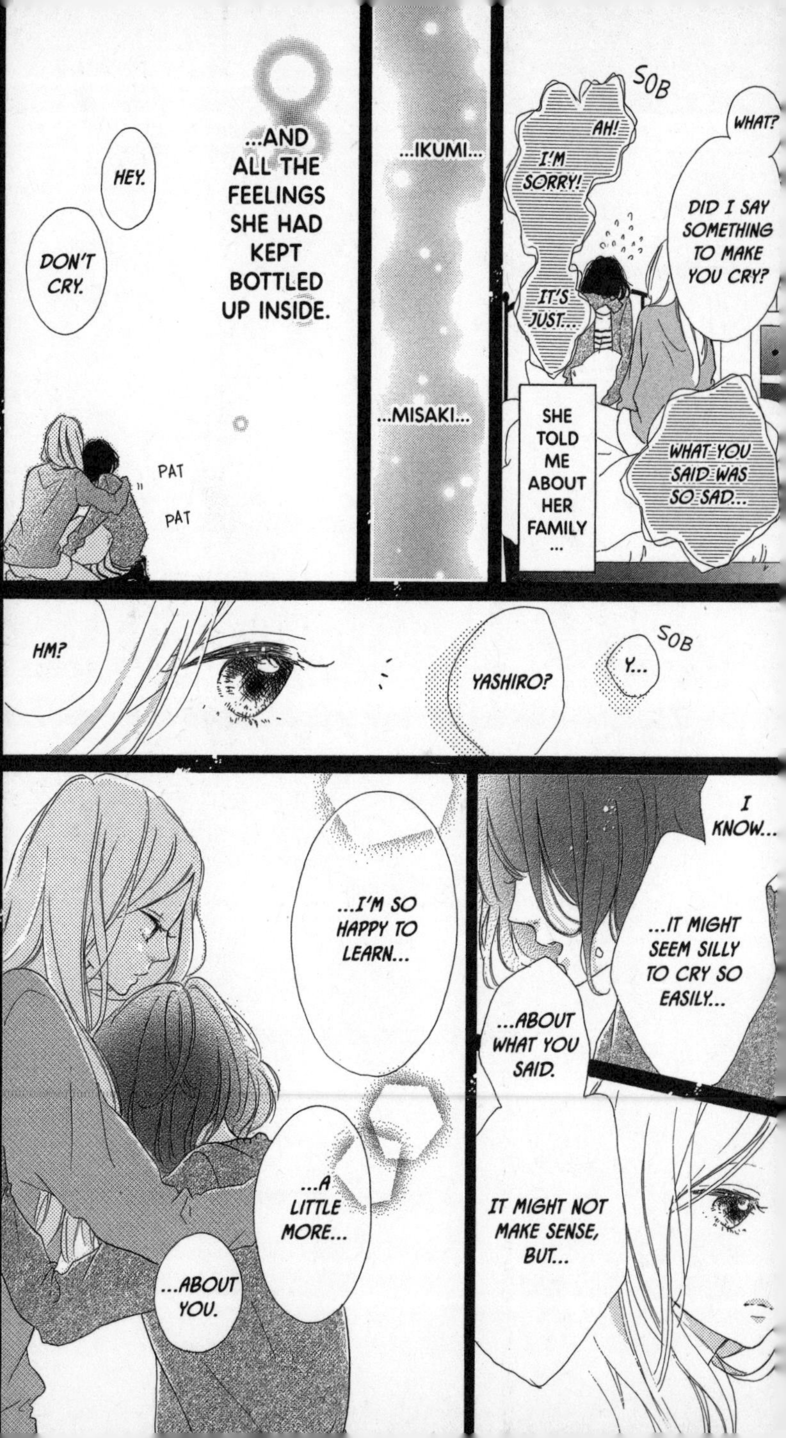
SOB
WHAT?
DID I SAY SOMETHING TO MAKE YOU CRY?
AH! I'M SORRY!
IT'S JUST...
WHAT YOU SAID WAS SO SAD...
SHE TOLD ME ABOUT HER FAMILY...
...IKUMI...
...MISAKI...
...AND ALL THE FEELINGS SHE HAD KEPT BOTTLED UP INSIDE.
HEY.
DON'T CRY.
PAT
PAT
SOB
Y...
YASHIRO?
HM?
I KNOW...
...IT MIGHT SEEM SILLY TO CRY SO EASILY...
...ABOUT WHAT YOU SAID.
IT MIGHT NOT MAKE SENSE, BUT...
...I'M SO HAPPY TO LEARN...
...A LITTLE MORE...
...ABOUT YOU.

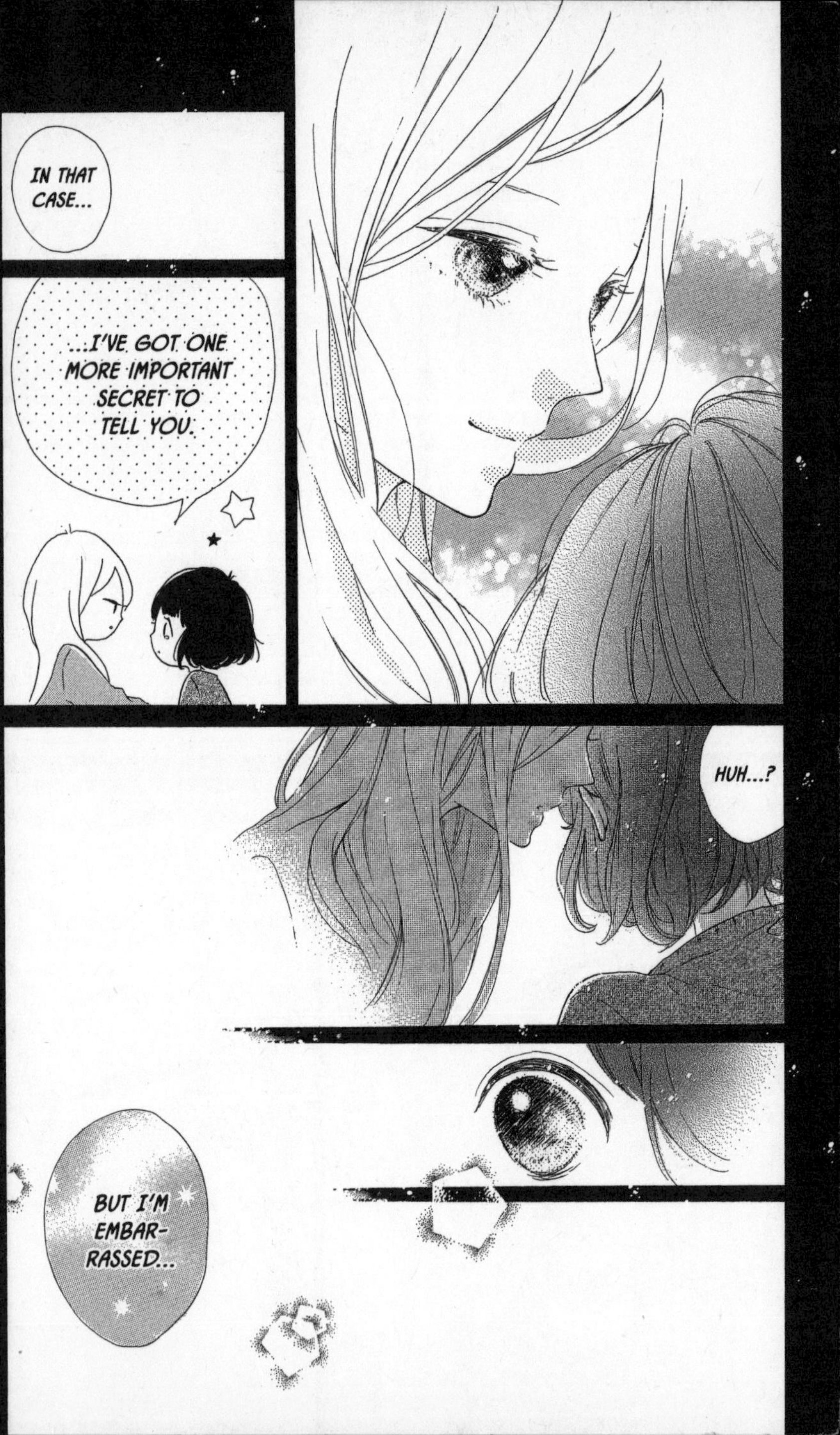
IN THAT CASE...
...I'VE GOT ONE MORE IMPORTANT SECRET TO TELL YOU.
HUH...?
BUT I'M EMBARRASSED...

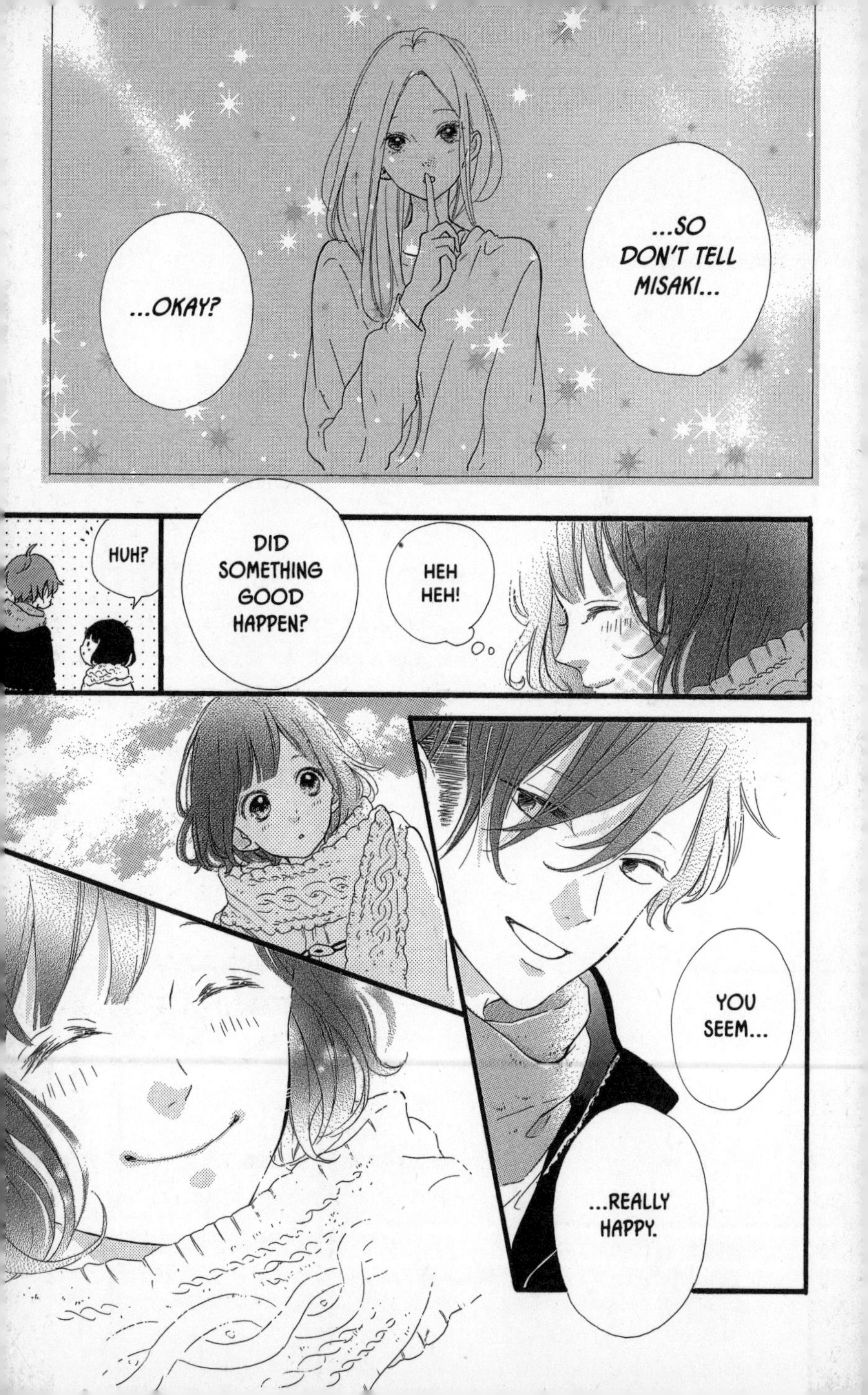
...SO DON'T TELL MISAKI...
...OKAY?
HEH HEH!
DID SOMETHING GOOD HAPPEN?
HUH?
YOU SEEM...
...REALLY HAPPY.

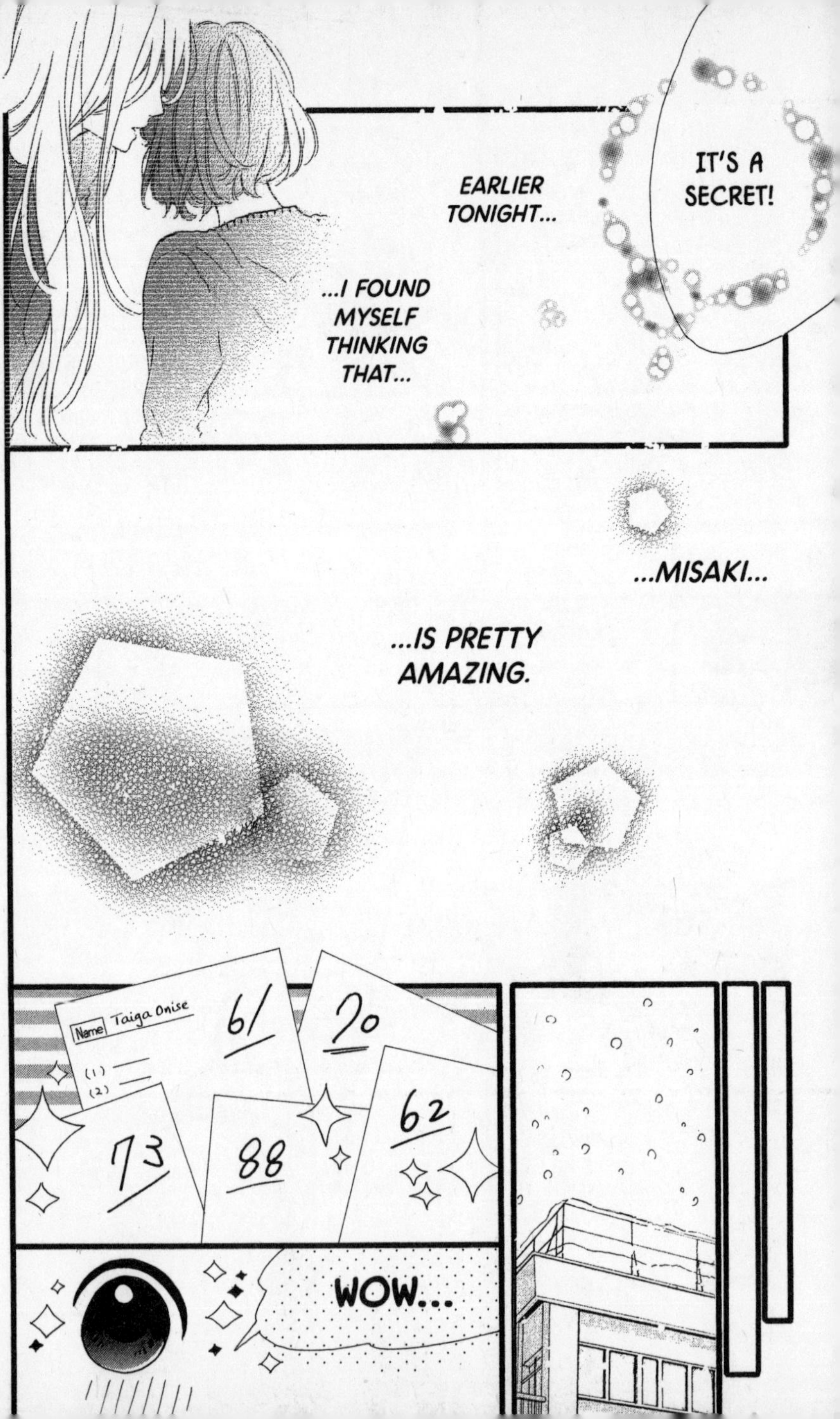
IT'S A SECRET!
EARLIER TONIGHT...
...I FOUND MYSELF THINKING THAT...
...MISAKI...
...IS PRETTY AMAZING.
Name Taiga Onise
(1)
(2)
61
70
62
88
73
WOW...

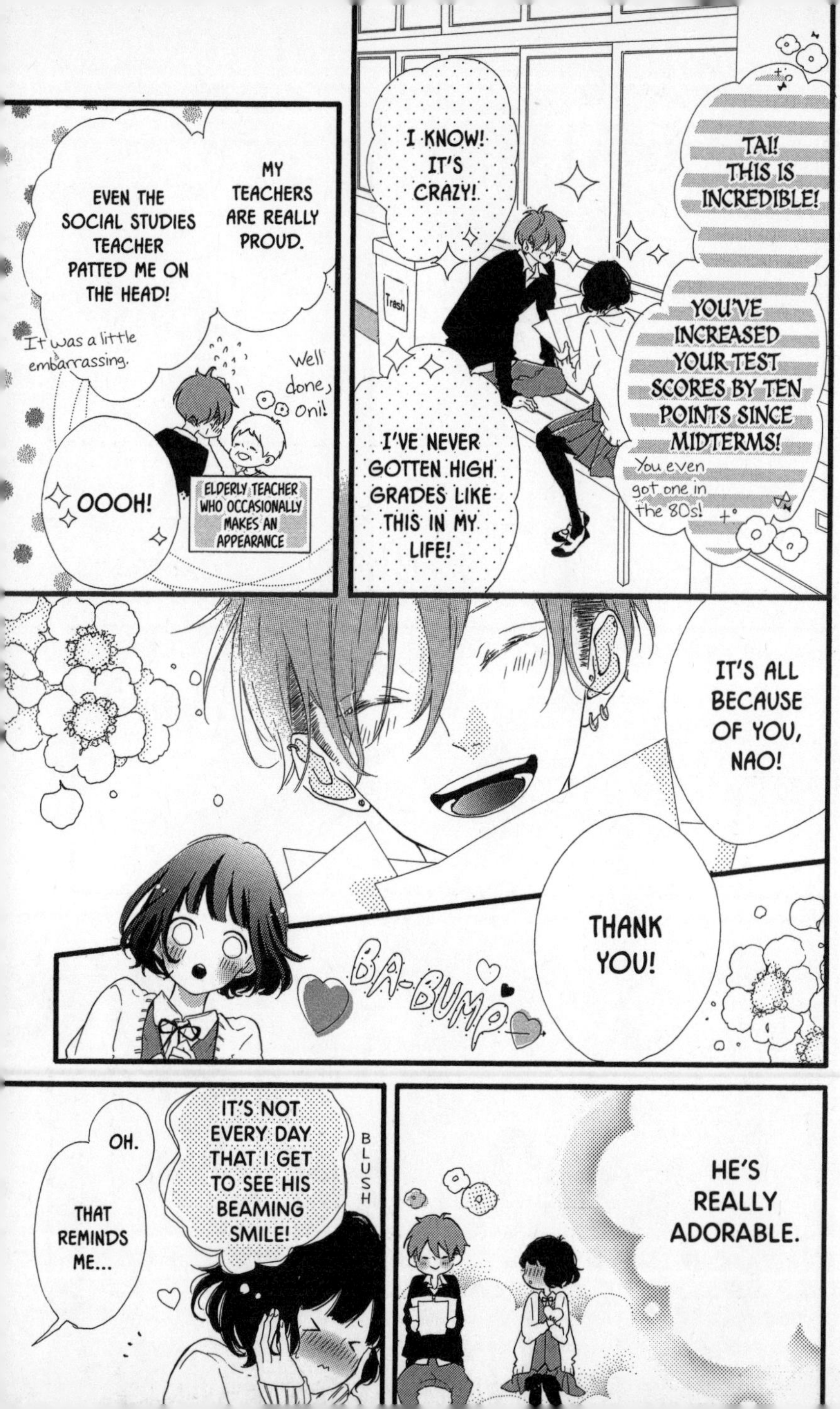
TAI! THIS IS INCREDIBLE!
YOU'VE INCREASED YOUR TEST SCORES BY TEN POINTS SINCE MIDTERMS!
You even got one in the 80s!
I KNOW! IT'S CRAZY!
I'VE NEVER GOTTEN HIGH GRADES LIKE THIS IN MY LIFE!
Trash
MY TEACHERS ARE REALLY PROUD.
EVEN THE SOCIAL STUDIES TEACHER PATTED ME ON THE HEAD!
It was a little embarrassing.
Well done, Oni!
ELDERLY TEACHER WHO OCCASIONALLY MAKES AN APPEARANCE
OOOH!
IT'S ALL BECAUSE OF YOU, NAO!
THANK YOU!
BA-BUMP
HE'S REALLY ADORABLE.
IT'S NOT EVERY DAY THAT I GET TO SEE HIS BEAMING SMILE!
BLUSH
OH.
THAT REMINDS ME...

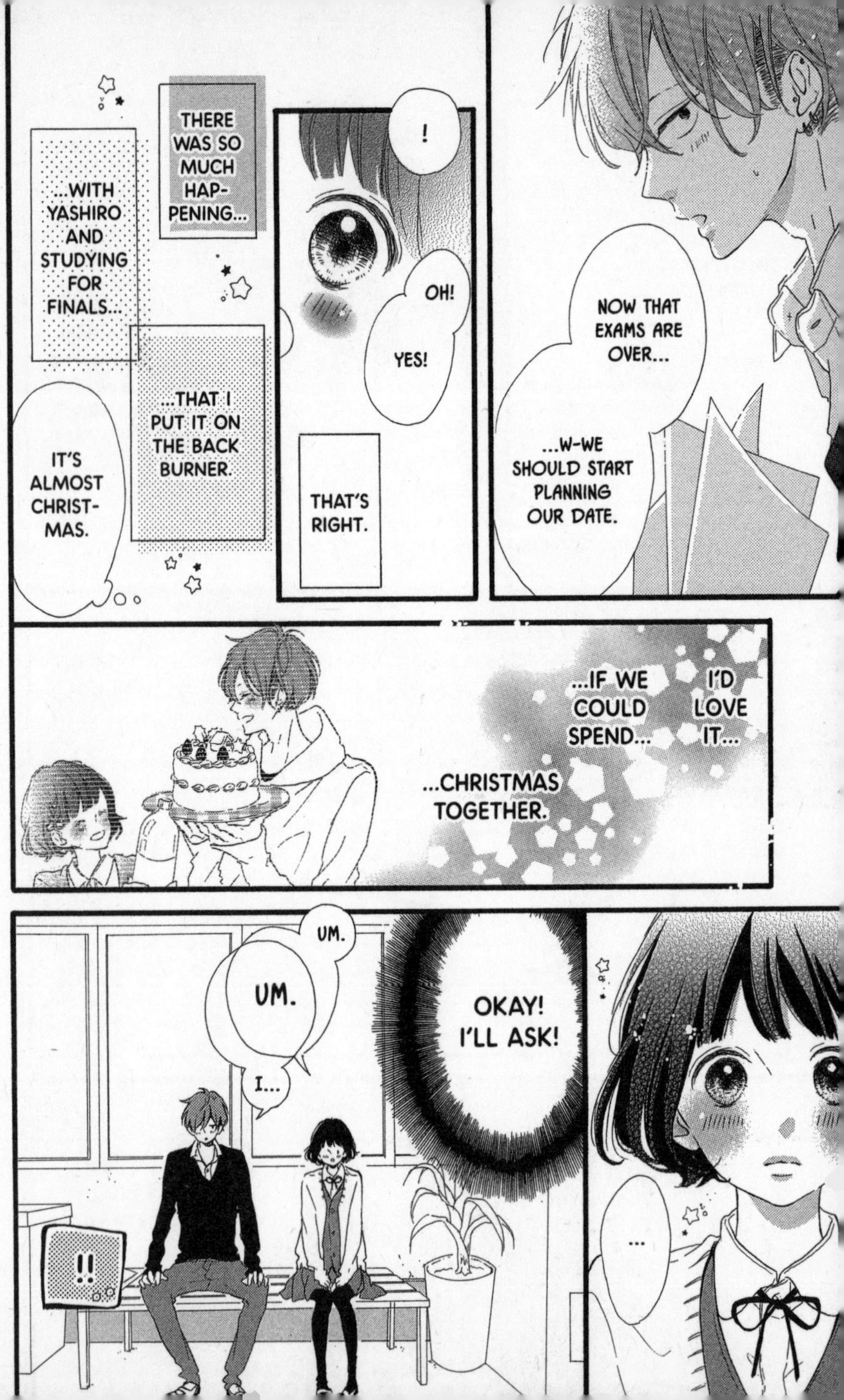
NOW THAT EXAMS ARE OVER...
...W-WE SHOULD START PLANNING OUR DATE.
!
OH!
YES!
THAT'S RIGHT.
THERE WAS SO MUCH HAP-PENING...
...WITH YASHIRO AND STUDYING FOR FINALS...
...THAT I PUT IT ON THE BACK BURNER.
IT'S ALMOST CHRIST-MAS.
I'D LOVE IT...
...IF WE COULD SPEND...
...CHRISTMAS TOGETHER.
...
OKAY! I'LL ASK!
UM.
UM.
I...
!!

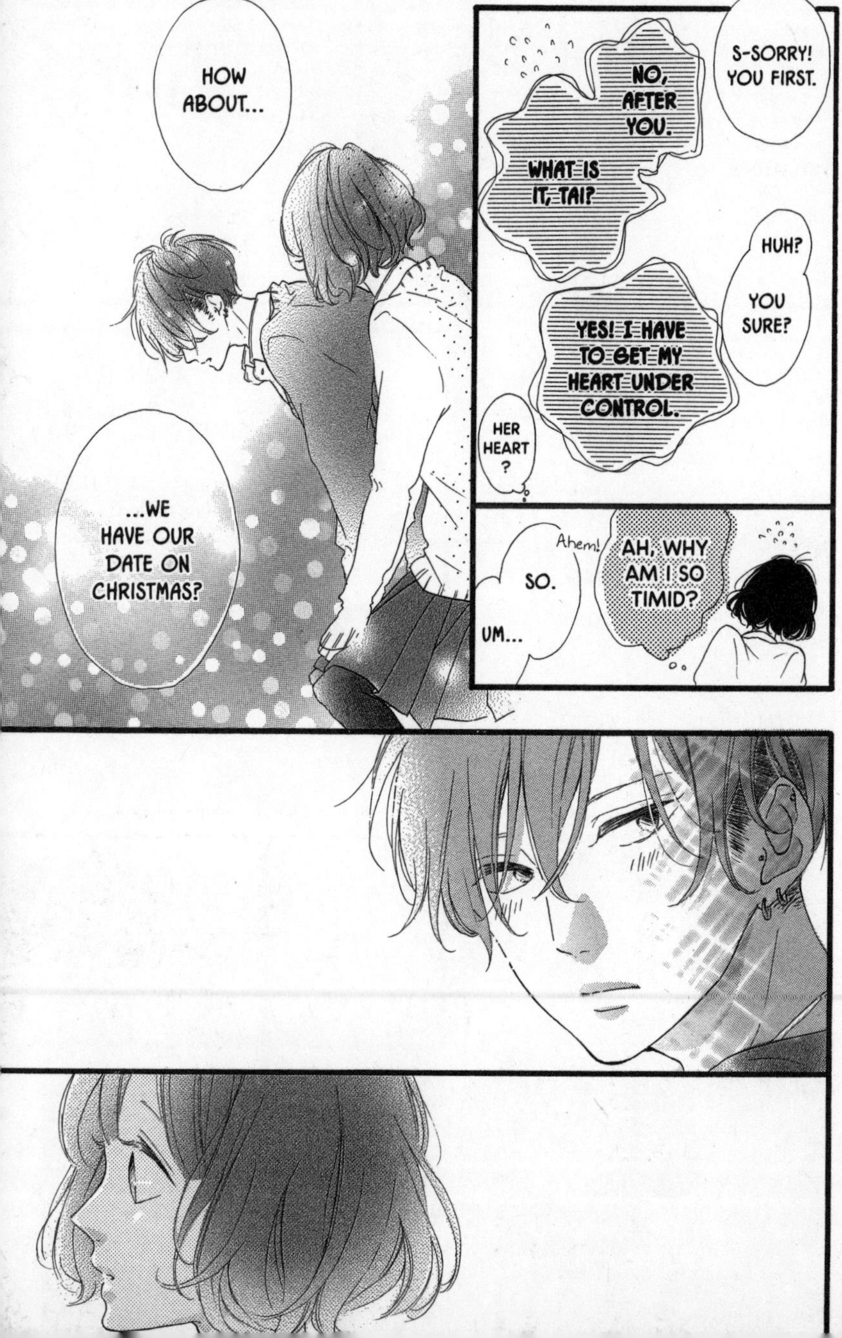
S-SORRY! YOU FIRST.
NO, AFTER YOU.
WHAT IS IT, TAI?
HUH? YOU SURE?
YES! I HAVE TO GET MY HEART UNDER CONTROL.
HER HEART?
AH, WHY AM I SO TIMID?
Ahem!
SO. UM...
HOW ABOUT...
...WE HAVE OUR DATE ON CHRISTMAS?

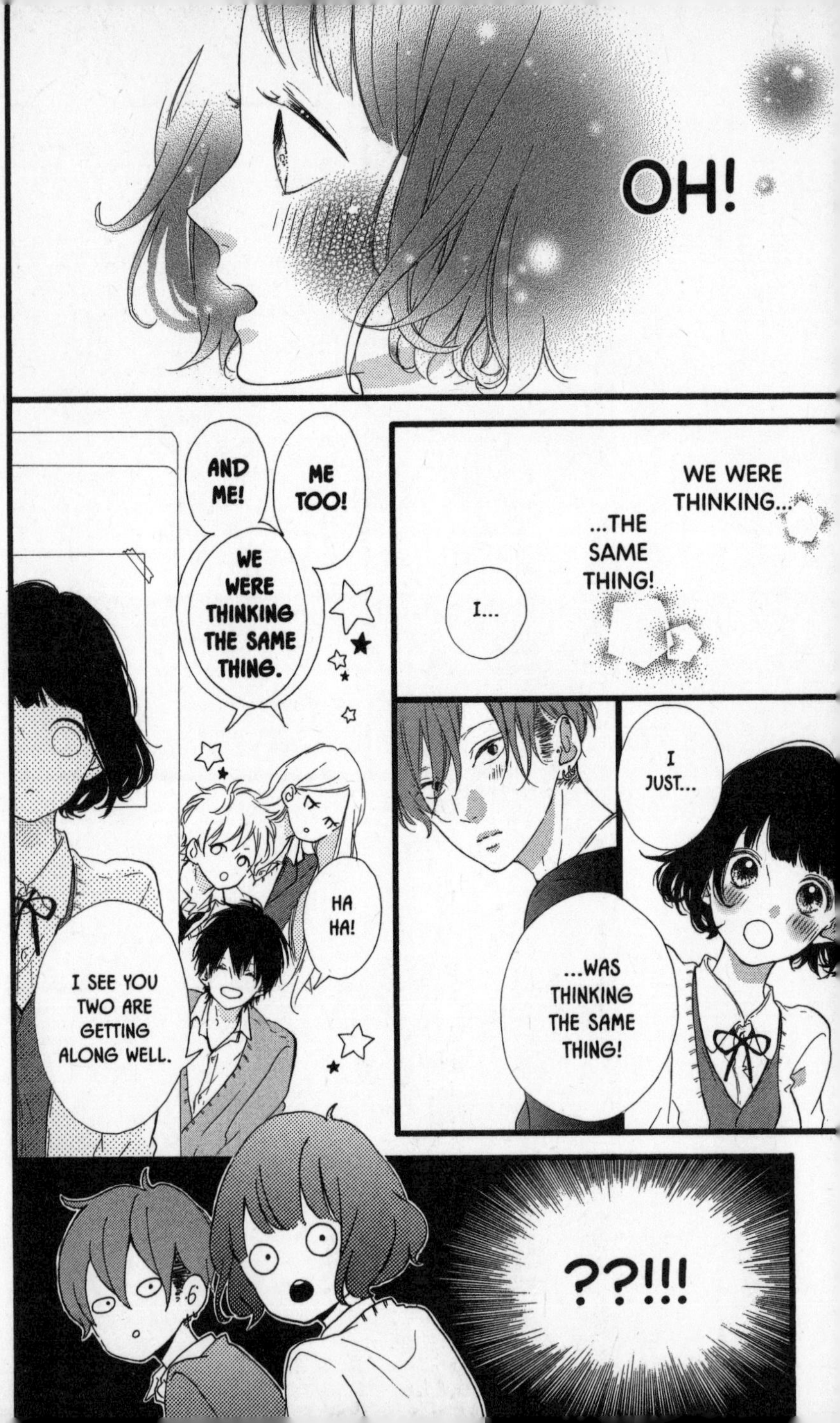
OH!
WE WERE THINKING...
...THE SAME THING!
I...
I JUST...
...WAS THINKING THE SAME THING!
ME TOO!
AND ME!
WE WERE THINKING THE SAME THING.
HA HA!
I SEE YOU TWO ARE GETTING ALONG WELL.
??!!!

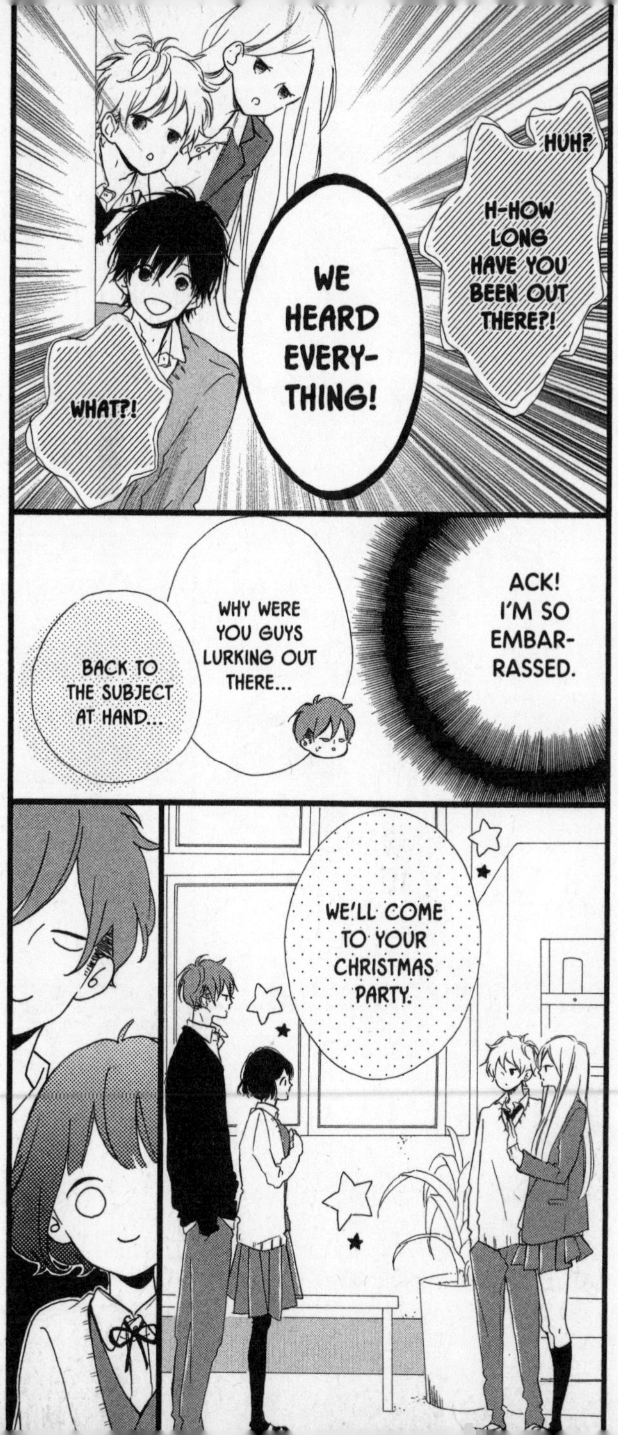
HUH?
H-HOW LONG HAVE YOU BEEN OUT THERE?!
WE HEARD EVERY-THING!
WHAT?!
ACK! I'M SO EMBAR-RASSED.
WHY WERE YOU GUYS LURKING OUT THERE...
BACK TO THE SUBJECT AT HAND...
WE'LL COME TO YOUR CHRISTMAS PARTY.

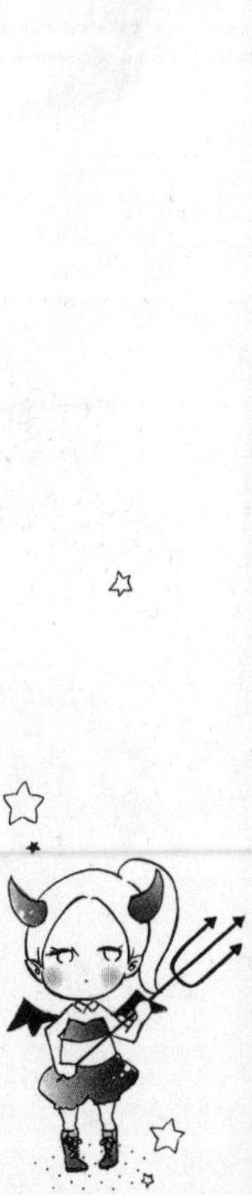

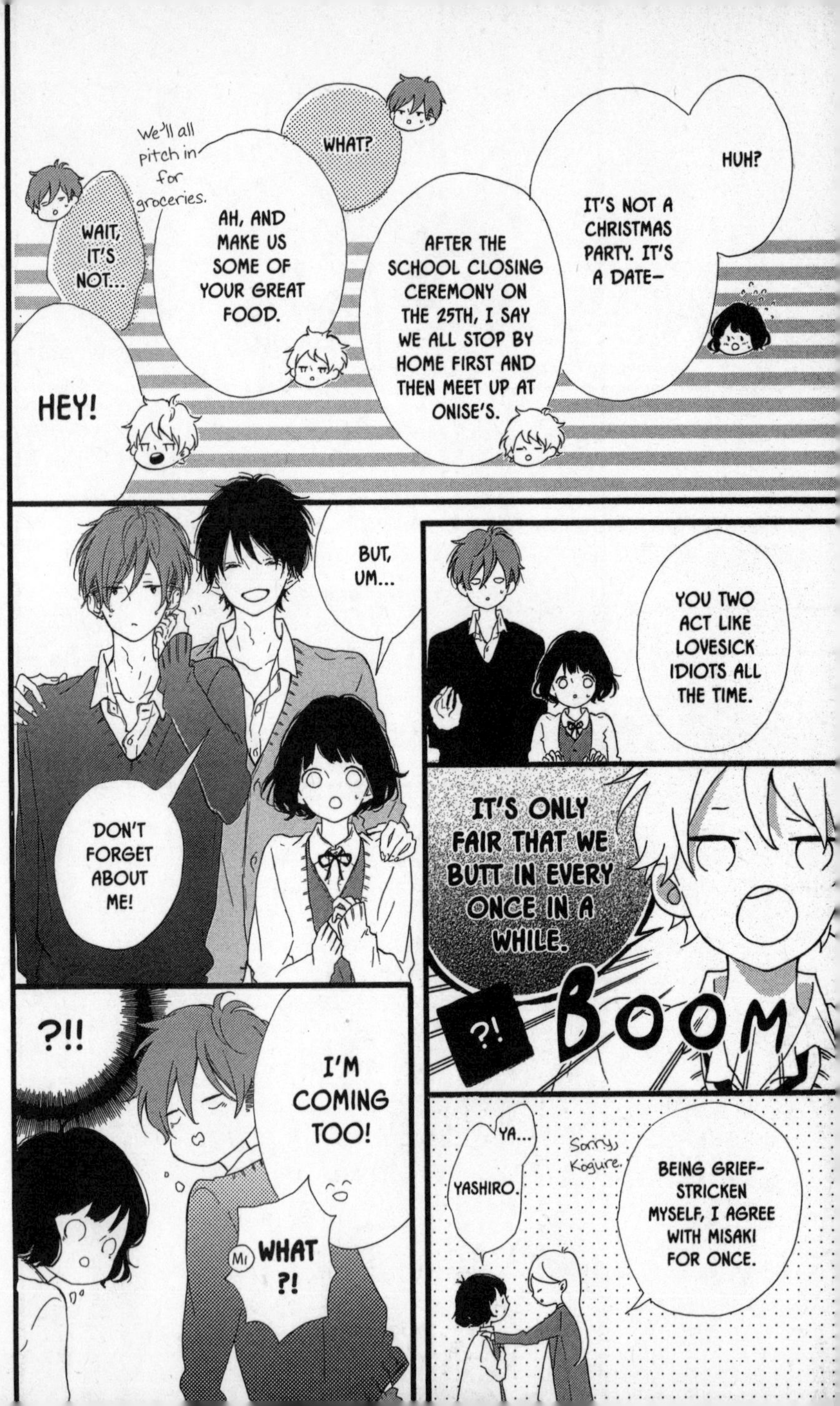
HUH?
IT'S NOT A CHRISTMAS PARTY. IT'S A DATE—
WHAT?
AFTER THE SCHOOL CLOSING CEREMONY ON THE 25TH, I SAY WE ALL STOP BY HOME FIRST AND THEN MEET UP AT ONISE'S.
AH, AND MAKE US SOME OF YOUR GREAT FOOD.
We'll all pitch in for groceries.
WAIT, IT'S NOT...
HEY!
YOU TWO ACT LIKE LOVESICK IDIOTS ALL THE TIME.
IT'S ONLY FAIR THAT WE BUTT IN EVERY ONCE IN A WHILE.
?!
BOOM
BUT, UM...
DON'T FORGET ABOUT ME!
BEING GRIEF-STRICKEN MYSELF, I AGREE WITH MISAKI FOR ONCE.
Sorry, Kogure.
YA...
YASHIRO.
?!!
I'M COMING TOO!
MI
WHAT ?!

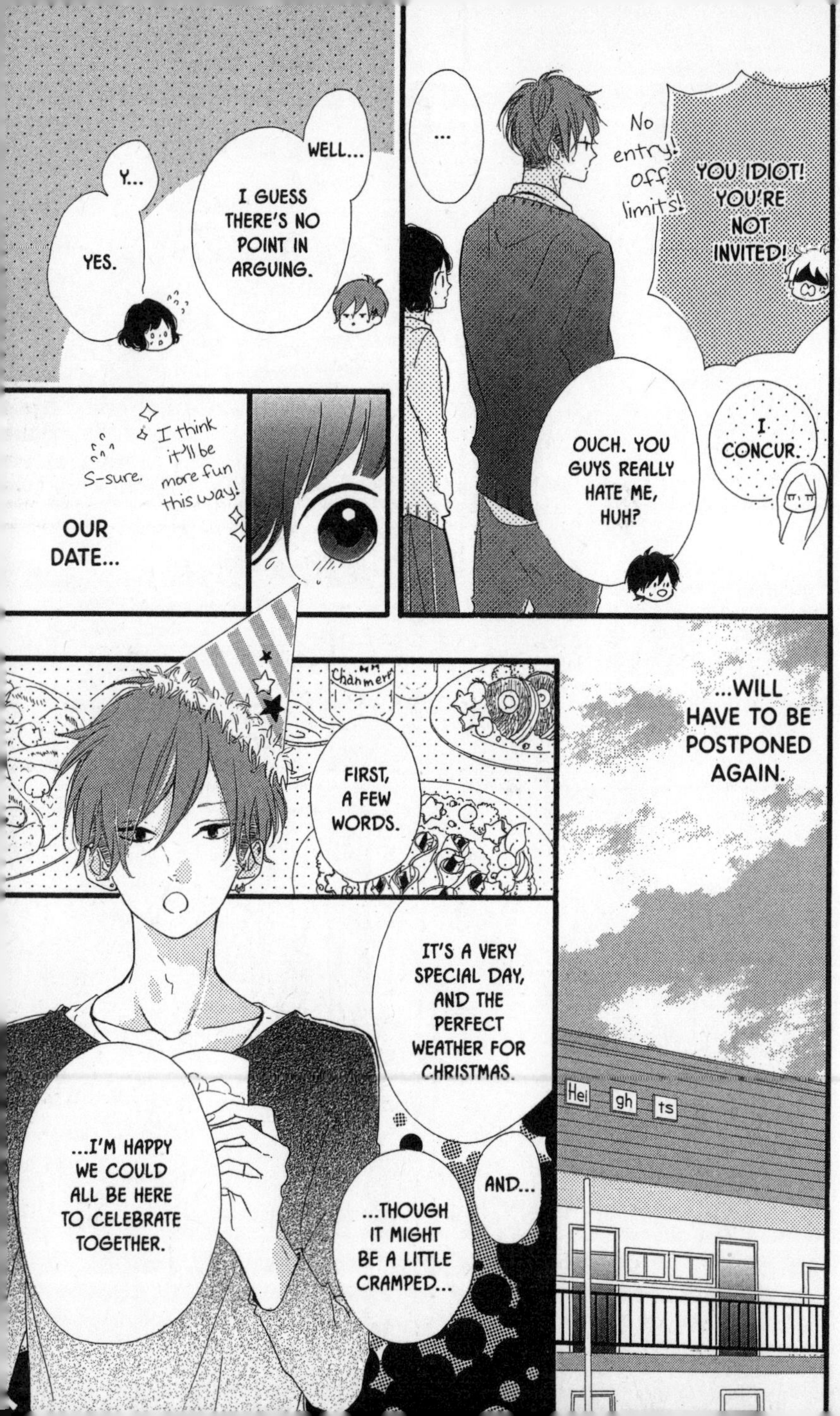
YOU IDIOT! YOU'RE NOT INVITED!
No entry! Off limits!
...
I CONCUR.
OUCH. YOU GUYS REALLY HATE ME, HUH?
WELL... I GUESS THERE'S NO POINT IN ARGUING.
Y... YES.
I think it'll be more fun this way!
S-sure.
OUR DATE...
...WILL HAVE TO BE POSTPONED AGAIN.
FIRST, A FEW WORDS.
IT'S A VERY SPECIAL DAY, AND THE PERFECT WEATHER FOR CHRISTMAS.
Hei gh ts
AND...
...THOUGH IT MIGHT BE A LITTLE CRAMPED...
...I'M HAPPY WE COULD ALL BE HERE TO CELEBRATE TOGETHER.

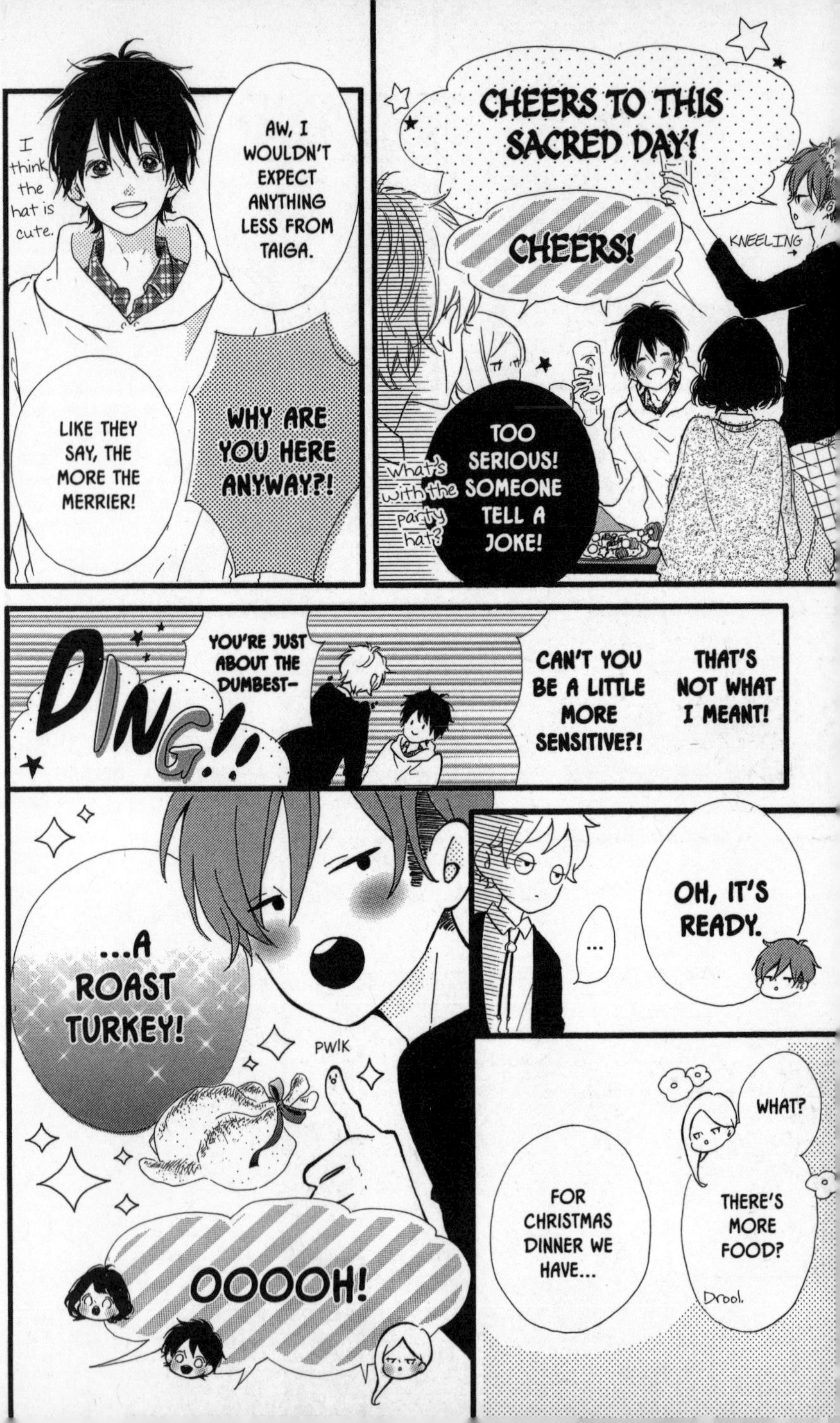
CHEERS TO THIS SACRED DAY!
KNEELING
CHEERS!
TOO SERIOUS! SOMEONE TELL A JOKE!
What's with the party hat?
AW, I WOULDN'T EXPECT ANYTHING LESS FROM TAIGA.
I think the hat is cute.
WHY ARE YOU HERE ANYWAY?!
LIKE THEY SAY, THE MORE THE MERRIER!
THAT'S NOT WHAT I MEANT!
CAN'T YOU BE A LITTLE MORE SENSITIVE?!
YOU'RE JUST ABOUT THE DUMBEST—
DING!!
OH, IT'S READY.
...
WHAT?
THERE'S MORE FOOD?
Drool.
FOR CHRISTMAS DINNER WE HAVE...
...A ROAST TURKEY!
PWIK
OOOOH!

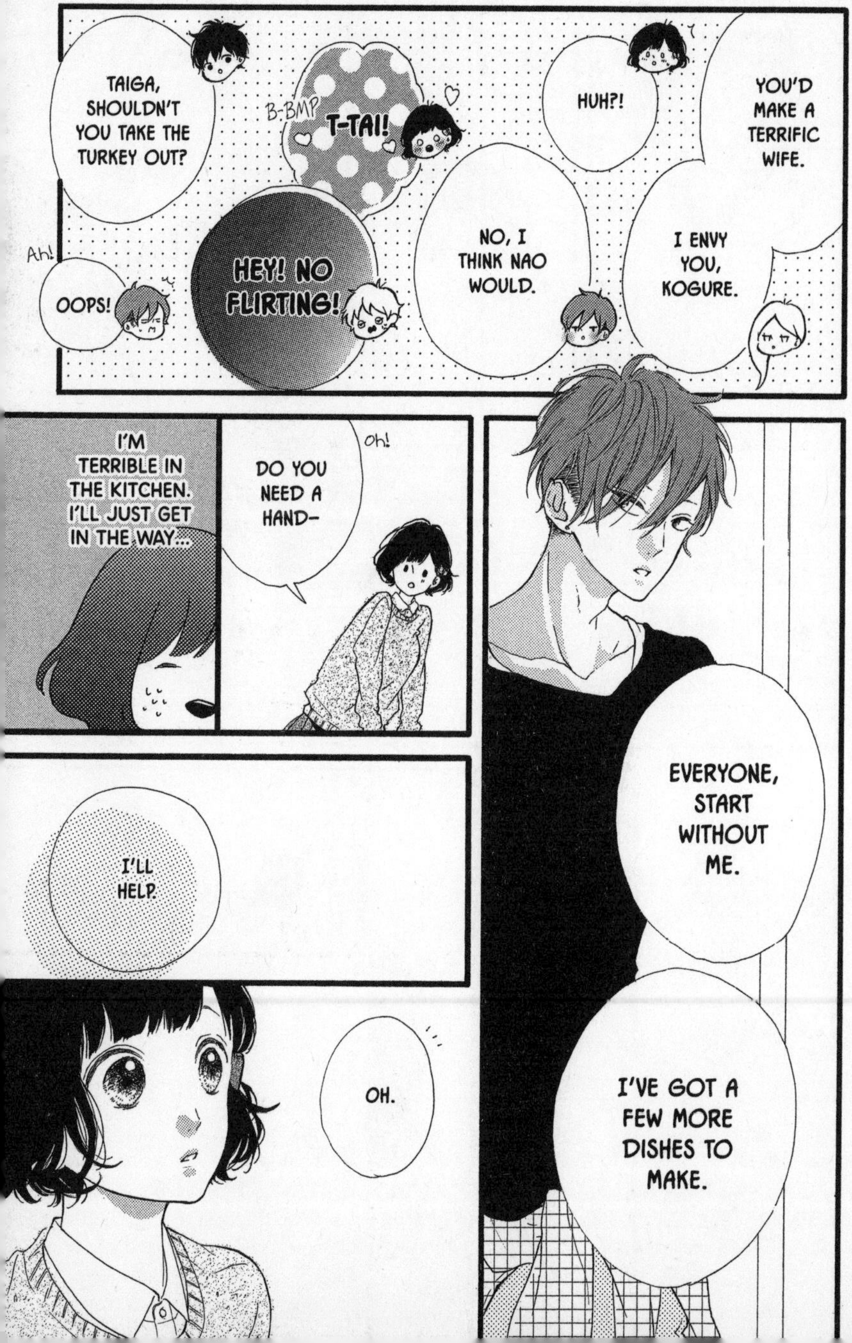
YOU'D MAKE A TERRIFIC WIFE.
I ENVY YOU, KOGURE.
HUH?!
NO, I THINK NAO WOULD.
T-TAI!
B-BMP
HEY! NO FLIRTING!
TAIGA, SHOULDN'T YOU TAKE THE TURKEY OUT?
Ah!
OOPS!
EVERYONE, START WITHOUT ME.
I'VE GOT A FEW MORE DISHES TO MAKE.
Oh!
DO YOU NEED A HAND—
I'M TERRIBLE IN THE KITCHEN. I'LL JUST GET IN THE WAY...
I'LL HELP.
OH.

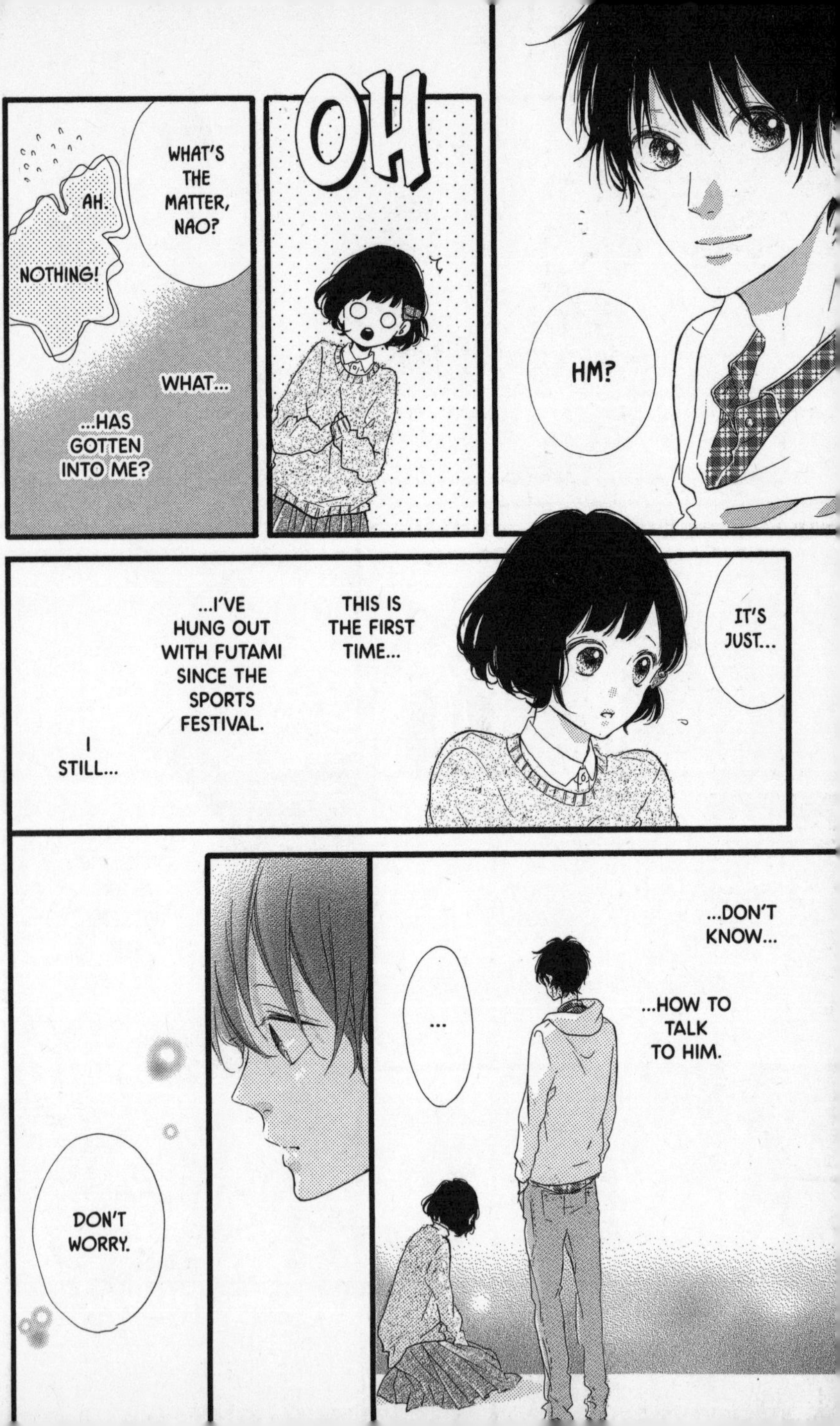
HM?
OH
WHAT'S THE MATTER, NAO?
AH.
NOTHING!
WHAT...
...HAS GOTTEN INTO ME?
IT'S JUST...
THIS IS THE FIRST TIME...
...I'VE HUNG OUT WITH FUTAMI SINCE THE SPORTS FESTIVAL.
I STILL...
...DON'T KNOW...
...HOW TO TALK TO HIM.
...
DON'T WORRY.

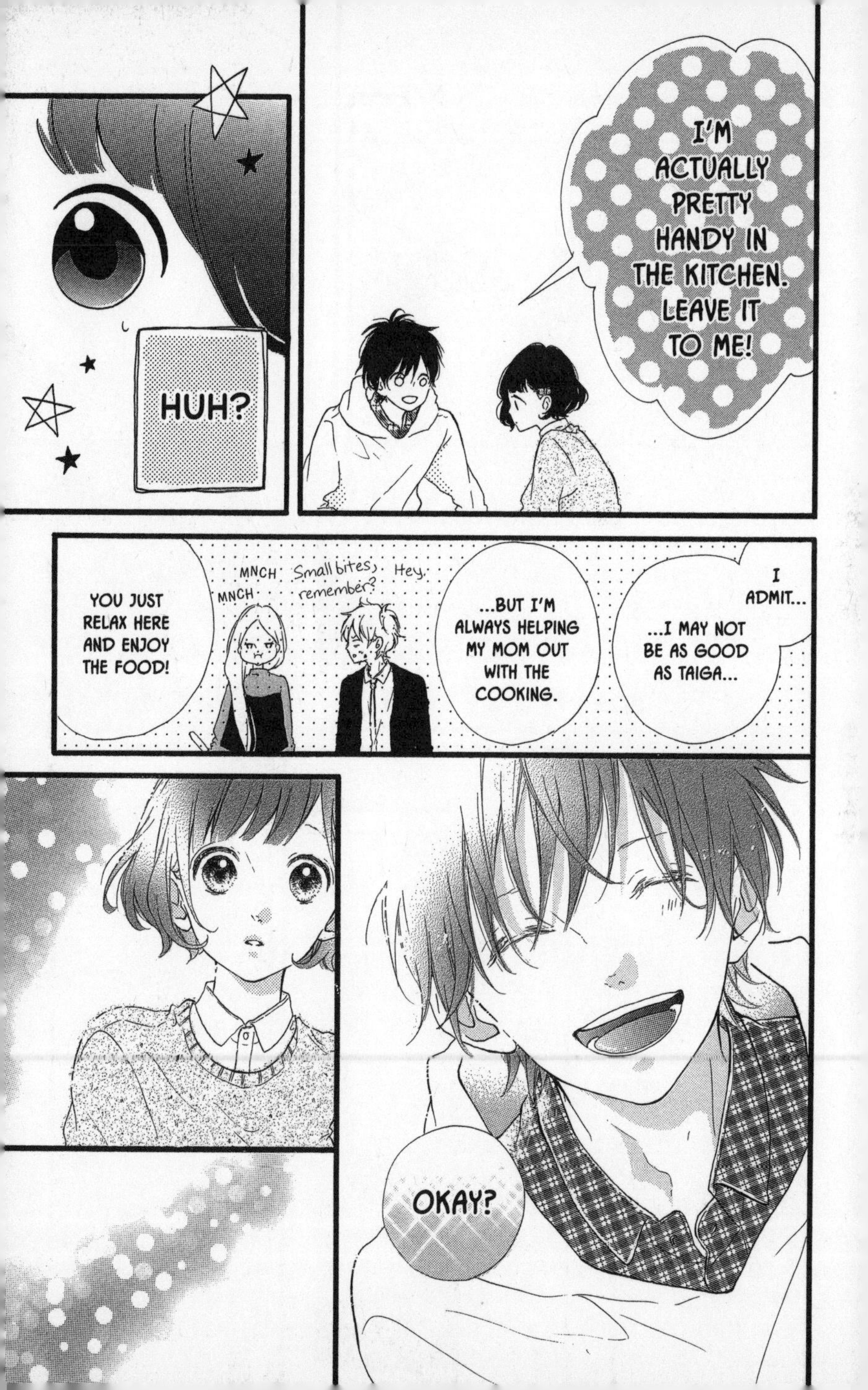
I'M ACTUALLY PRETTY HANDY IN THE KITCHEN. LEAVE IT TO ME!
HUH?
I ADMIT...
...I MAY NOT BE AS GOOD AS TAIGA...
...BUT I'M ALWAYS HELPING MY MOM OUT WITH THE COOKING.
Hey.
Small bites, remember?
MNCH MNCH
YOU JUST RELAX HERE AND ENJOY THE FOOD!
OKAY?

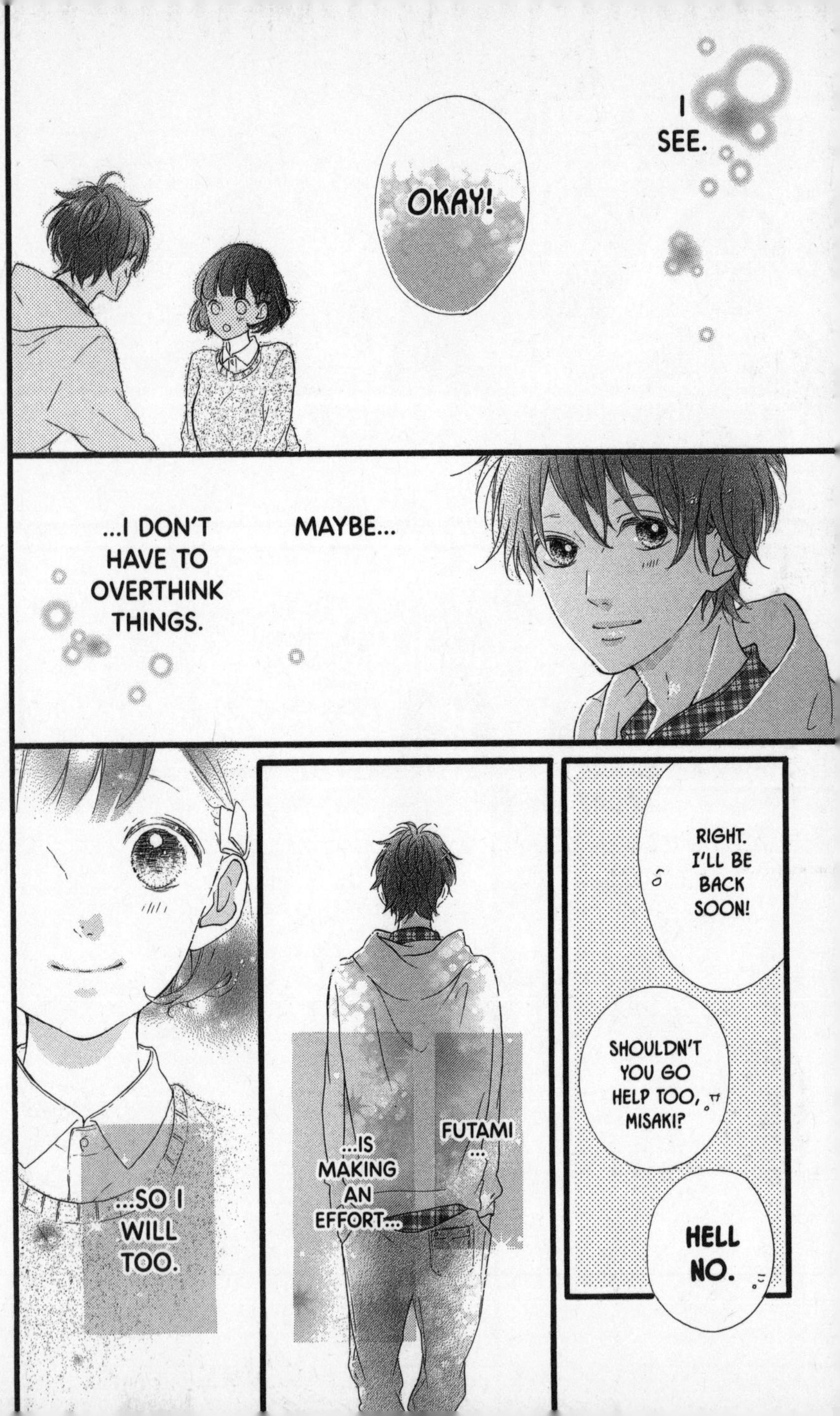
I SEE.
OKAY!
MAYBE...
...I DON'T HAVE TO OVERTHINK THINGS.
RIGHT. I'LL BE BACK SOON!
SHOULDN'T YOU GO HELP TOO, MISAKI?
HELL NO.
FUTAMI...
...IS MAKING AN EFFORT...
...SO I WILL TOO.

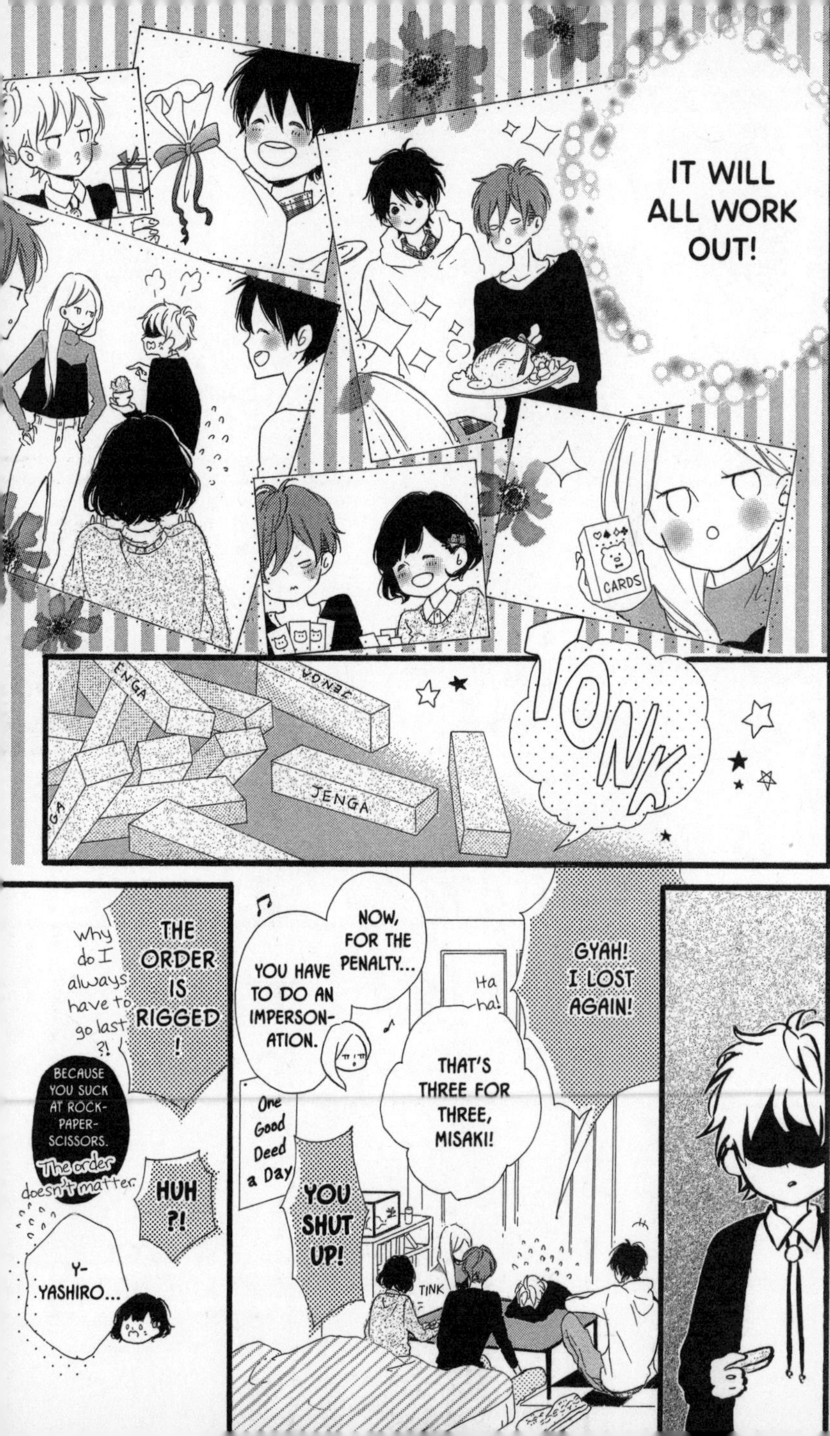
IT WILL ALL WORK OUT!
CARDS
TONK
JENGA
GYAH! I LOST AGAIN!
NOW, FOR THE PENALTY...
YOU HAVE TO DO AN IMPERSON-ATION.
Ha ha!
THAT'S THREE FOR THREE, MISAKI!
One Good Deed a Day
YOU SHUT UP!
TINK
THE ORDER IS RIGGED!
Why do I always have to go last?!
BECAUSE YOU SUCK AT ROCK-PAPER-SCISSORS.
The order doesn't matter.
HUH?!
Y-YASHIRO...

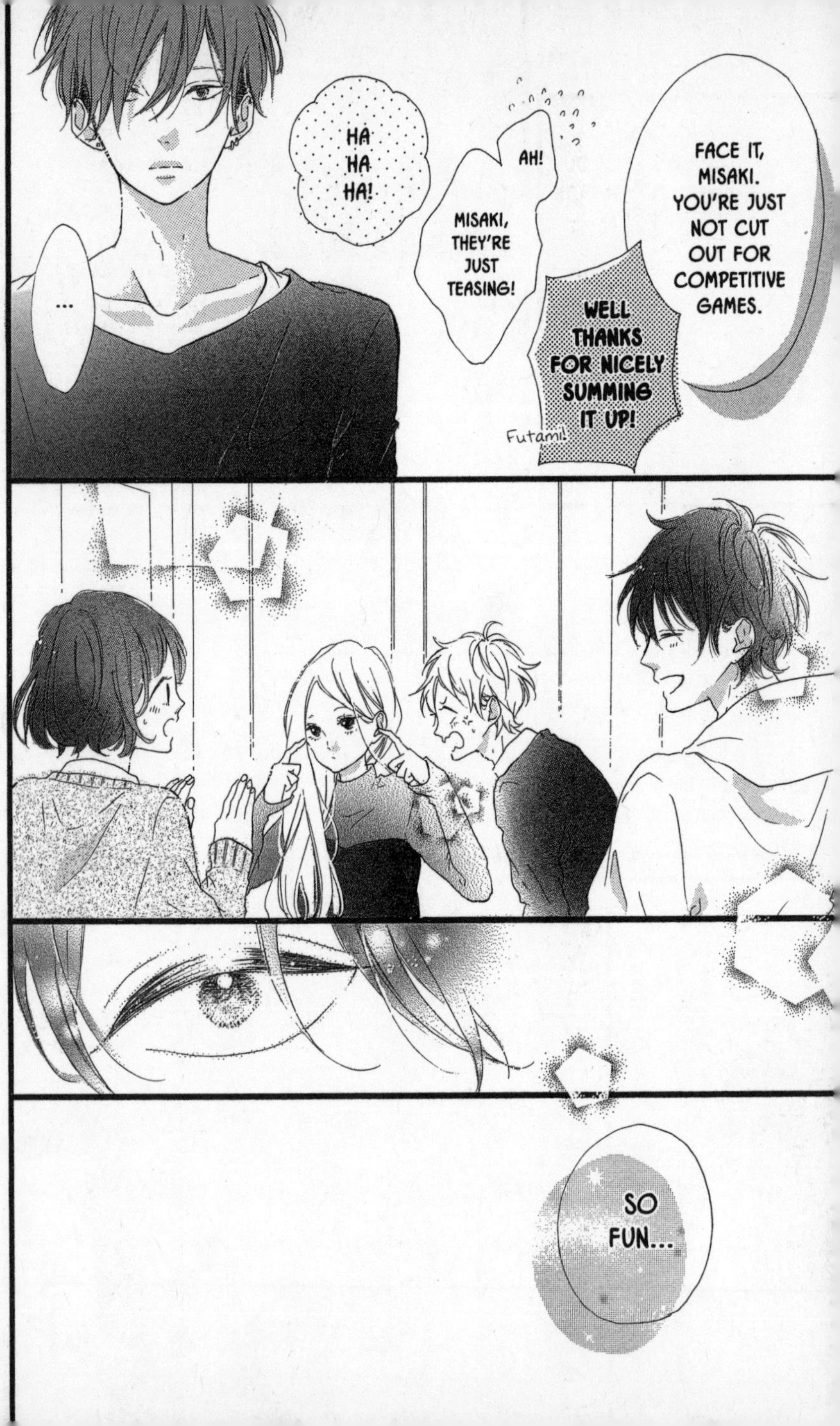
FACE IT, MISAKI. YOU'RE JUST NOT CUT OUT FOR COMPETITIVE GAMES.
WELL THANKS FOR NICELY SUMMING IT UP!
Futami!
AH!
MISAKI, THEY'RE JUST TEASING!
HA HA HA!
...
SO FUN...

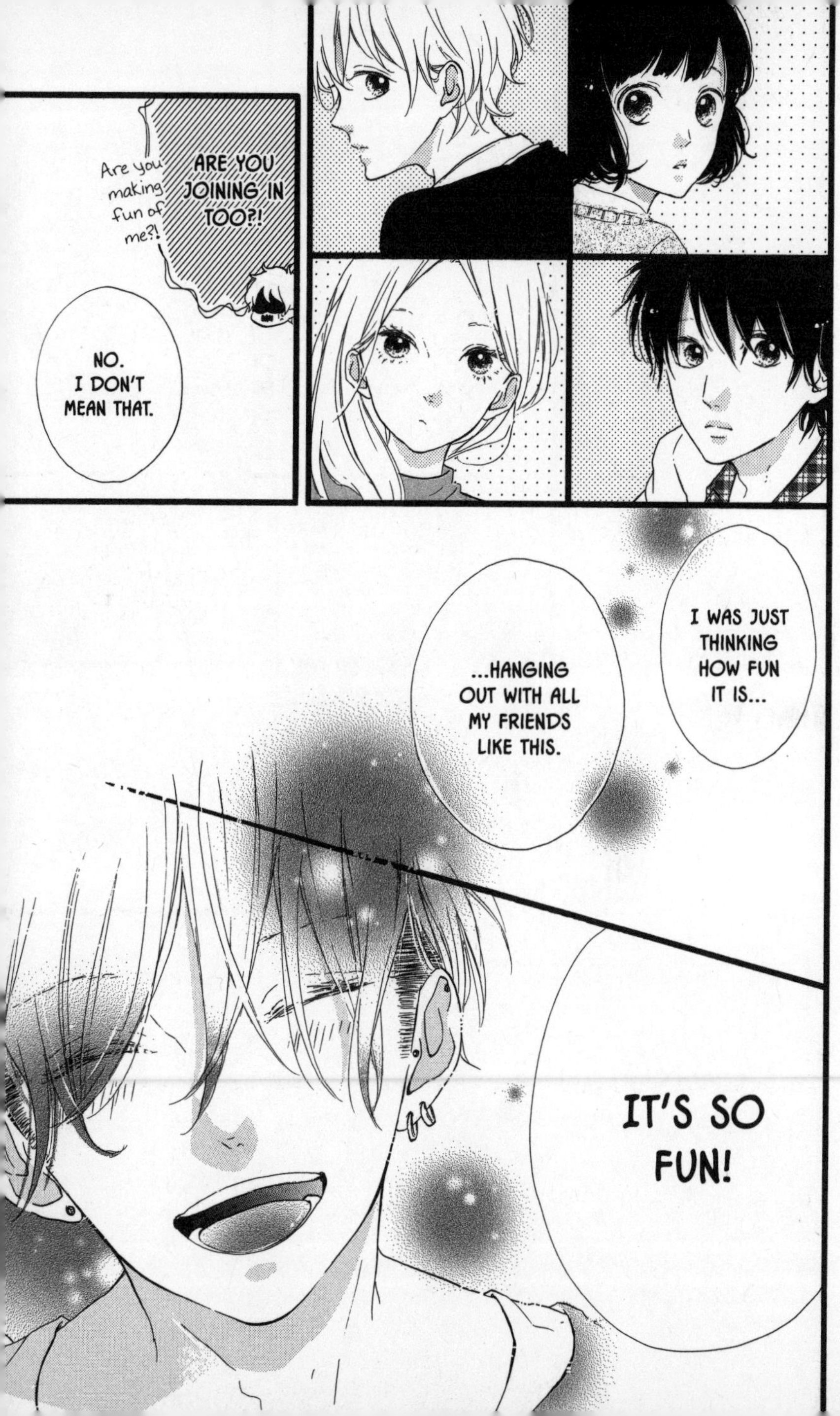
ARE YOU JOINING IN TOO?!
Are you making fun of me?!
NO. I DON'T MEAN THAT.
I WAS JUST THINKING HOW FUN IT IS...
...HANGING OUT WITH ALL MY FRIENDS LIKE THIS.
IT'S SO FUN!

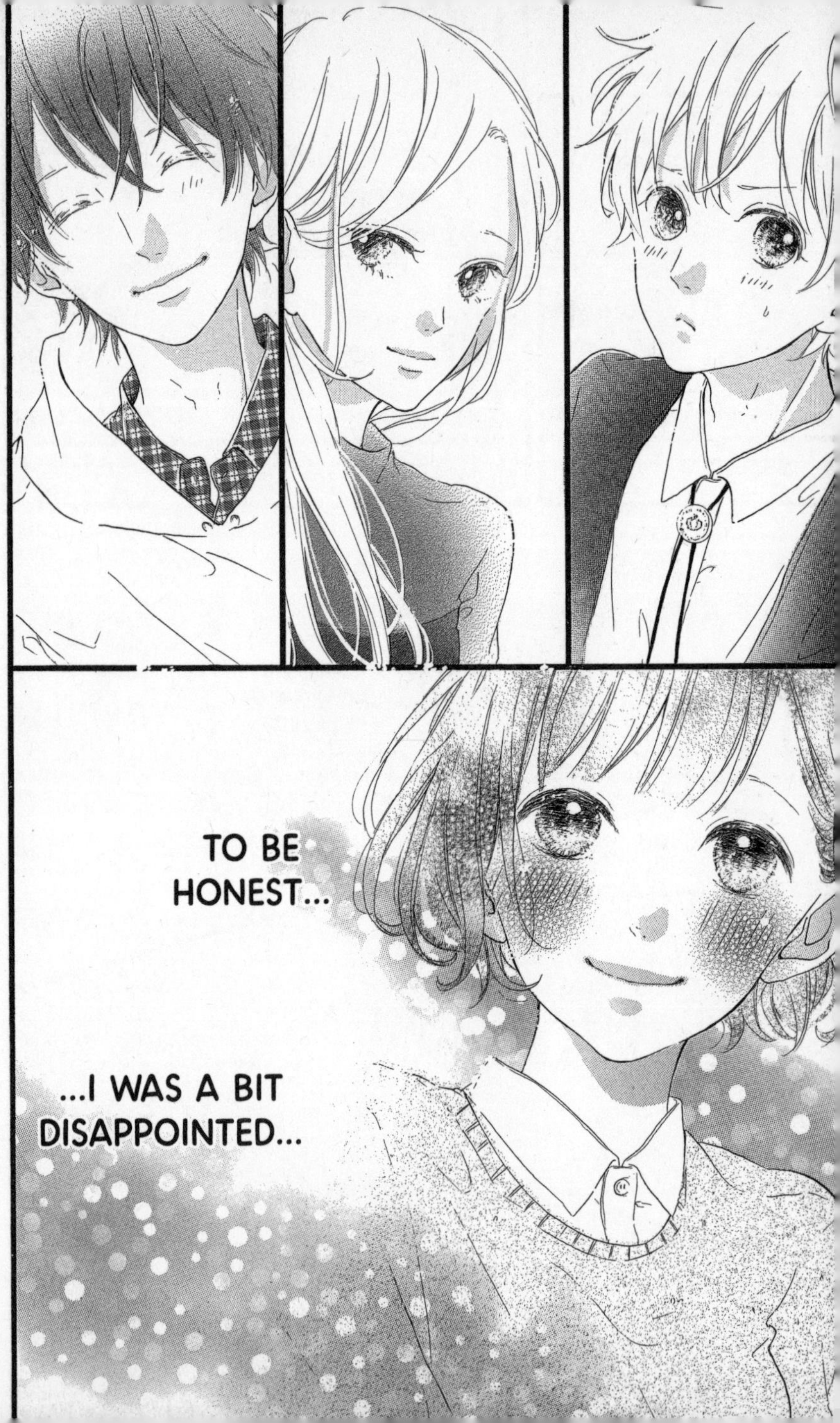
TO BE HONEST...
...I WAS A BIT DISAPPOINTED...

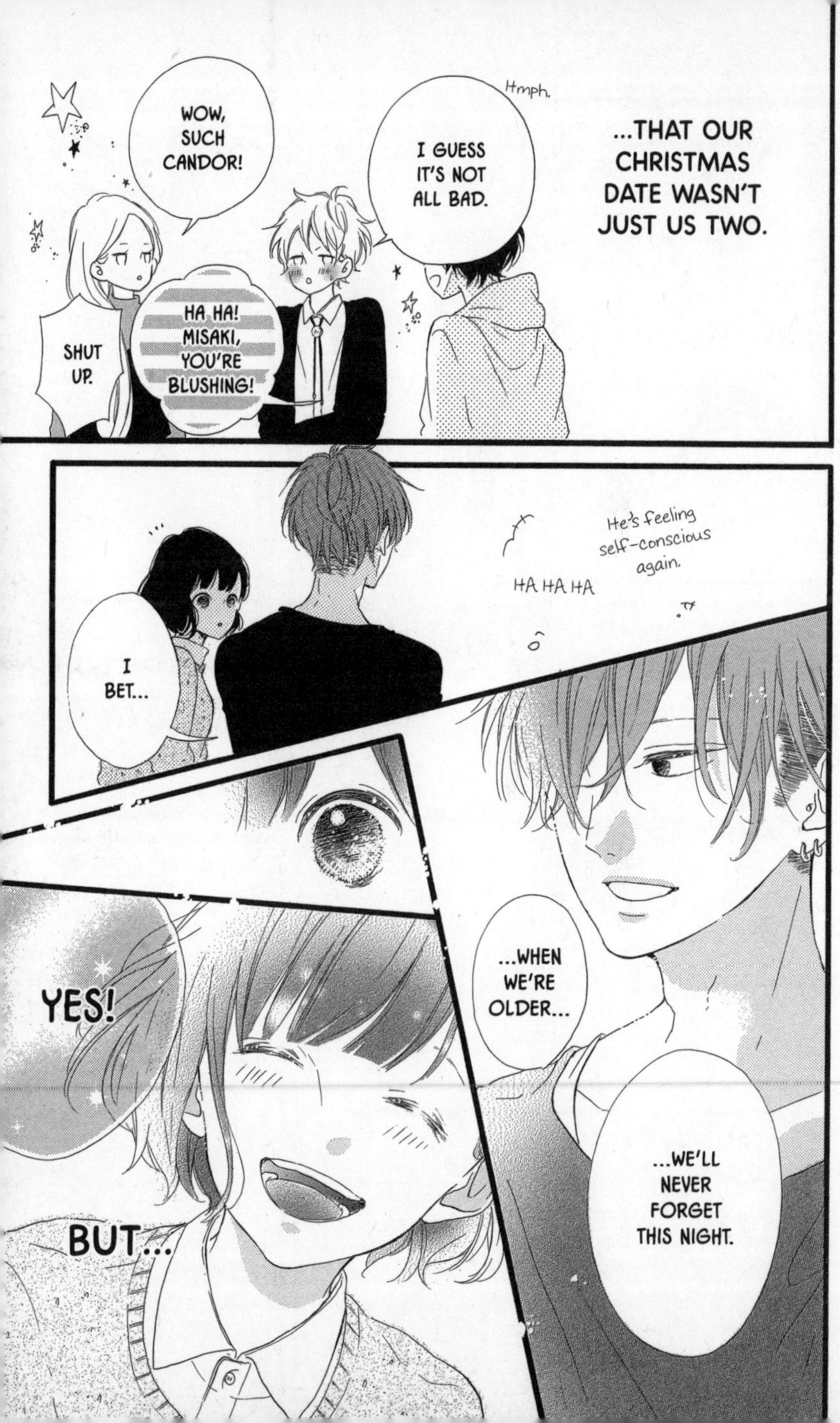
...THAT OUR CHRISTMAS DATE WASN'T JUST US TWO.
Hmph.
I GUESS IT'S NOT ALL BAD.
WOW, SUCH CANDOR!
HA HA! MISAKI, YOU'RE BLUSHING!
SHUT UP.
He's feeling self-conscious again.
HA HA HA
I BET...
...WHEN WE'RE OLDER...
...WE'LL NEVER FORGET THIS NIGHT.
YES!
BUT...

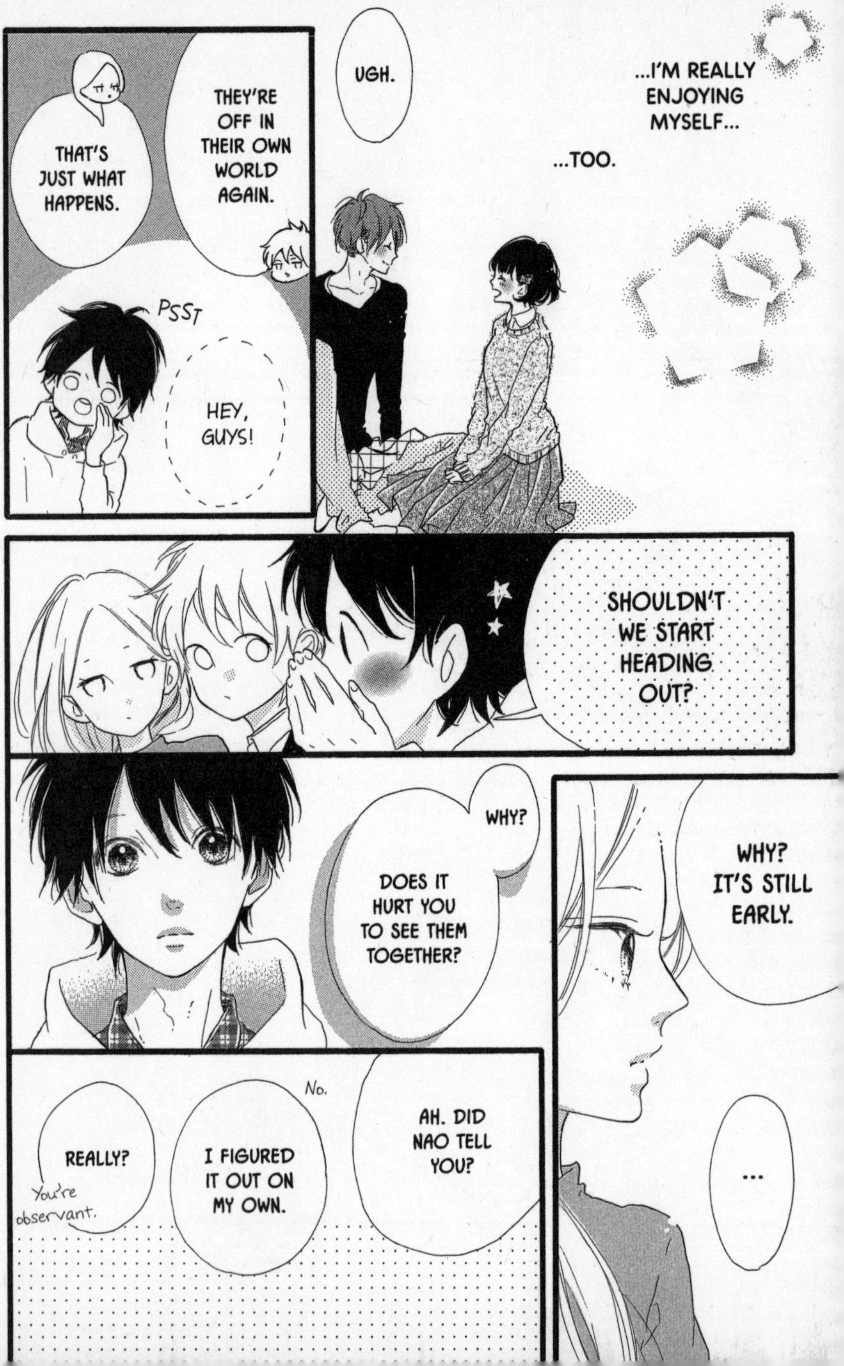
...I'M REALLY ENJOYING MYSELF...
...TOO.
UGH.
THEY'RE OFF IN THEIR OWN WORLD AGAIN.
THAT'S JUST WHAT HAPPENS.
PSST
HEY, GUYS!
SHOULDN'T WE START HEADING OUT?
WHY? IT'S STILL EARLY.
...
WHY?
DOES IT HURT YOU TO SEE THEM TOGETHER?
AH. DID NAO TELL YOU?
No.
I FIGURED IT OUT ON MY OWN.
REALLY?
You're observant.

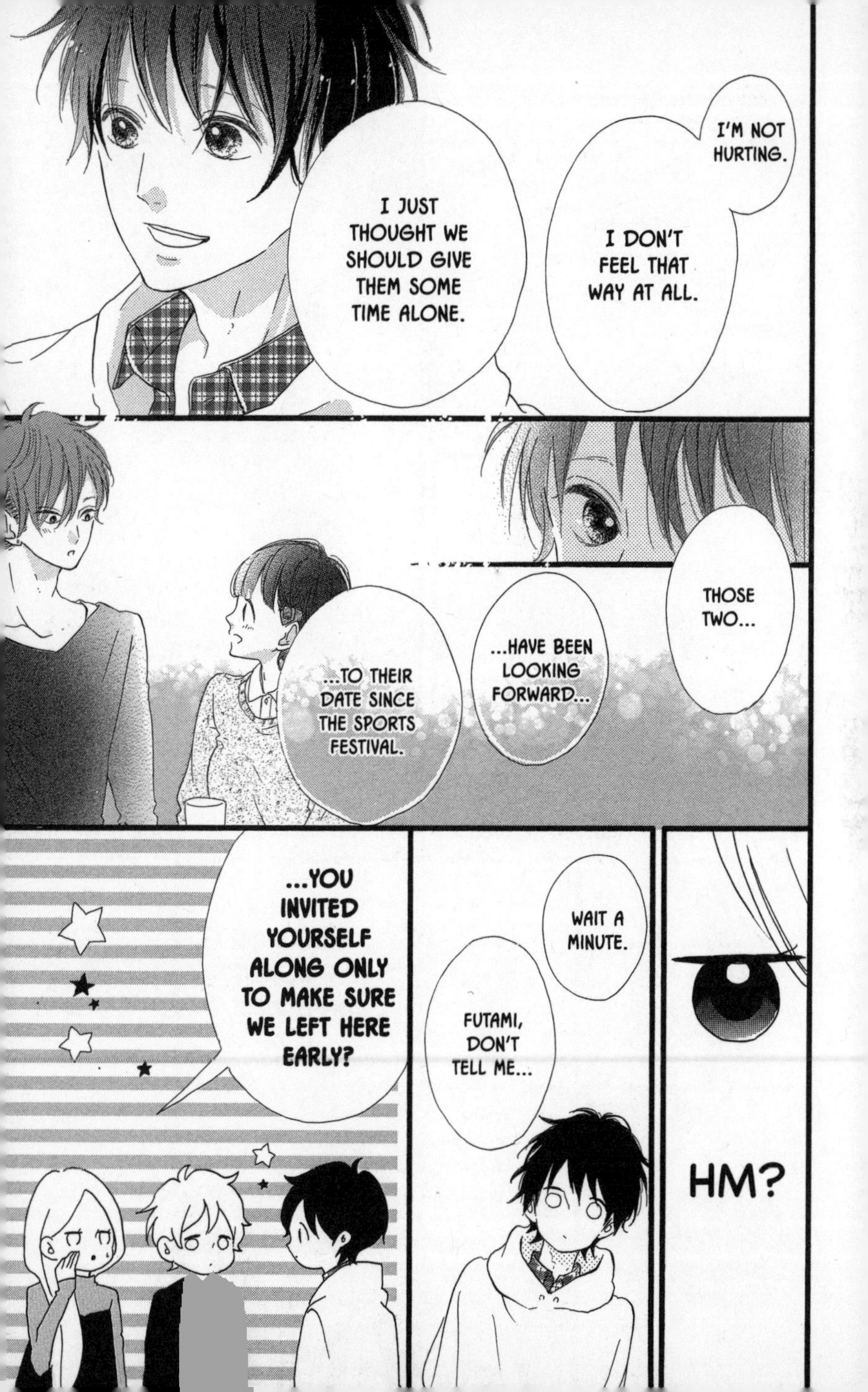
I'M NOT HURTING.
I DON'T FEEL THAT WAY AT ALL.
I JUST THOUGHT WE SHOULD GIVE THEM SOME TIME ALONE.
THOSE TWO...
...HAVE BEEN LOOKING FORWARD...
...TO THEIR DATE SINCE THE SPORTS FESTIVAL.
HM?
WAIT A MINUTE.
FUTAMI, DON'T TELL ME...
...YOU INVITED YOURSELF ALONG ONLY TO MAKE SURE WE LEFT HERE EARLY?

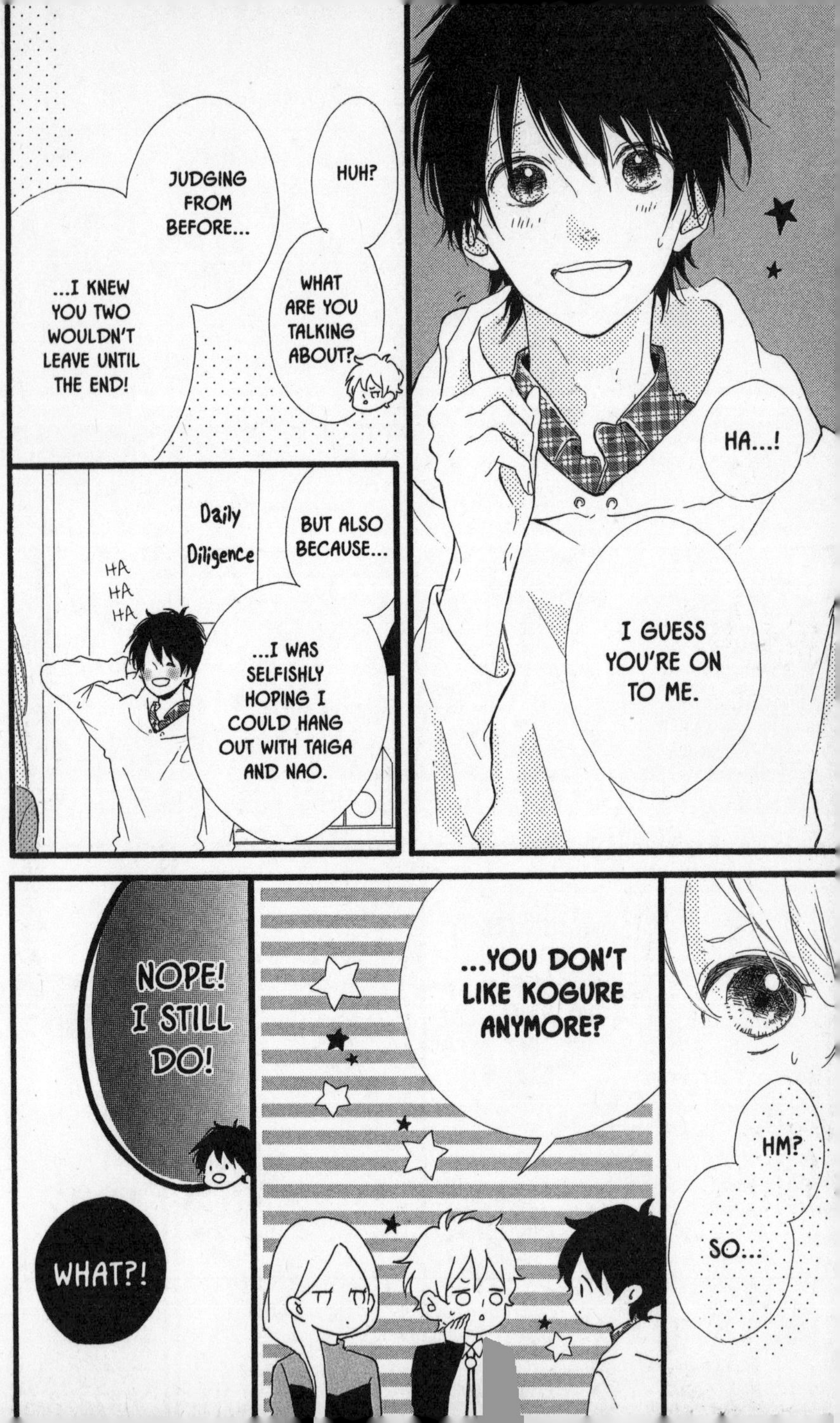
HA...!
I GUESS YOU'RE ON TO ME.
HUH?
WHAT ARE YOU TALKING ABOUT?
JUDGING FROM BEFORE...
...I KNEW YOU TWO WOULDN'T LEAVE UNTIL THE END!
BUT ALSO BECAUSE...
Daily Diligence
...I WAS SELFISHLY HOPING I COULD HANG OUT WITH TAIGA AND NAO.
HA HA HA
HM?
SO...
...YOU DON'T LIKE KOGURE ANYMORE?
NOPE! I STILL DO!
WHAT?!

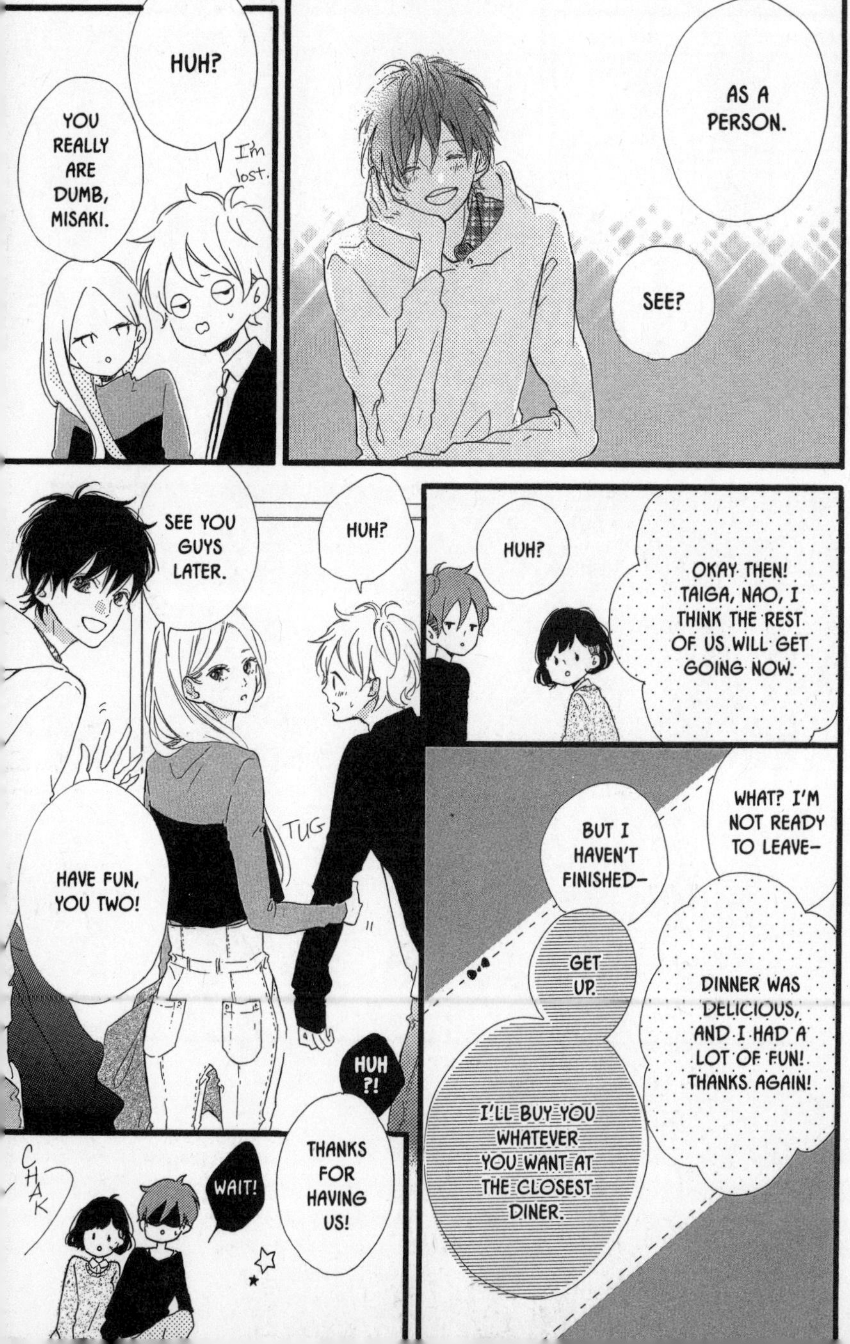
AS A PERSON.
SEE?
HUH?
I'm lost.
YOU REALLY ARE DUMB, MISAKI.
OKAY THEN! TAIGA, NAO, I THINK THE REST OF US WILL GET GOING NOW.
HUH?
WHAT? I'M NOT READY TO LEAVE–
BUT I HAVEN'T FINISHED–
DINNER WAS DELICIOUS, AND I HAD A LOT OF FUN! THANKS AGAIN!
GET UP.
I'LL BUY YOU WHATEVER YOU WANT AT THE CLOSEST DINER.
HUH?
SEE YOU GUYS LATER.
TUG
HAVE FUN, YOU TWO!
HUH ?!
THANKS FOR HAVING US!
WAIT!
CHAK

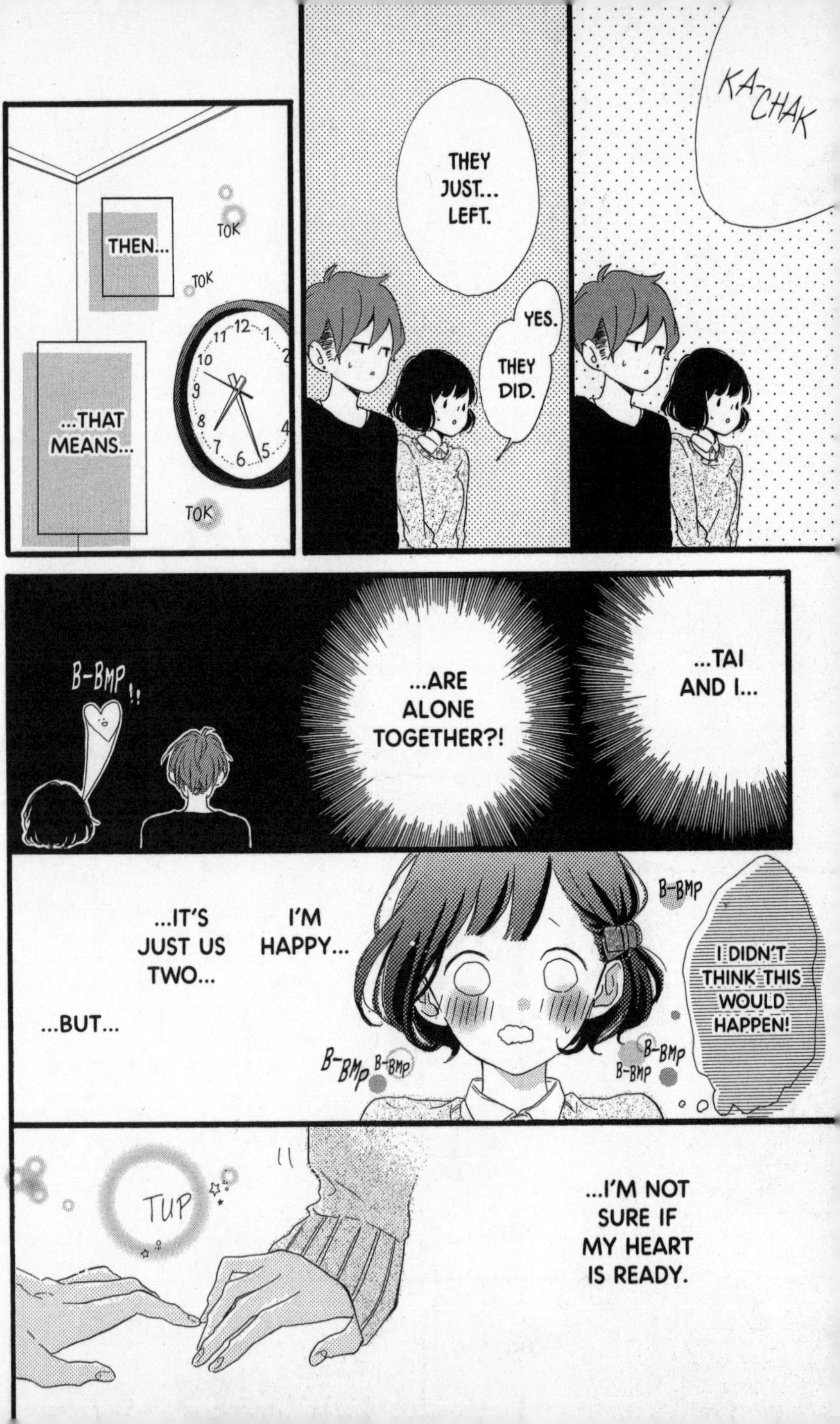
KA-CHAK
THEY JUST... LEFT.
YES.
THEY DID.
TOK
THEN...
TOK
...THAT MEANS...
TOK
...TAI AND I...
...ARE ALONE TOGETHER?!
B-BMP!!
B-BMP
I DIDN'T THINK THIS WOULD HAPPEN!
B-BMP
B-BMP
B-BMP B-BMP
I'M HAPPY...
...IT'S JUST US TWO...
...BUT...
...I'M NOT SURE IF MY HEART IS READY.
TUP

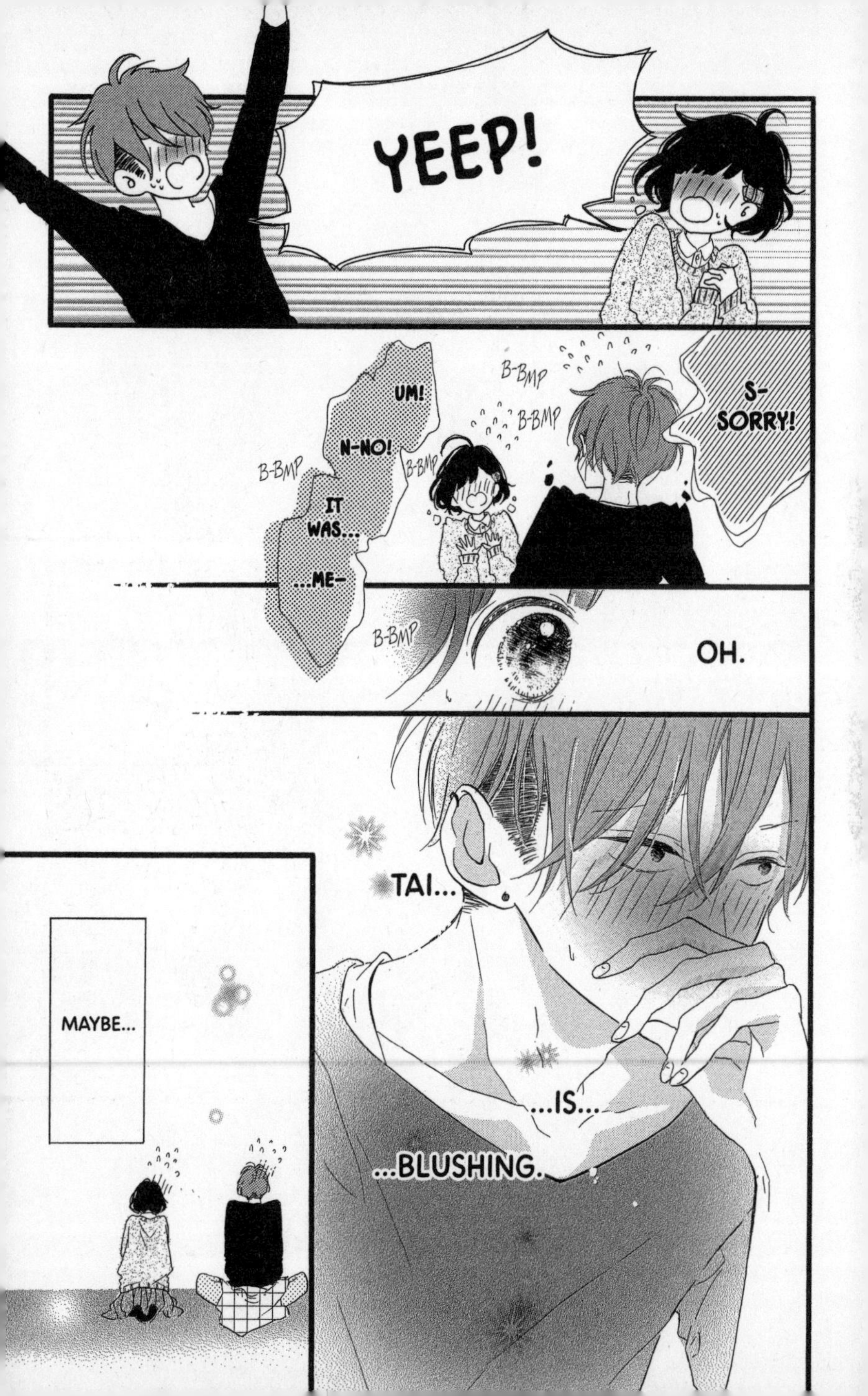
YEEP!
S-SORRY!
B-BMP
B-BMP
UM!
N-NO!
B-BMP
B-BMP
IT WAS...
...ME-
B-BMP
OH.
TAI...
...IS...
...BLUSHING.
MAYBE...

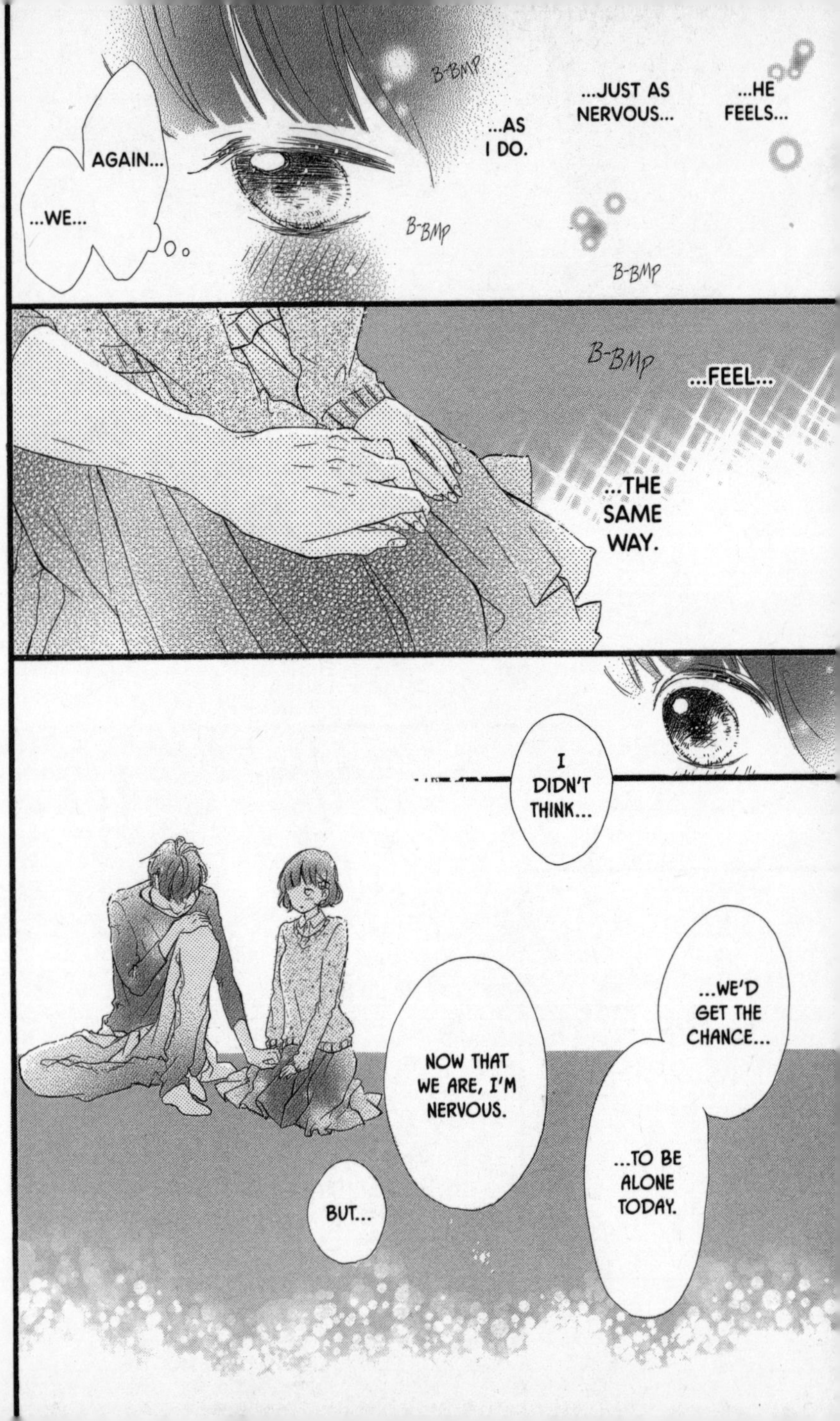
B-BMP
...HE FEELS...
...JUST AS NERVOUS...
...AS I DO.
B-BMP
AGAIN...
...WE...
B-BMP
B-BMP
...FEEL...
...THE SAME WAY.
I DIDN'T THINK...
...WE'D GET THE CHANCE...
...TO BE ALONE TODAY.
NOW THAT WE ARE, I'M NERVOUS.
BUT...

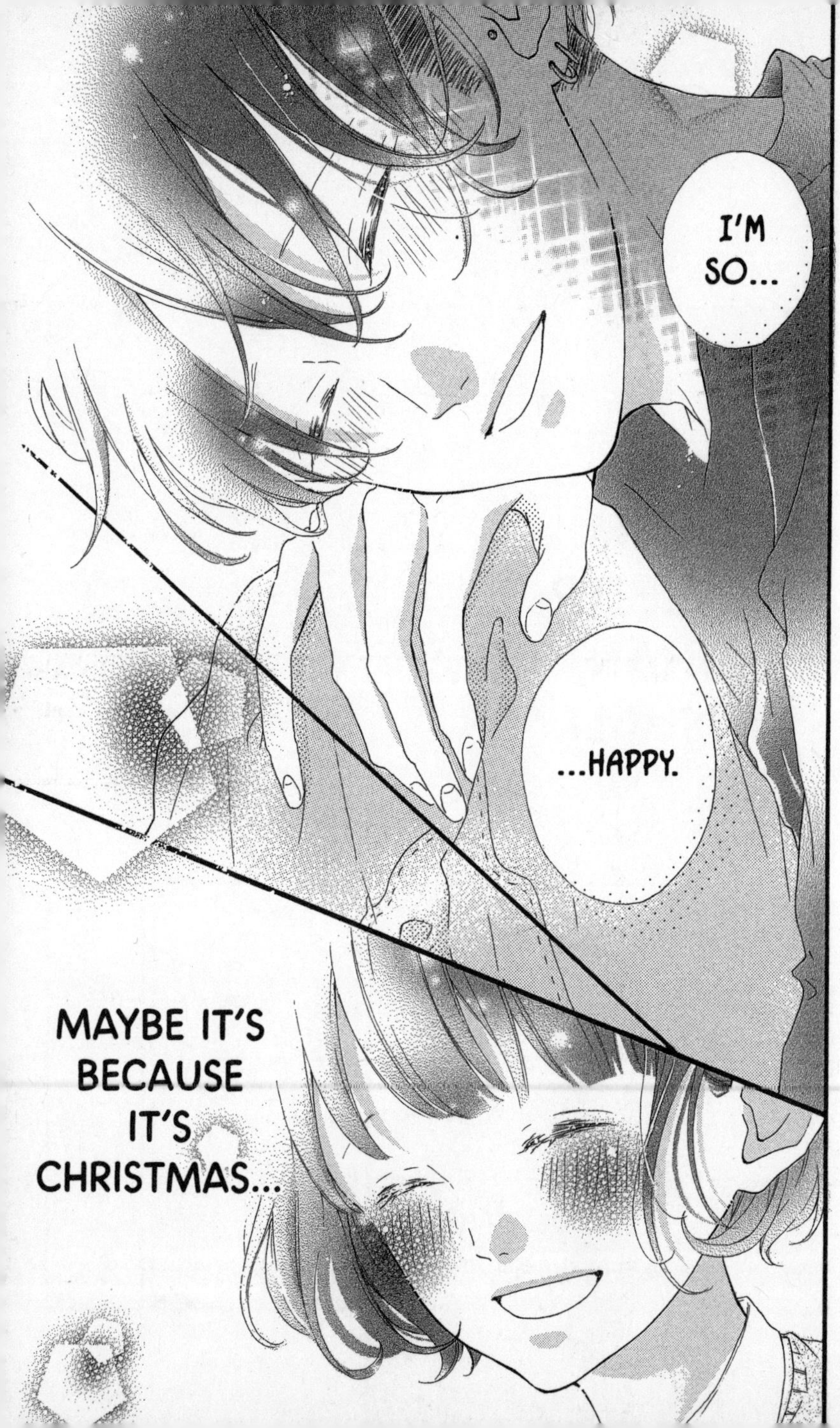
I'M SO...
...HAPPY.
MAYBE IT'S BECAUSE IT'S CHRISTMAS...

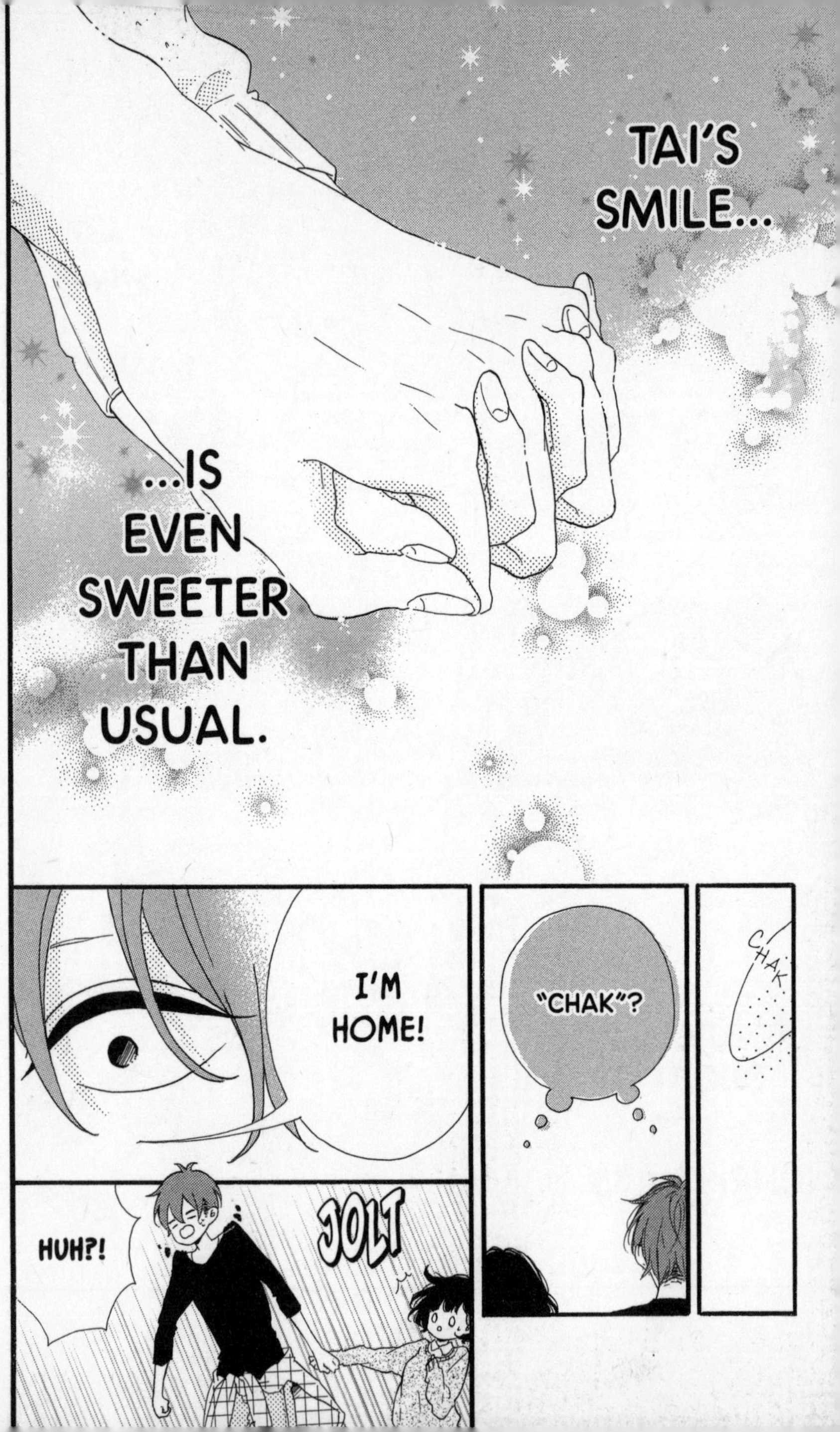
TAI'S SMILE...
...IS EVEN SWEETER THAN USUAL.
CHAK
"CHAK"?
I'M HOME!
JOLT
HUH?!

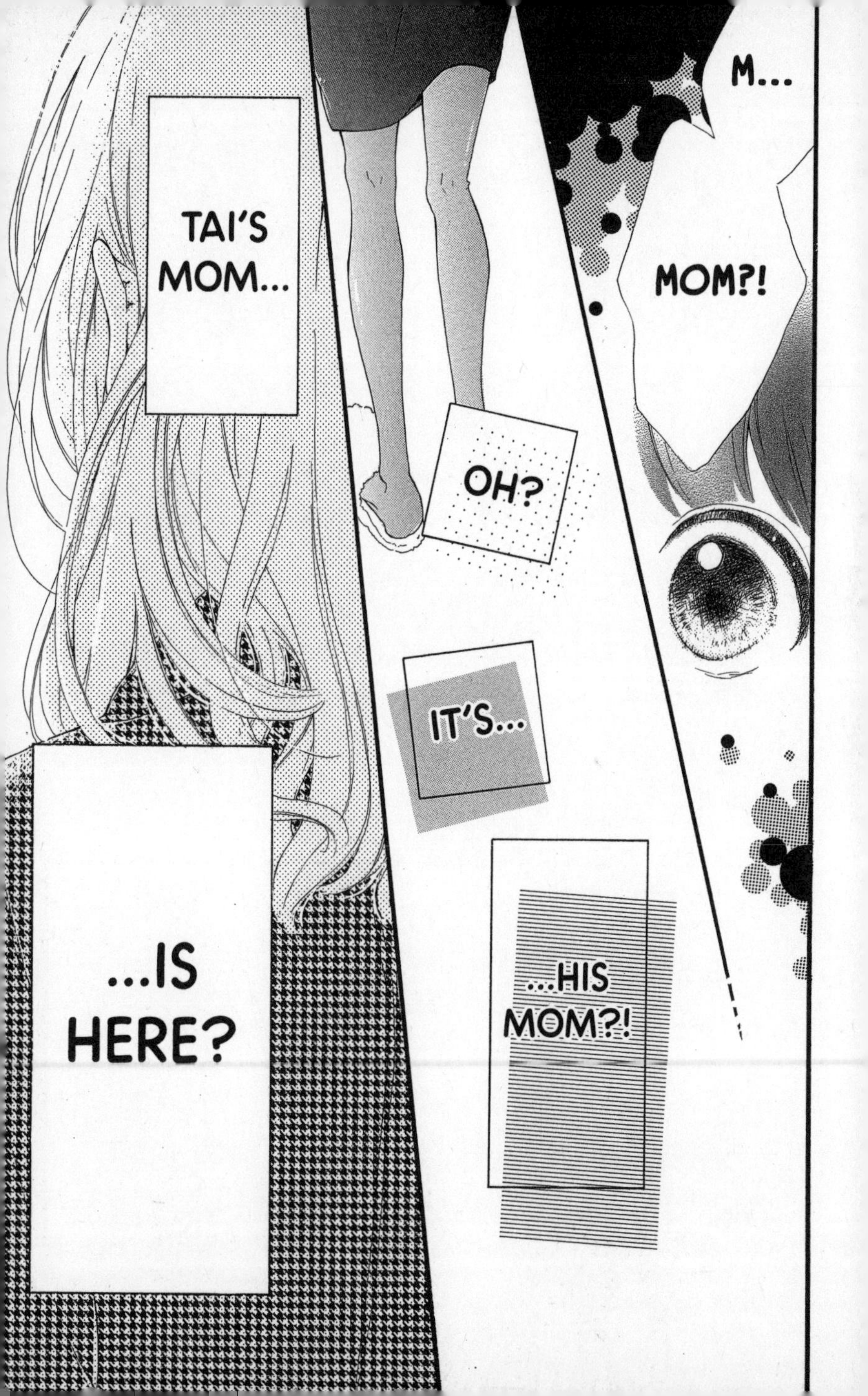
M...
MOM?!
OH?
IT'S...
...HIS MOM?!
TAI'S MOM...
...IS HERE?

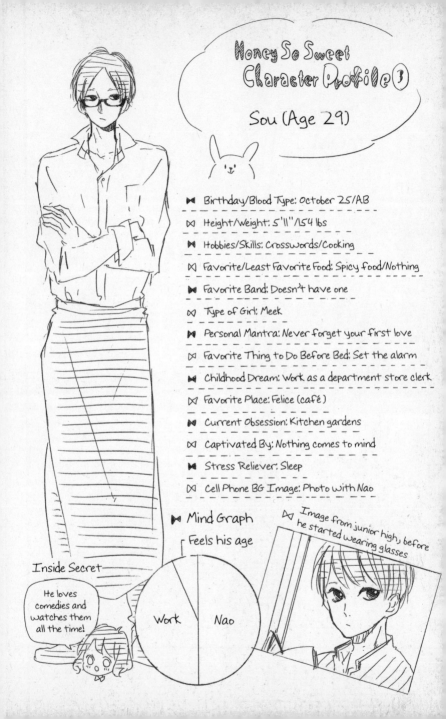

Honey So Sweet Character Profile 3

Sou (Age 29)

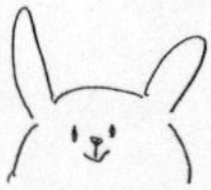

- Birthday/Blood Type: October 25/AB
- Height/Weight: 5'11"/154 lbs
- Hobbies/Skills: Crosswords/Cooking
- Favorite/Least Favorite Food: Spicy food/Nothing
- Favorite Band: Doesn't have one
- Type of Girl: Meek
- Personal Mantra: Never forget your first love
- Favorite Thing to Do Before Bed: Set the alarm
- Childhood Dream: Work as a department store clerk
- Favorite Place: Felice (café)
- Current Obsession: Kitchen gardens
- Captivated By: Nothing comes to mind
- Stress Reliever: Sleep
- Cell Phone BG Image: Photo with Nao

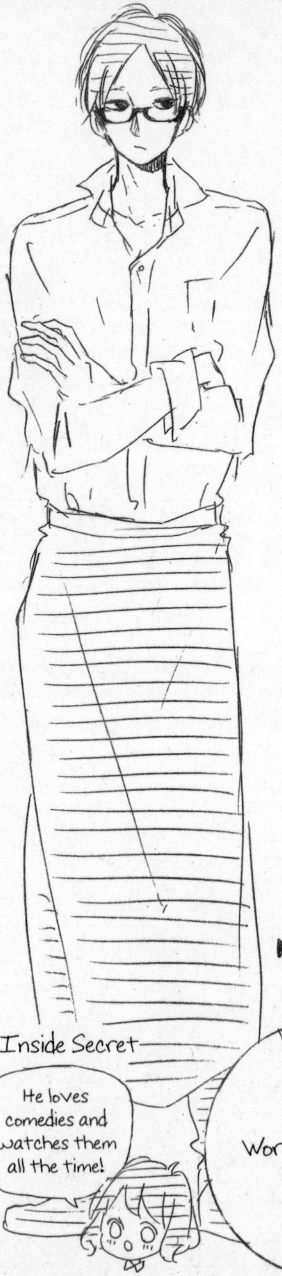

Inside Secret

He loves comedies and watches them all the time!

Mind Graph

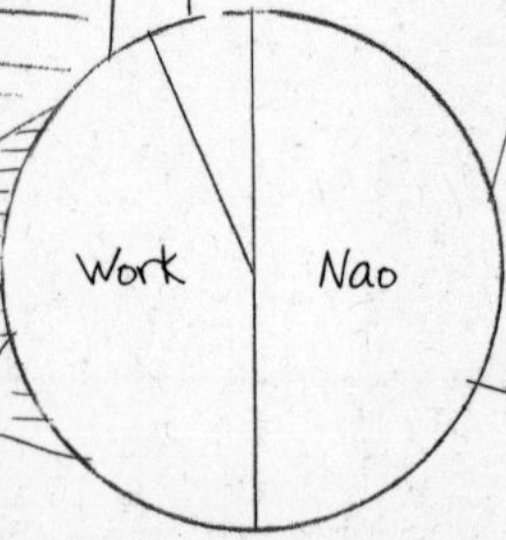
Feels his age
Work
Nao

Image from junior high, before he started wearing glasses

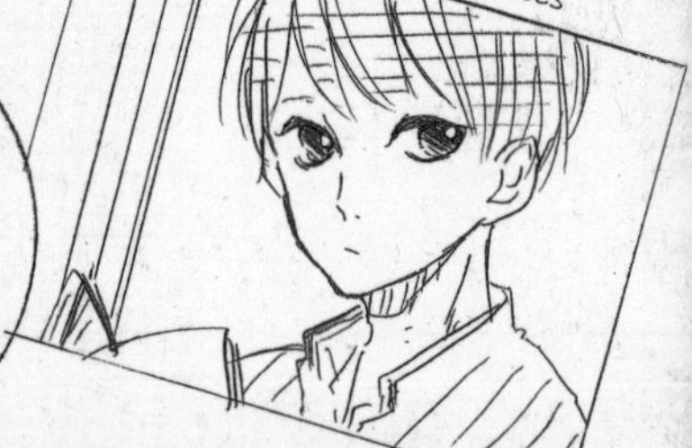

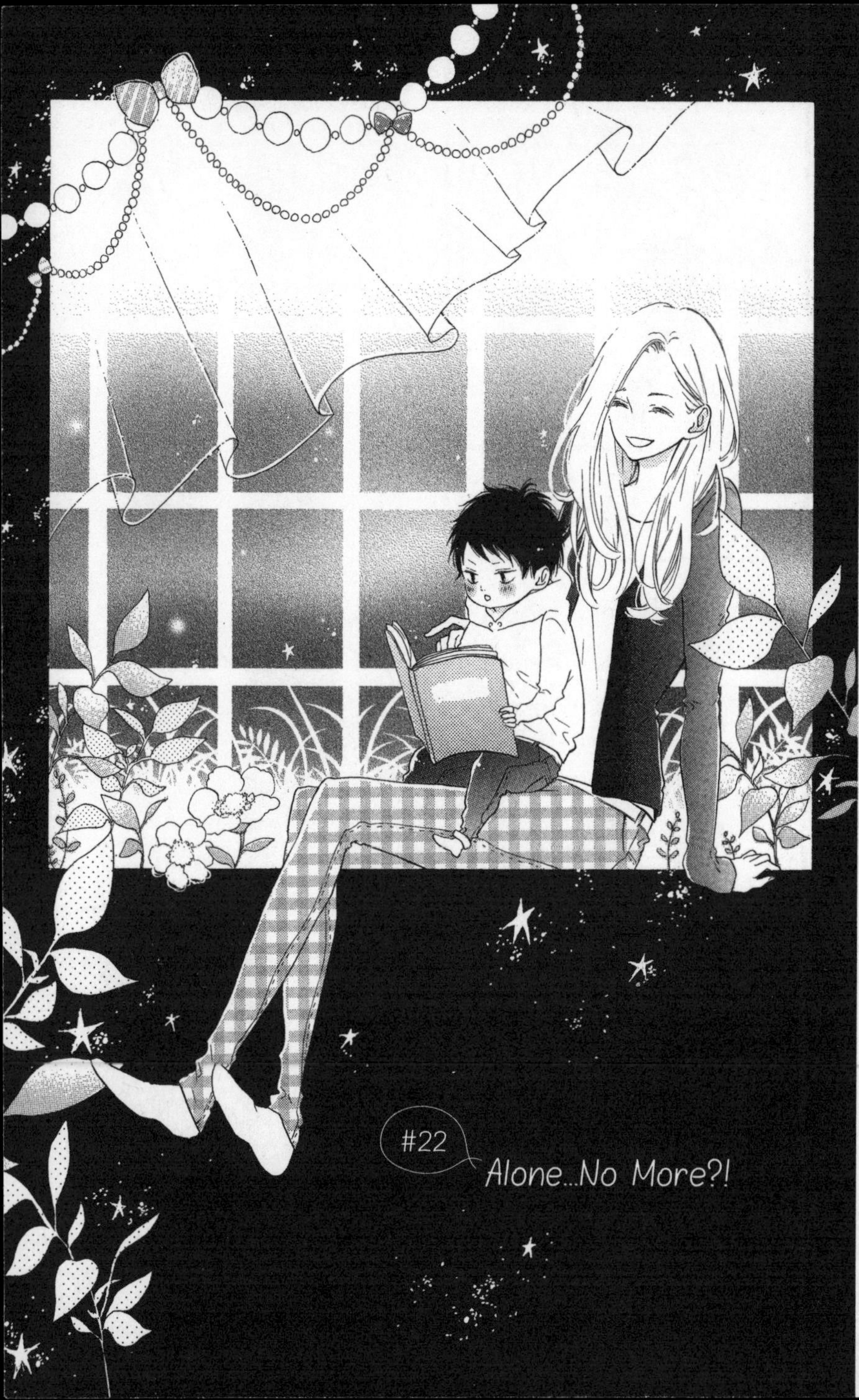
#22
Alone...No More?!

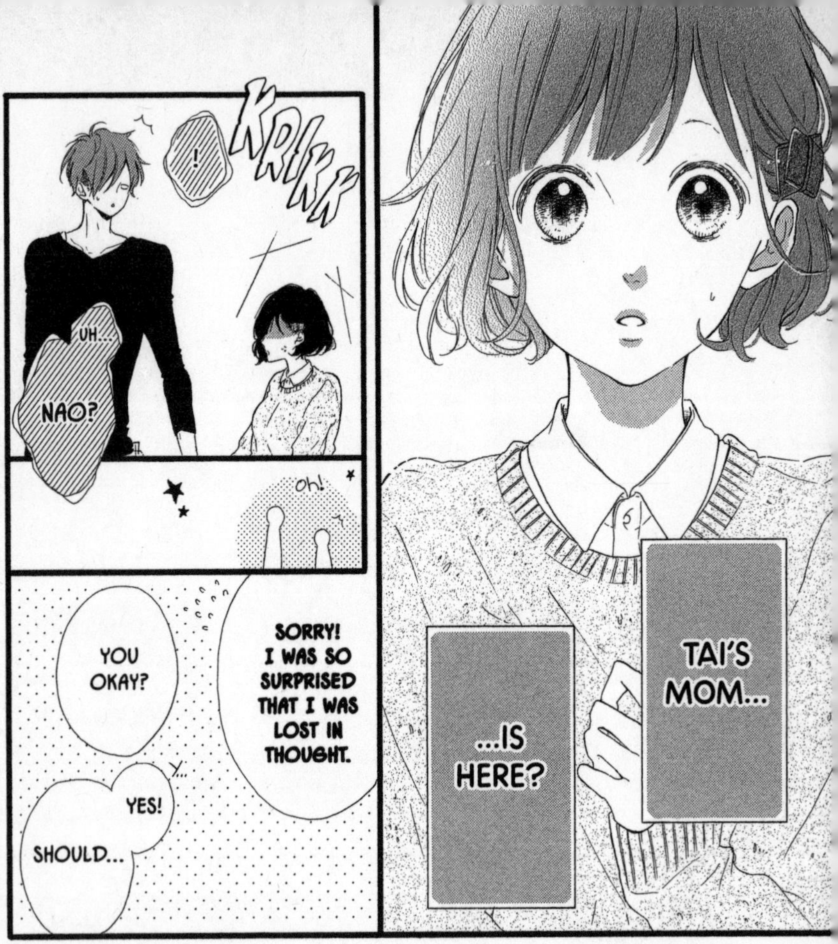
TAI'S MOM...
...IS HERE?
!
KRIKK
UH...
NAO?
OH!
SORRY! I WAS SO SURPRISED THAT I WAS LOST IN THOUGHT.
YOU OKAY?
Y...
YES!
SHOULD...

Around a year ago my friend who's a novelist got me into "Hello! Project" idols. I love many of the bands, but my favorite is Morning Musume. '14 and °C-ute are good too, and I often watch DVDs of their shows while working. (ˇᴗˇ) I'm still pretty new to it, but the groups are so cute and fun! If you're ever curious, I highly recommend you check them out!

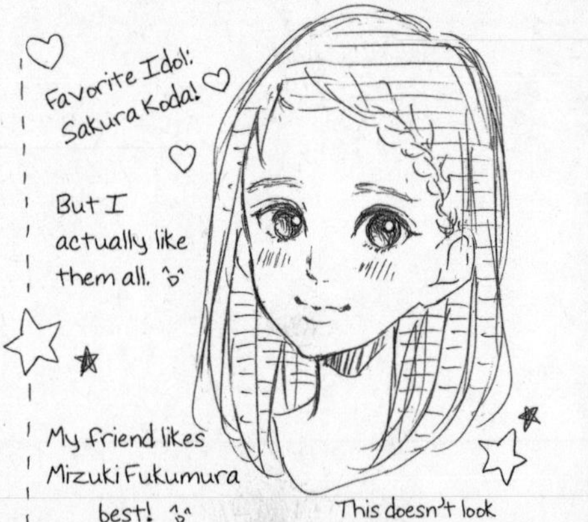
Favorite Idol: Sakura Koda!
But I actually like them all.
My friend likes Mizuki Fukumura best!
This doesn't look like her at all...

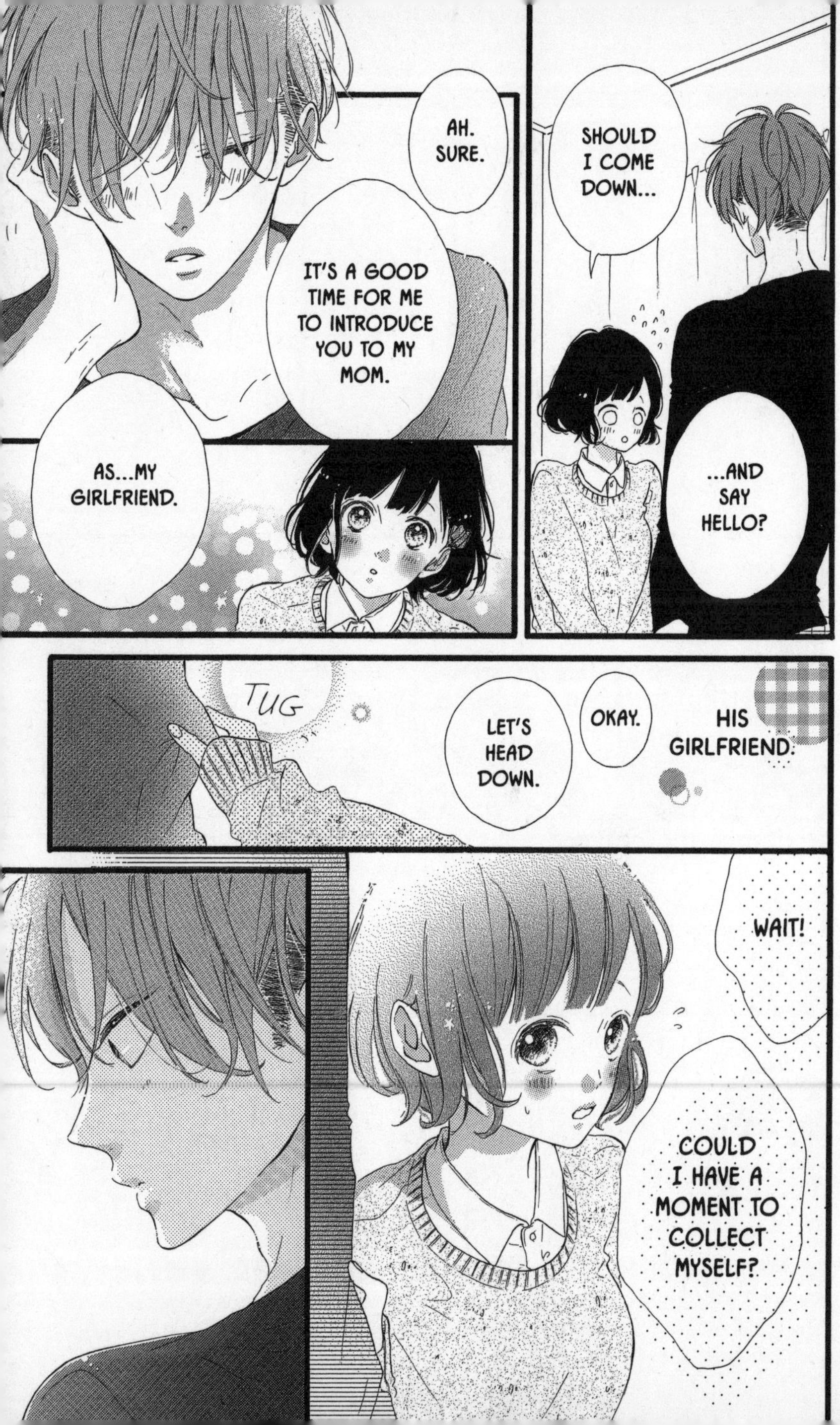
SHOULD I COME DOWN...
...AND SAY HELLO?
AH. SURE.
IT'S A GOOD TIME FOR ME TO INTRODUCE YOU TO MY MOM.
AS...MY GIRLFRIEND.
HIS GIRLFRIEND.
OKAY.
LET'S HEAD DOWN.
TUG
WAIT!
COULD I HAVE A MOMENT TO COLLECT MYSELF?

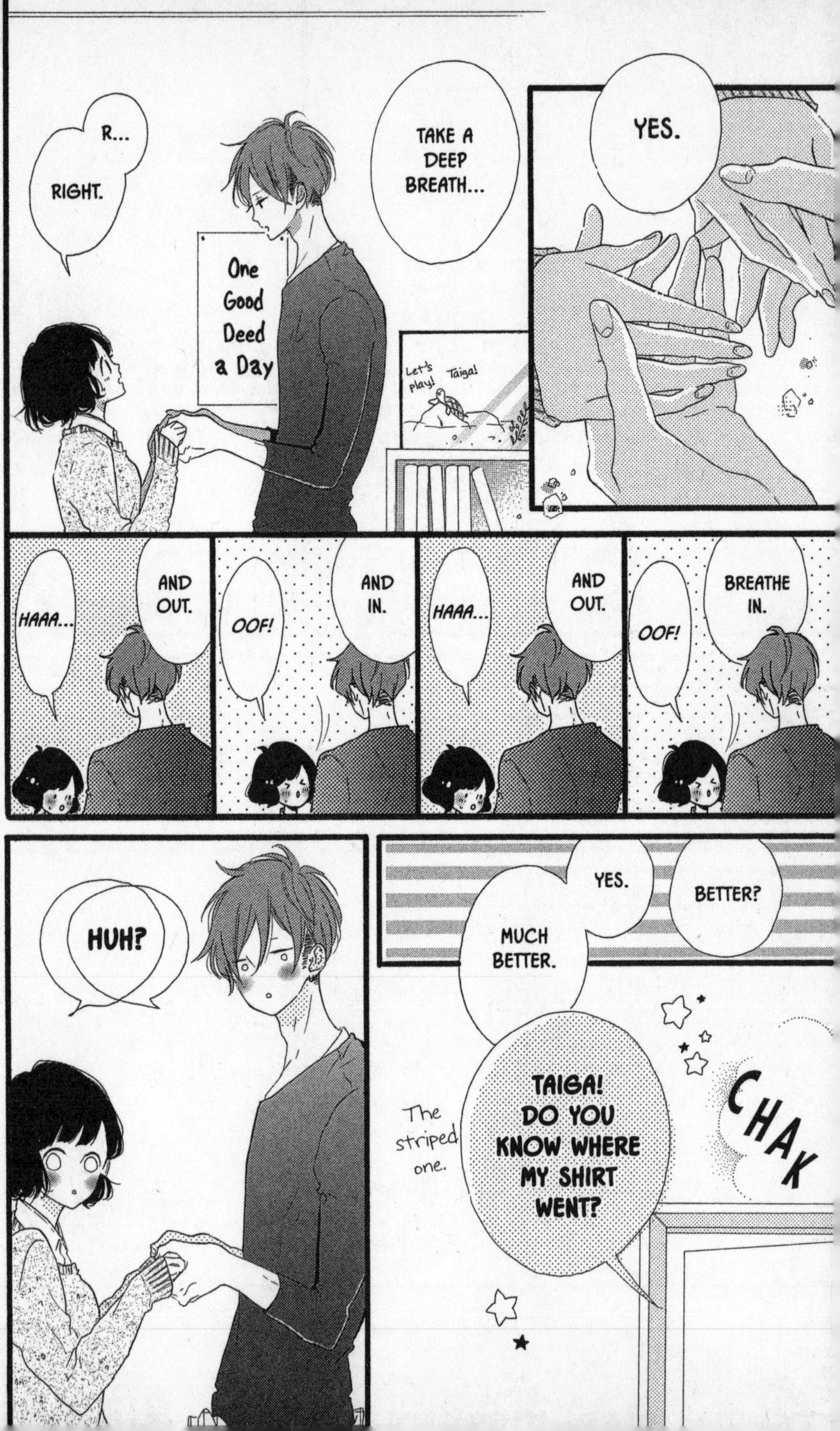
YES.
TAKE A DEEP BREATH...
R... RIGHT.
One Good Deed a Day
Let's play! Taiga!
BREATHE IN.
OOF!
AND OUT.
HAAA...
AND IN.
OOF!
AND OUT.
HAAA...
BETTER?
YES. MUCH BETTER.
CHAK
TAIGA! DO YOU KNOW WHERE MY SHIRT WENT?
The striped one.
HUH?

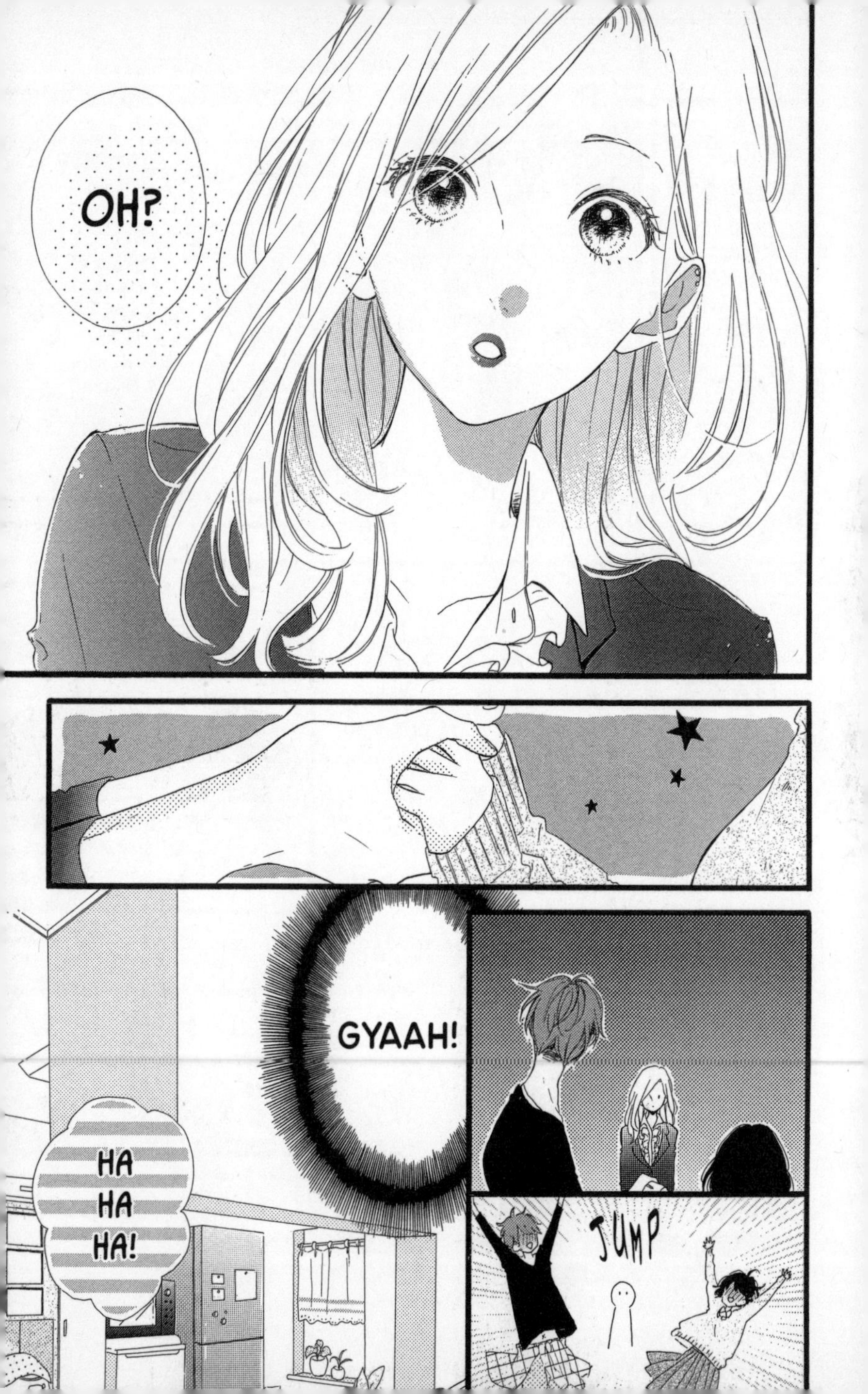
OH?
GYAAH!
HA
HA
HA!
JUMP

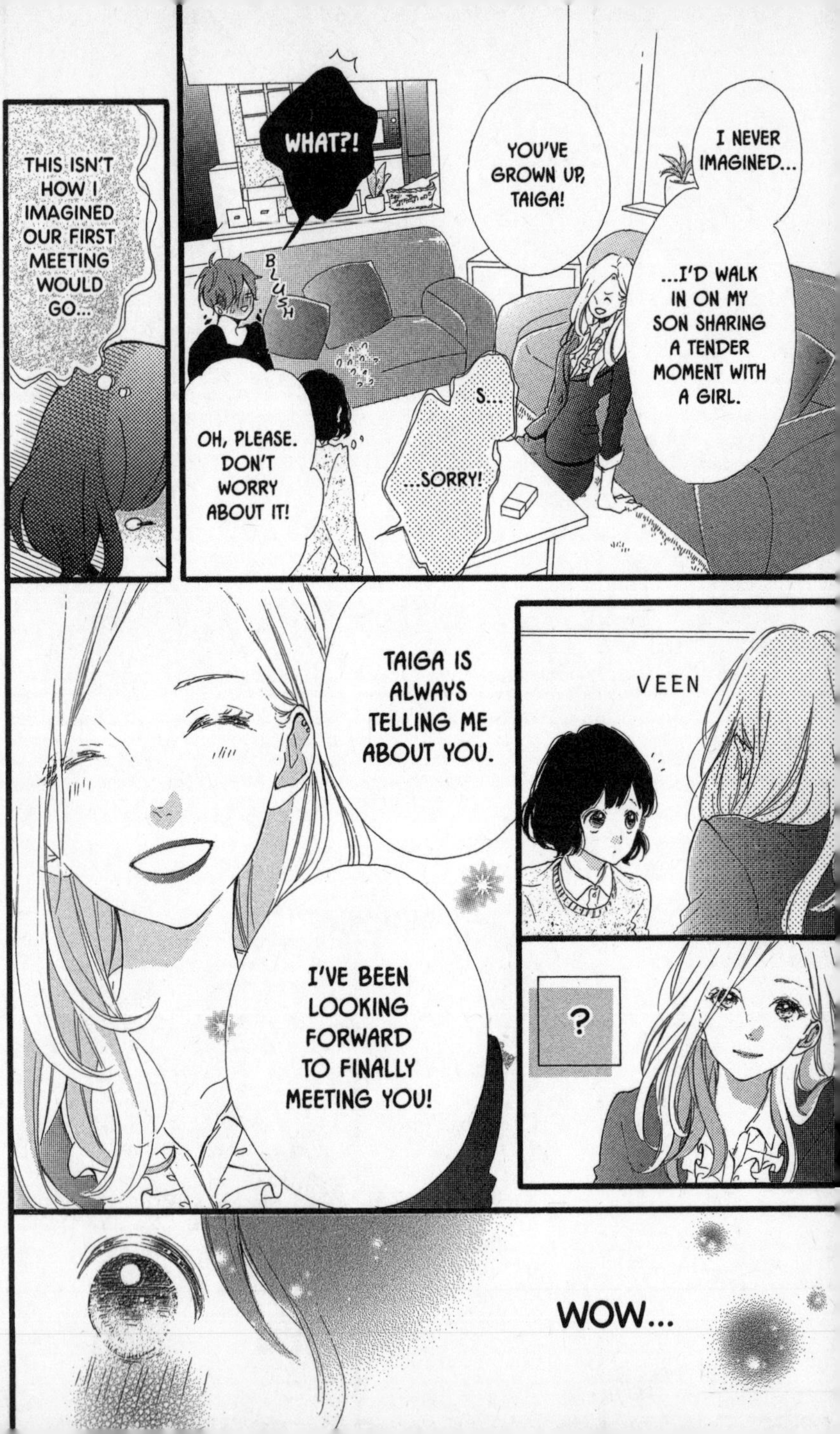
I NEVER IMAGINED...
...I'D WALK IN ON MY SON SHARING A TENDER MOMENT WITH A GIRL.
YOU'VE GROWN UP, TAIGA!
WHAT?!
BLUSH
S...
...SORRY!
OH, PLEASE. DON'T WORRY ABOUT IT!
THIS ISN'T HOW I IMAGINED OUR FIRST MEETING WOULD GO...
VEEN
?
TAIGA IS ALWAYS TELLING ME ABOUT YOU.
I'VE BEEN LOOKING FORWARD TO FINALLY MEETING YOU!
WOW...

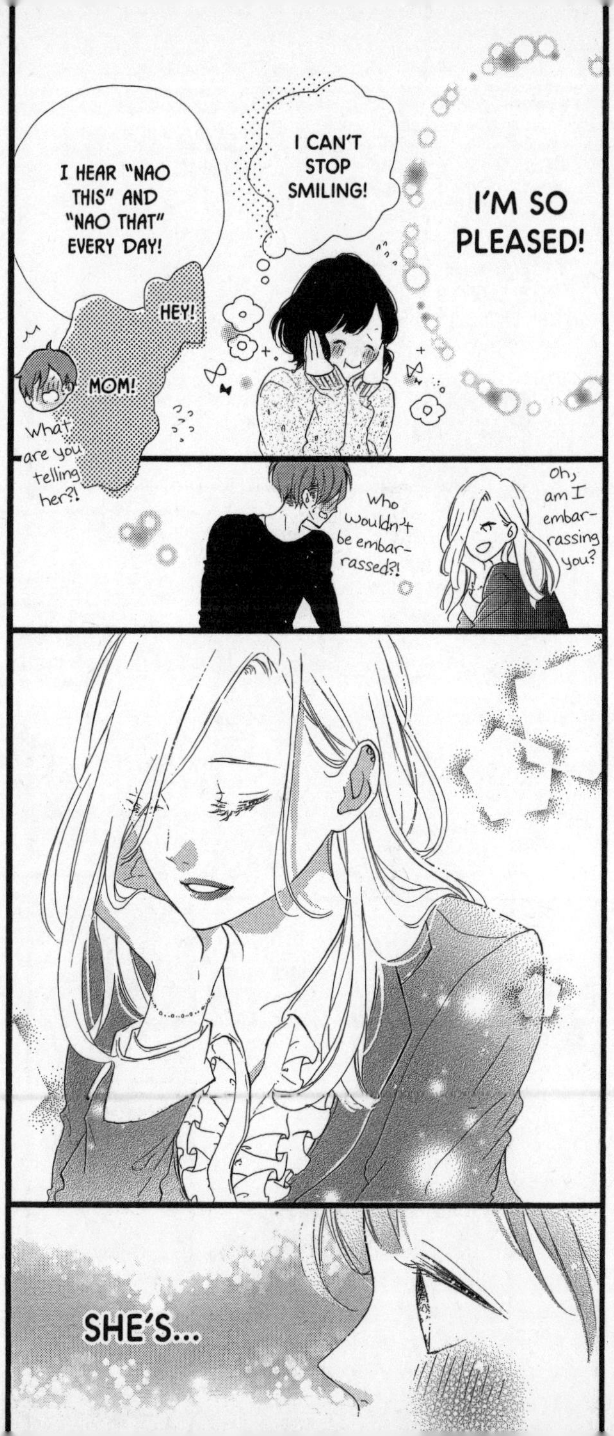
I'M SO PLEASED!
I CAN'T STOP SMILING!
I HEAR "NAO THIS" AND "NAO THAT" EVERY DAY!
HEY!
MOM!
What are you telling her?!
Oh, am I embar-rassing you?
Who wouldn't be embar-rassed?!
SHE'S...
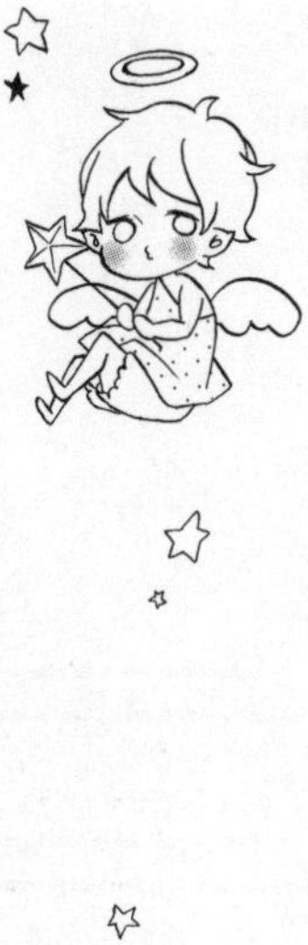

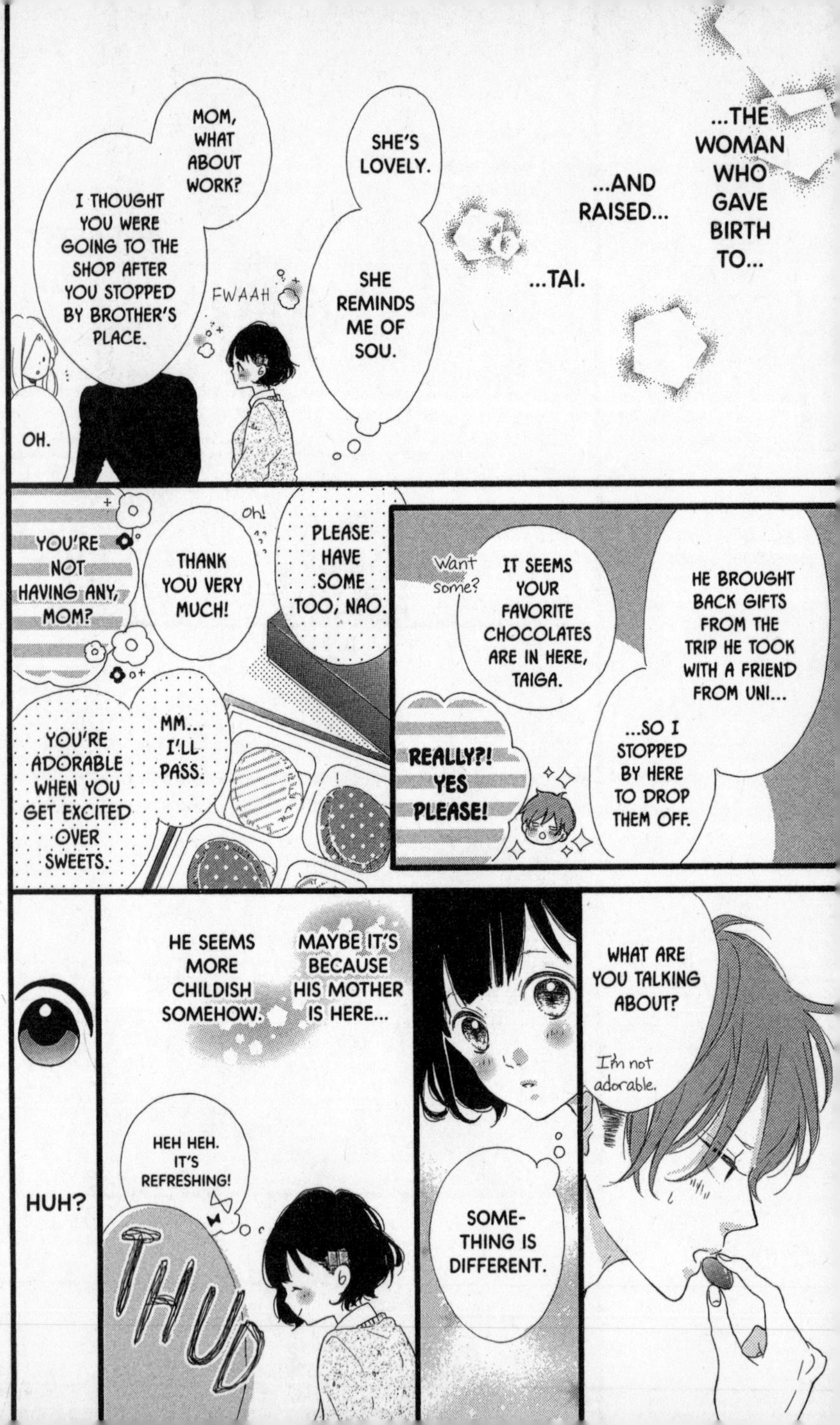
...THE WOMAN WHO GAVE BIRTH TO...
...AND RAISED...
...TAI.
SHE'S LOVELY.
SHE REMINDS ME OF SOU.
FWAAH
MOM, WHAT ABOUT WORK?
I THOUGHT YOU WERE GOING TO THE SHOP AFTER YOU STOPPED BY BROTHER'S PLACE.
OH.
HE BROUGHT BACK GIFTS FROM THE TRIP HE TOOK WITH A FRIEND FROM UNI...
...SO I STOPPED BY HERE TO DROP THEM OFF.
IT SEEMS YOUR FAVORITE CHOCOLATES ARE IN HERE, TAIGA.
Want some?
REALLY?! YES PLEASE!
PLEASE HAVE SOME TOO, NAO.
Oh!
THANK YOU VERY MUCH!
YOU'RE NOT HAVING ANY, MOM?
MM... I'LL PASS.
YOU'RE ADORABLE WHEN YOU GET EXCITED OVER SWEETS.
WHAT ARE YOU TALKING ABOUT?
I'm not adorable.
SOME-THING IS DIFFERENT.
MAYBE IT'S BECAUSE HIS MOTHER IS HERE...
HE SEEMS MORE CHILDISH SOMEHOW.
HEH HEH. IT'S REFRESHING!
THUD
HUH?

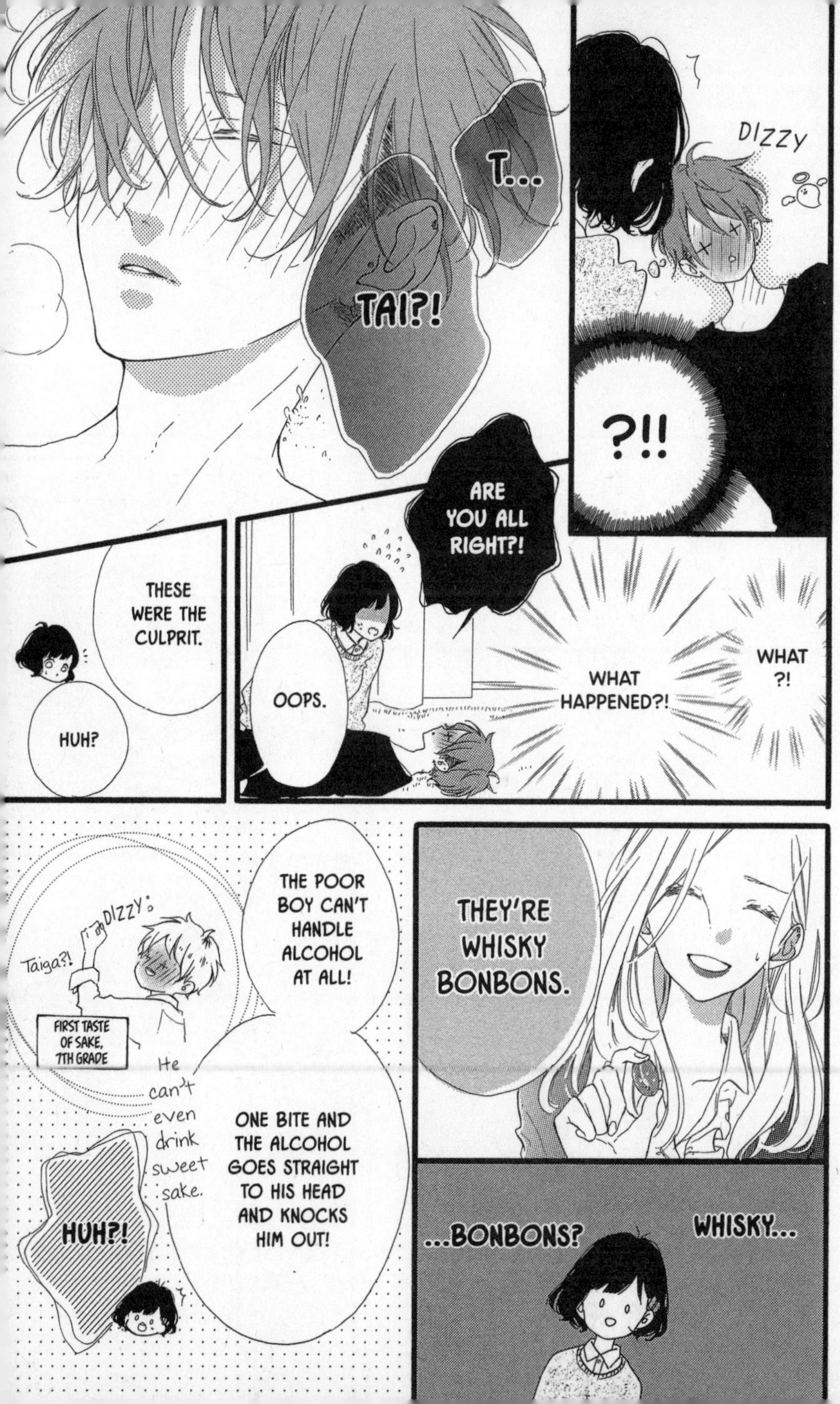
DIZZY
?!!
T...
TAI?!
ARE YOU ALL RIGHT?!
WHAT ?!
WHAT HAPPENED?!
OOPS.
THESE WERE THE CULPRIT.
HUH?
THEY'RE WHISKY BONBONS.
WHISKY...
...BONBONS?
THE POOR BOY CAN'T HANDLE ALCOHOL AT ALL!
Taiga?!
DIZZY
FIRST TASTE OF SAKE, 7TH GRADE
He can't even drink sweet sake.
ONE BITE AND THE ALCOHOL GOES STRAIGHT TO HIS HEAD AND KNOCKS HIM OUT!
HUH?!

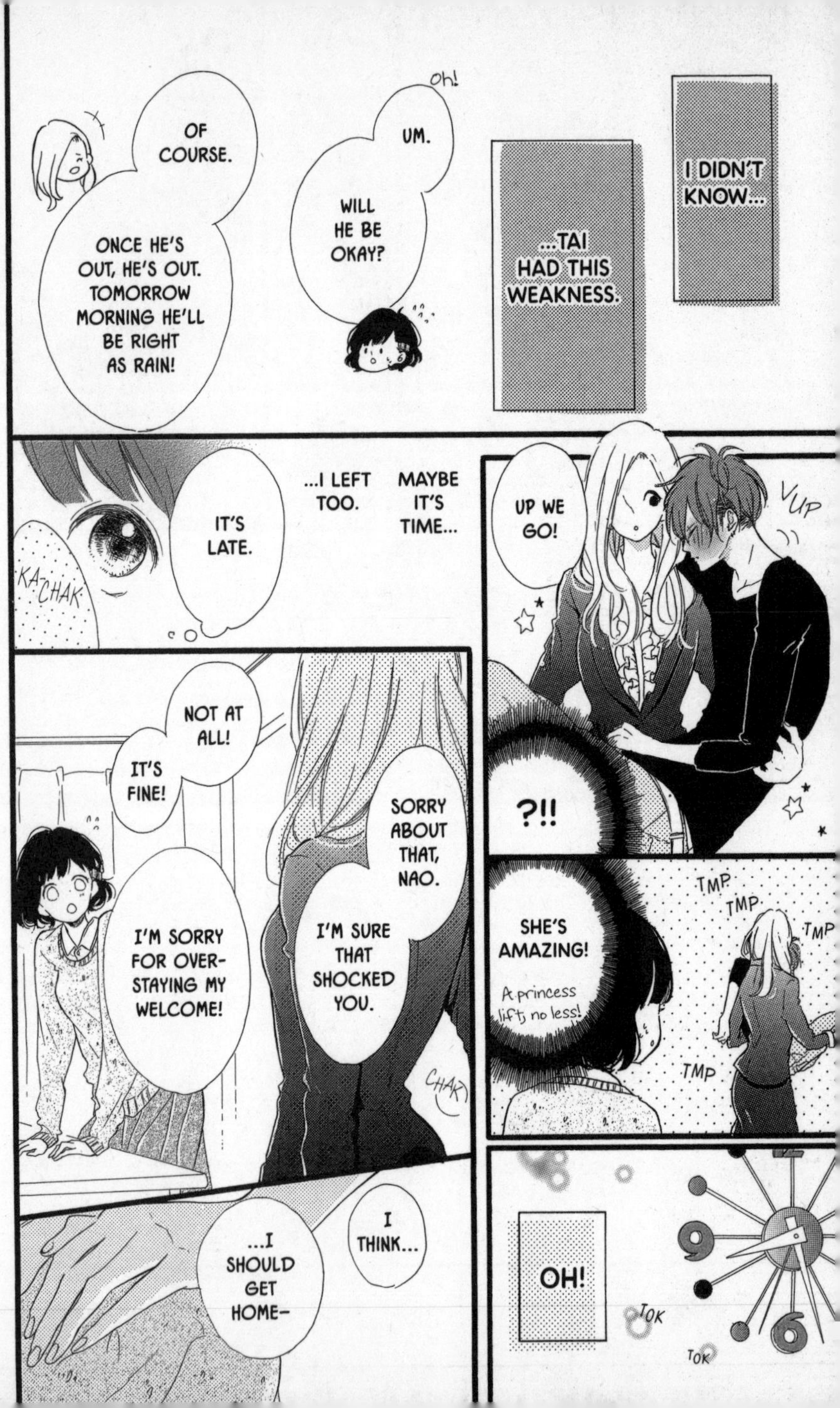
I DIDN'T KNOW...
...TAI HAD THIS WEAKNESS.
Oh!
UM.
WILL HE BE OKAY?
OF COURSE.
ONCE HE'S OUT, HE'S OUT. TOMORROW MORNING HE'LL BE RIGHT AS RAIN!
VUP
UP WE GO!
?!!
TMP TMP TMP TMP
SHE'S AMAZING!
A princess lift, no less!
TOK TOK
OH!
MAYBE IT'S TIME...
...I LEFT TOO.
IT'S LATE.
KA-CHAK
SORRY ABOUT THAT, NAO.
I'M SURE THAT SHOCKED YOU.
NOT AT ALL!
IT'S FINE!
I'M SORRY FOR OVER-STAYING MY WELCOME!
CHAK
I THINK...
...I SHOULD GET HOME-

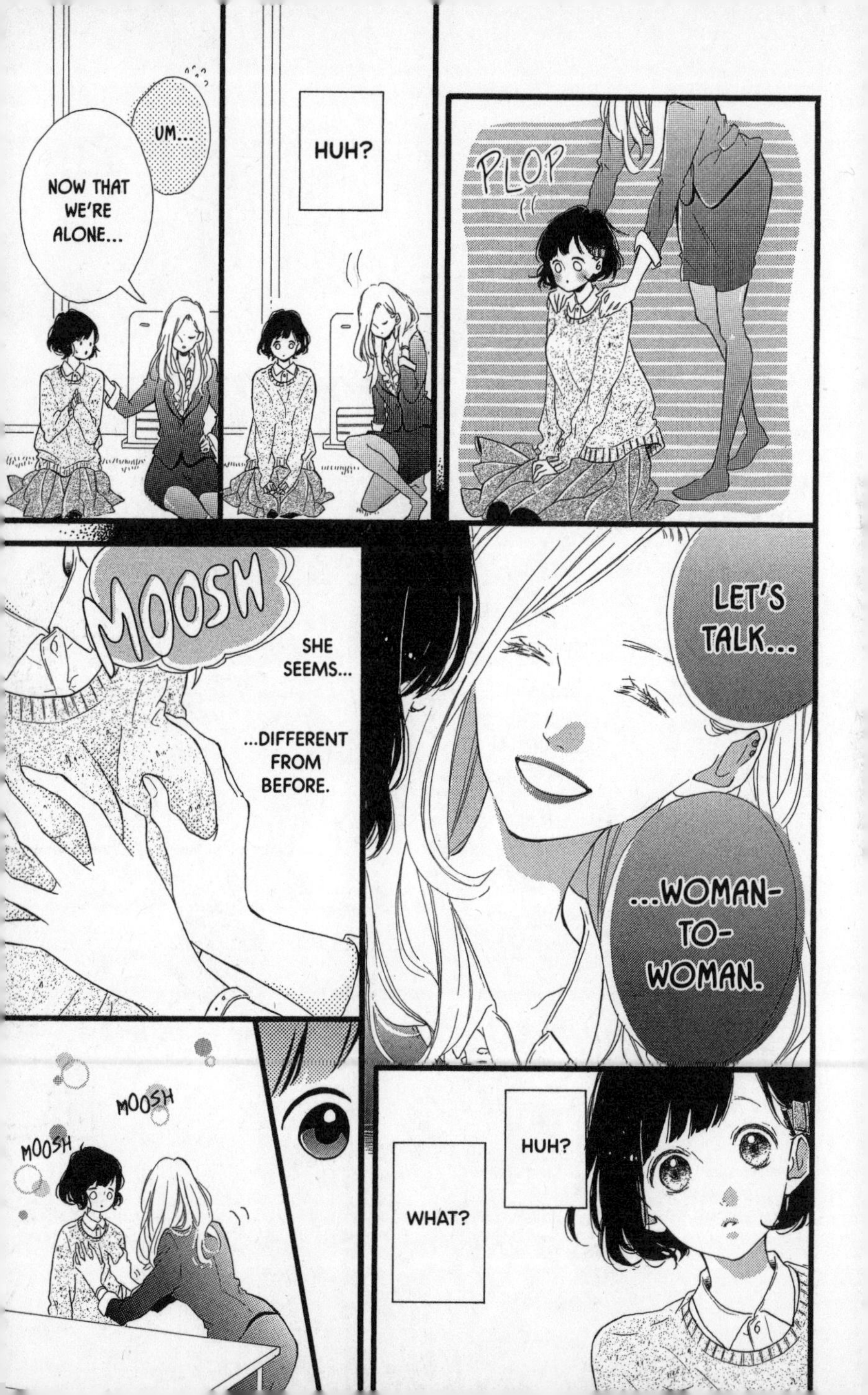
PLOP
HUH?
UM...
NOW THAT WE'RE ALONE...
LET'S TALK...
...WOMAN-TO-WOMAN.
MOOSH
SHE SEEMS...
...DIFFERENT FROM BEFORE.
HUH?
WHAT?
MOOSH
MOOSH

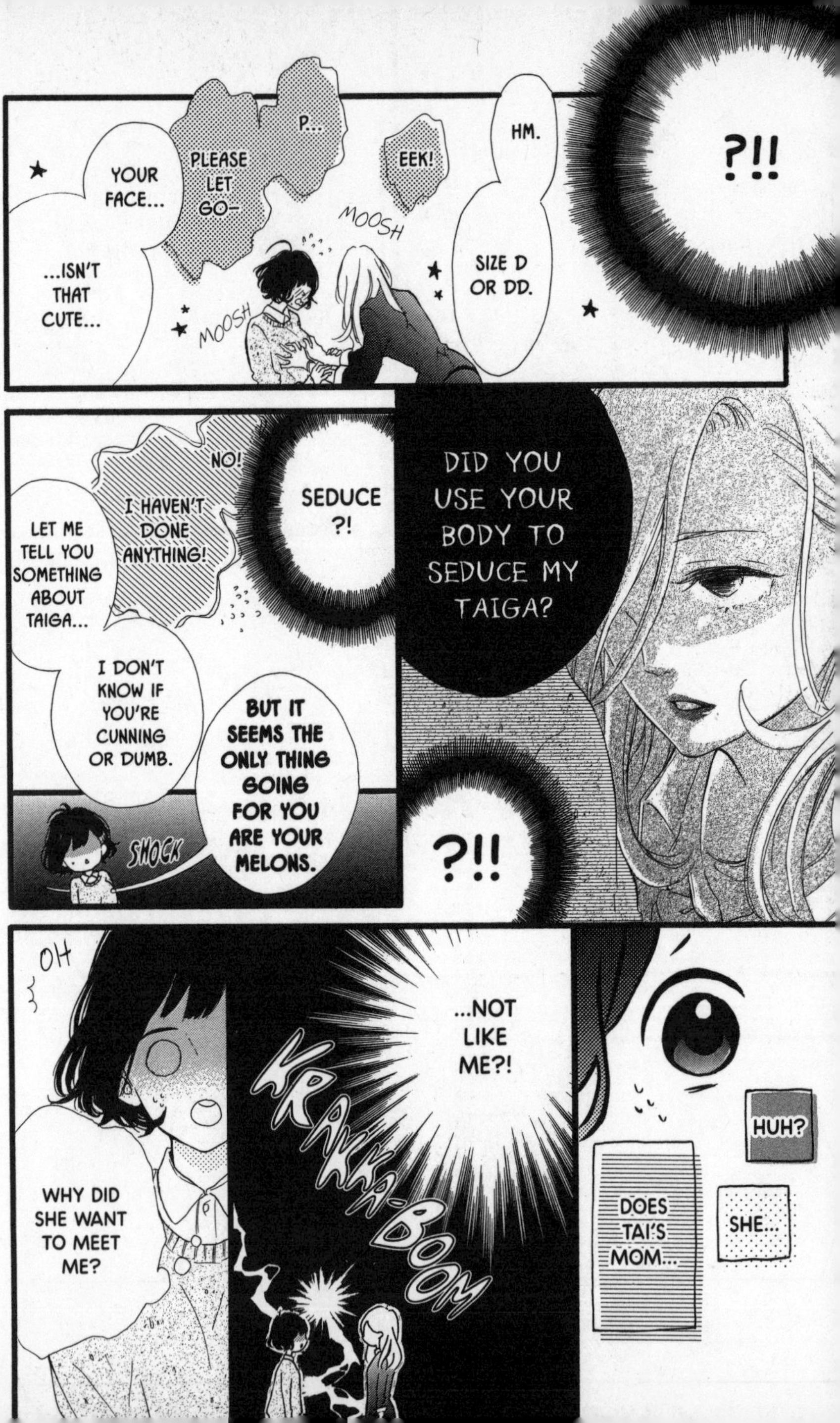
?!!
HM.
SIZE D OR DD.
EEK!
P...
MOOSH
PLEASE LET GO–
YOUR FACE...
...ISN'T THAT CUTE...
MOOSH
DID YOU USE YOUR BODY TO SEDUCE MY TAIGA?
?!!
SEDUCE?!
NO!
I HAVEN'T DONE ANYTHING!
LET ME TELL YOU SOMETHING ABOUT TAIGA...
I DON'T KNOW IF YOU'RE CUNNING OR DUMB.
BUT IT SEEMS THE ONLY THING GOING FOR YOU ARE YOUR MELONS.
SHOCK
HUH?
SHE...
DOES TAI'S MOM...
...NOT LIKE ME?!
KRAKKA-BOOM
OH
WHY DID SHE WANT TO MEET ME?

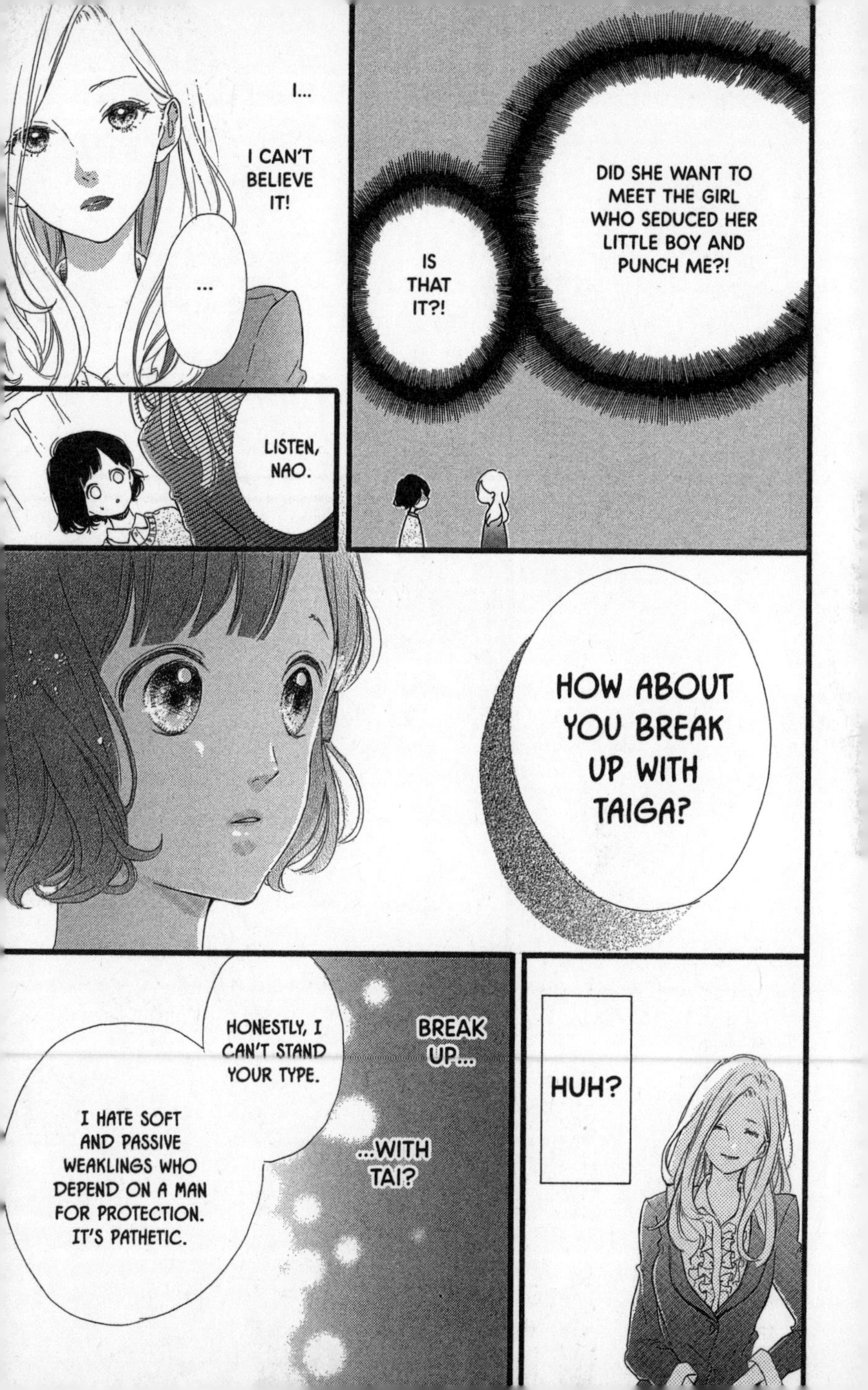
DID SHE WANT TO MEET THE GIRL WHO SEDUCED HER LITTLE BOY AND PUNCH ME?!
IS THAT IT?!
I...
I CAN'T BELIEVE IT!
...
LISTEN, NAO.
HOW ABOUT YOU BREAK UP WITH TAIGA?
HUH?
BREAK UP...
HONESTLY, I CAN'T STAND YOUR TYPE.
...WITH TAI?
I HATE SOFT AND PASSIVE WEAKLINGS WHO DEPEND ON A MAN FOR PROTECTION. IT'S PATHETIC.

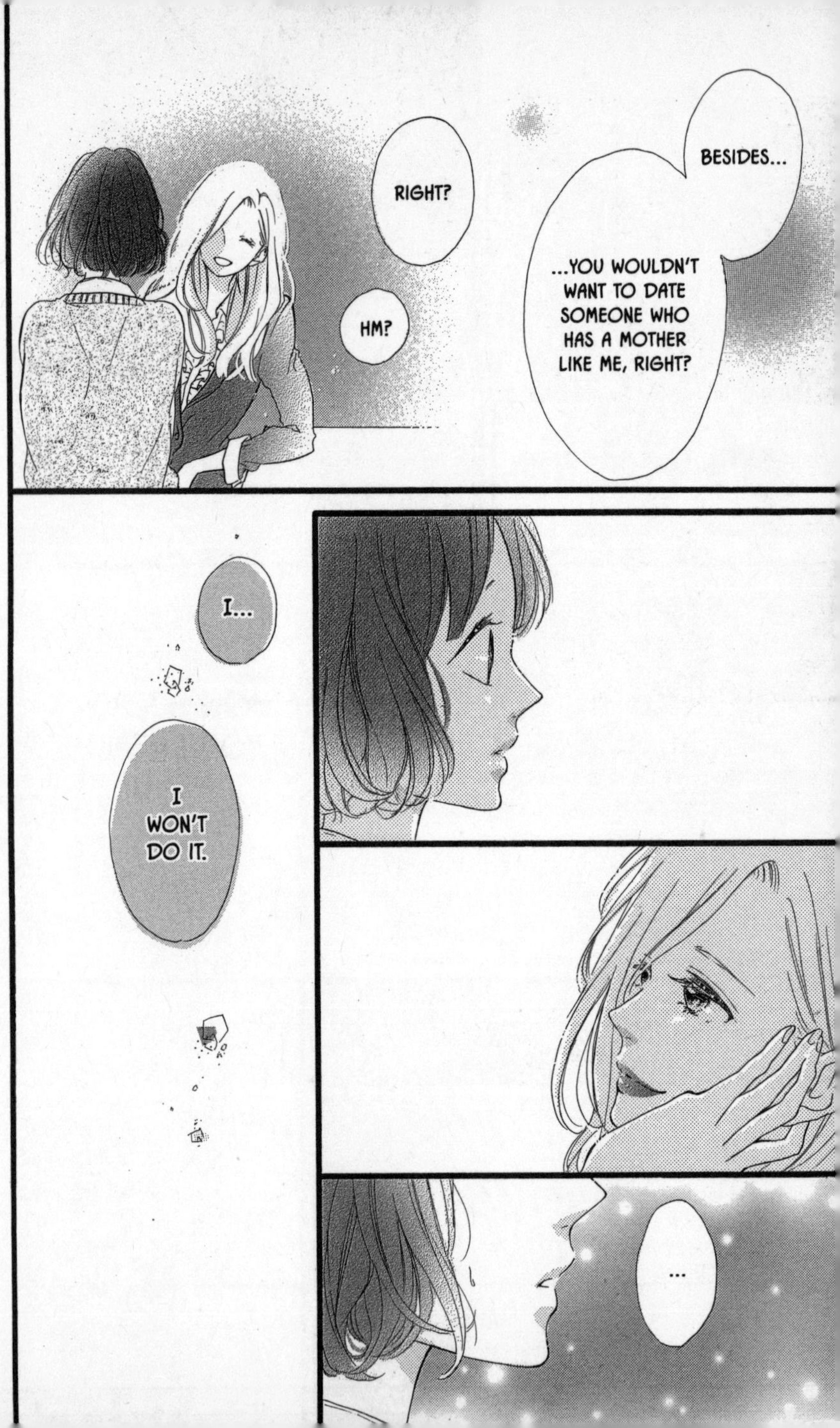
BESIDES...
...YOU WOULDN'T WANT TO DATE SOMEONE WHO HAS A MOTHER LIKE ME, RIGHT?
RIGHT?
HM?
I...
I WON'T DO IT.
...

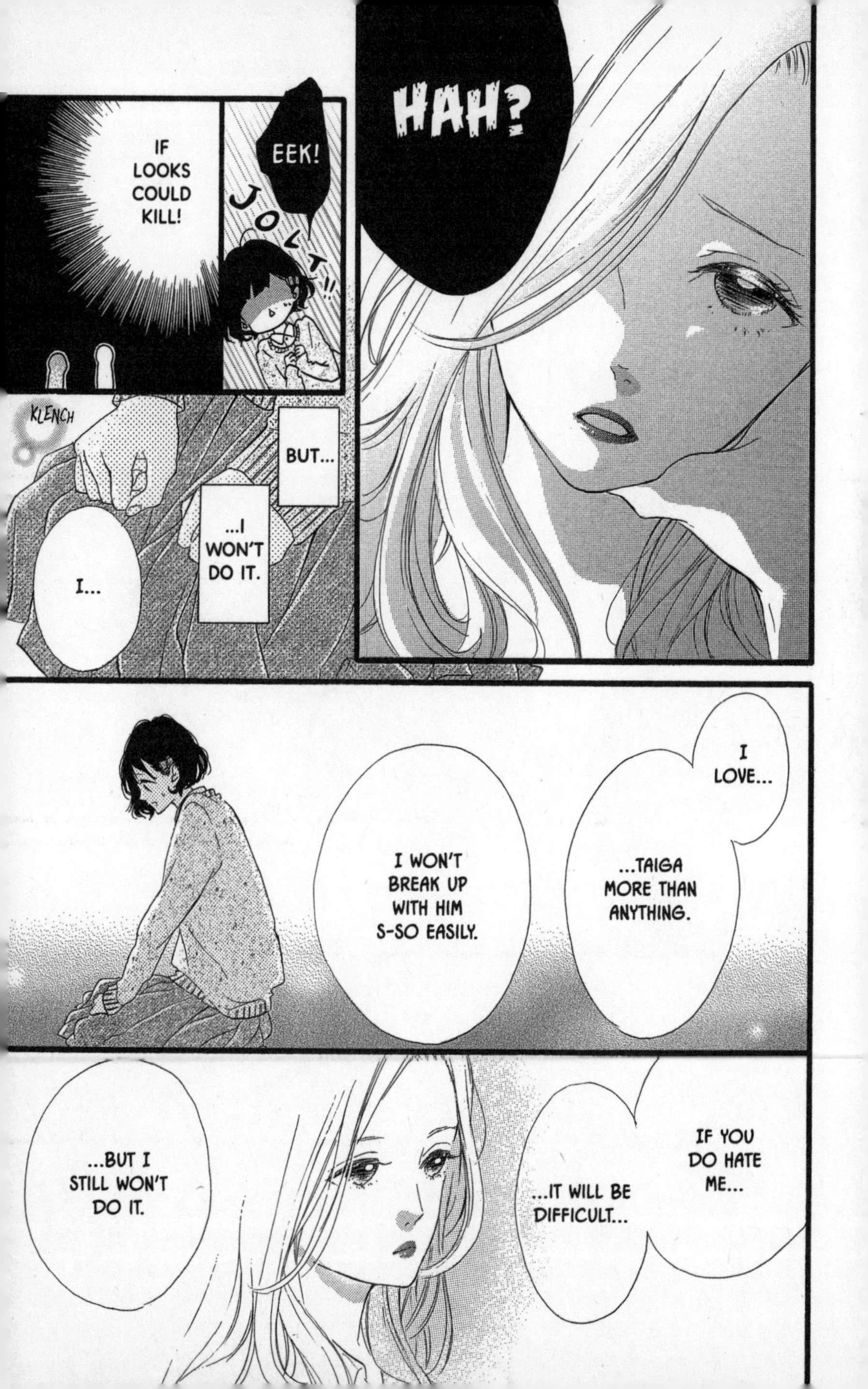
HAH?
EEK!
JOLT!!
IF LOOKS COULD KILL!
BUT...
...I WON'T DO IT.
KLENCH
I...
I LOVE...
...TAIGA MORE THAN ANYTHING.
I WON'T BREAK UP WITH HIM S-SO EASILY.
IF YOU DO HATE ME...
...IT WILL BE DIFFICULT...
...BUT I STILL WON'T DO IT.

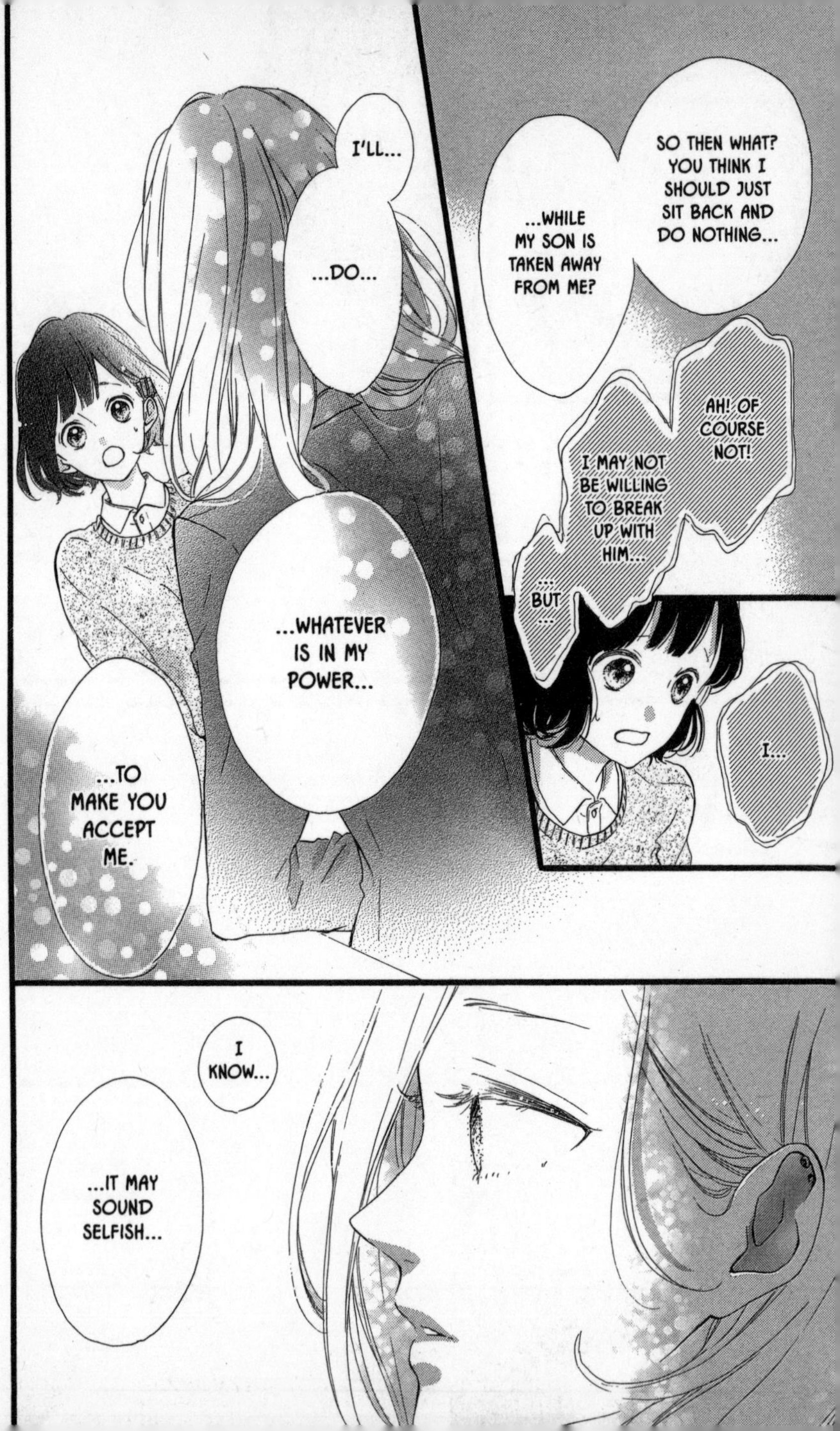
SO THEN WHAT? YOU THINK I SHOULD JUST SIT BACK AND DO NOTHING...
...WHILE MY SON IS TAKEN AWAY FROM ME?
AH! OF COURSE NOT!
I MAY NOT BE WILLING TO BREAK UP WITH HIM...
...BUT...
I...
I'LL...
...DO...
...WHATEVER IS IN MY POWER...
...TO MAKE YOU ACCEPT ME.
I KNOW...
...IT MAY SOUND SELFISH...

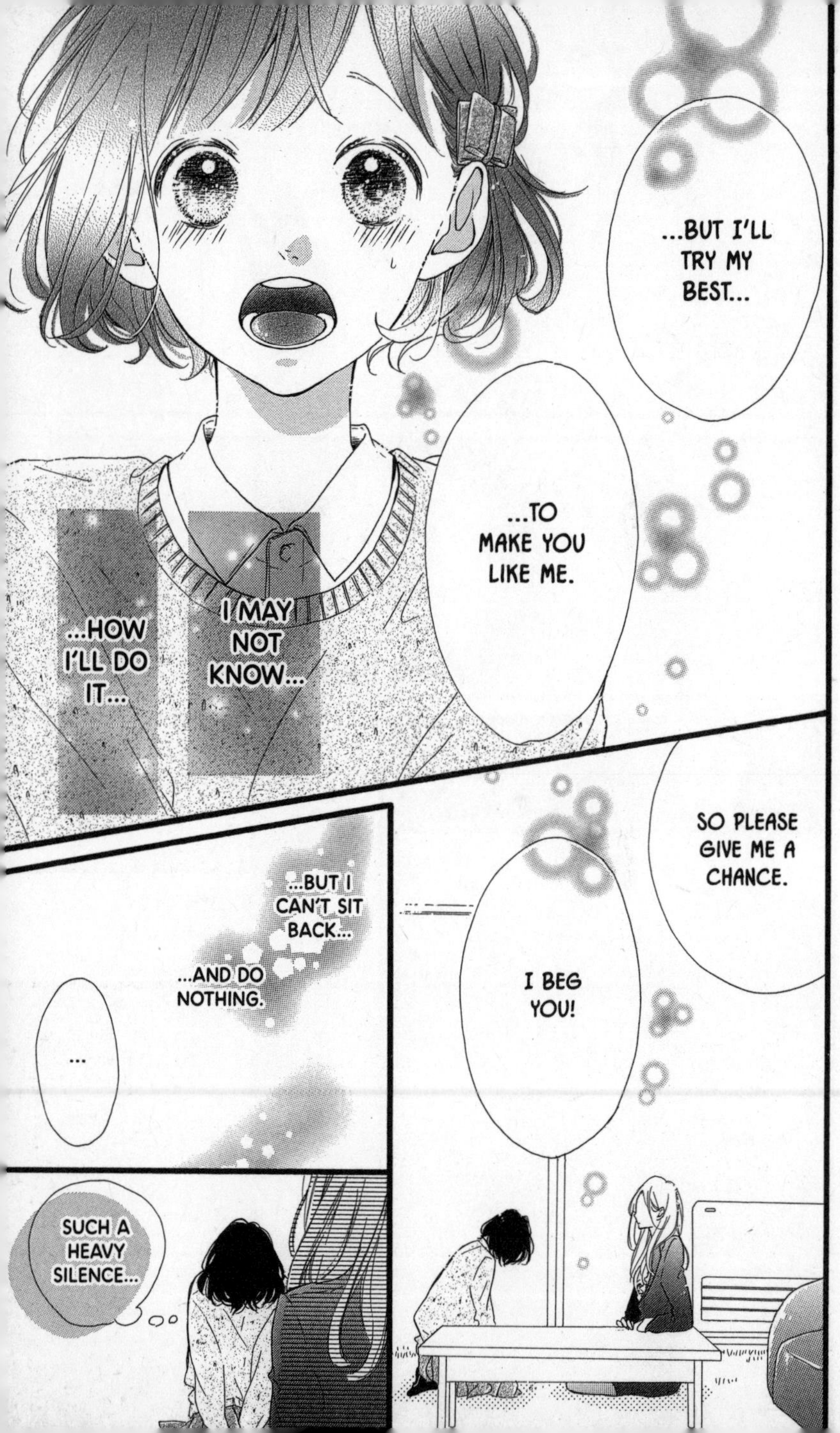
...BUT I'LL TRY MY BEST...
...TO MAKE YOU LIKE ME.
I MAY NOT KNOW...
...HOW I'LL DO IT...
SO PLEASE GIVE ME A CHANCE.
I BEG YOU!
...BUT I CAN'T SIT BACK...
...AND DO NOTHING.
...
SUCH A HEAVY SILENCE...

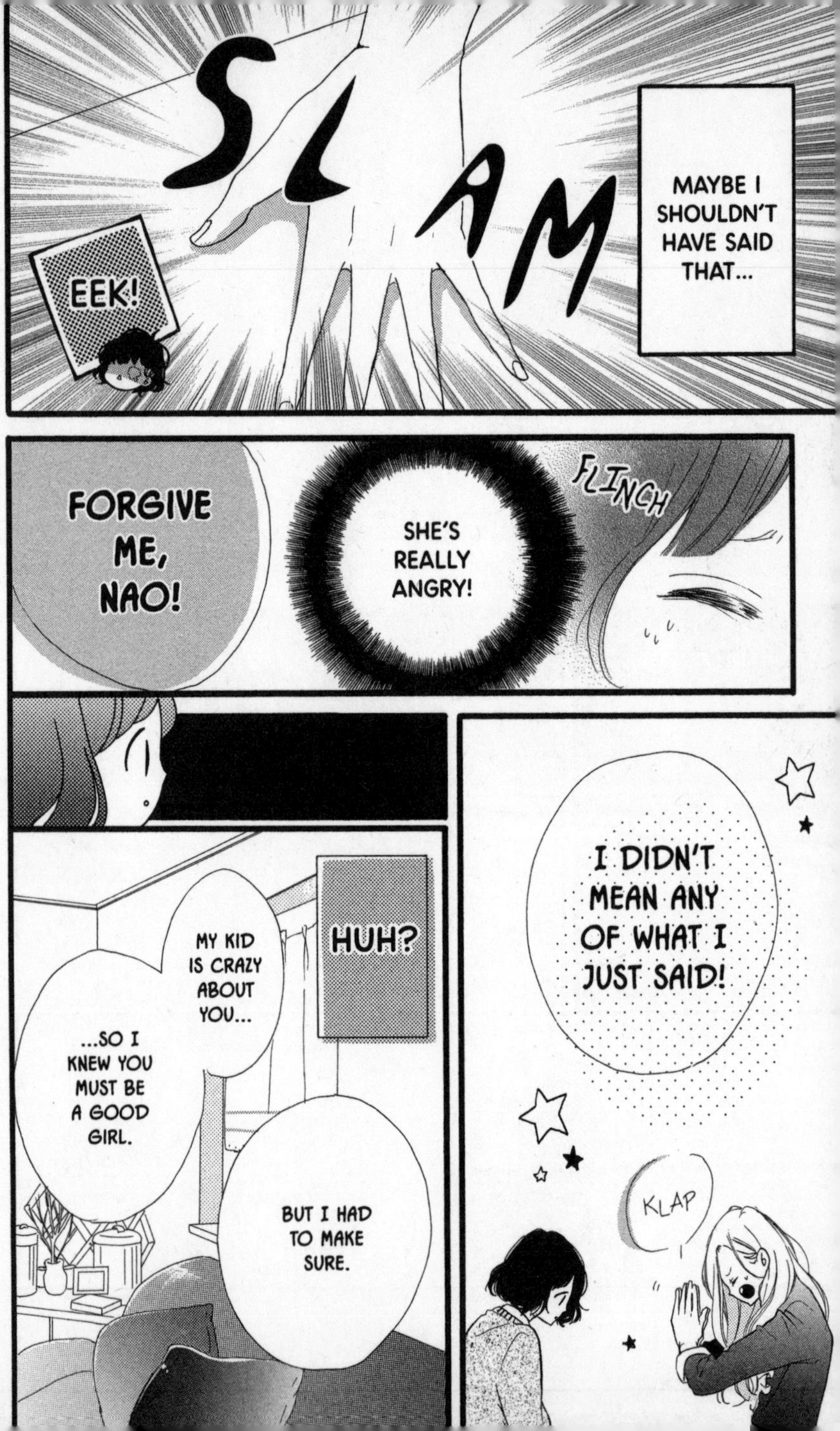
MAYBE I SHOULDN'T HAVE SAID THAT...
SLAM
EEK!
FLINCH
SHE'S REALLY ANGRY!
FORGIVE ME, NAO!
I DIDN'T MEAN ANY OF WHAT I JUST SAID!
KLAP
HUH?
MY KID IS CRAZY ABOUT YOU...
...SO I KNEW YOU MUST BE A GOOD GIRL.
BUT I HAD TO MAKE SURE.

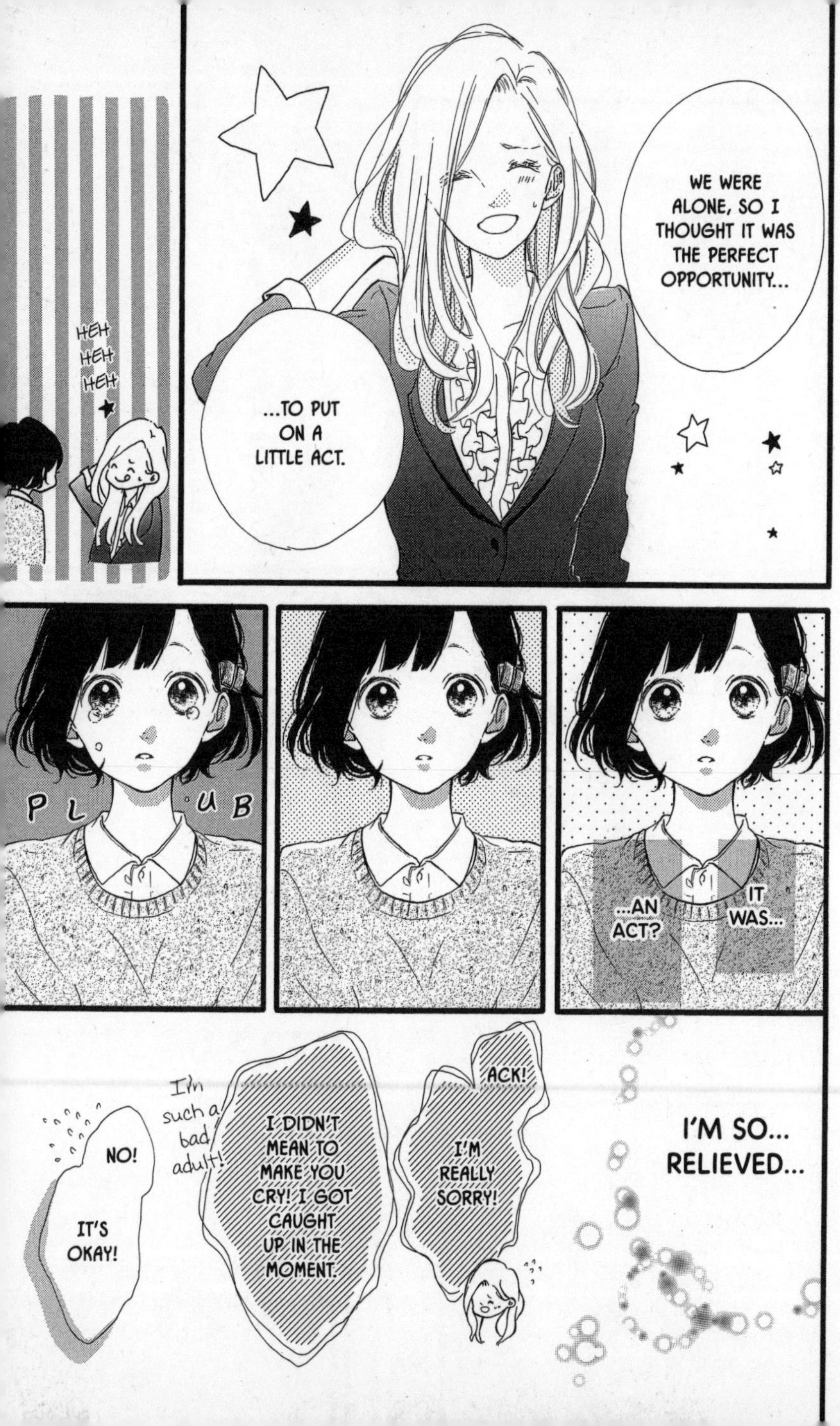
WE WERE ALONE, SO I THOUGHT IT WAS THE PERFECT OPPORTUNITY...
...TO PUT ON A LITTLE ACT.
HEH HEH HEH
IT WAS...
...AN ACT?
PLUB
I'M SO... RELIEVED...
ACK!
I'M REALLY SORRY!
I DIDN'T MEAN TO MAKE YOU CRY! I GOT CAUGHT UP IN THE MOMENT.
I'm such a bad adult!
NO!
IT'S OKAY!

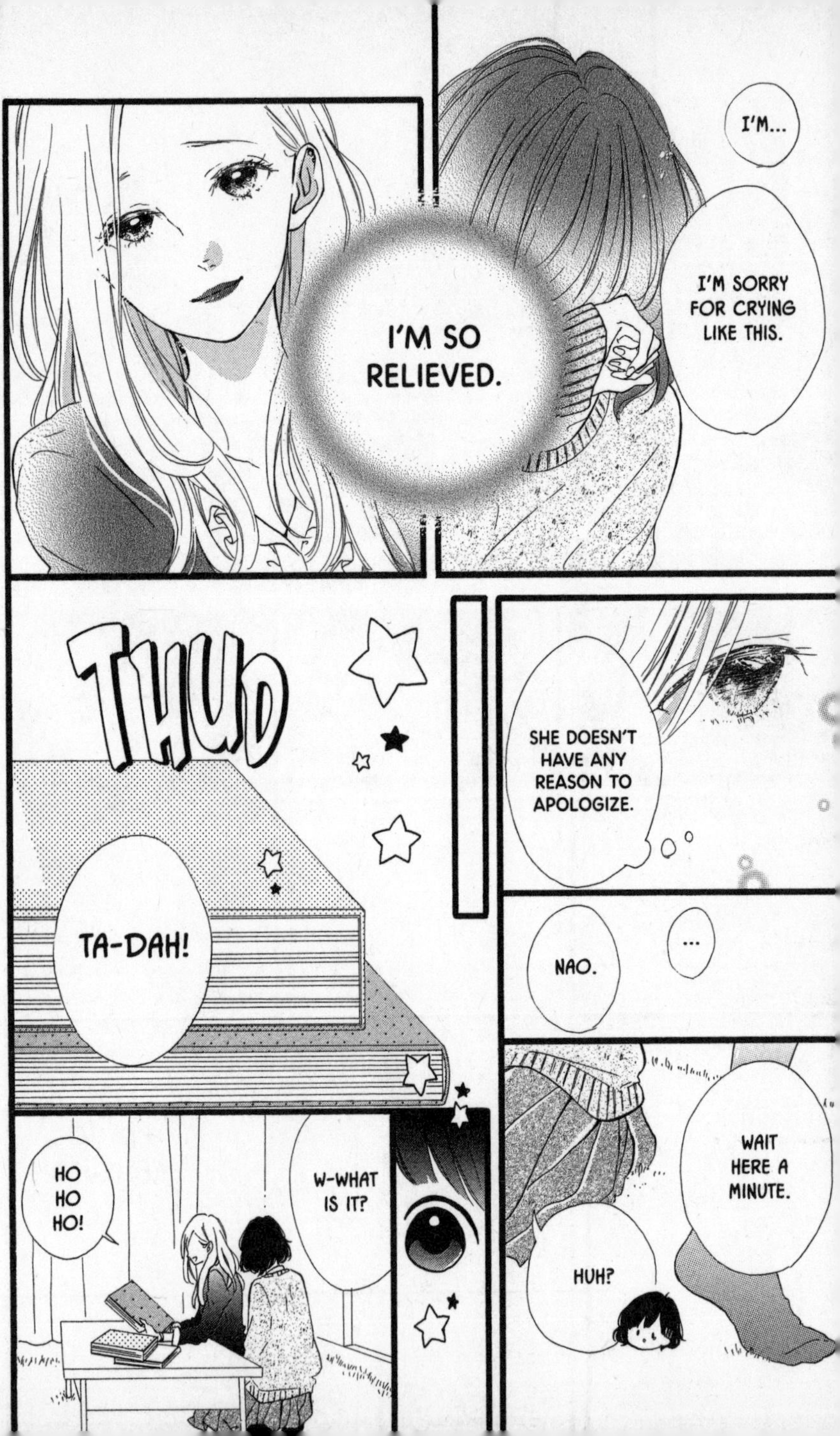
I'M...
I'M SORRY FOR CRYING LIKE THIS.
I'M SO RELIEVED.
SHE DOESN'T HAVE ANY REASON TO APOLOGIZE.
...
NAO.
WAIT HERE A MINUTE.
HUH?
THUD
TA-DAH!
W-WHAT IS IT?
HO HO HO!

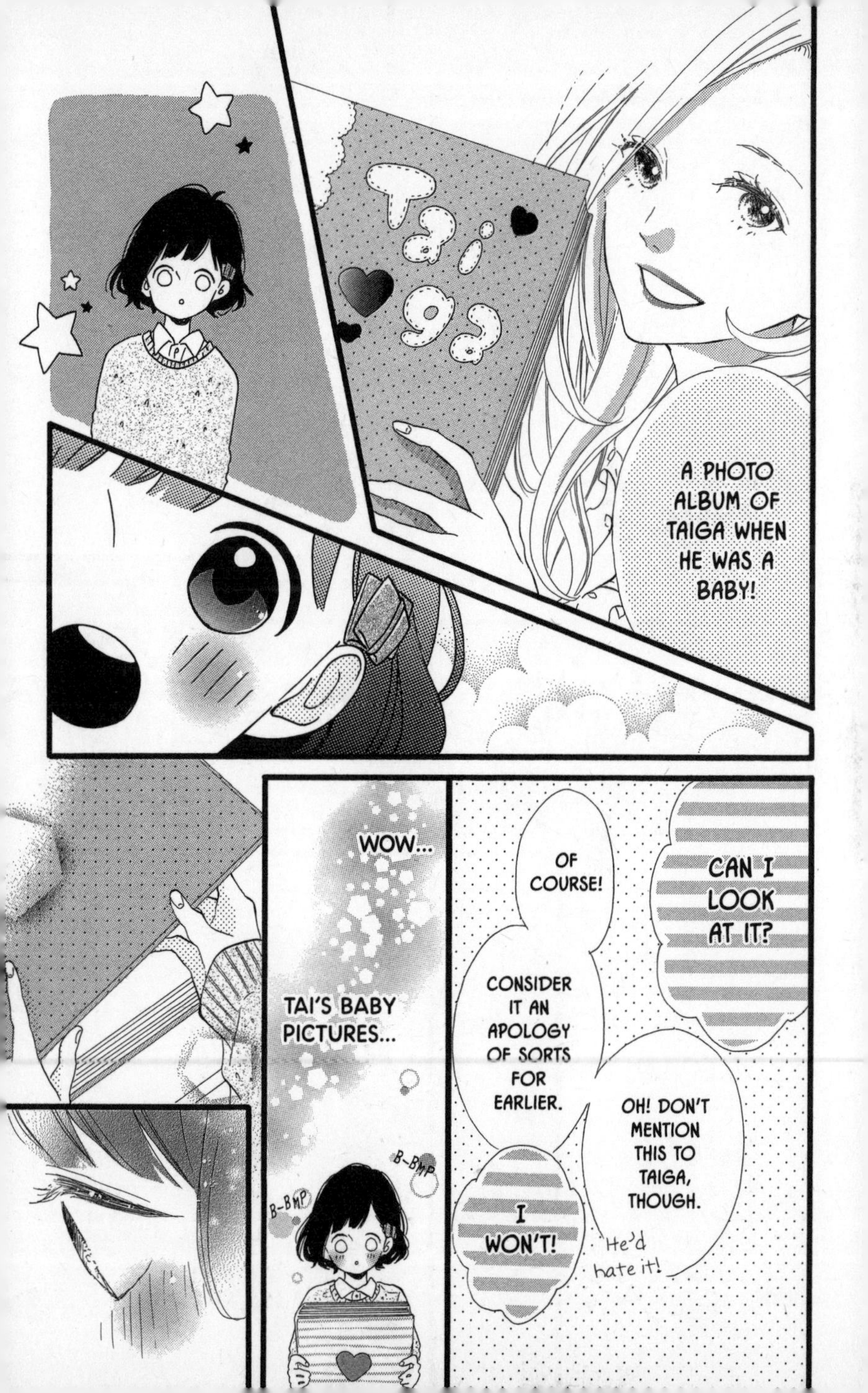
Taiga
A PHOTO ALBUM OF TAIGA WHEN HE WAS A BABY!
CAN I LOOK AT IT?
OF COURSE!
CONSIDER IT AN APOLOGY OF SORTS FOR EARLIER.
OH! DON'T MENTION THIS TO TAIGA, THOUGH.
He'd hate it!
I WON'T!
WOW...
TAI'S BABY PICTURES...
B-BMP
B-BMP

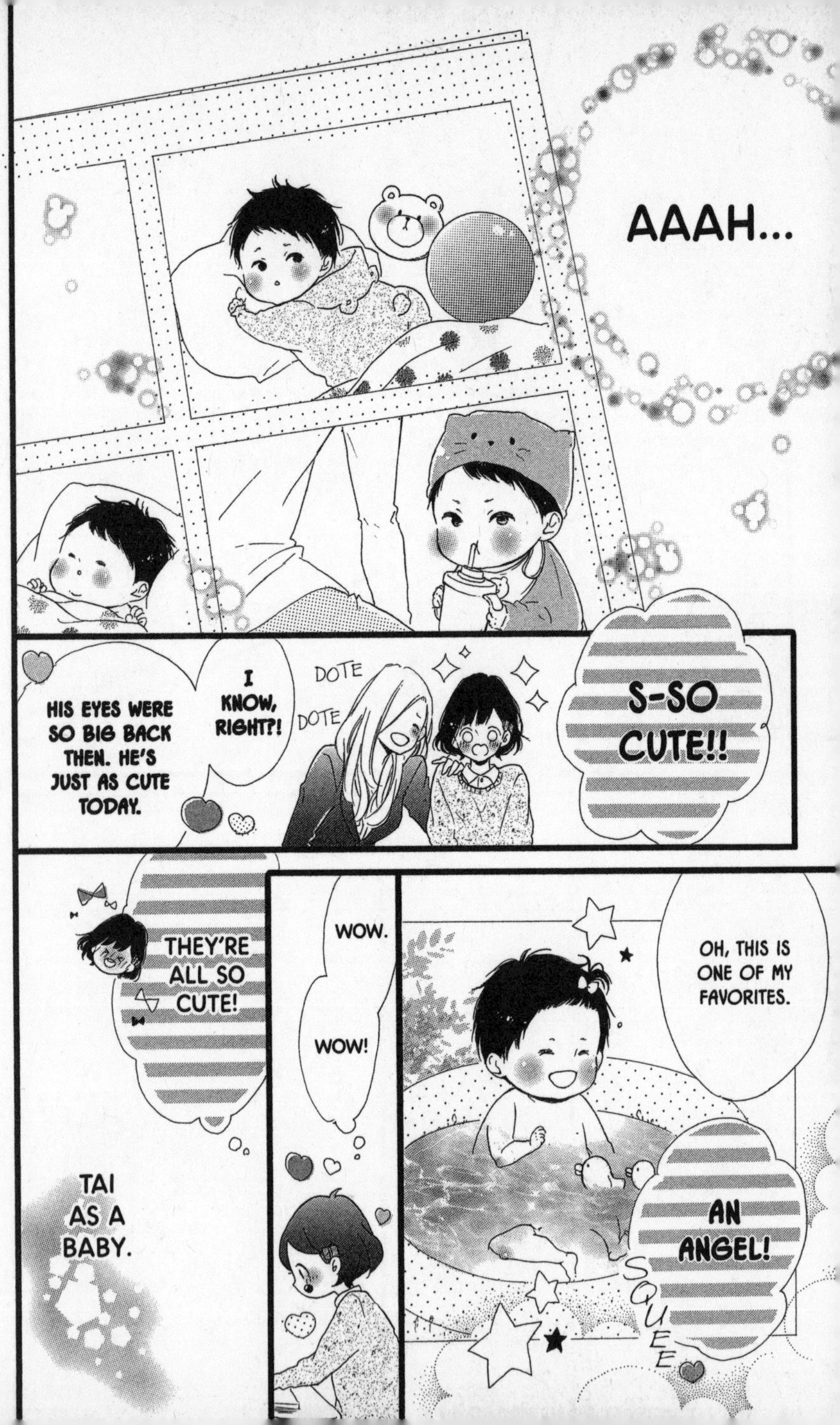
AAAH...
S-SO CUTE!!
DOTE
DOTE
I KNOW, RIGHT?!
HIS EYES WERE SO BIG BACK THEN. HE'S JUST AS CUTE TODAY.
OH, THIS IS ONE OF MY FAVORITES.
AN ANGEL!
SQUEE
WOW.
WOW!
THEY'RE ALL SO CUTE!
TAI AS A BABY.

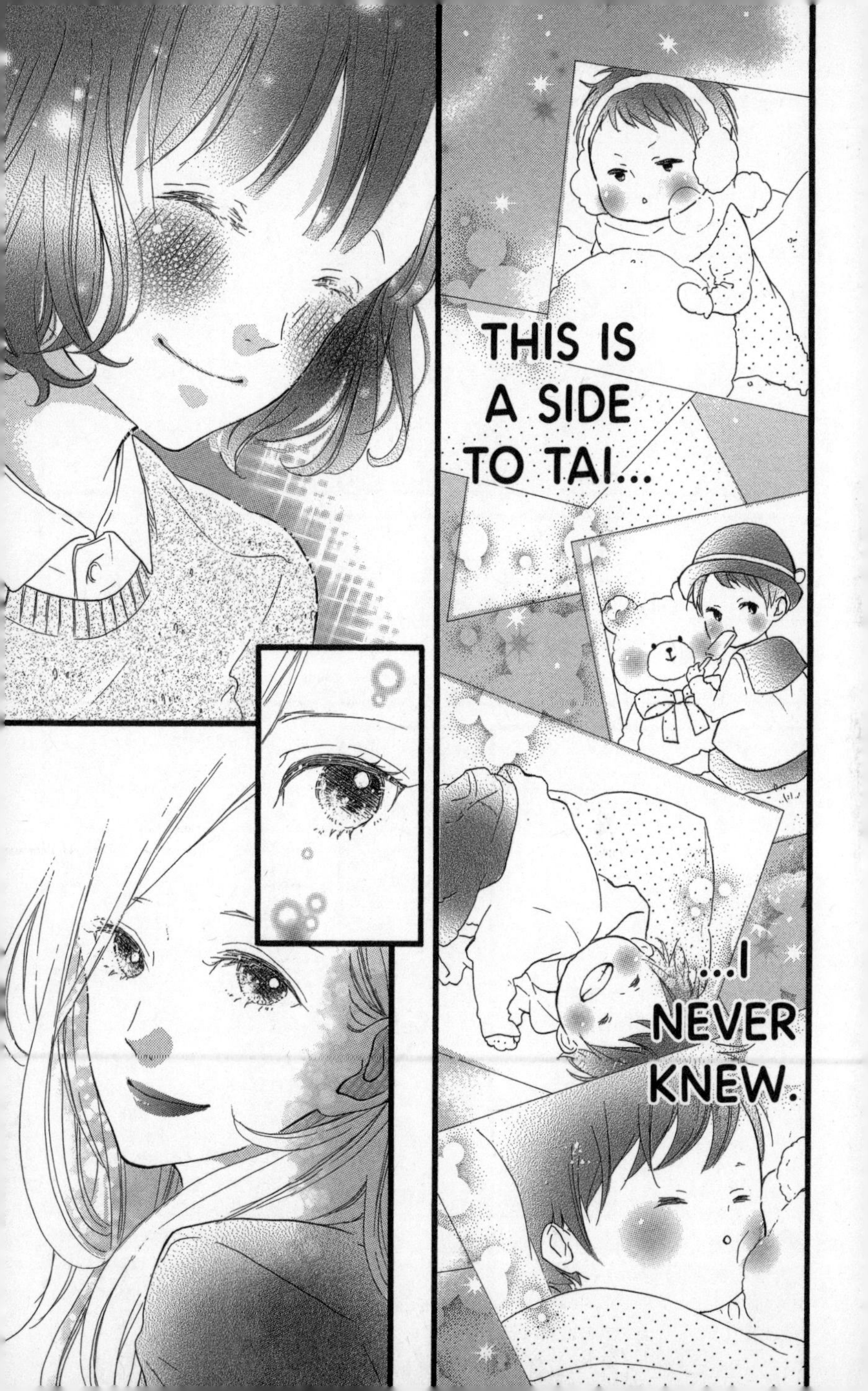
THIS IS A SIDE TO TAI...
...I NEVER KNEW.

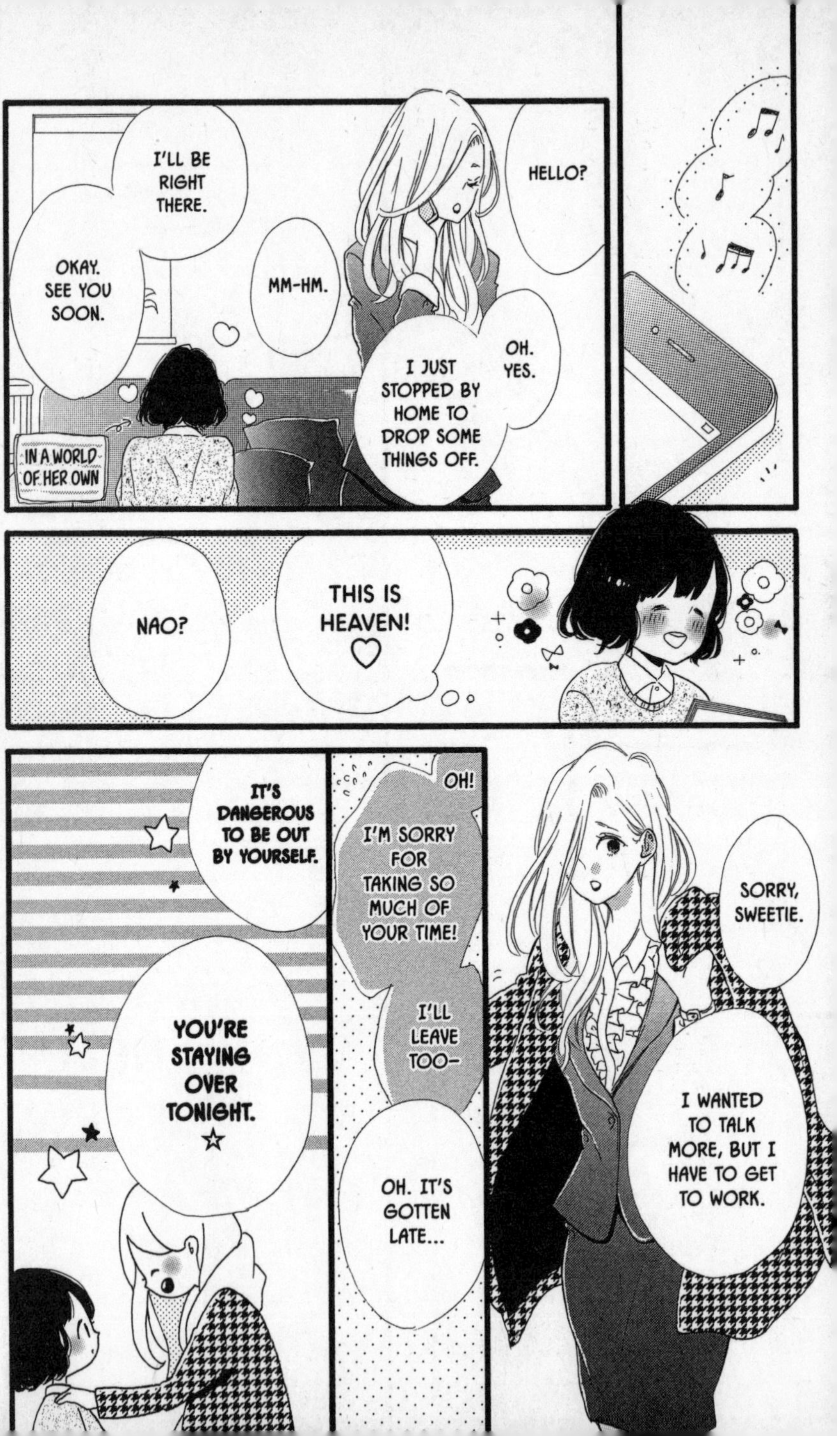
HELLO?
OH. YES.
I JUST STOPPED BY HOME TO DROP SOME THINGS OFF.
MM-HM.
I'LL BE RIGHT THERE.
OKAY. SEE YOU SOON.
IN A WORLD OF HER OWN
THIS IS HEAVEN! ♡
NAO?
SORRY, SWEETIE.
I WANTED TO TALK MORE, BUT I HAVE TO GET TO WORK.
OH!
I'M SORRY FOR TAKING SO MUCH OF YOUR TIME!
I'LL LEAVE TOO—
OH. IT'S GOTTEN LATE...
IT'S DANGEROUS TO BE OUT BY YOURSELF.
YOU'RE STAYING OVER TONIGHT. ☆

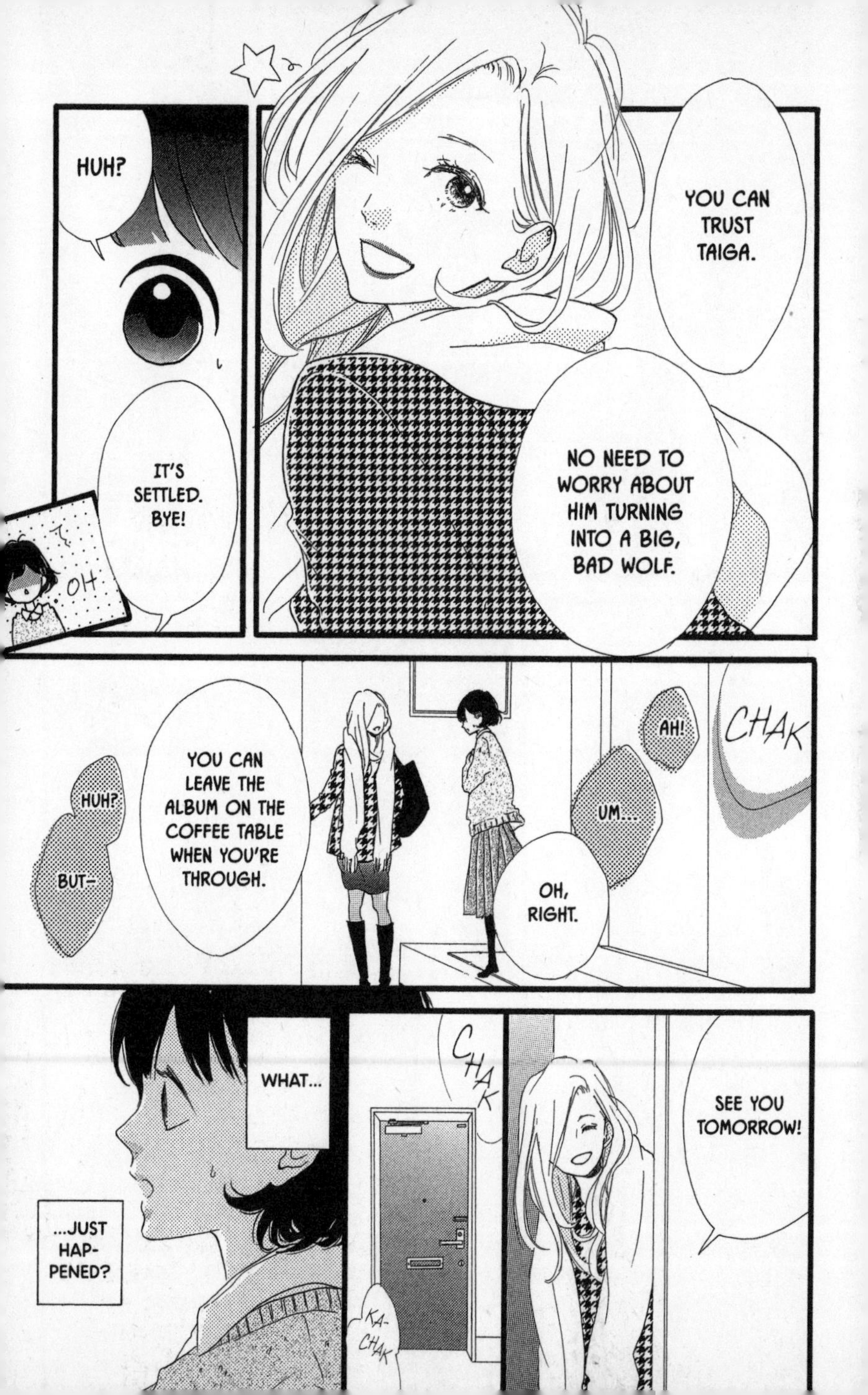
YOU CAN TRUST TAIGA.
NO NEED TO WORRY ABOUT HIM TURNING INTO A BIG, BAD WOLF.
HUH?
IT'S SETTLED. BYE!
OH
CHAK
AH!
UM...
OH, RIGHT.
YOU CAN LEAVE THE ALBUM ON THE COFFEE TABLE WHEN YOU'RE THROUGH.
HUH?
BUT–
SEE YOU TOMORROW!
CHAK
KA-CHAK
WHAT...
...JUST HAP-PENED?

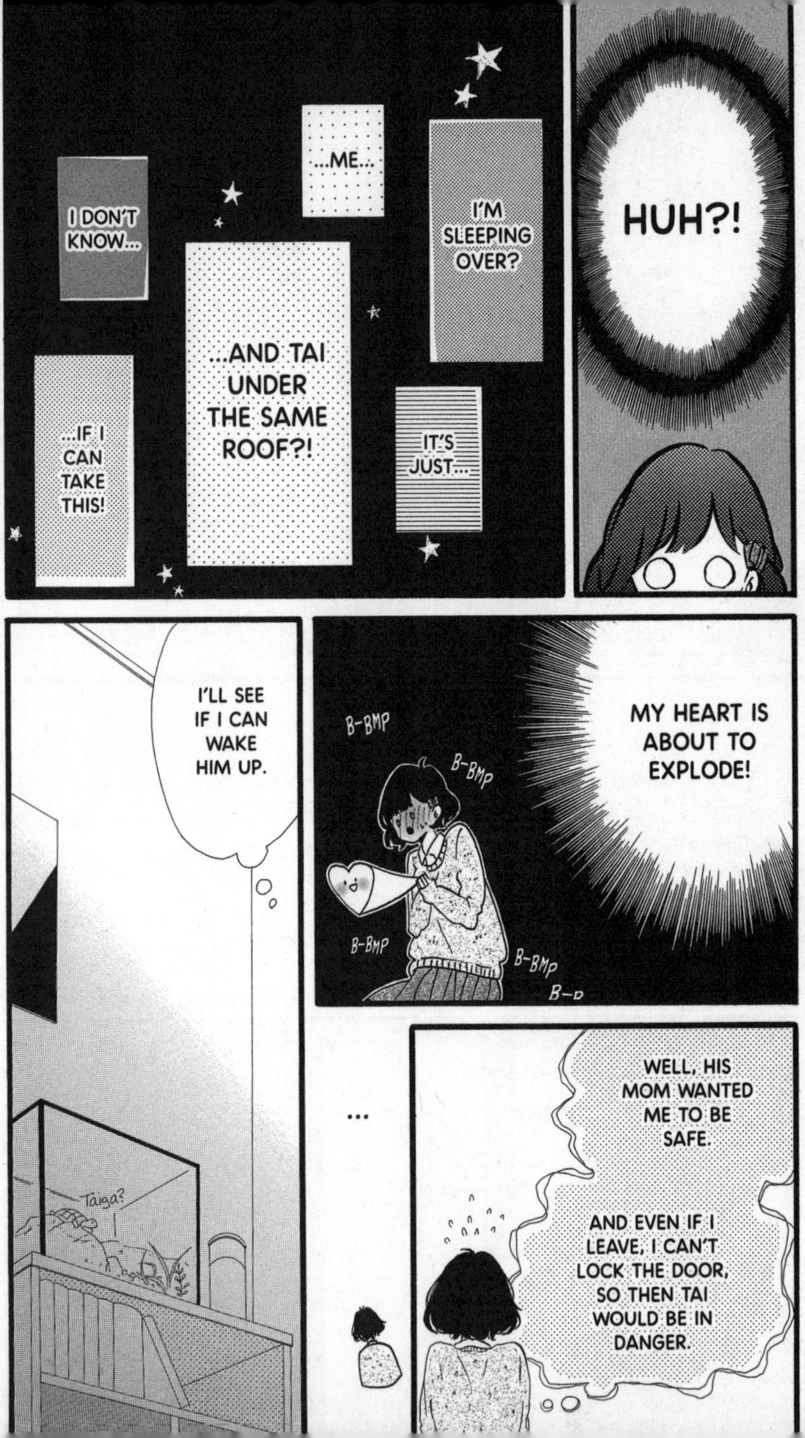
HUH?!
I'M SLEEPING OVER?
...ME...
...AND TAI UNDER THE SAME ROOF?!
IT'S JUST...
I DON'T KNOW...
...IF I CAN TAKE THIS!
MY HEART IS ABOUT TO EXPLODE!
B-BMP
B-BMP
B-BMP
B-BMP
...
WELL, HIS MOM WANTED ME TO BE SAFE.
AND EVEN IF I LEAVE, I CAN'T LOCK THE DOOR, SO THEN TAI WOULD BE IN DANGER.
I'LL SEE IF I CAN WAKE HIM UP.
Taiga?

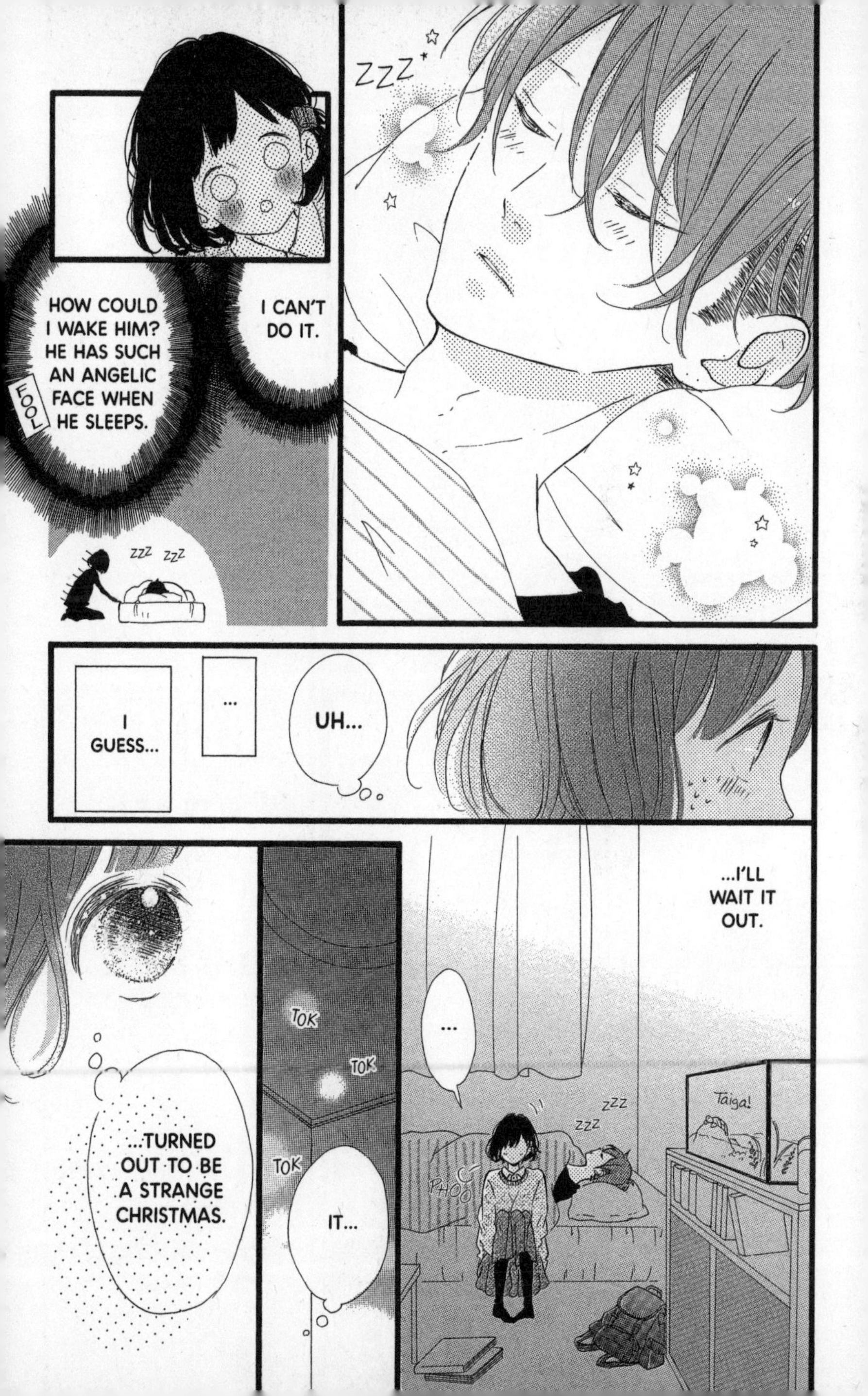
ZZZ
I CAN'T DO IT.
HOW COULD I WAKE HIM? HE HAS SUCH AN ANGELIC FACE WHEN HE SLEEPS.
FOOL
ZZZ ZZZ
UH...
...
I GUESS...
...I'LL WAIT IT OUT.
...
ZZZ
ZZZ
Taiga!
PHOO
TOK
TOK
TOK
IT...
...TURNED OUT TO BE A STRANGE CHRISTMAS.

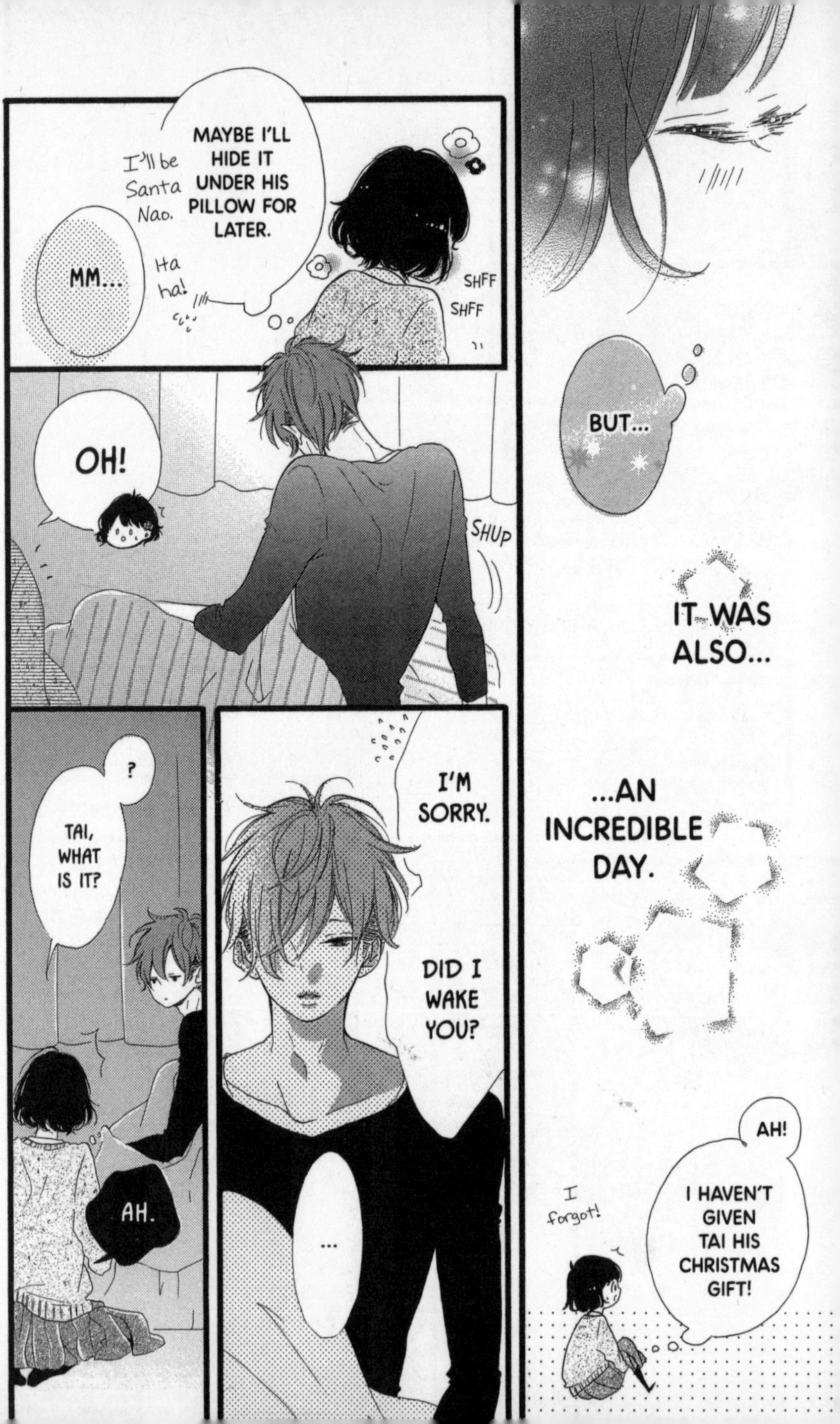
BUT...
IT WAS ALSO...
...AN INCREDIBLE DAY.
AH!
I HAVEN'T GIVEN TAI HIS CHRISTMAS GIFT!
I forgot!
MAYBE I'LL HIDE IT UNDER HIS PILLOW FOR LATER.
I'll be Santa Nao.
SHFF
SHFF
MM...
Ha ha!
SHUP
OH!
I'M SORRY.
DID I WAKE YOU?
...
?
TAI, WHAT IS IT?
AH.

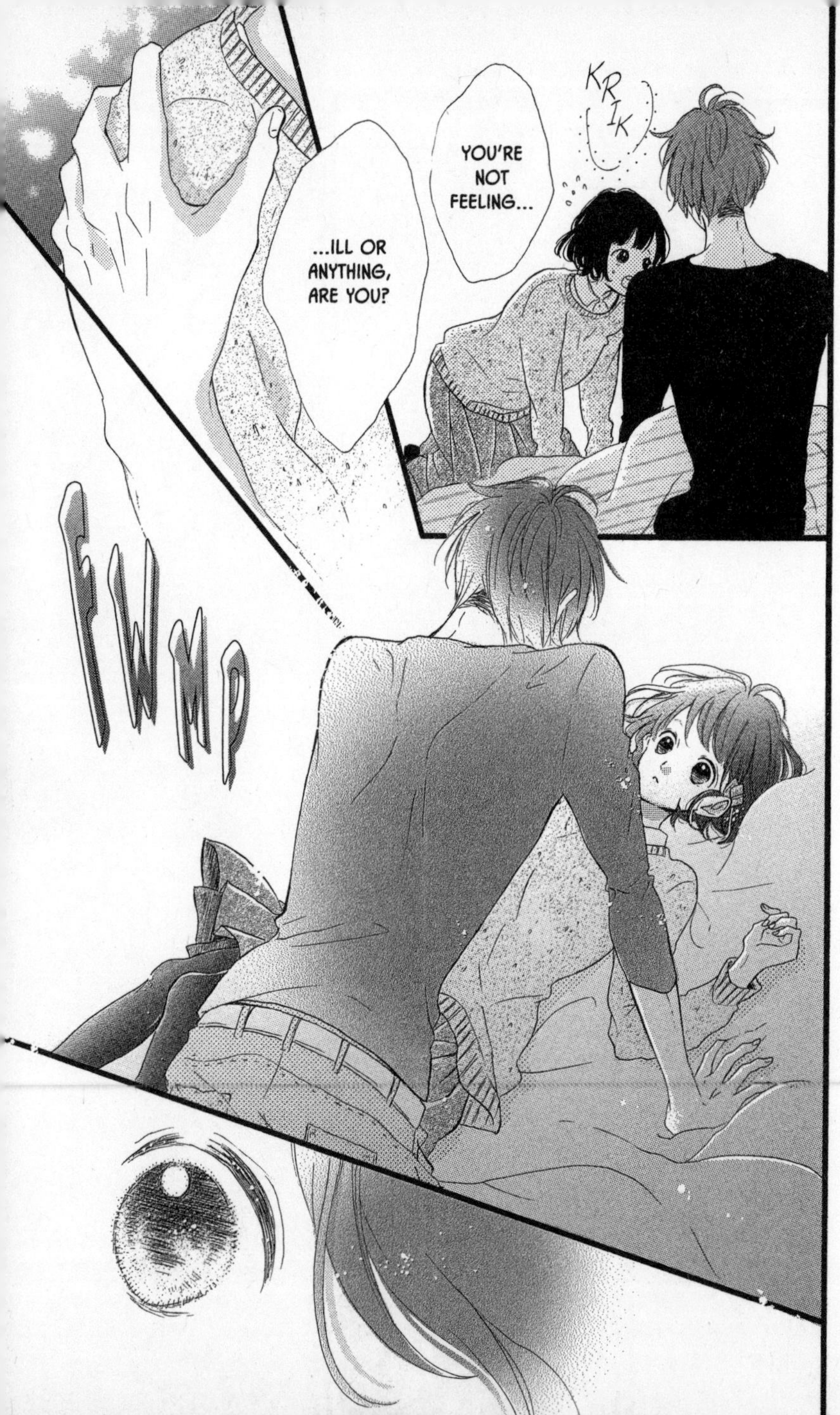
KRIK
YOU'RE NOT FEELING...
...ILL OR ANYTHING, ARE YOU?
FWMP

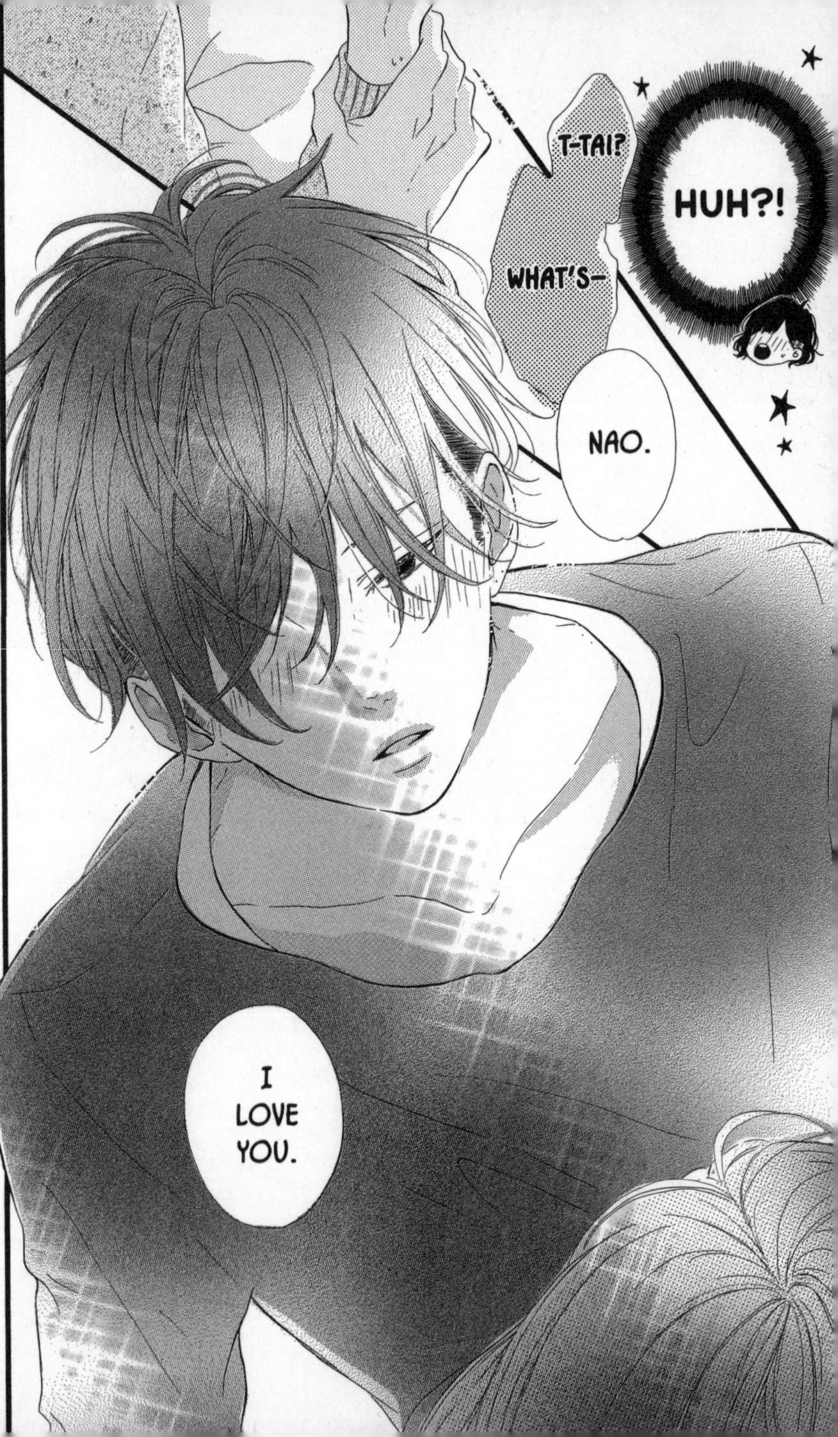
HUH?!
T-TAI?
WHAT'S-
NAO.
I LOVE YOU.

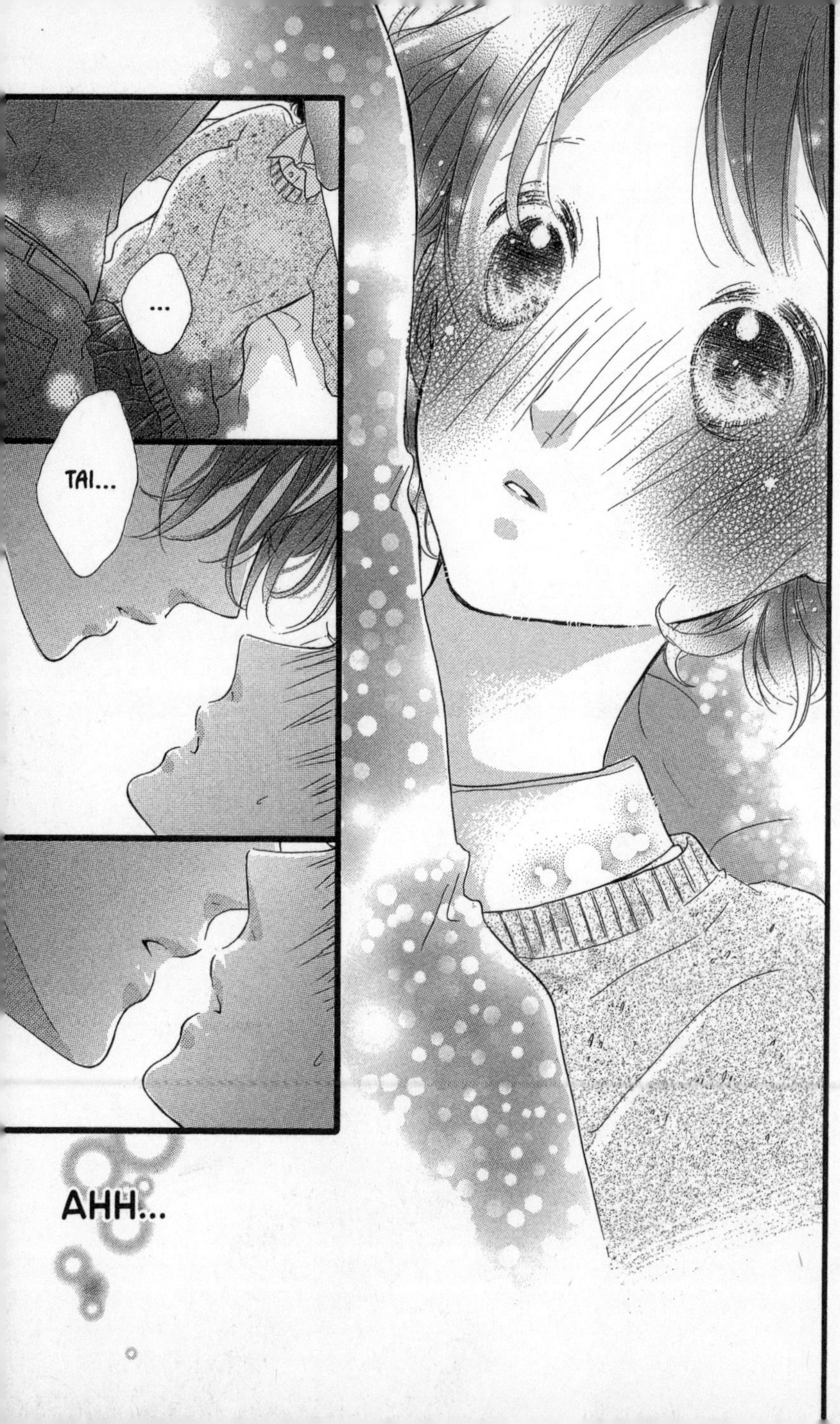
...
TAI...
AHH...

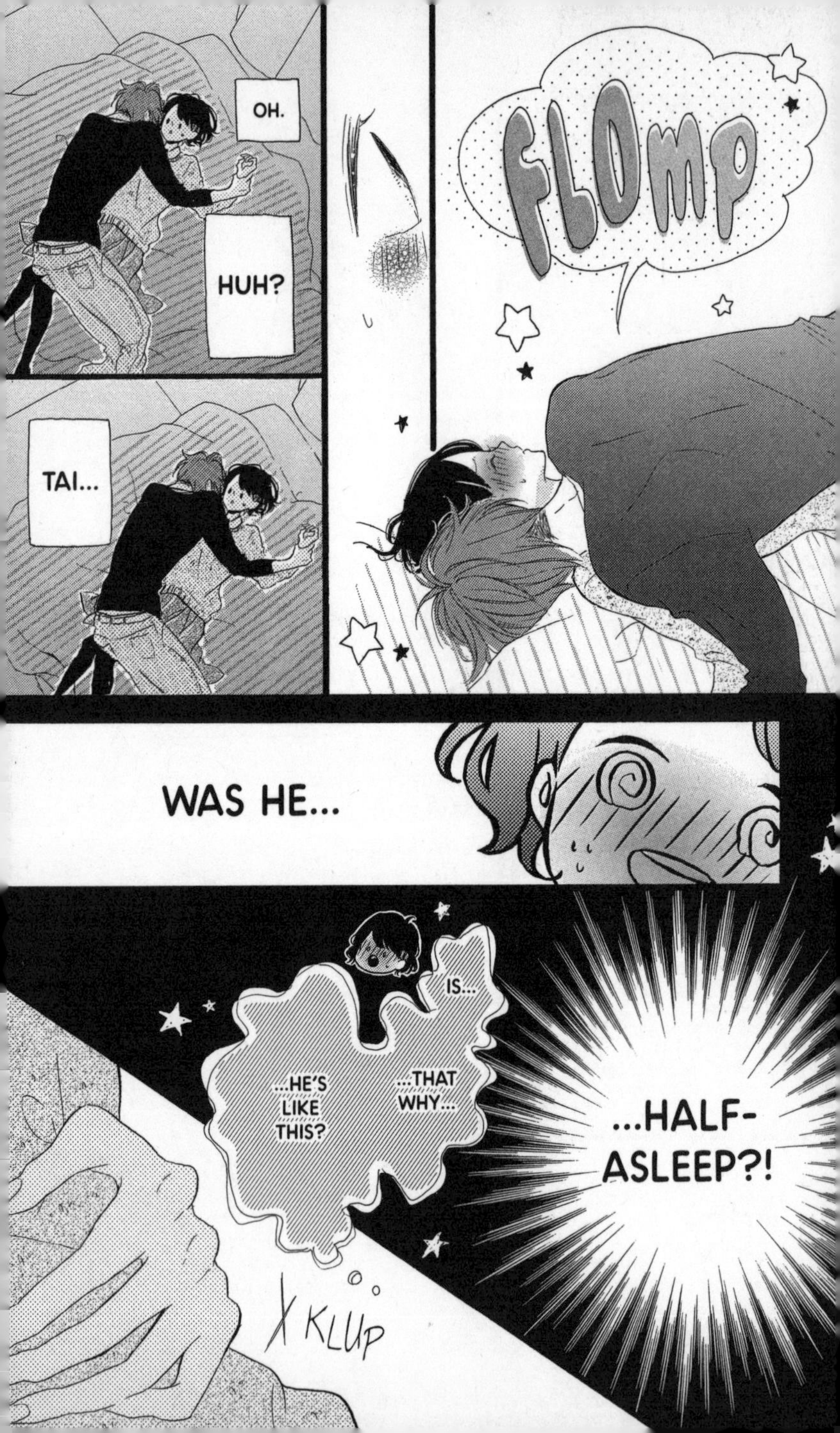
FLOMP
OH.
HUH?
TAI...
WAS HE...
...HALF-ASLEEP?!
IS...
...THAT WHY...
...HE'S LIKE THIS?
KLUP

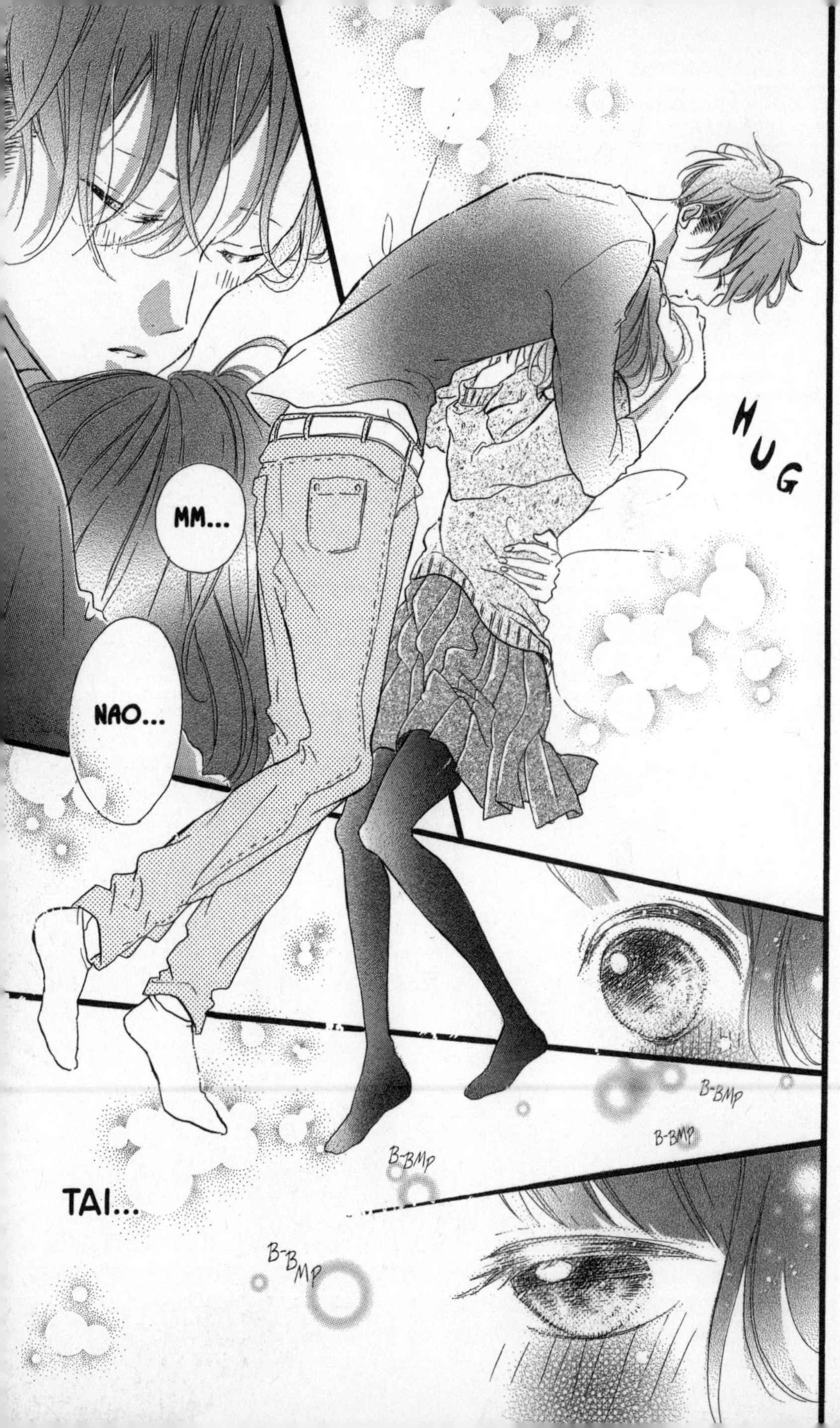
HUG
MM...
NAO...
B-BMP
B-BMP
B-BMP
TAI...
B-BMP

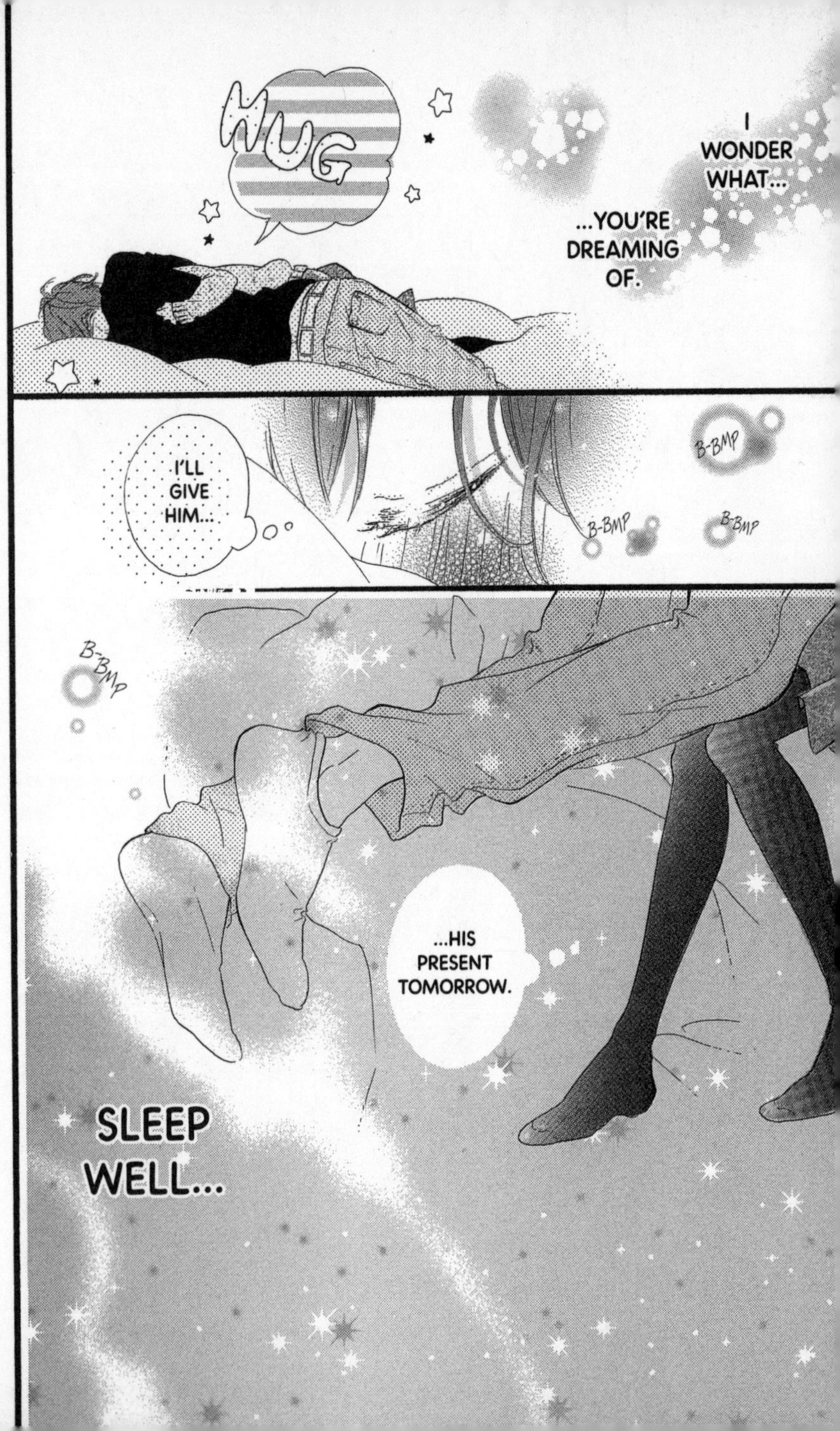
I WONDER WHAT...
...YOU'RE DREAMING OF.
HUG
B-BMP
B-BMP
B-BMP
I'LL GIVE HIM...
...HIS PRESENT TOMORROW.
B-BMP
SLEEP WELL...

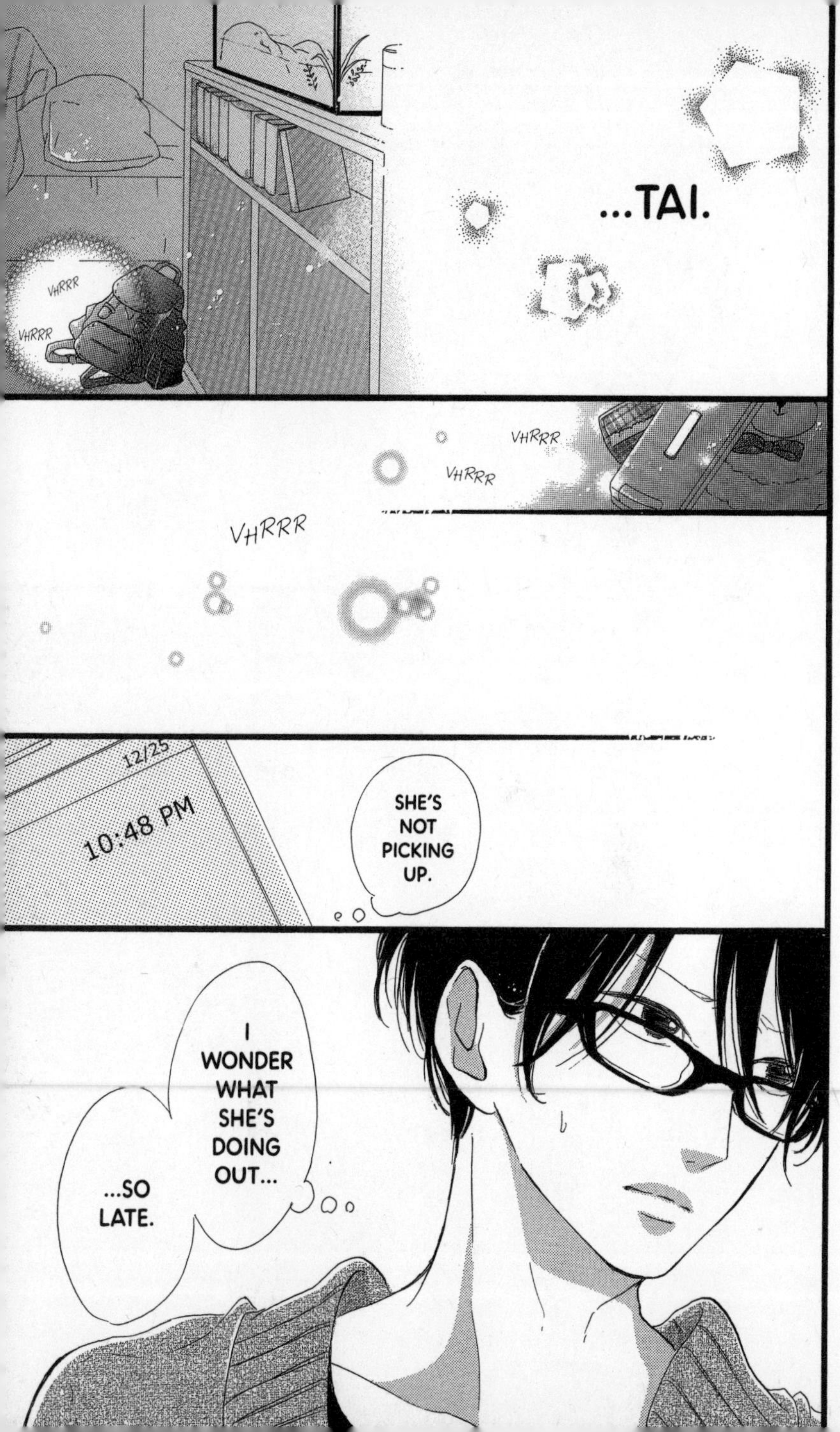
...TAI.
VHRRR
VHRRR
VHRRR
VHRRR
VHRRR
12/25
10:48 PM
SHE'S NOT PICKING UP.
I WONDER WHAT SHE'S DOING OUT...
...SO LATE.

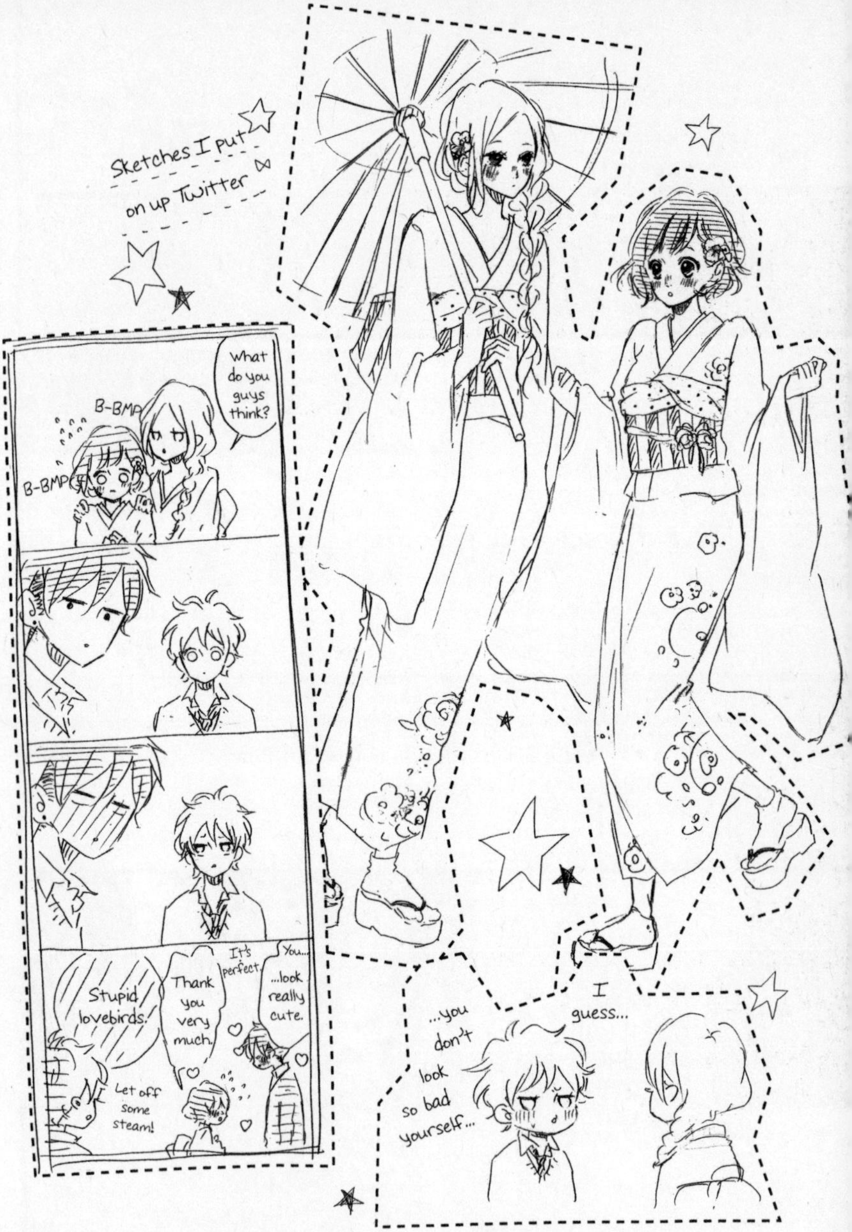
Sketches I put on up Twitter
...you don't look so bad yourself...
I guess...
What do you guys think?
B-BMP
B-BMP
You...
...look really cute.
It's perfect.
Thank you very much.
Stupid lovebirds.
Let off some steam!

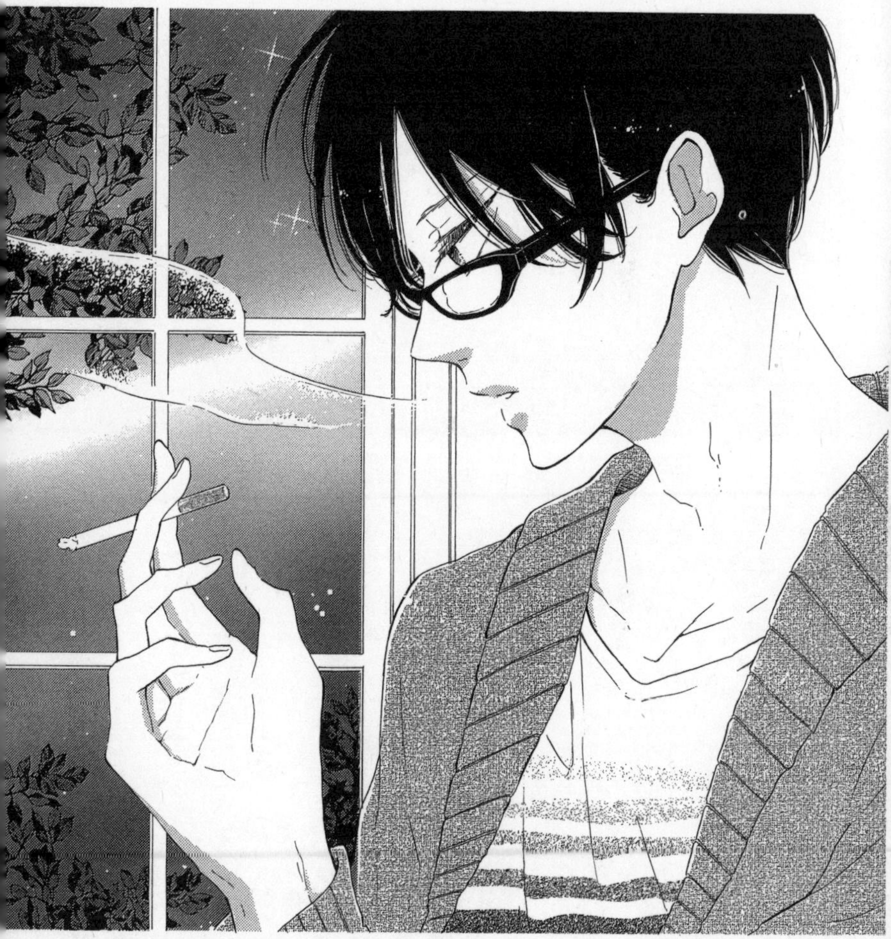

#23

Sou's Situation

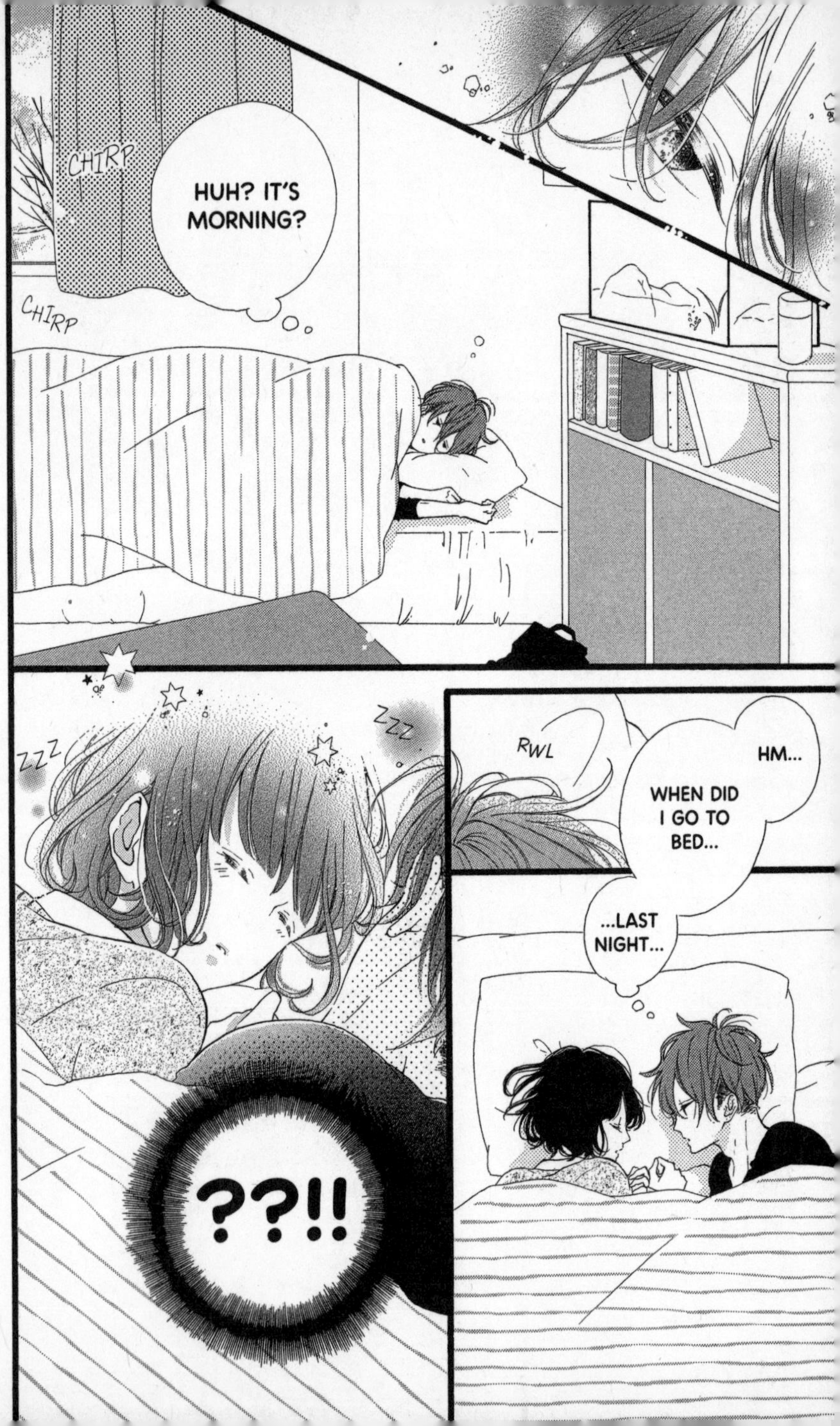
CHIRP
HUH? IT'S MORNING?
CHIRP
HM...
RWL
WHEN DID I GO TO BED...
...LAST NIGHT...
ZZZ
ZZZ
??!!

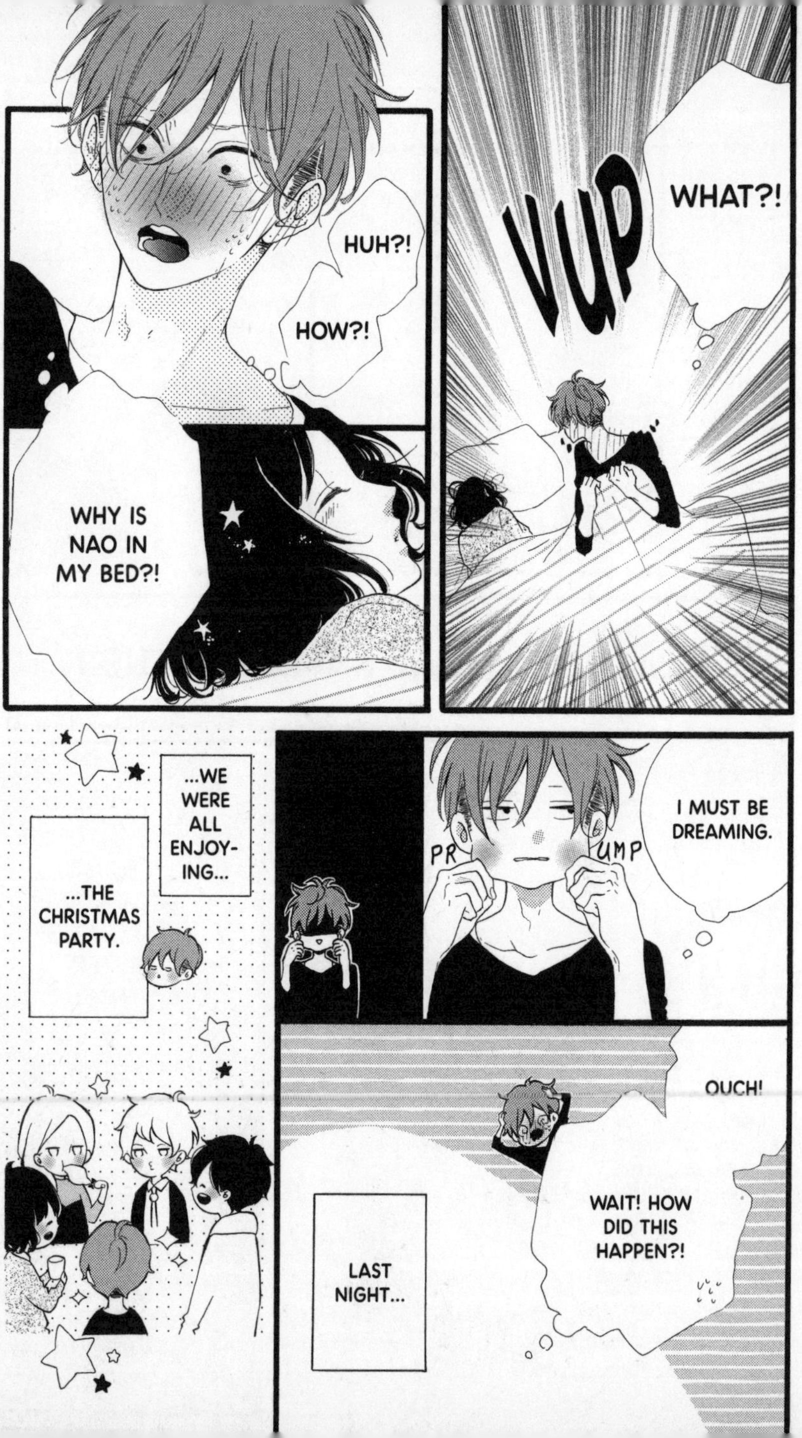
VUP
WHAT?!
HUH?!
HOW?!
WHY IS NAO IN MY BED?!
PRUMP
I MUST BE DREAMING.
OUCH!
WAIT! HOW DID THIS HAPPEN?!
LAST NIGHT...
...WE WERE ALL ENJOYING...
...THE CHRISTMAS PARTY.

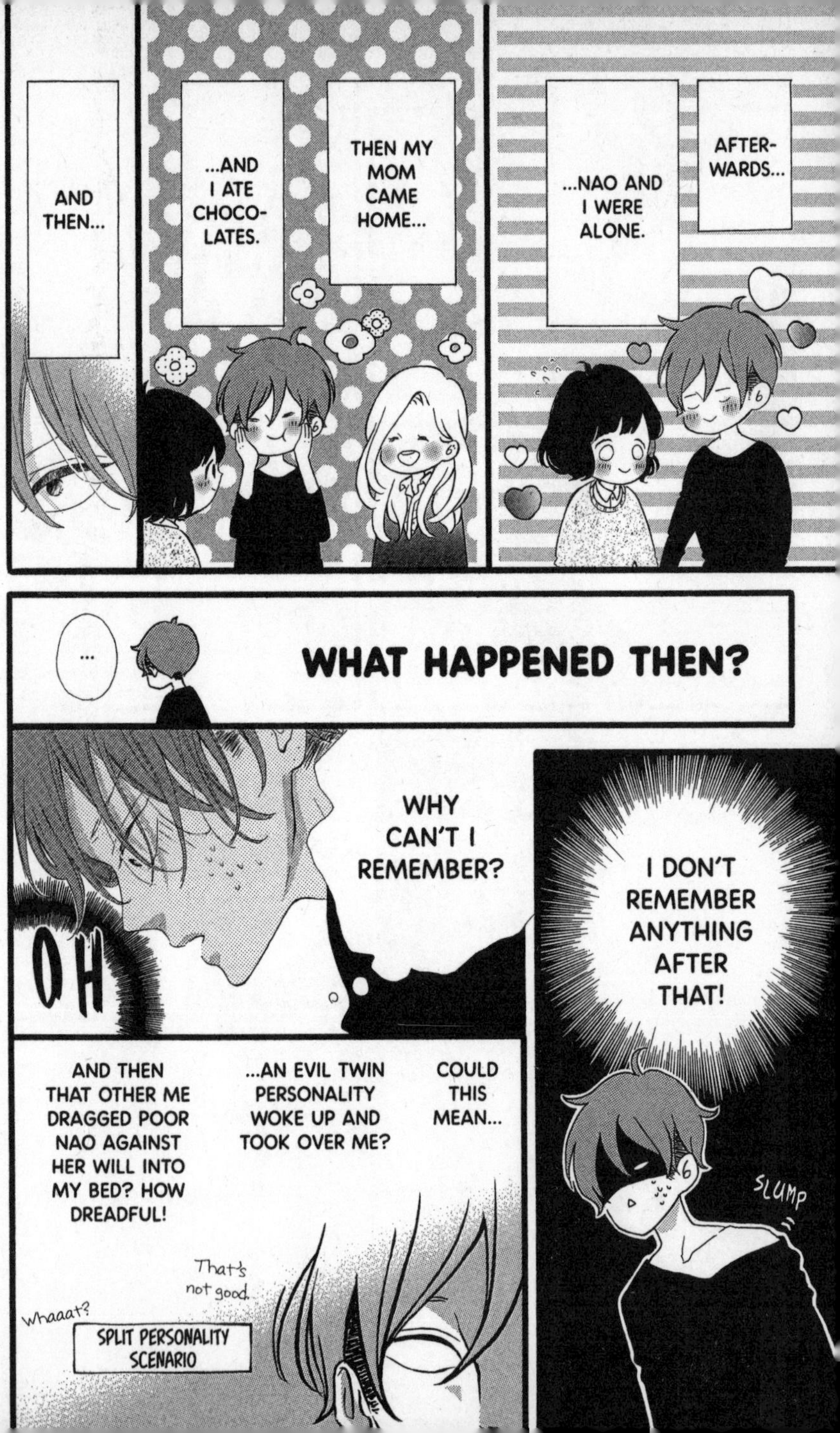
AFTER-WARDS...
...NAO AND I WERE ALONE.
THEN MY MOM CAME HOME...
...AND I ATE CHOCO-LATES.
AND THEN...
WHAT HAPPENED THEN?
...
I DON'T REMEMBER ANYTHING AFTER THAT!
SLUMP
WHY CAN'T I REMEMBER?
OH
COULD THIS MEAN...
...AN EVIL TWIN PERSONALITY WOKE UP AND TOOK OVER ME?
AND THEN THAT OTHER ME DRAGGED POOR NAO AGAINST HER WILL INTO MY BED? HOW DREADFUL!
That's not good.
Whaaat?
SPLIT PERSONALITY SCENARIO

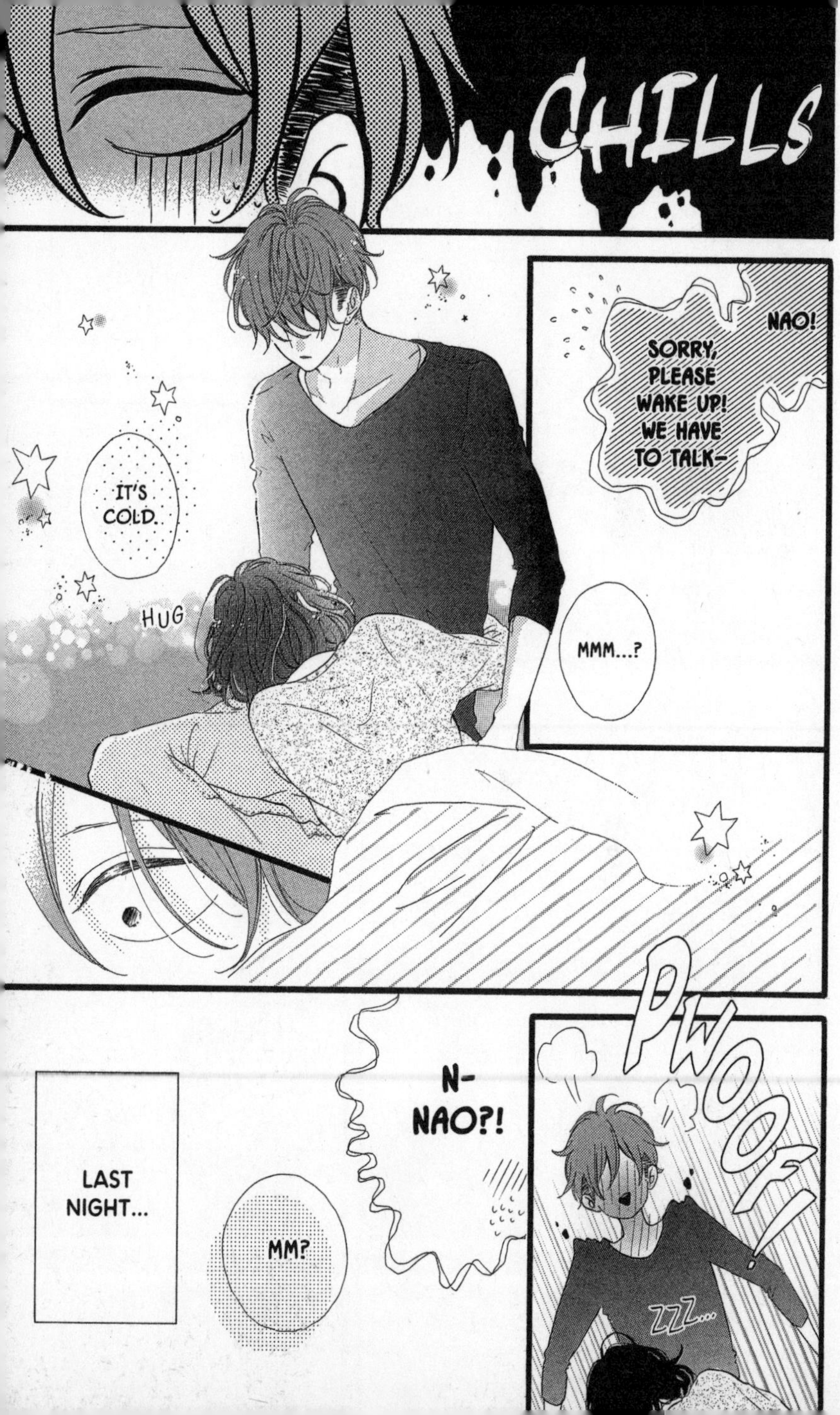
CHILLS
NAO!
SORRY, PLEASE WAKE UP! WE HAVE TO TALK—
MMM...?
IT'S COLD...
HUG
PWOOF!
ZZZ...
N- NAO?!
MM?
LAST NIGHT...

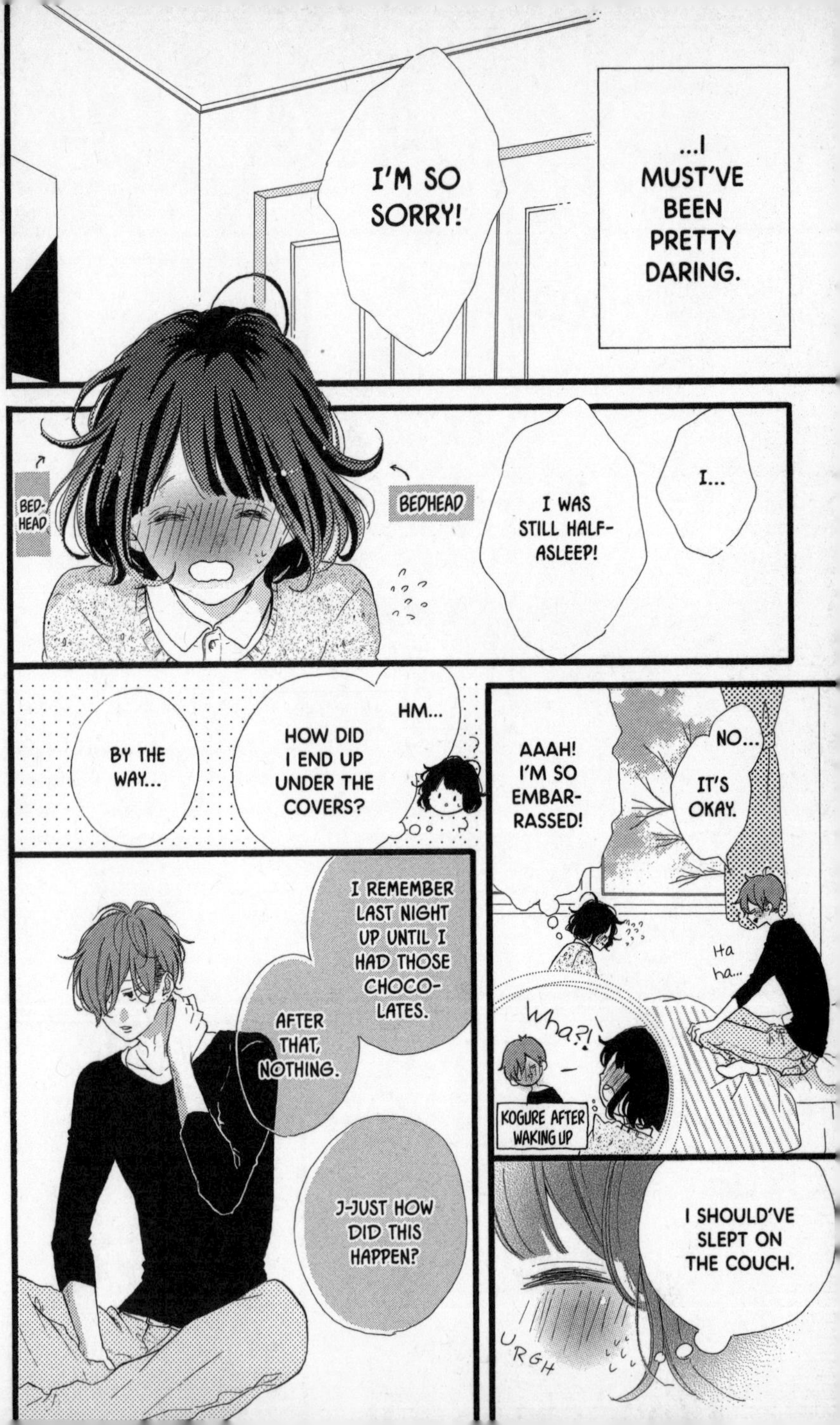
...I MUST'VE BEEN PRETTY DARING.
I'M SO SORRY!
I...
I WAS STILL HALF-ASLEEP!
BEDHEAD
BED-HEAD
NO... IT'S OKAY.
AAAH! I'M SO EMBARRASSED!
Ha ha...
Wha?!
KOGURE AFTER WAKING UP
I SHOULD'VE SLEPT ON THE COUCH.
URGH
HM...
HOW DID I END UP UNDER THE COVERS?
BY THE WAY...
I REMEMBER LAST NIGHT UP UNTIL I HAD THOSE CHOCOLATES.
AFTER THAT, NOTHING.
J-JUST HOW DID THIS HAPPEN?

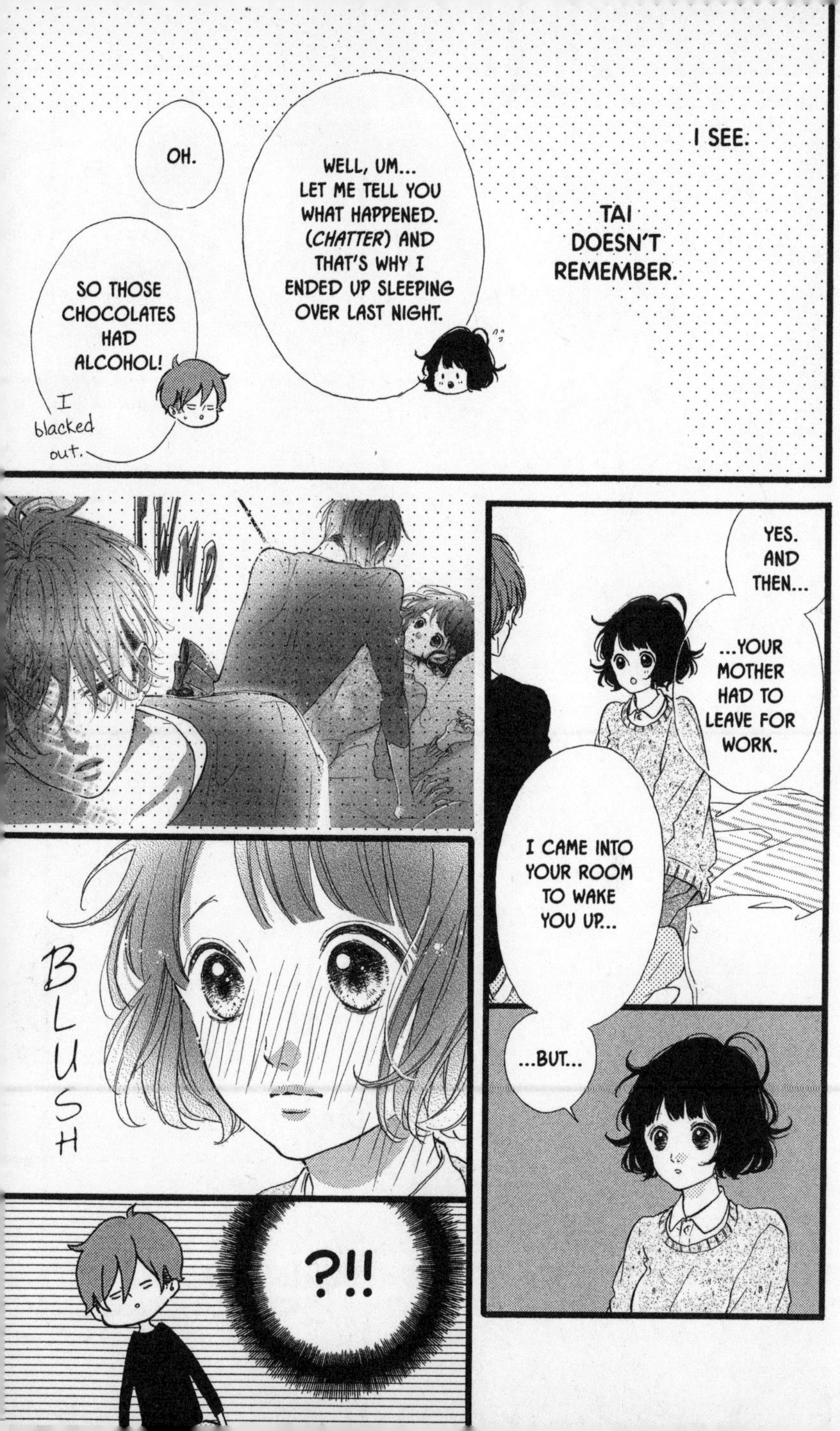
I SEE.
TAI DOESN'T REMEMBER.
WELL, UM... LET ME TELL YOU WHAT HAPPENED. (CHATTER) AND THAT'S WHY I ENDED UP SLEEPING OVER LAST NIGHT.
OH.
SO THOSE CHOCOLATES HAD ALCOHOL!
I blacked out.
YES. AND THEN...
...YOUR MOTHER HAD TO LEAVE FOR WORK.
I CAME INTO YOUR ROOM TO WAKE YOU UP...
...BUT...
WMP
BLUSH
?!!

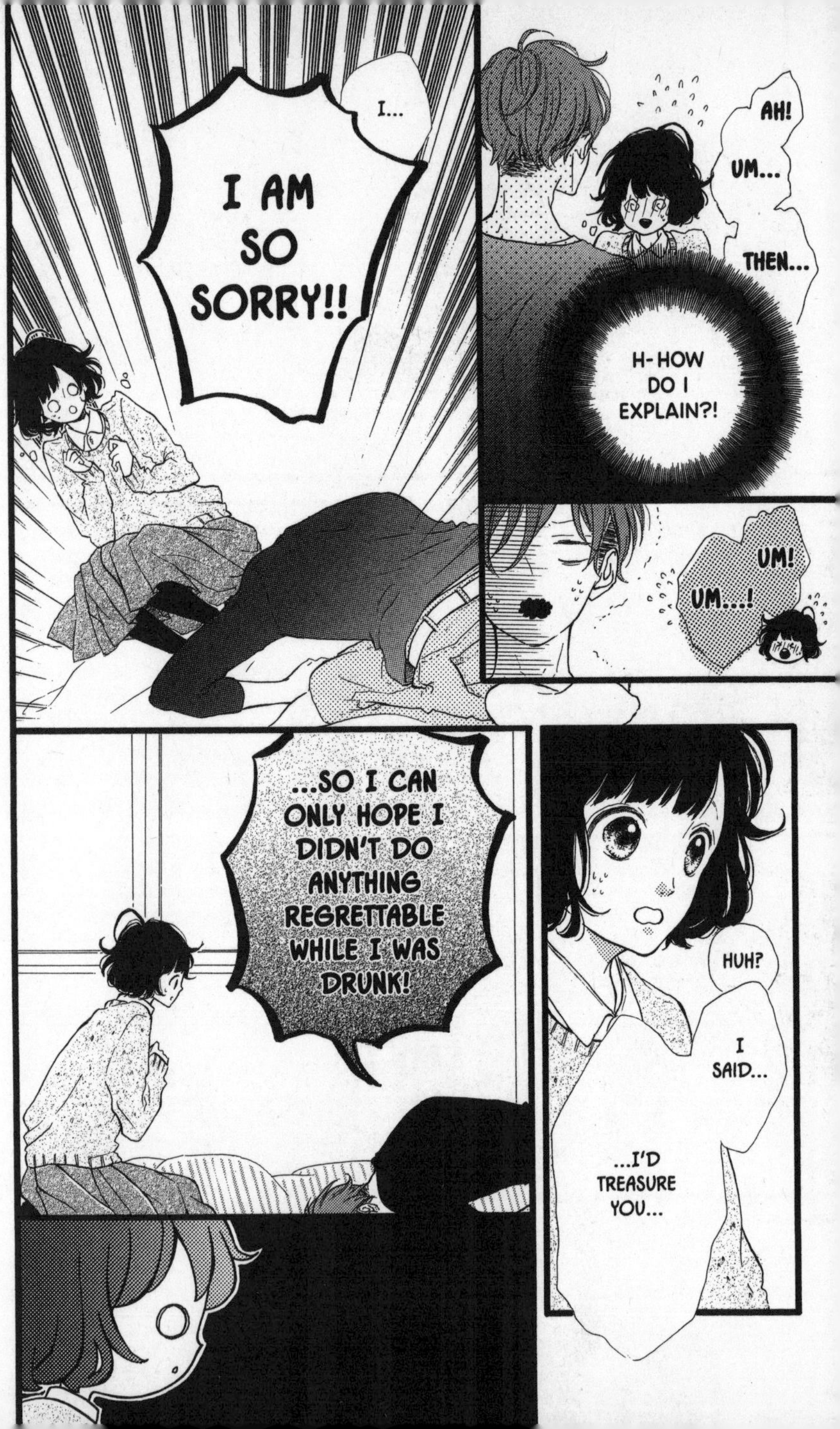
AH!
UM...
THEN...
H-HOW DO I EXPLAIN?!
UM!
UM...!
I...
I AM SO SORRY!!
HUH?
I SAID...
...I'D TREASURE YOU...
...SO I CAN ONLY HOPE I DIDN'T DO ANYTHING REGRETTABLE WHILE I WAS DRUNK!

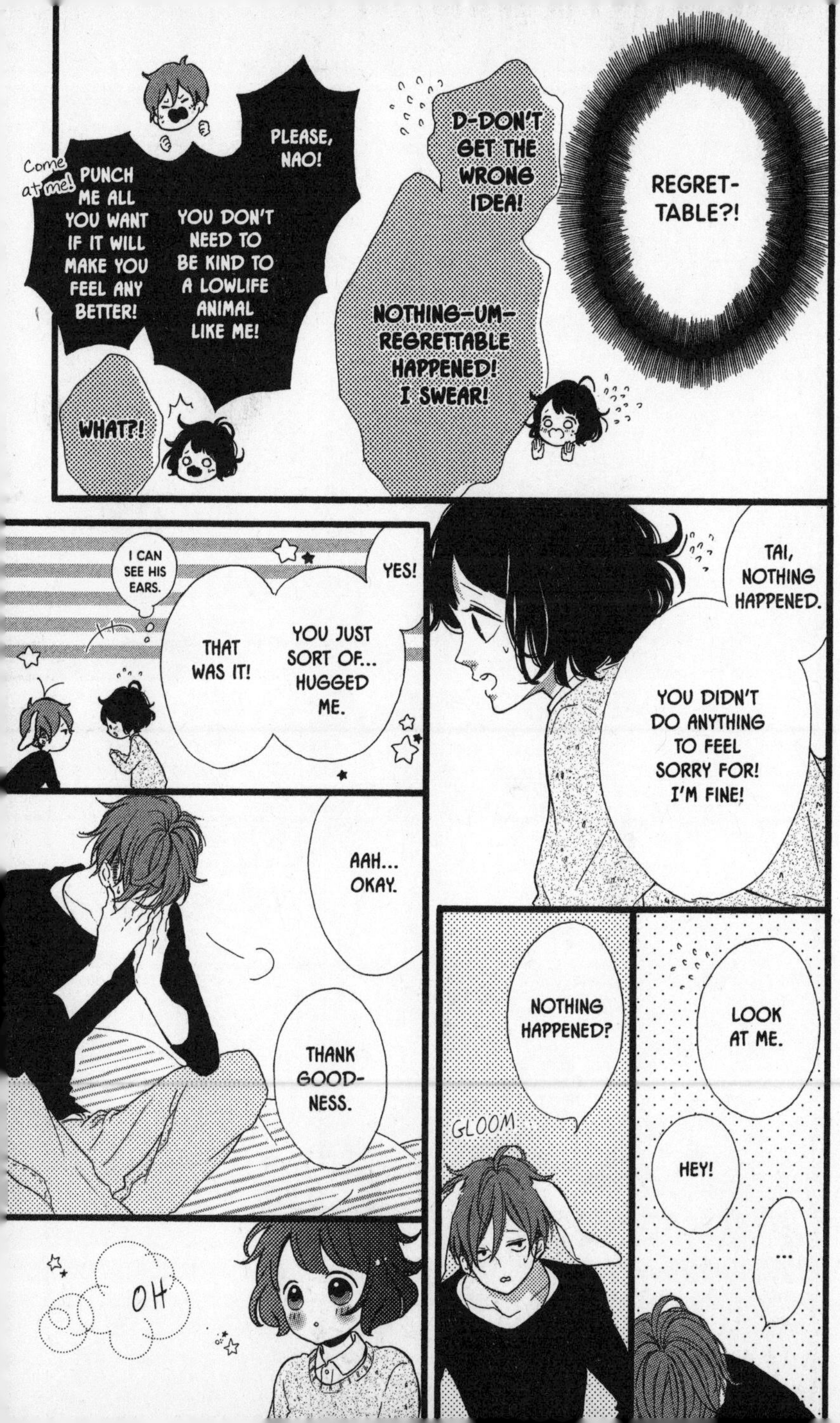
REGRET-TABLE?!
D-DON'T GET THE WRONG IDEA!
NOTHING—UM—REGRETTABLE HAPPENED! I SWEAR!
PLEASE, NAO!
YOU DON'T NEED TO BE KIND TO A LOWLIFE ANIMAL LIKE ME!
PUNCH ME ALL YOU WANT IF IT WILL MAKE YOU FEEL ANY BETTER!
Come at me!
WHAT?!
TAI, NOTHING HAPPENED.
YOU DIDN'T DO ANYTHING TO FEEL SORRY FOR! I'M FINE!
YES!
YOU JUST SORT OF... HUGGED ME.
THAT WAS IT!
I CAN SEE HIS EARS.
AAH... OKAY.
THANK GOODNESS.
LOOK AT ME.
HEY!
...
NOTHING HAPPENED?
GLOOM
OH

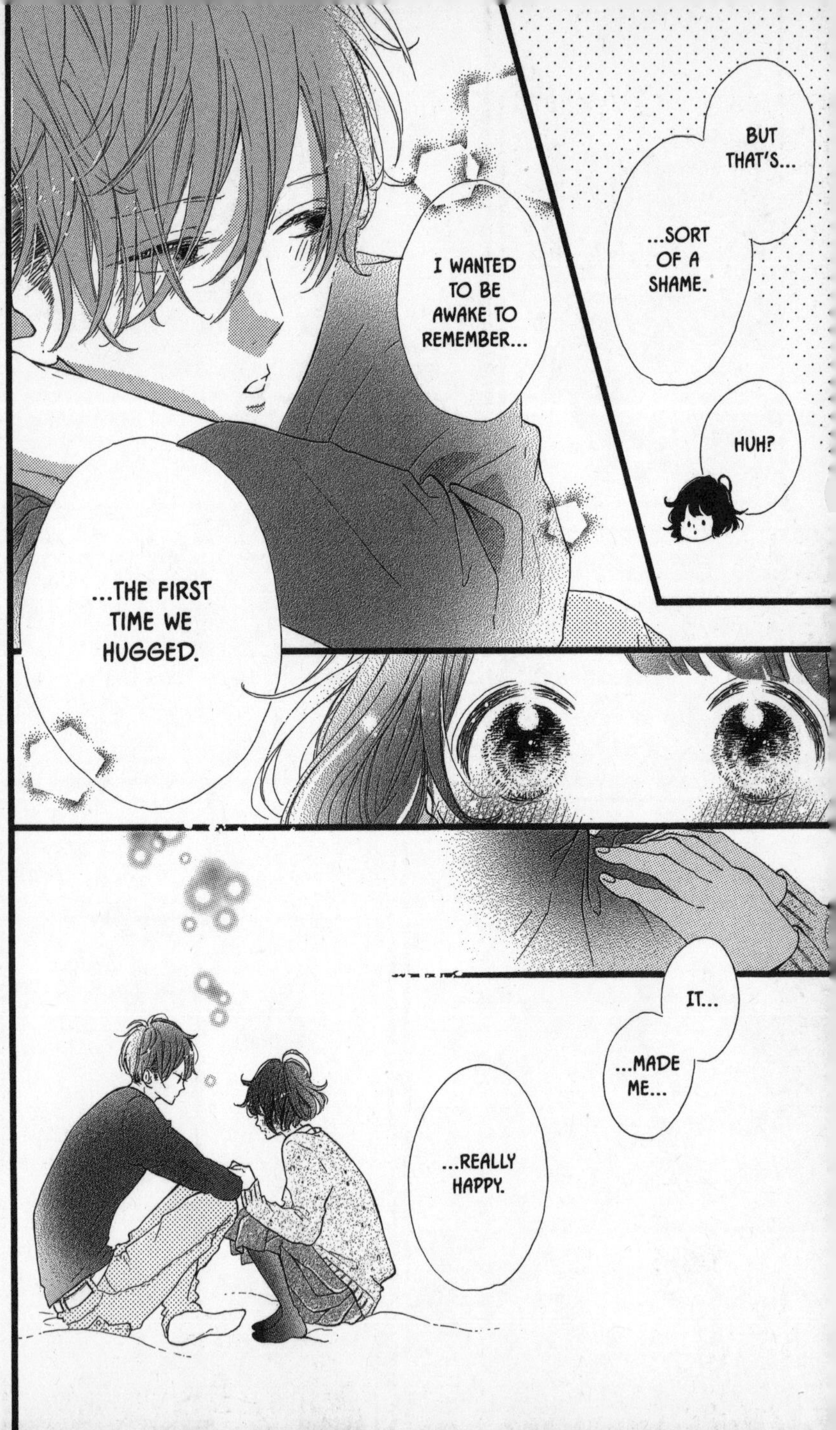
BUT THAT'S...
...SORT OF A SHAME.
HUH?
I WANTED TO BE AWAKE TO REMEMBER...
...THE FIRST TIME WE HUGGED.
IT...
...MADE ME...
...REALLY HAPPY.

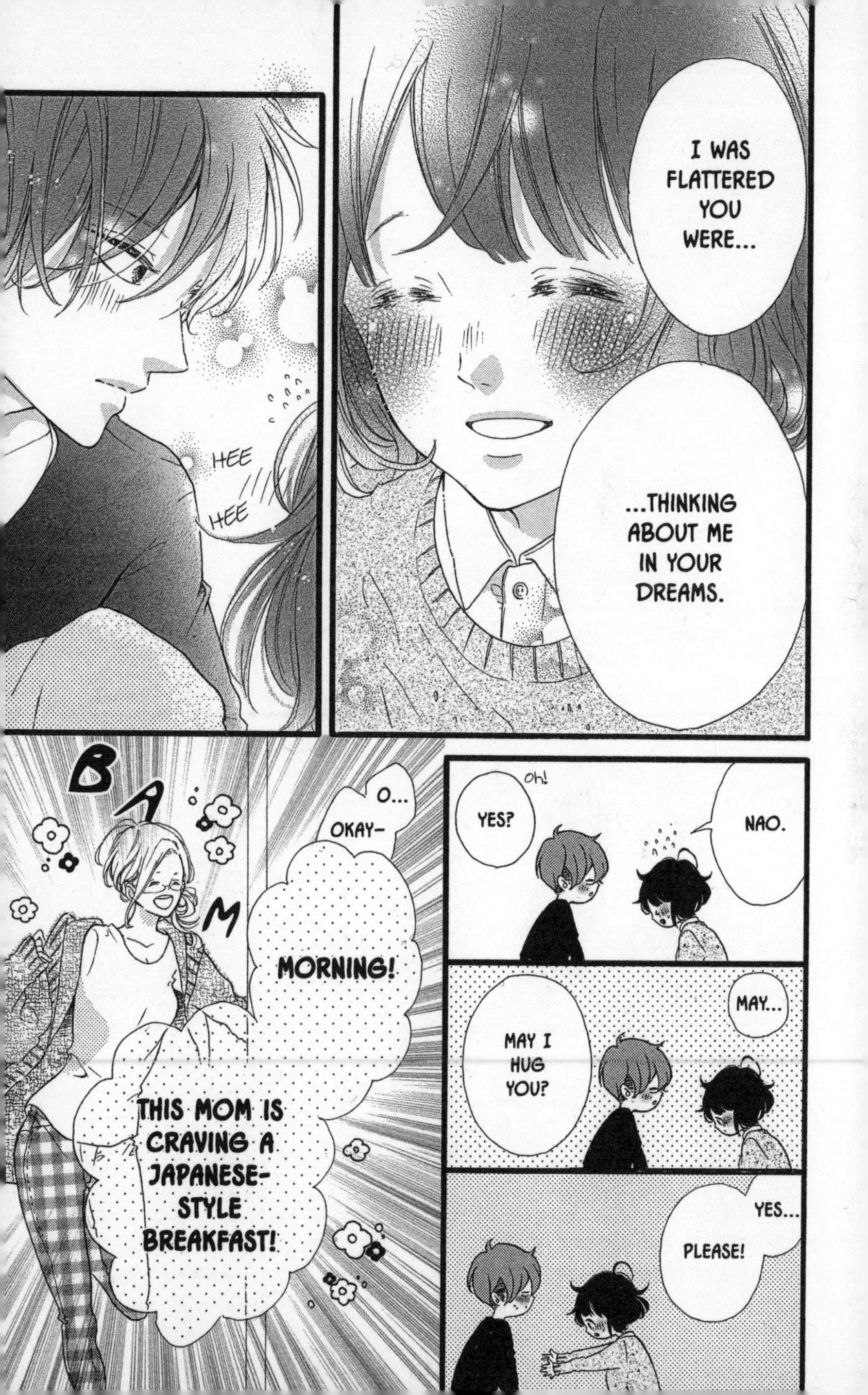
I WAS FLATTERED YOU WERE...
...THINKING ABOUT ME IN YOUR DREAMS.
HEE HEE
NAO.
Oh!
YES?
MAY...
MAY I HUG YOU?
YES... PLEASE!
O... OKAY-
BAM
MORNING!
THIS MOM IS CRAVING A JAPANESE-STYLE BREAKFAST!

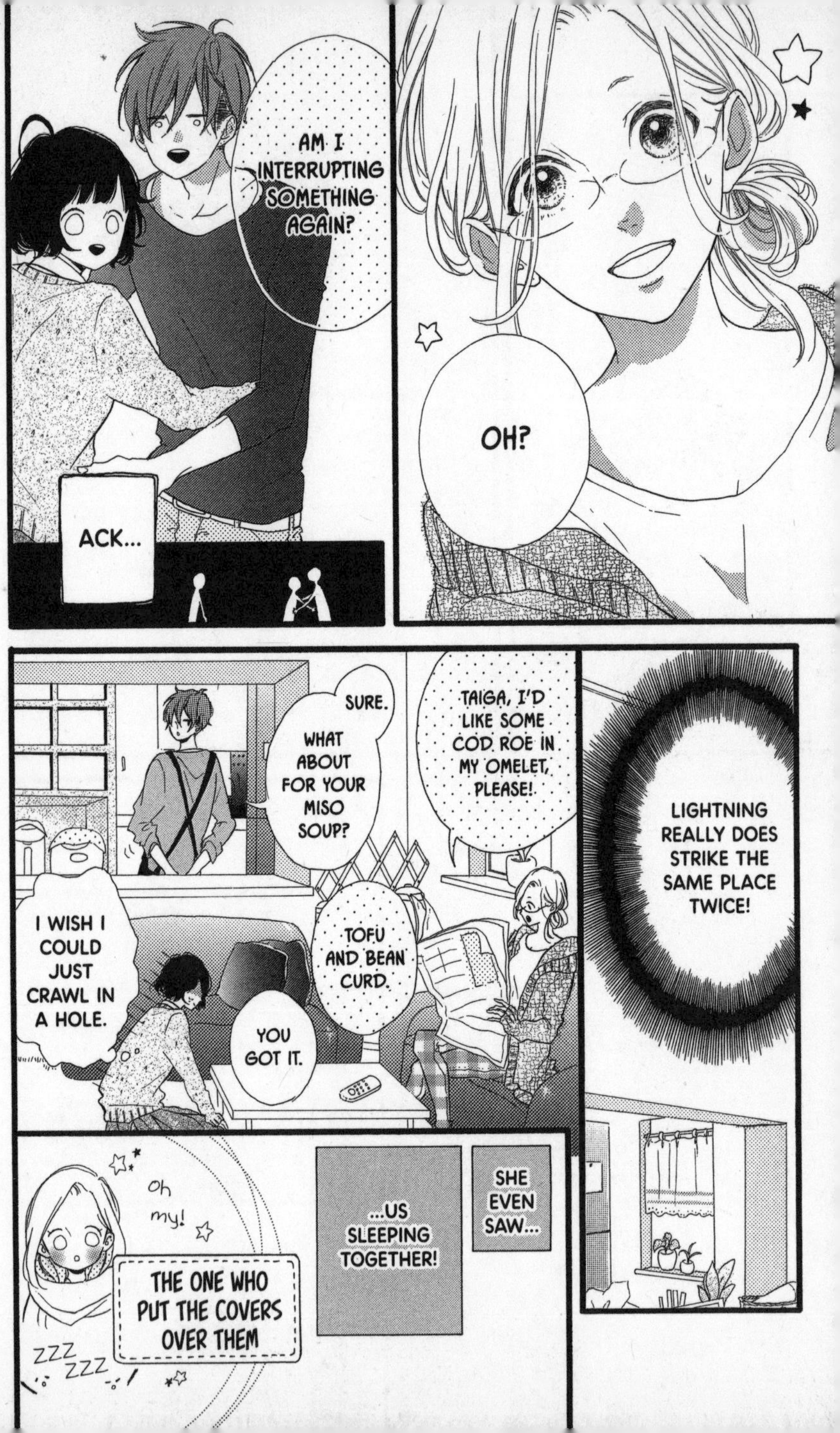
OH?
AM I INTERRUPTING SOMETHING AGAIN?
ACK...
LIGHTNING REALLY DOES STRIKE THE SAME PLACE TWICE!
TAIGA, I'D LIKE SOME COD ROE IN MY OMELET, PLEASE!
SURE.
WHAT ABOUT FOR YOUR MISO SOUP?
TOFU AND BEAN CURD.
YOU GOT IT.
I WISH I COULD JUST CRAWL IN A HOLE.
SHE EVEN SAW...
...US SLEEPING TOGETHER!
Oh my!
THE ONE WHO PUT THE COVERS OVER THEM
ZZZ ZZZ

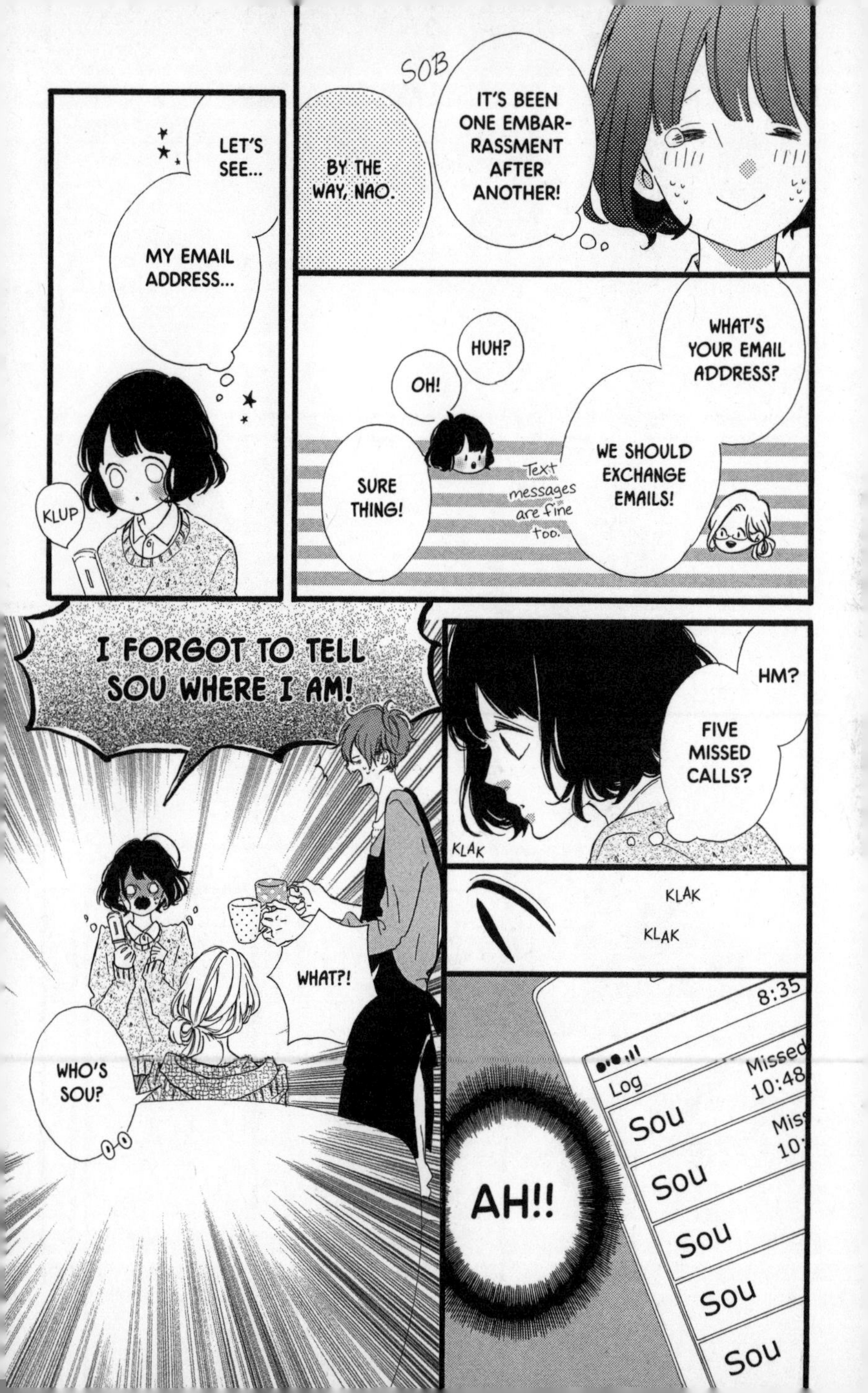
SOB
IT'S BEEN ONE EMBARRASSMENT AFTER ANOTHER!
BY THE WAY, NAO.
WHAT'S YOUR EMAIL ADDRESS?
WE SHOULD EXCHANGE EMAILS!
Text messages are fine too.
HUH?
OH!
SURE THING!
LET'S SEE...
MY EMAIL ADDRESS...
KLUP
HM?
FIVE MISSED CALLS?
KLAK
KLAK
KLAK
8:35
Log
Missed
10:48
Sou
Sou
Sou
Sou
Sou
AH!!
I FORGOT TO TELL SOU WHERE I AM!
WHAT?!
WHO'S SOU?

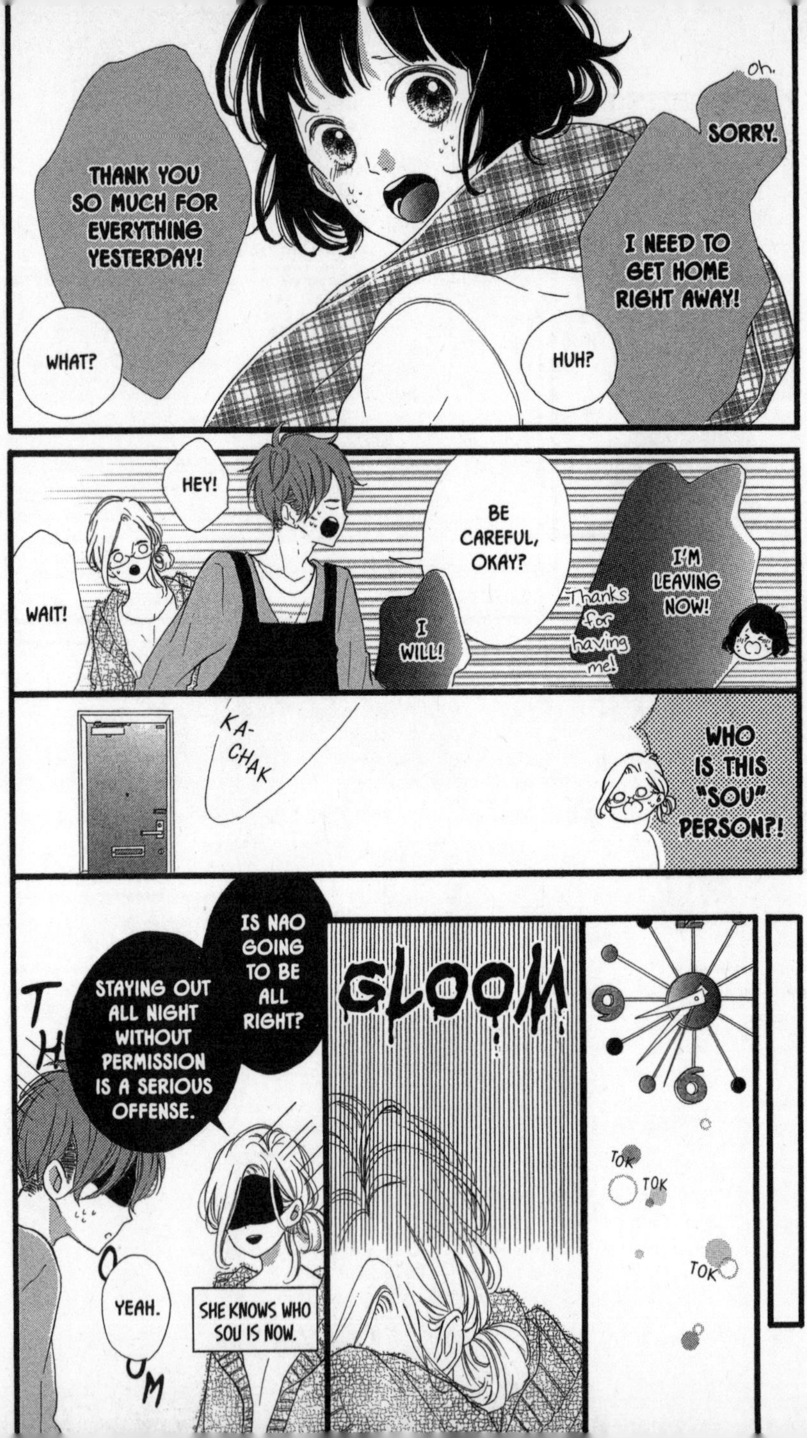
Oh.
SORRY.
I NEED TO GET HOME RIGHT AWAY!
HUH?
THANK YOU SO MUCH FOR EVERYTHING YESTERDAY!
WHAT?
I'M LEAVING NOW!
Thanks for having me!
BE CAREFUL, OKAY?
I WILL!
HEY!
WAIT!
WHO IS THIS "SOU" PERSON?!
KA-CHAK
TOK
TOK
TOK
GLOOM
IS NAO GOING TO BE ALL RIGHT?
STAYING OUT ALL NIGHT WITHOUT PERMISSION IS A SERIOUS OFFENSE.
YEAH.
SHE KNOWS WHO SOU IS NOW.

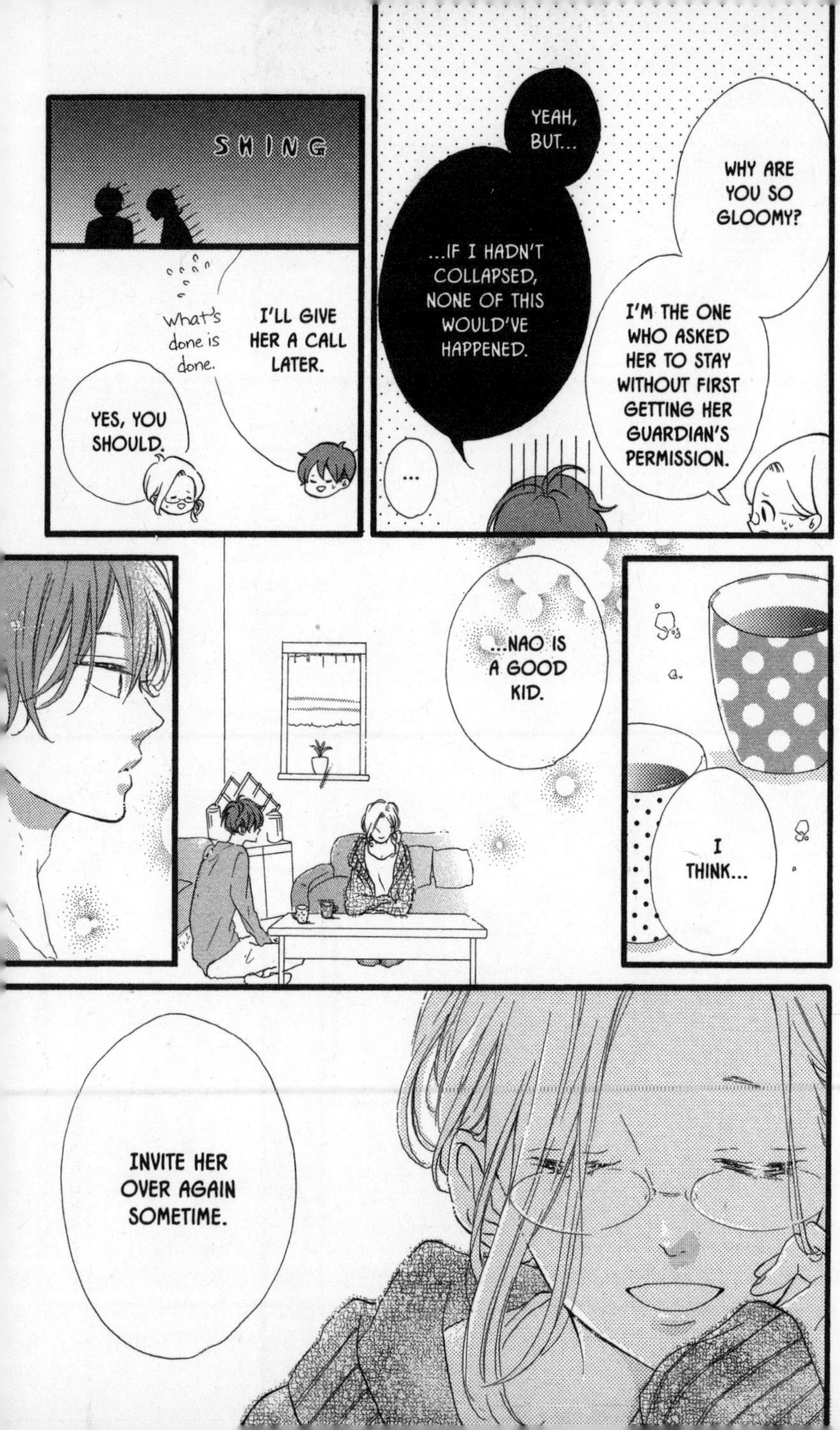
...
WHY ARE YOU SO GLOOMY?
YEAH, BUT...
...IF I HADN'T COLLAPSED, NONE OF THIS WOULD'VE HAPPENED.
I'M THE ONE WHO ASKED HER TO STAY WITHOUT FIRST GETTING HER GUARDIAN'S PERMISSION.
SHING
I'LL GIVE HER A CALL LATER.
What's done is done.
YES, YOU SHOULD.
I THINK...
...NAO IS A GOOD KID.
INVITE HER OVER AGAIN SOMETIME.

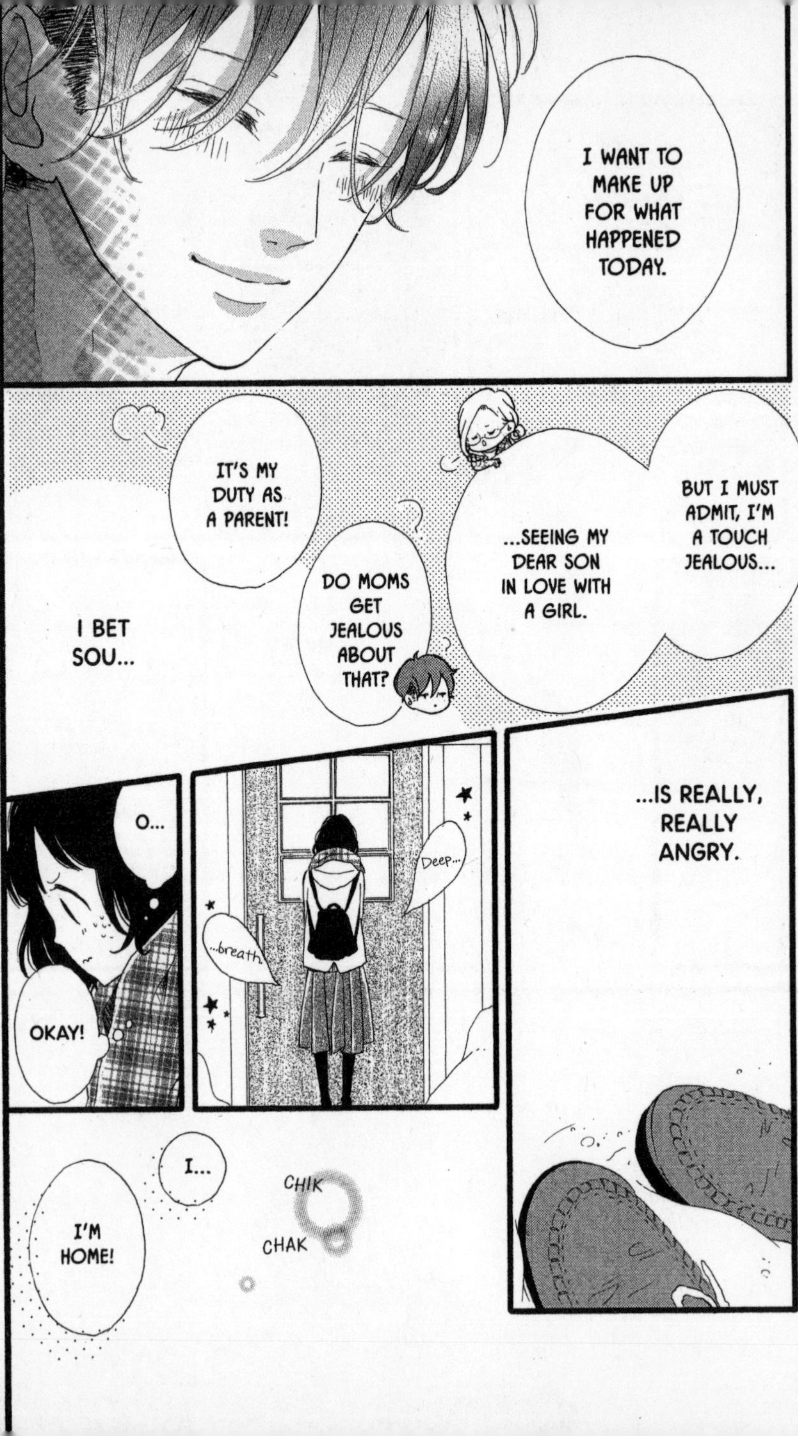

I WANT TO MAKE UP FOR WHAT HAPPENED TODAY.
BUT I MUST ADMIT, I'M A TOUCH JEALOUS...
...SEEING MY DEAR SON IN LOVE WITH A GIRL.
IT'S MY DUTY AS A PARENT!
DO MOMS GET JEALOUS ABOUT THAT?
I BET SOU...
...IS REALLY, REALLY ANGRY.
Deep...
...breath
O...
OKAY!
I...
I'M HOME!
CHIK
CHAK

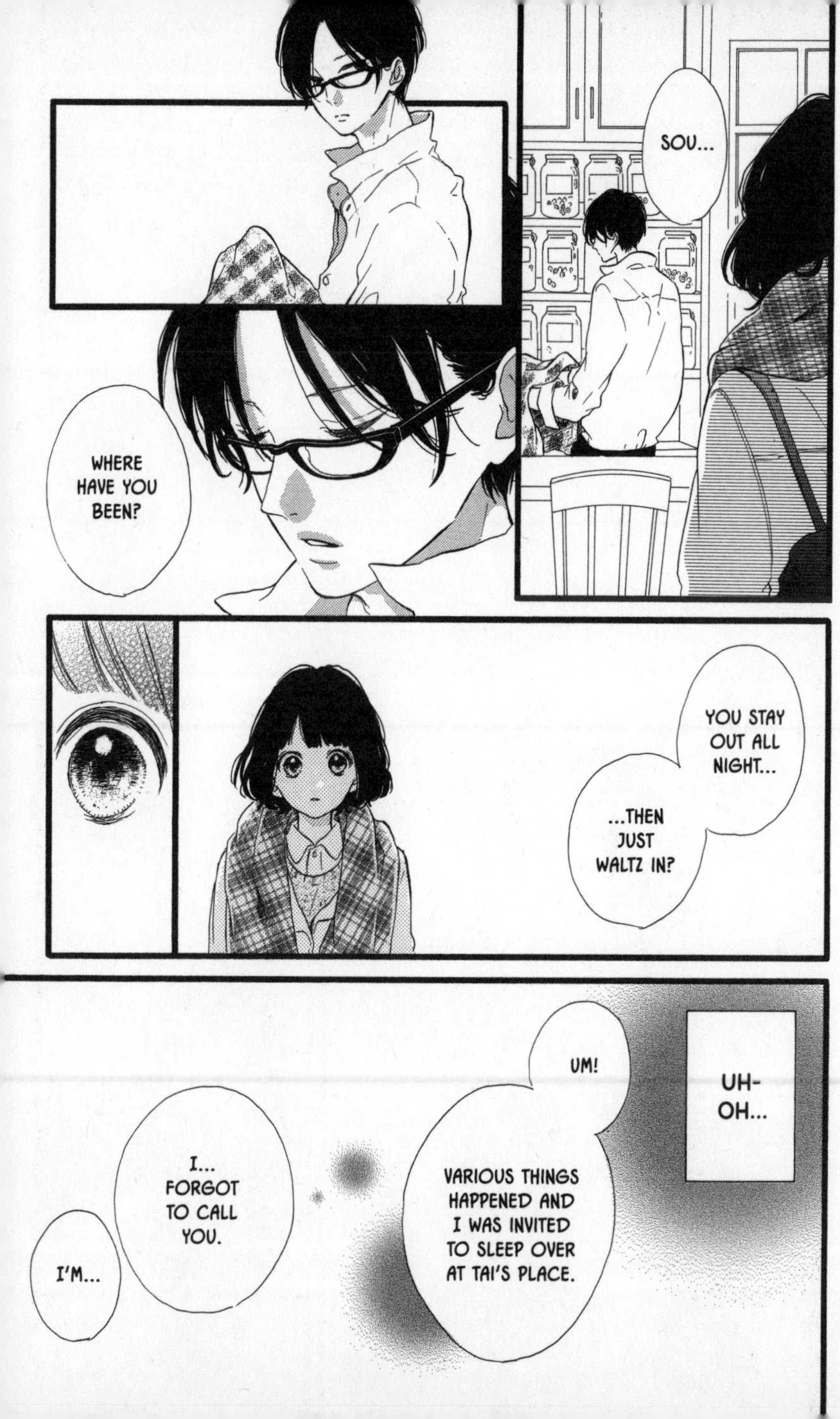
SOU...
WHERE HAVE YOU BEEN?
YOU STAY OUT ALL NIGHT...
...THEN JUST WALTZ IN?
UH-OH...
UM!
VARIOUS THINGS HAPPENED AND I WAS INVITED TO SLEEP OVER AT TAI'S PLACE.
I... FORGOT TO CALL YOU.
I'M...

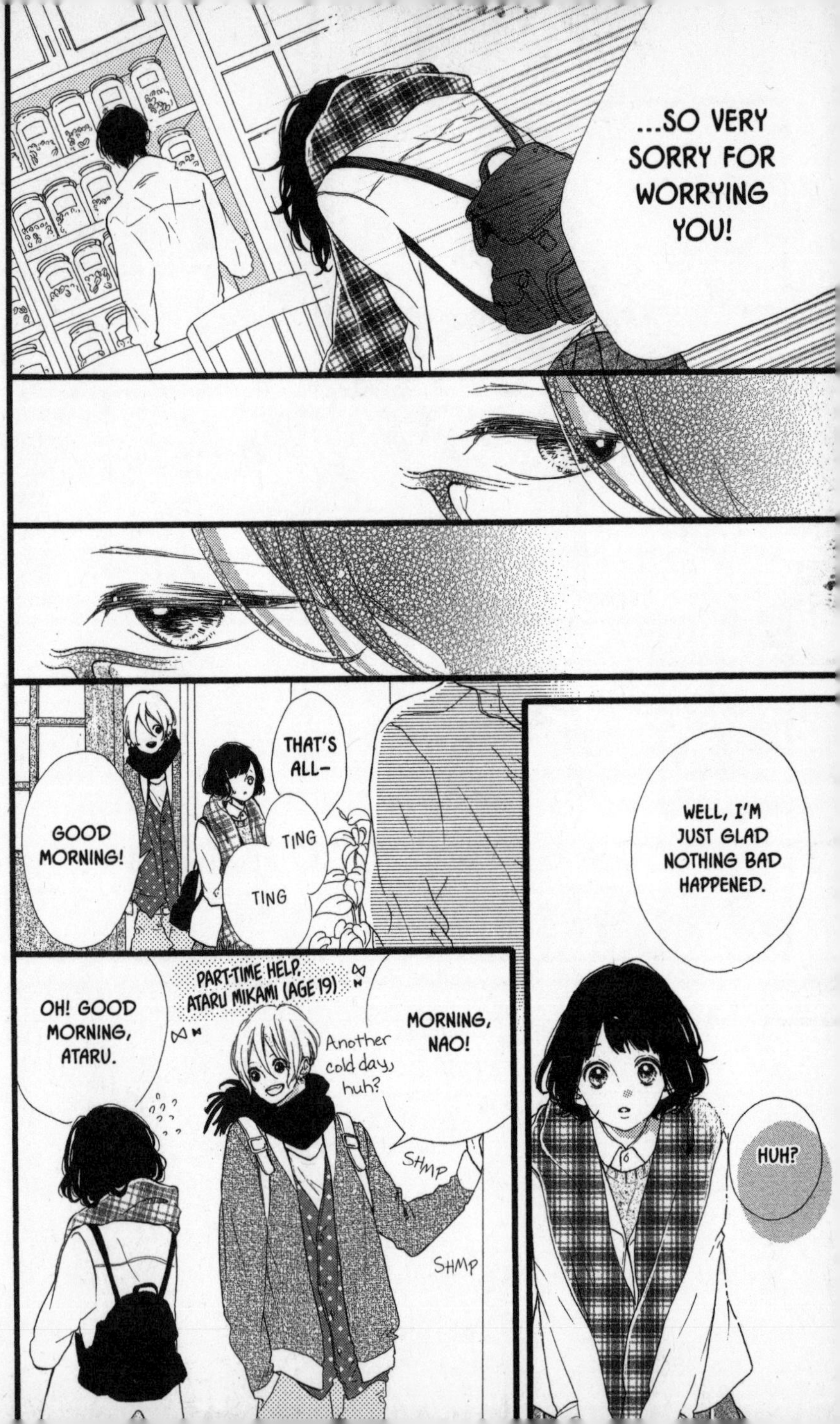
...SO VERY SORRY FOR WORRYING YOU!
WELL, I'M JUST GLAD NOTHING BAD HAPPENED.
HUH?
THAT'S ALL—
TING
TING
GOOD MORNING!
PART-TIME HELP, ATARU MIKAMI (AGE 19)
MORNING, NAO!
Another cold day, huh?
SHMP
SHMP
OH! GOOD MORNING, ATARU.

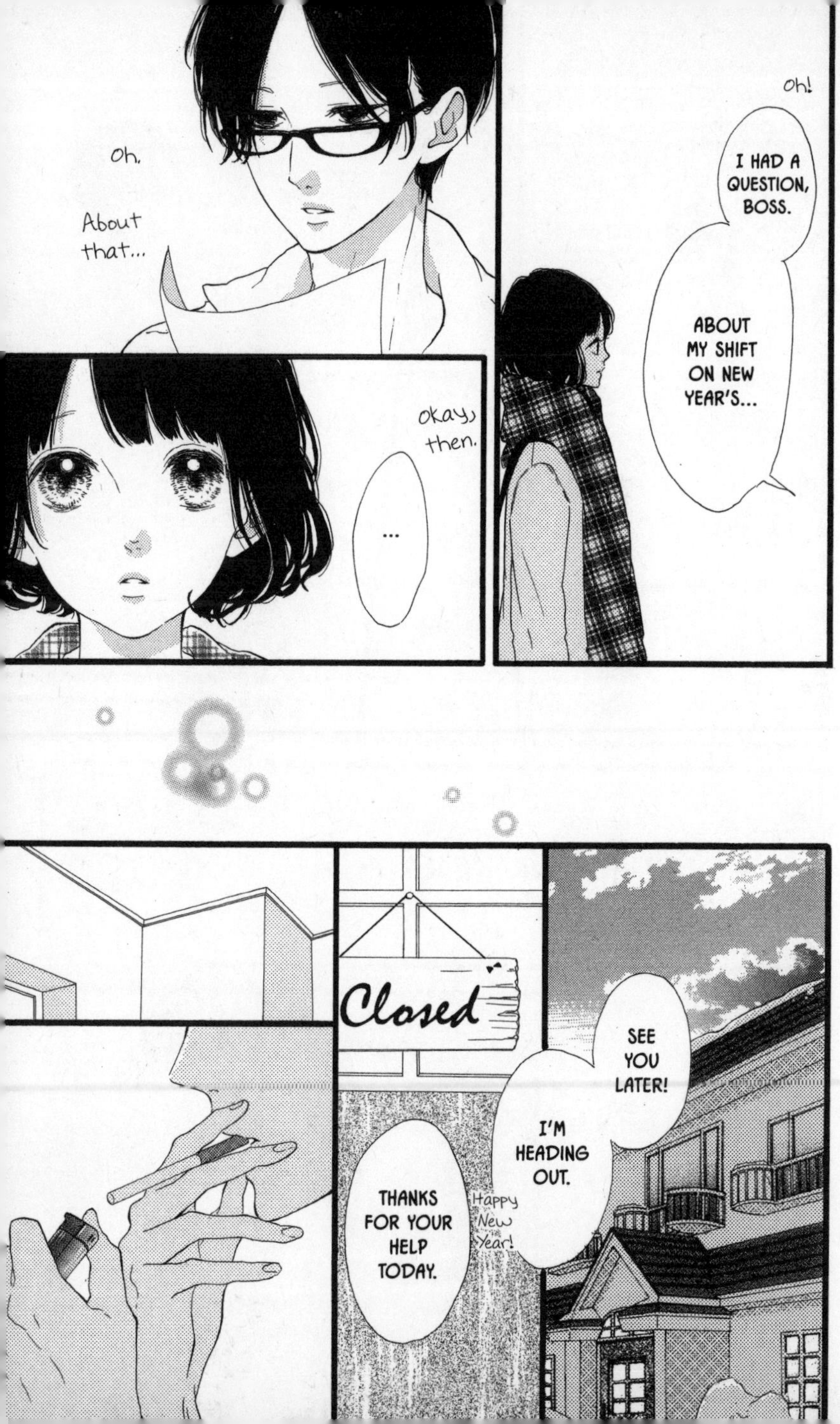
Oh!
I HAD A QUESTION, BOSS.
ABOUT MY SHIFT ON NEW YEAR'S...
Oh.
About that...
Okay, then.
...
SEE YOU LATER!
I'M HEADING OUT.
Closed
Happy New Year!
THANKS FOR YOUR HELP TODAY.

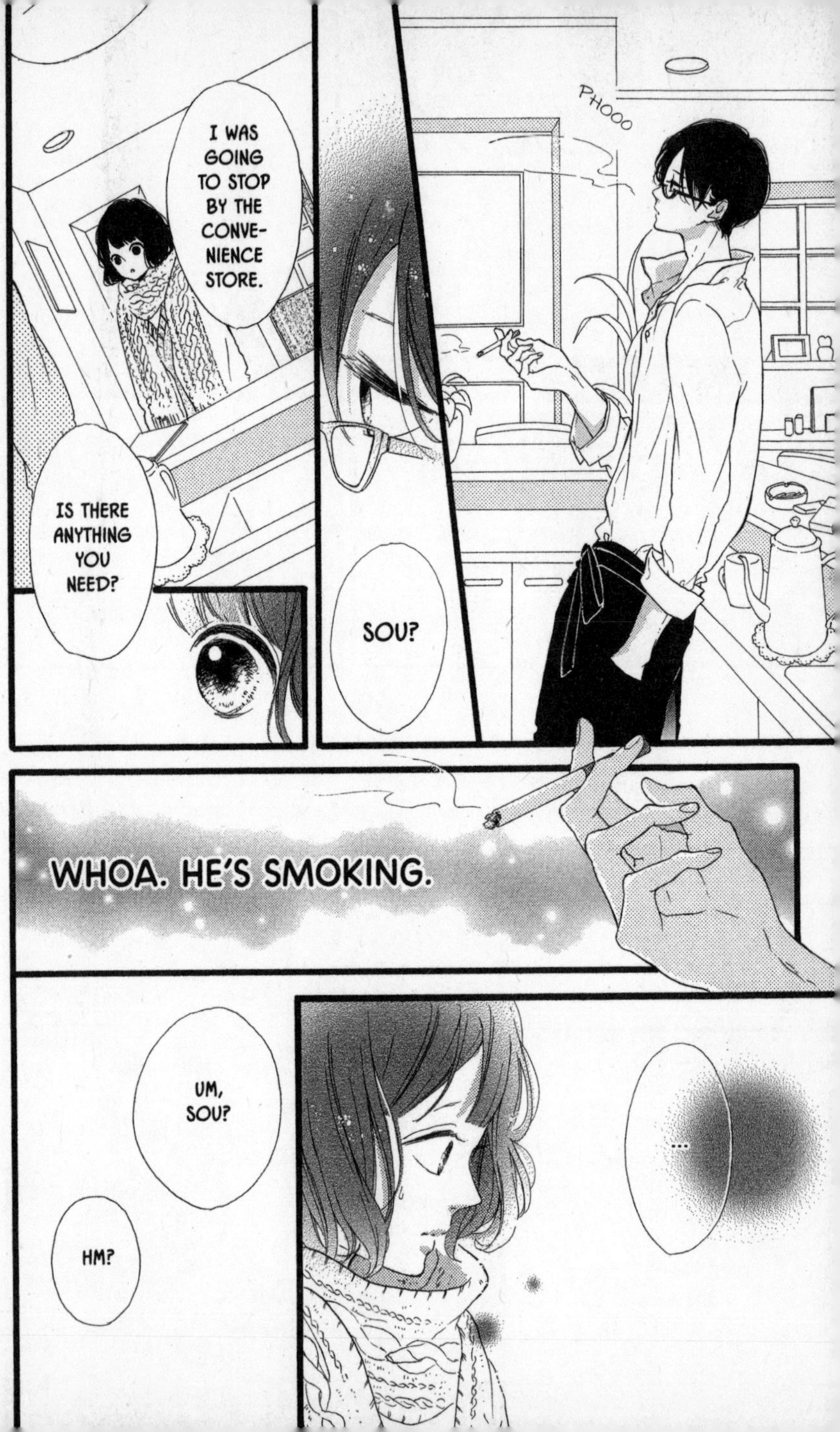
PHOOO
SOU?
I WAS GOING TO STOP BY THE CONVENIENCE STORE.
IS THERE ANYTHING YOU NEED?
WHOA. HE'S SMOKING.
...
UM, SOU?
HM?

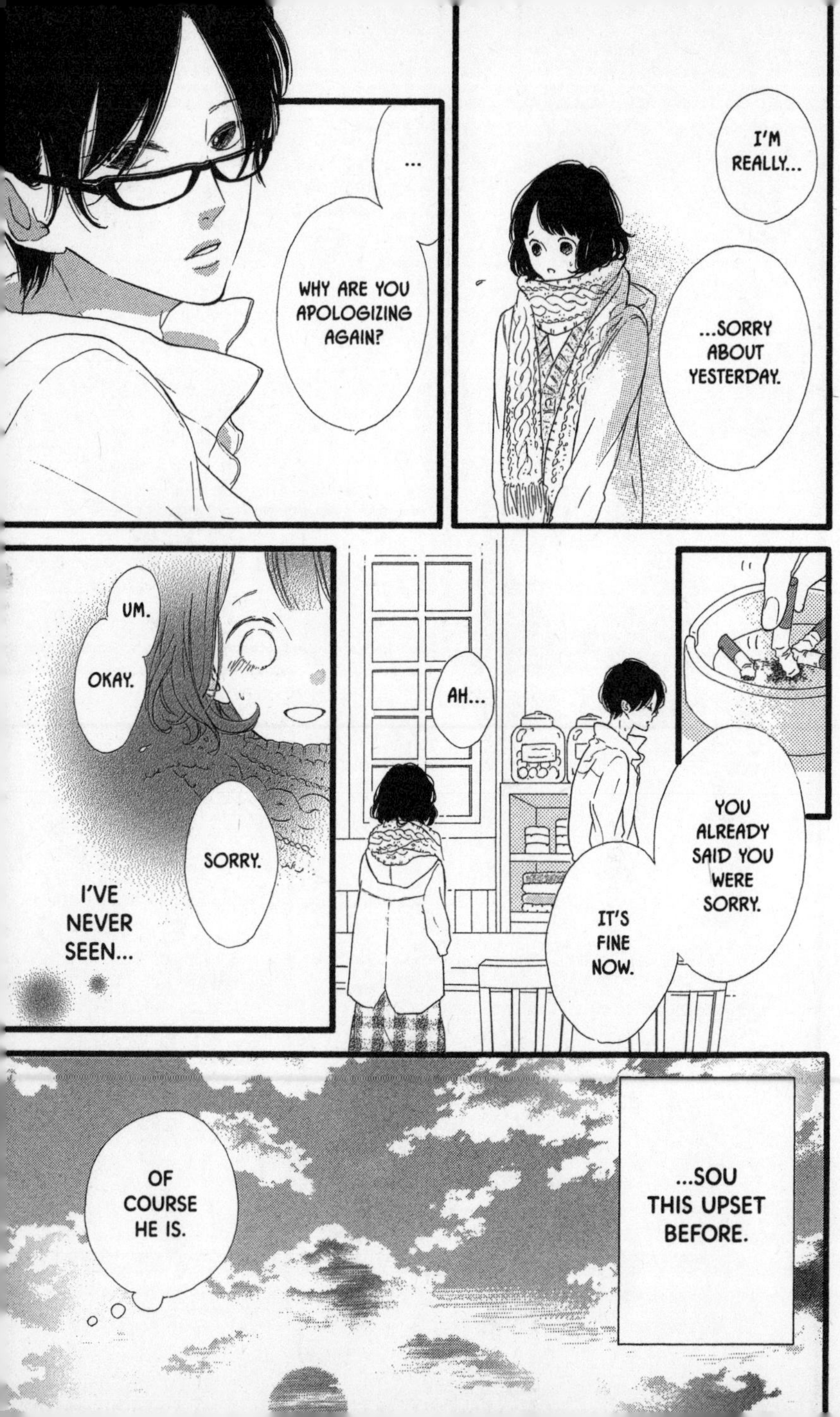
I'M REALLY...
...SORRY ABOUT YESTERDAY.
...
WHY ARE YOU APOLOGIZING AGAIN?
AH...
YOU ALREADY SAID YOU WERE SORRY.
IT'S FINE NOW.
UM.
OKAY.
SORRY.
I'VE NEVER SEEN...
...SOU THIS UPSET BEFORE.
OF COURSE HE IS.

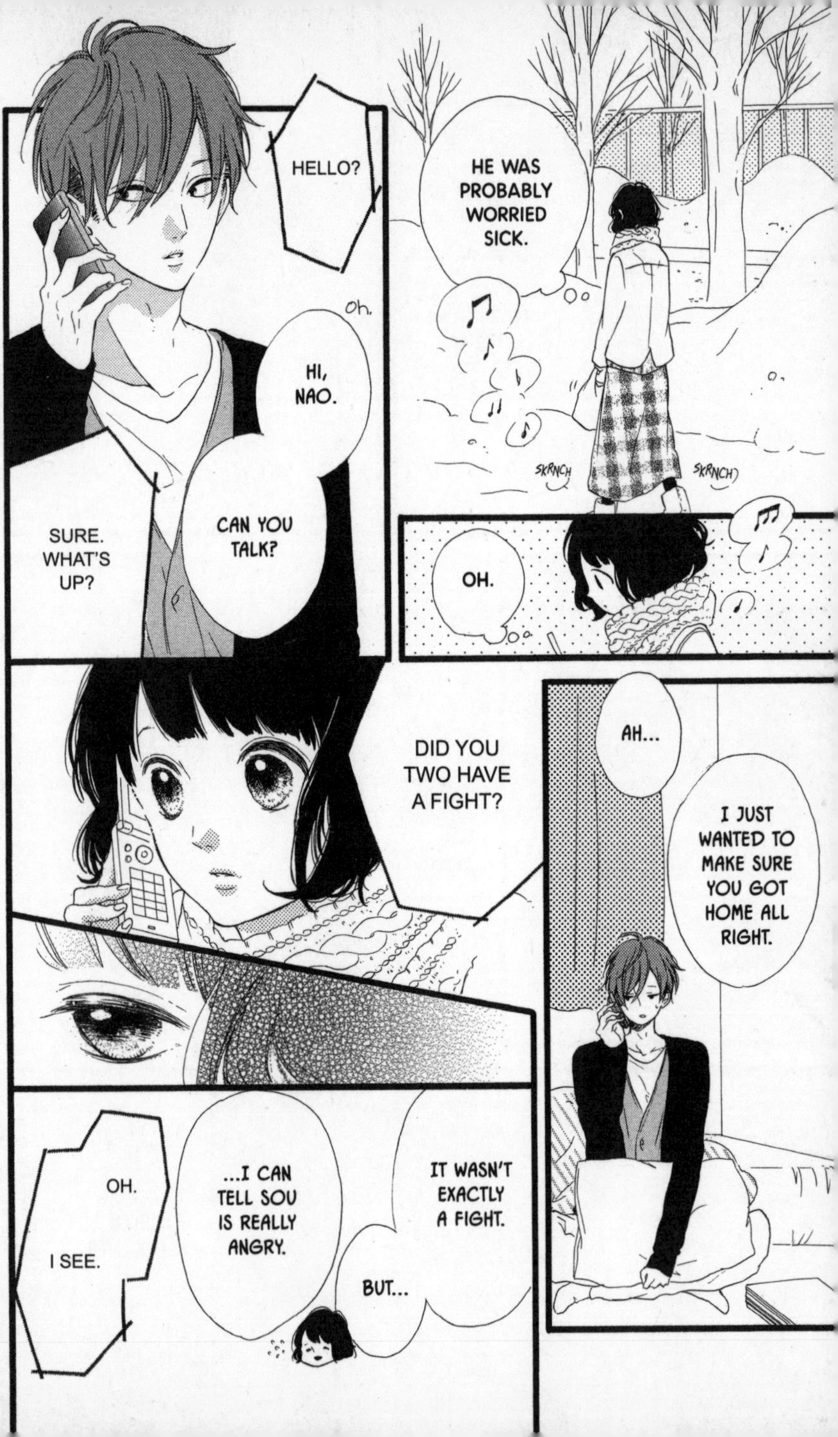
HE WAS PROBABLY WORRIED SICK.
SKRNCH
SKRNCH
OH.
HELLO?
Oh.
HI, NAO.
CAN YOU TALK?
SURE. WHAT'S UP?
AH...
I JUST WANTED TO MAKE SURE YOU GOT HOME ALL RIGHT.
DID YOU TWO HAVE A FIGHT?
IT WASN'T EXACTLY A FIGHT.
BUT...
...I CAN TELL SOU IS REALLY ANGRY.
OH.
I SEE.

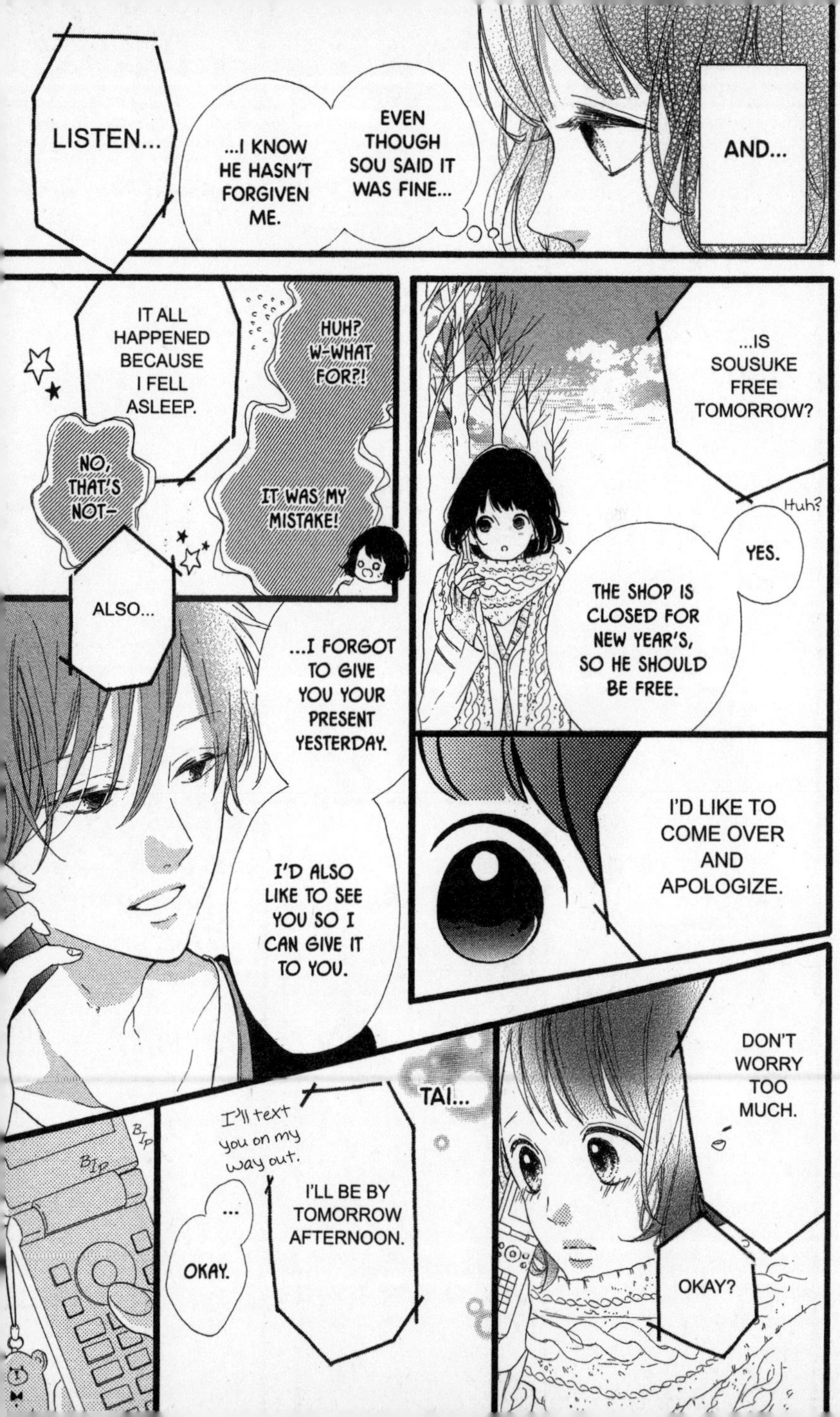
AND...
EVEN THOUGH SOU SAID IT WAS FINE...
...I KNOW HE HASN'T FORGIVEN ME.
LISTEN...
...IS SOUSUKE FREE TOMORROW?
Huh?
YES.
THE SHOP IS CLOSED FOR NEW YEAR'S, SO HE SHOULD BE FREE.
I'D LIKE TO COME OVER AND APOLOGIZE.
HUH? W-WHAT FOR?!
IT ALL HAPPENED BECAUSE I FELL ASLEEP.
IT WAS MY MISTAKE!
NO, THAT'S NOT-
ALSO...
...I FORGOT TO GIVE YOU YOUR PRESENT YESTERDAY.
I'D ALSO LIKE TO SEE YOU SO I CAN GIVE IT TO YOU.
DON'T WORRY TOO MUCH.
OKAY?
TAI...
I'LL BE BY TOMORROW AFTERNOON.
I'll text you on my way out.
...
OKAY.
BIP
BIP

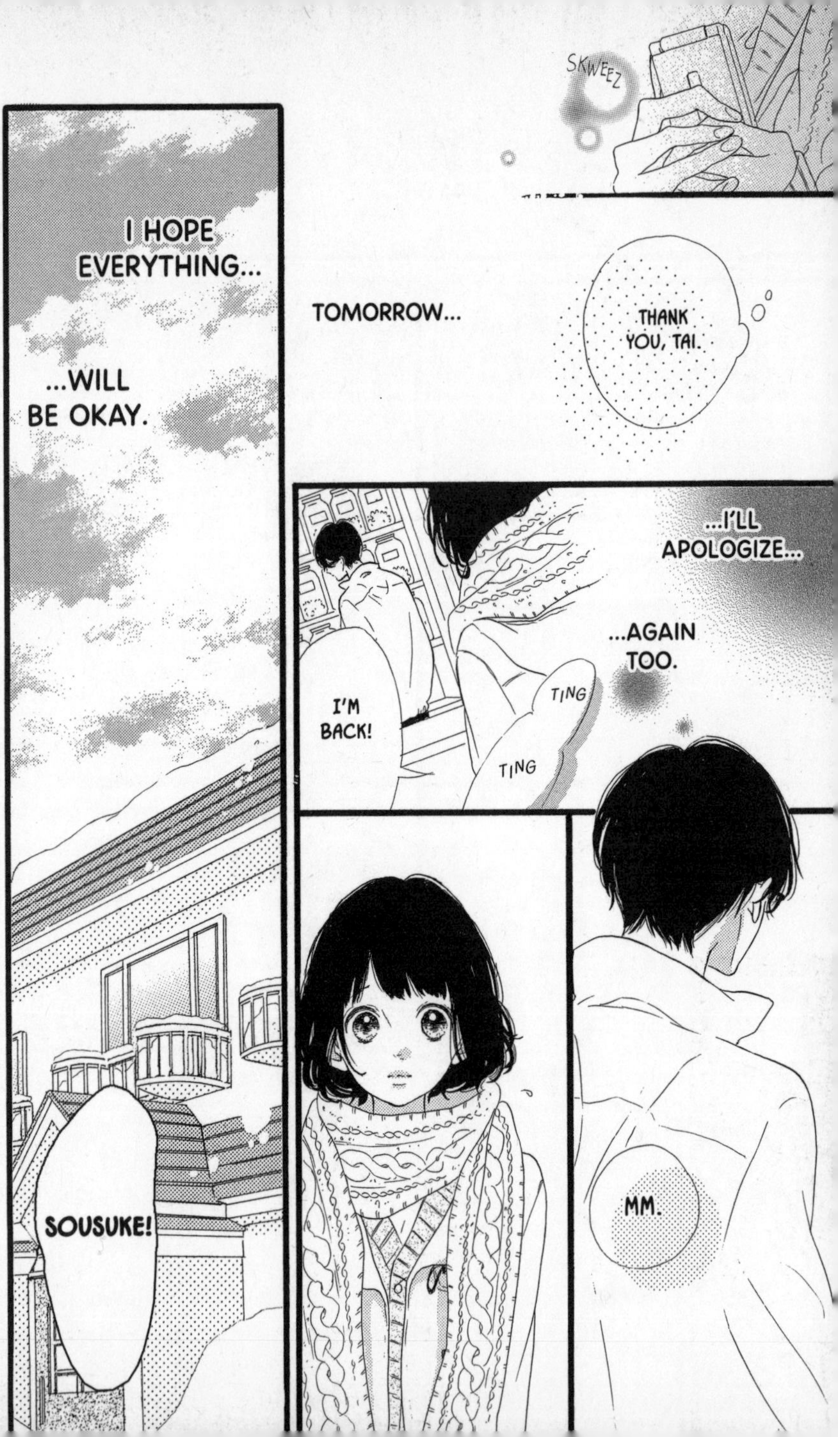
SKWEEZ
THANK YOU, TAI.
TOMORROW...
...I'LL APOLOGIZE...
...AGAIN TOO.
TING
I'M BACK!
TING
MM.
I HOPE EVERYTHING...
...WILL BE OKAY.
SOUSUKE!

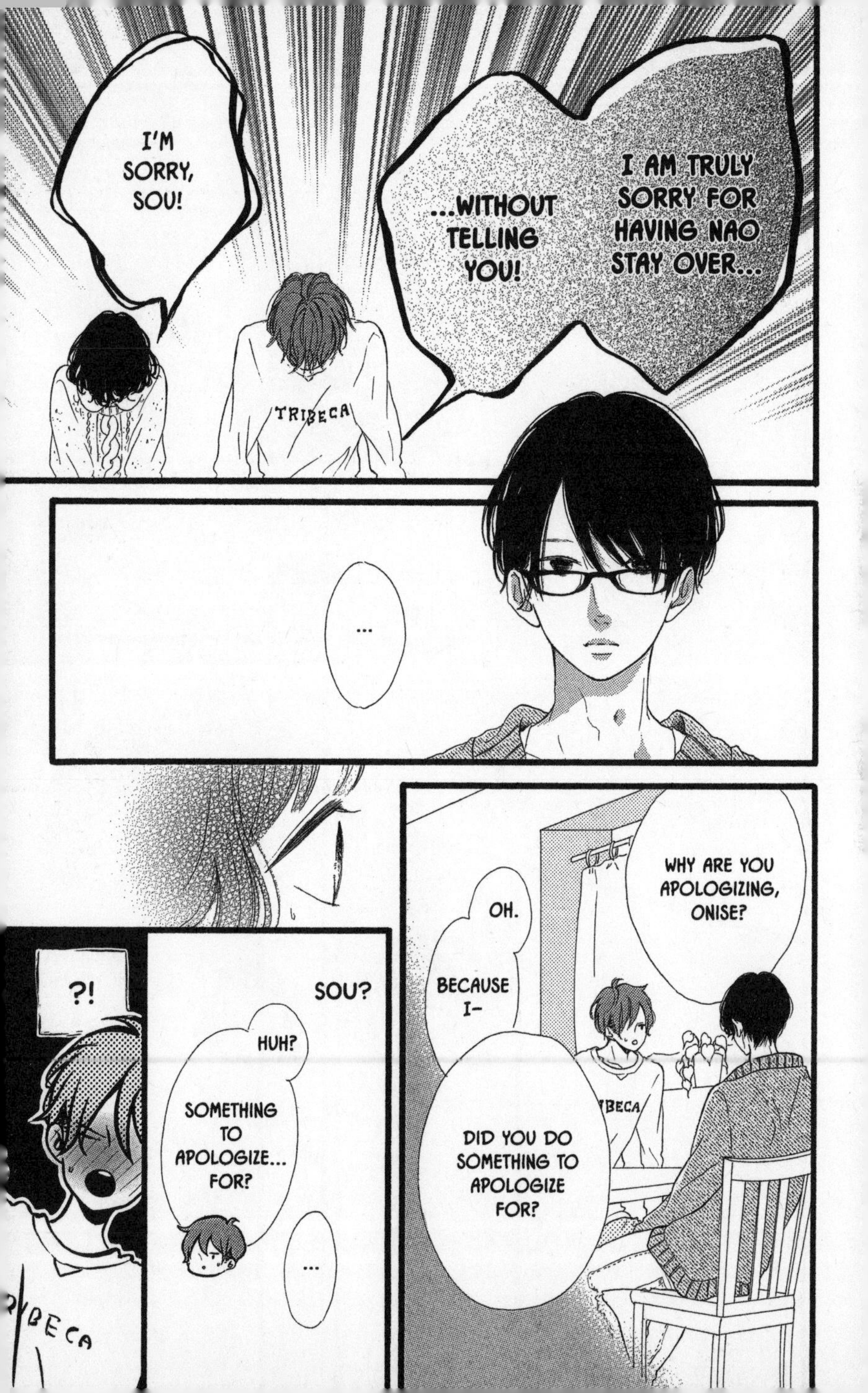
I AM TRULY SORRY FOR HAVING NAO STAY OVER...
...WITHOUT TELLING YOU!
I'M SORRY, SOU!
TRIBECA
...
WHY ARE YOU APOLOGIZING, ONISE?
OH.
BECAUSE I-
DID YOU DO SOMETHING TO APOLOGIZE FOR?
TRIBECA
SOU?
HUH?
SOMETHING TO APOLOGIZE... FOR?
...
?!
TRIBECA

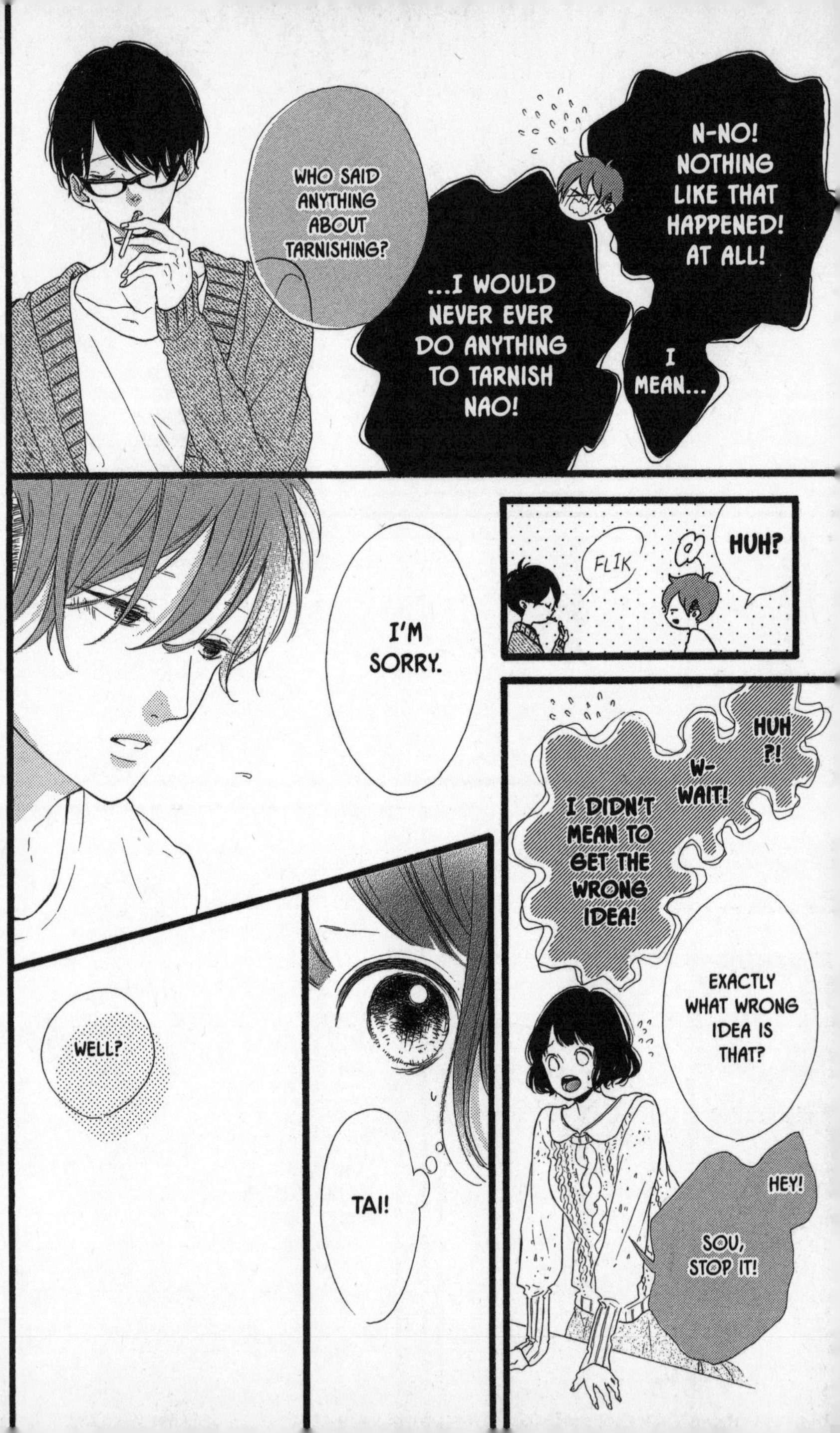
N-NO! NOTHING LIKE THAT HAPPENED! AT ALL!
I MEAN...
...I WOULD NEVER EVER DO ANYTHING TO TARNISH NAO!
WHO SAID ANYTHING ABOUT TARNISHING?
HUH?
FLIK
HUH?!
W-WAIT!
I DIDN'T MEAN TO GET THE WRONG IDEA!
EXACTLY WHAT WRONG IDEA IS THAT?
HEY!
SOU, STOP IT!
I'M SORRY.
TAI!
WELL?

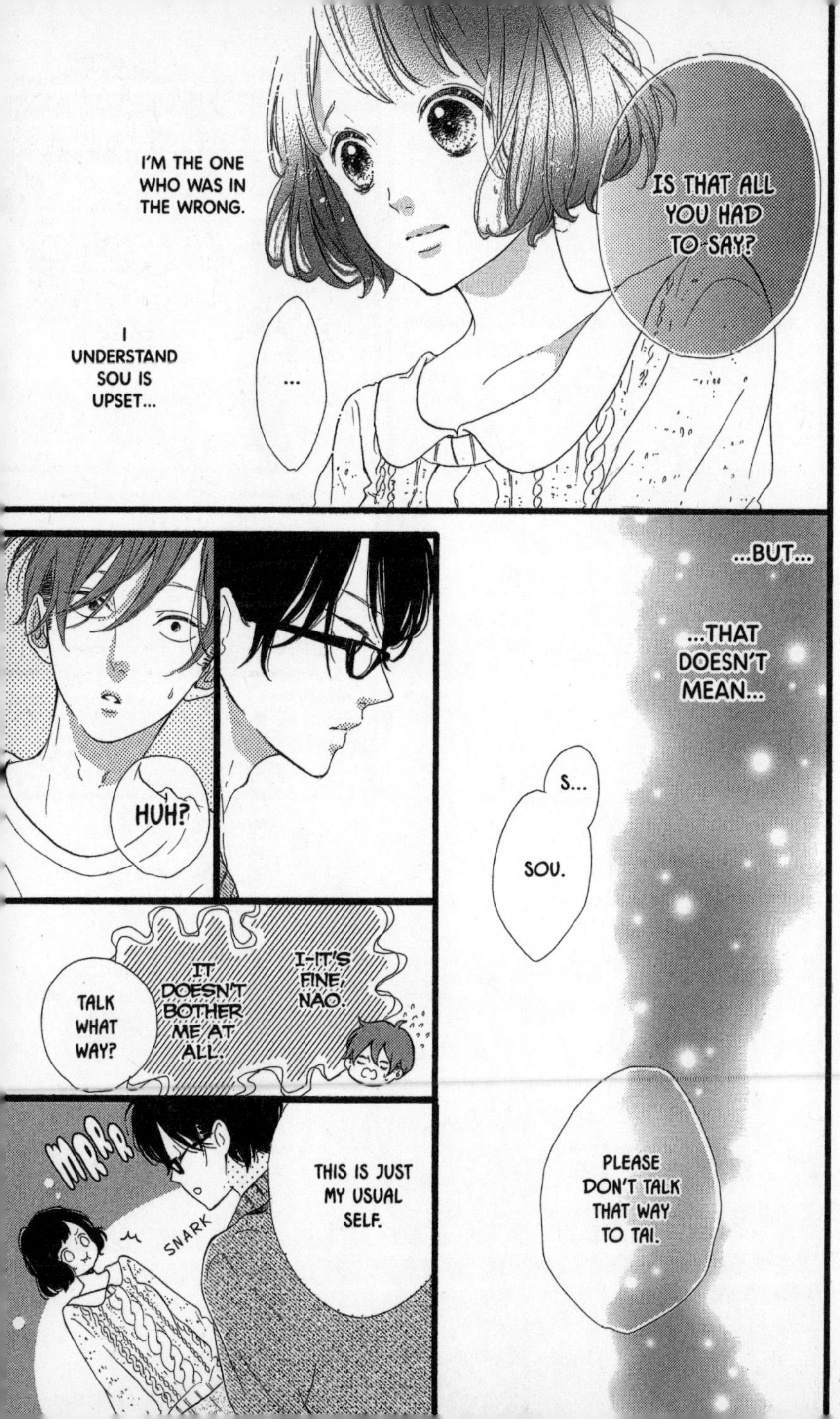
IS THAT ALL YOU HAD TO SAY?
...
I'M THE ONE WHO WAS IN THE WRONG.
I UNDERSTAND SOU IS UPSET...
...BUT...
...THAT DOESN'T MEAN...
S...
SOU.
PLEASE DON'T TALK THAT WAY TO TAI.
HUH?
I-IT'S FINE NAO.
IT DOESN'T BOTHER ME AT ALL.
TALK WHAT WAY?
THIS IS JUST MY USUAL SELF.
SNARK
MRRR

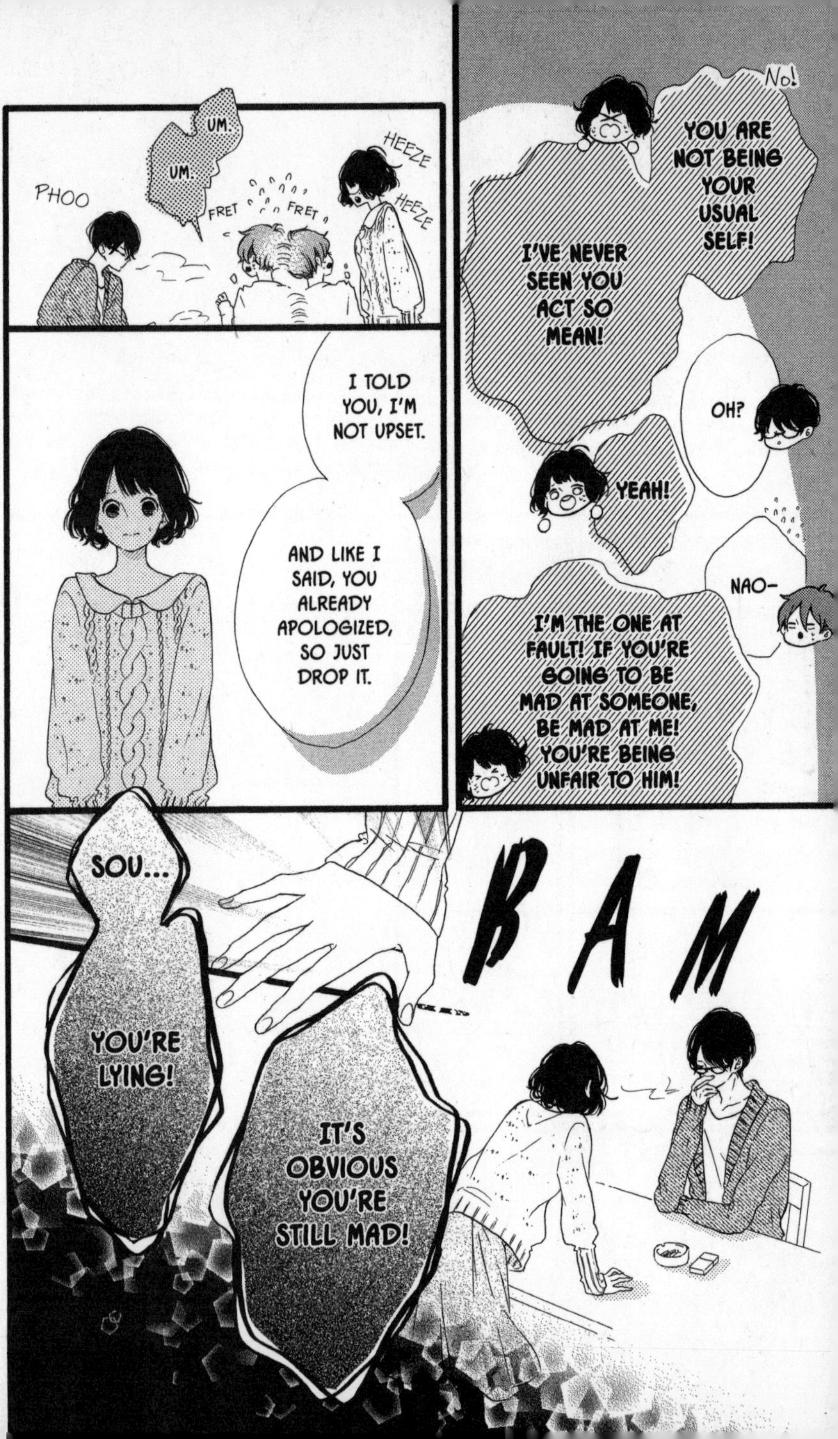
No!
YOU ARE NOT BEING YOUR USUAL SELF!
I'VE NEVER SEEN YOU ACT SO MEAN!
OH?
YEAH!
NAO-
I'M THE ONE AT FAULT! IF YOU'RE GOING TO BE MAD AT SOMEONE, BE MAD AT ME! YOU'RE BEING UNFAIR TO HIM!
HEEZE
HEEZE
UM.
UM.
FRET
FRET
PHOO
I TOLD YOU, I'M NOT UPSET.
AND LIKE I SAID, YOU ALREADY APOLOGIZED, SO JUST DROP IT.
BAM
SOU...
YOU'RE LYING!
IT'S OBVIOUS YOU'RE STILL MAD!

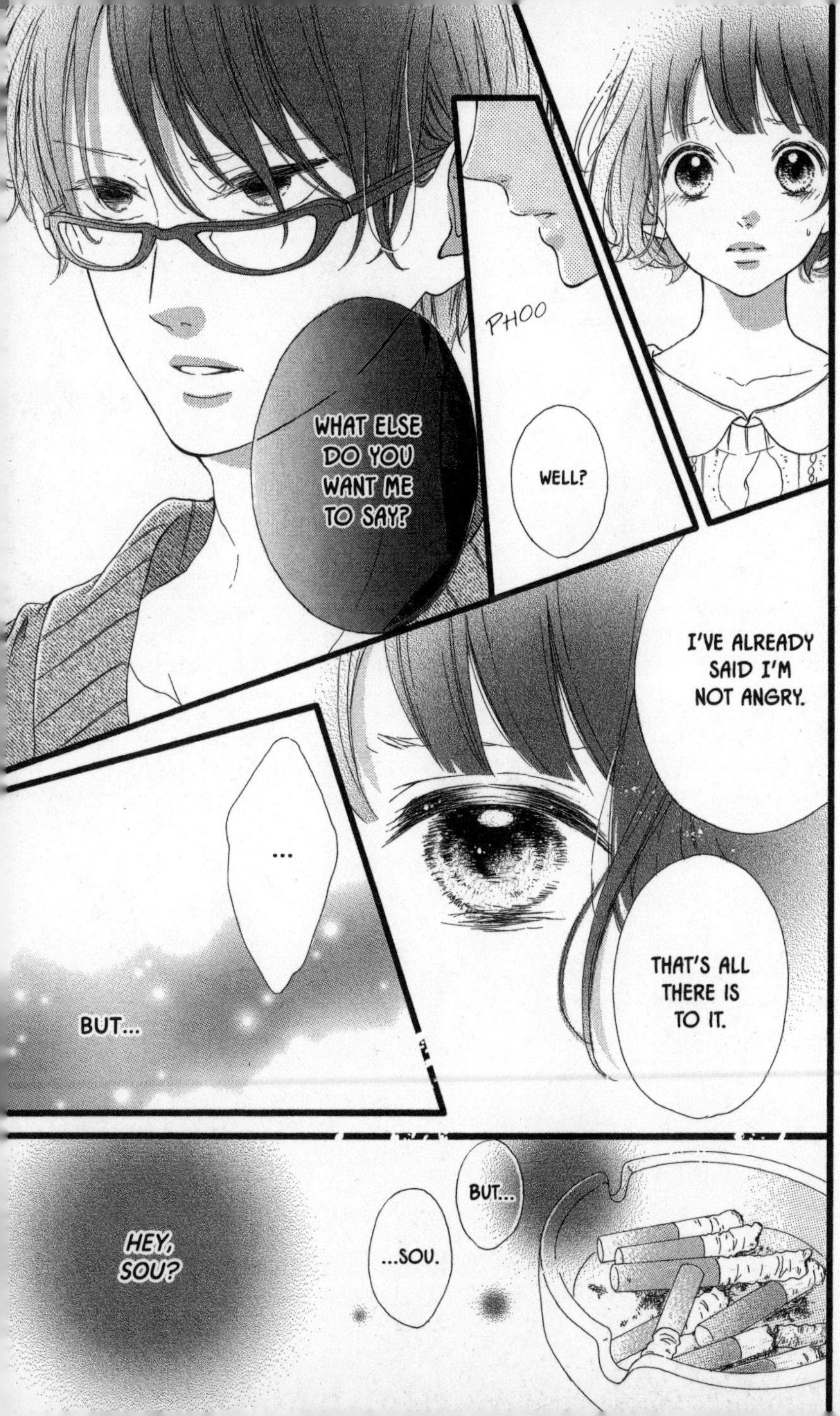
PHOO
WELL?
WHAT ELSE DO YOU WANT ME TO SAY?
I'VE ALREADY SAID I'M NOT ANGRY.
THAT'S ALL THERE IS TO IT.
...
BUT...
BUT...
...SOU.
HEY, SOU?

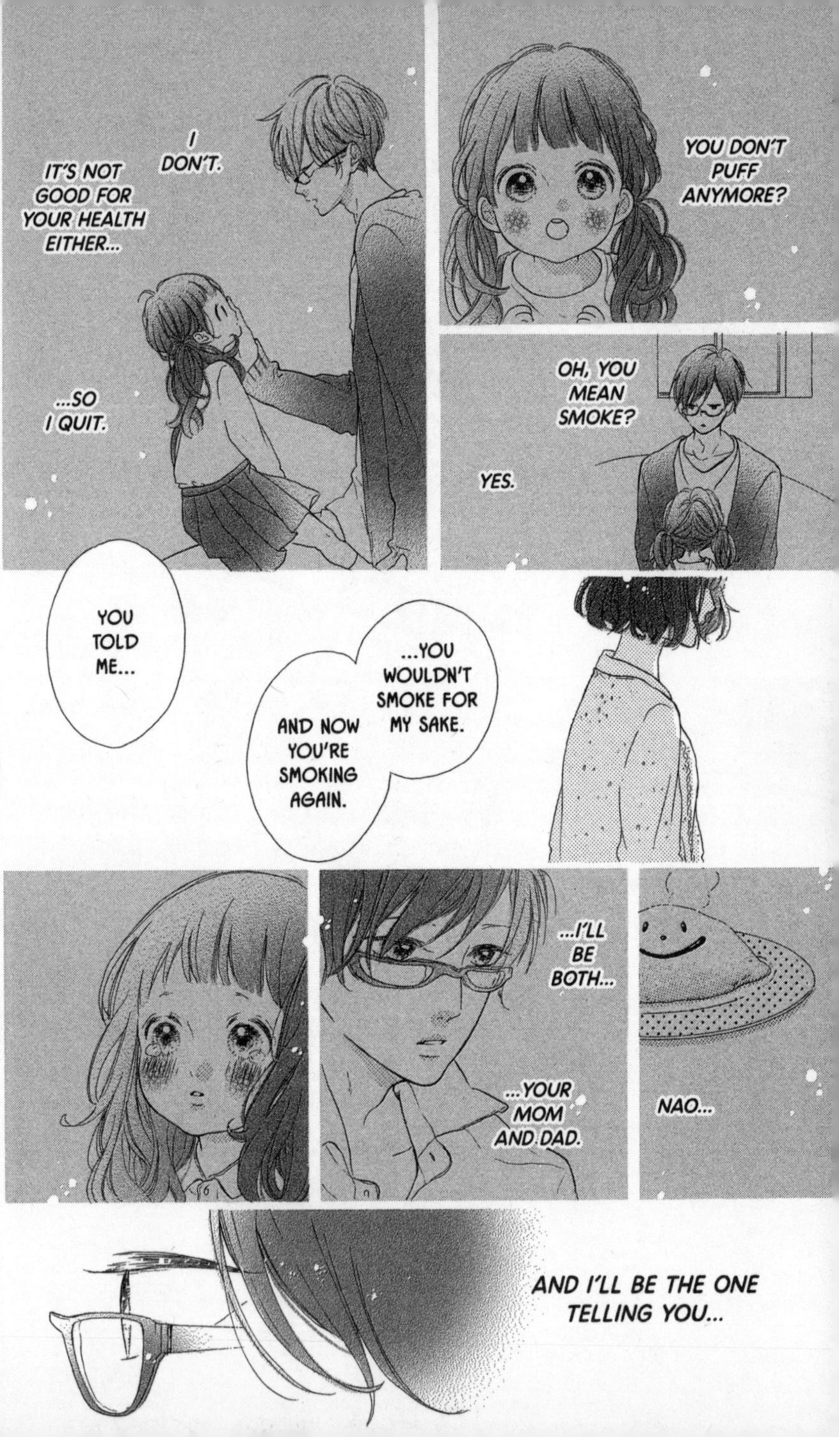
YOU DON'T PUFF ANYMORE?
OH, YOU MEAN SMOKE?
YES.
I DON'T.
IT'S NOT GOOD FOR YOUR HEALTH EITHER...
...SO I QUIT.
YOU TOLD ME...
...YOU WOULDN'T SMOKE FOR MY SAKE.
AND NOW YOU'RE SMOKING AGAIN.
NAO...
...I'LL BE BOTH...
...YOUR MOM AND DAD.
AND I'LL BE THE ONE TELLING YOU...

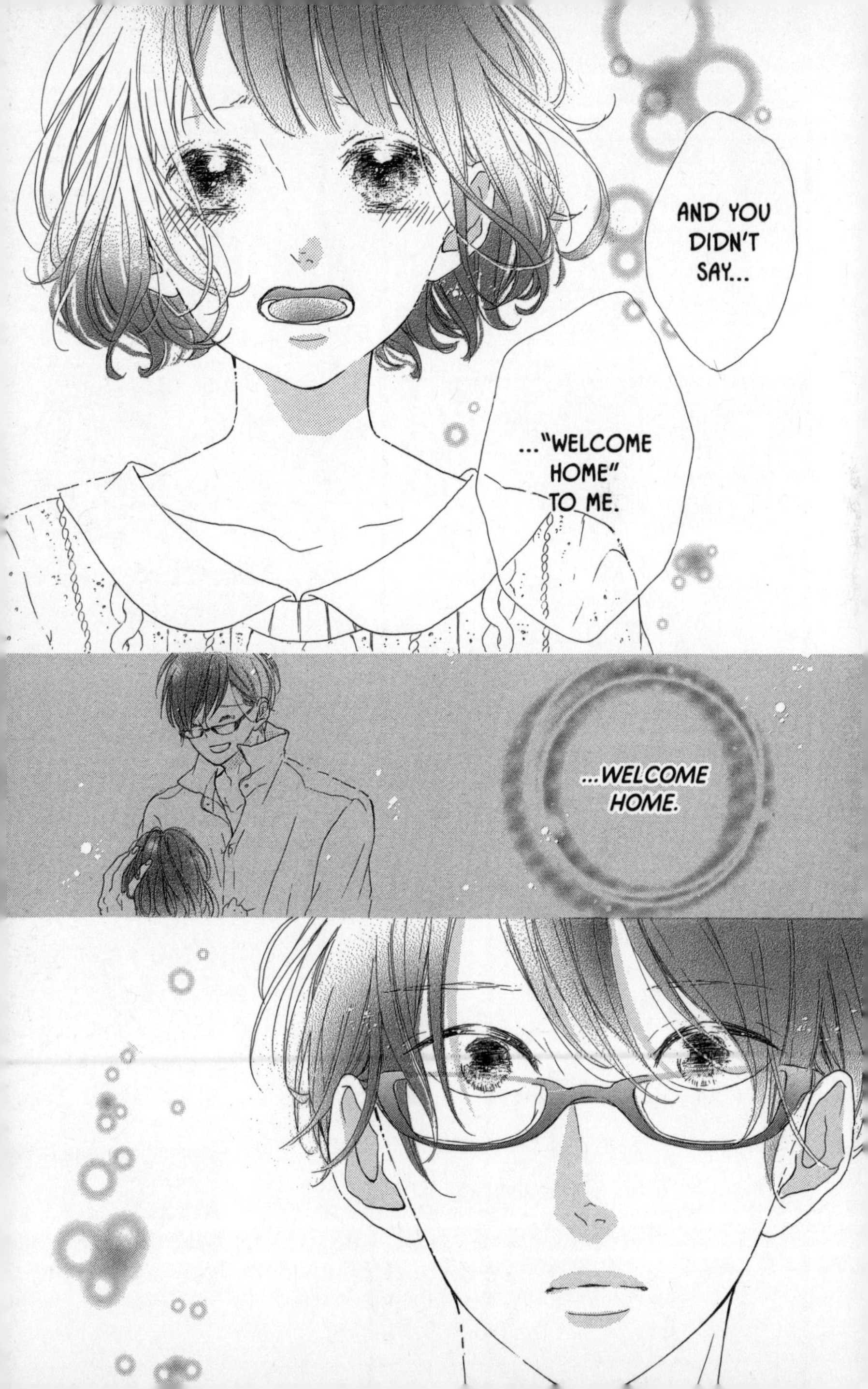
AND YOU DIDN'T SAY...
..."WELCOME HOME" TO ME.
...WELCOME HOME.

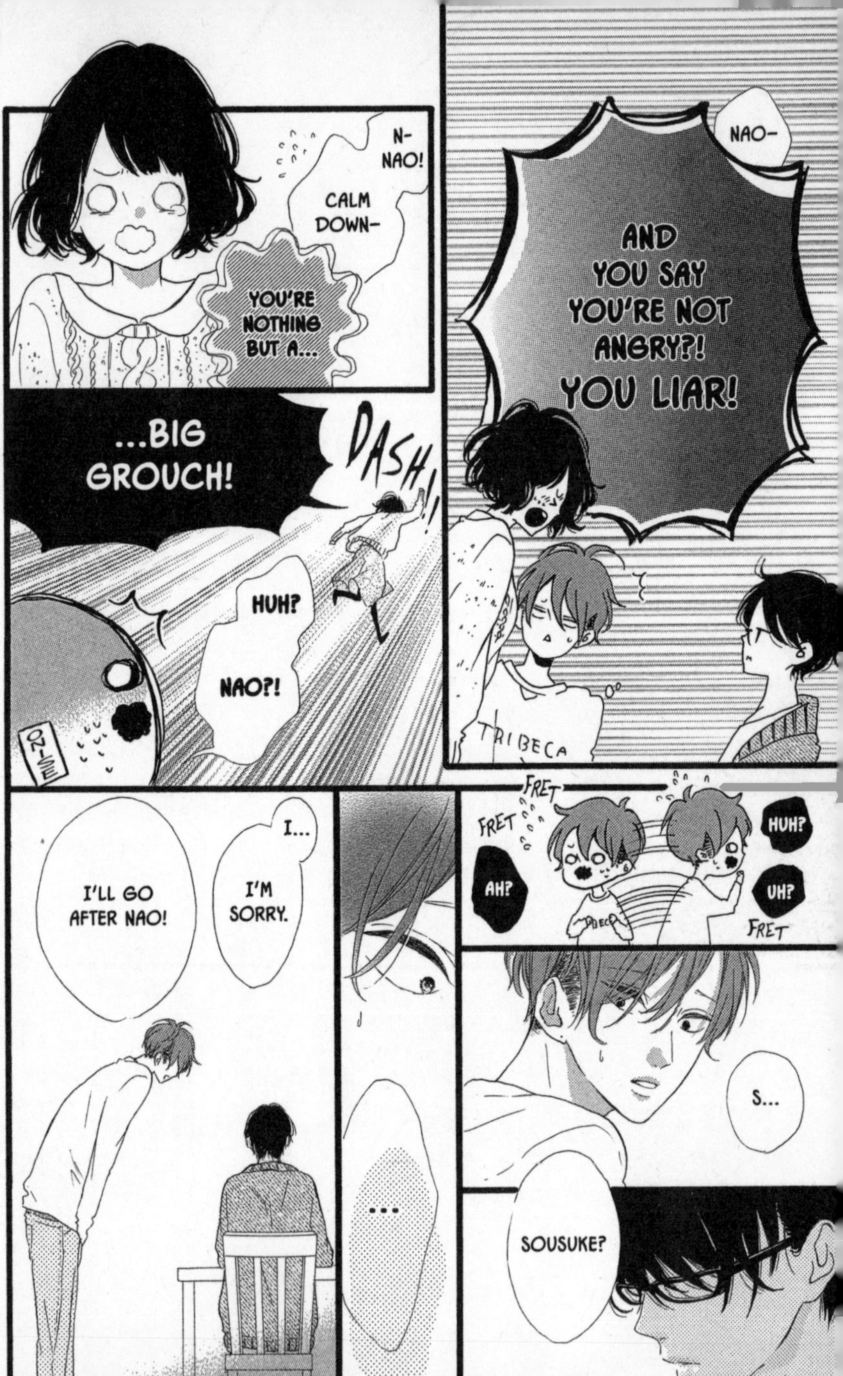
NAO–
AND YOU SAY YOU'RE NOT ANGRY?! YOU LIAR!
TRIBECA
N-NAO!
CALM DOWN–
YOU'RE NOTHING BUT A...
...BIG GROUCH!
DASH!!
HUH?
NAO?!
ONISE
FRET
FRET
HUH?
UH?
AH?
FRET
S...
SOUSUKE?
...
I...
I'M SORRY.
I'LL GO AFTER NAO!

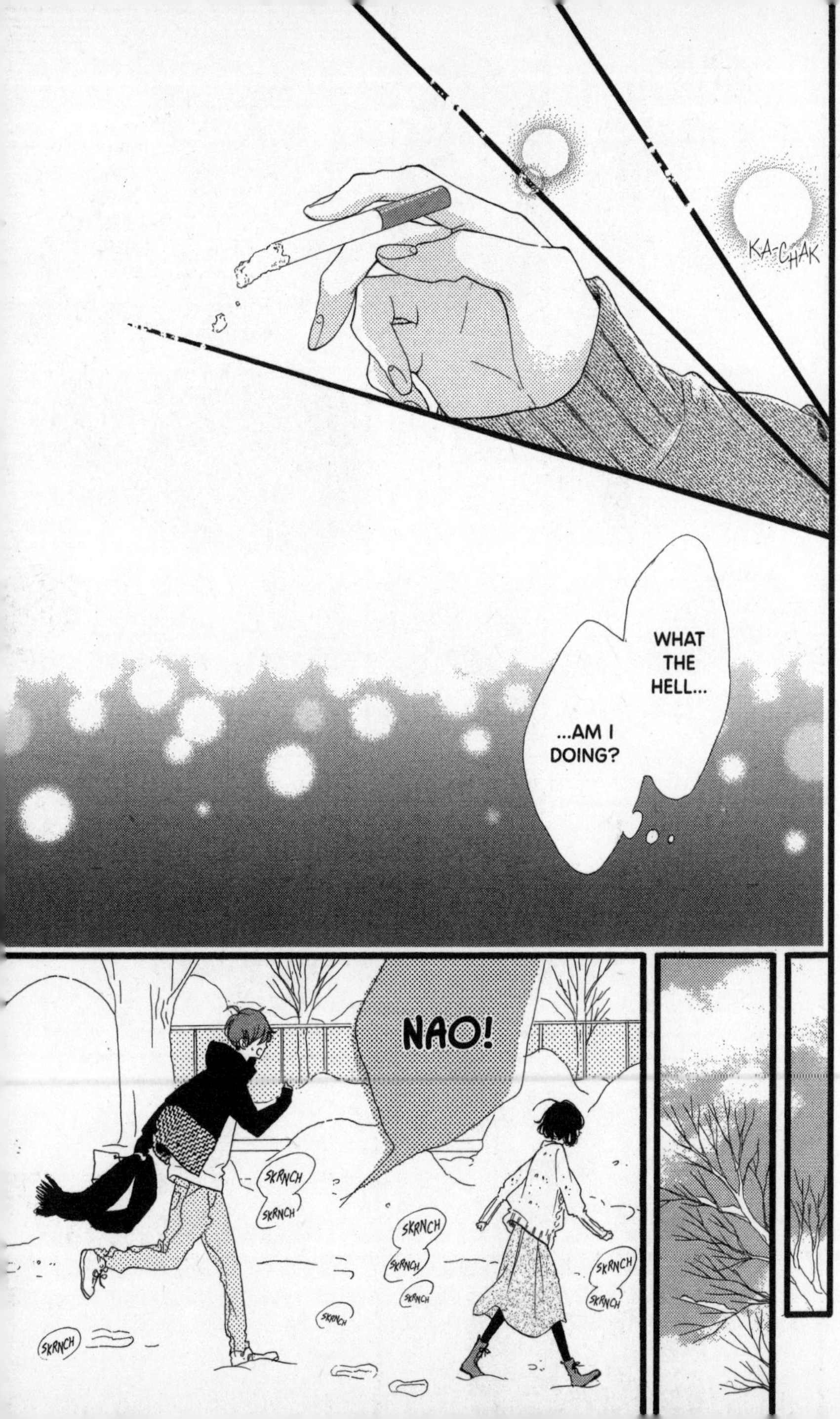
KA-CHAK
WHAT THE HELL...
...AM I DOING?
NAO!
SKRNCH
SKRNCH
SKRNCH
SKRNCH
SKRNCH
SKRNCH
SKRNCH
SKRNCH
SKRNCH
SKRNCH

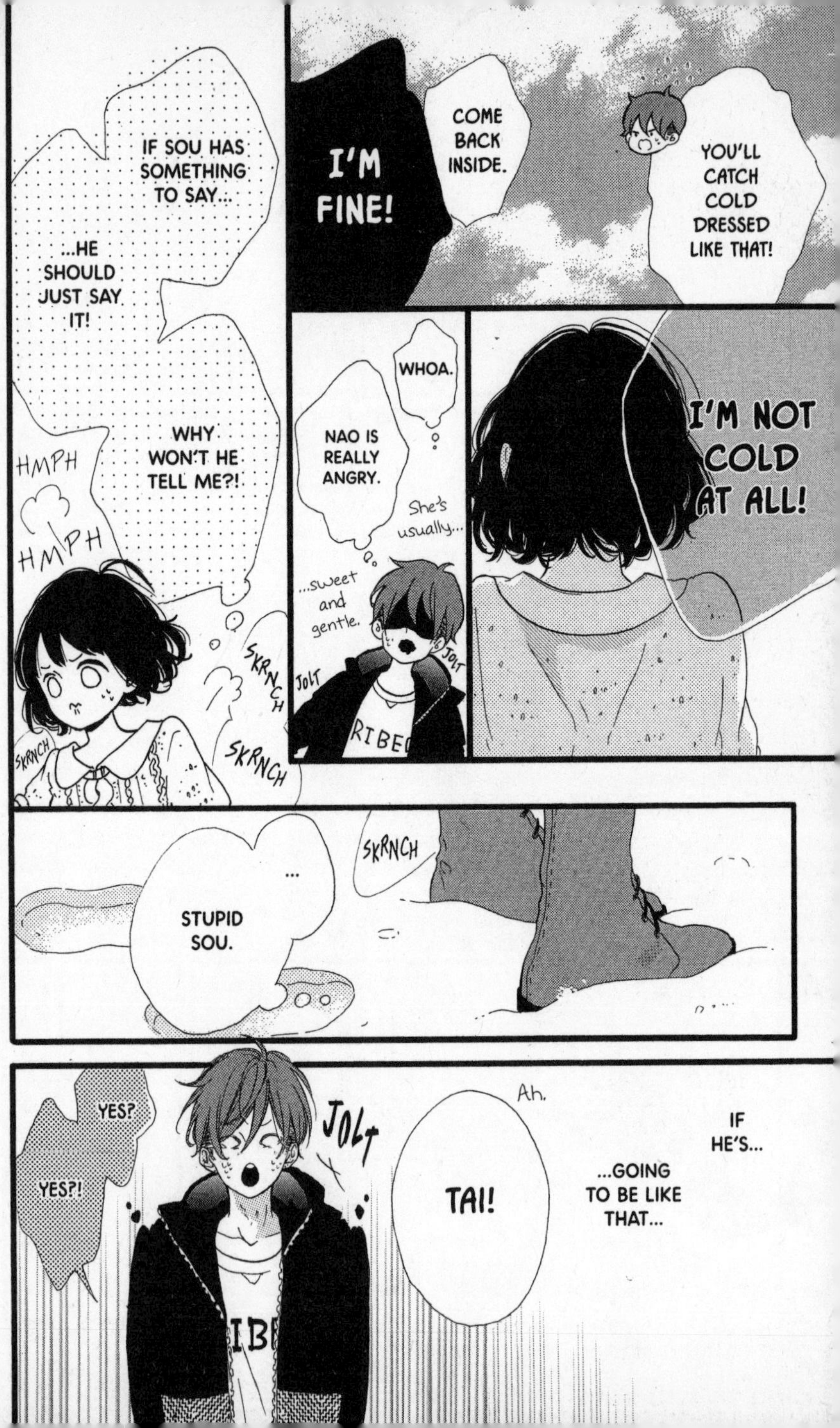
YOU'LL CATCH COLD DRESSED LIKE THAT!
COME BACK INSIDE.
I'M FINE!
I'M NOT COLD AT ALL!
WHOA.
NAO IS REALLY ANGRY.
She's usually...
...sweet and gentle.
JOLT
JOLT
IF SOU HAS SOMETHING TO SAY...
...HE SHOULD JUST SAY IT!
WHY WON'T HE TELL ME?!
HMPH
HMPH
SKRNCH
SKRNCH
SKRNCH
SKRNCH
...
STUPID SOU.
IF HE'S...
...GOING TO BE LIKE THAT...
TAI!
Ah.
JOLT
YES?
YES?!

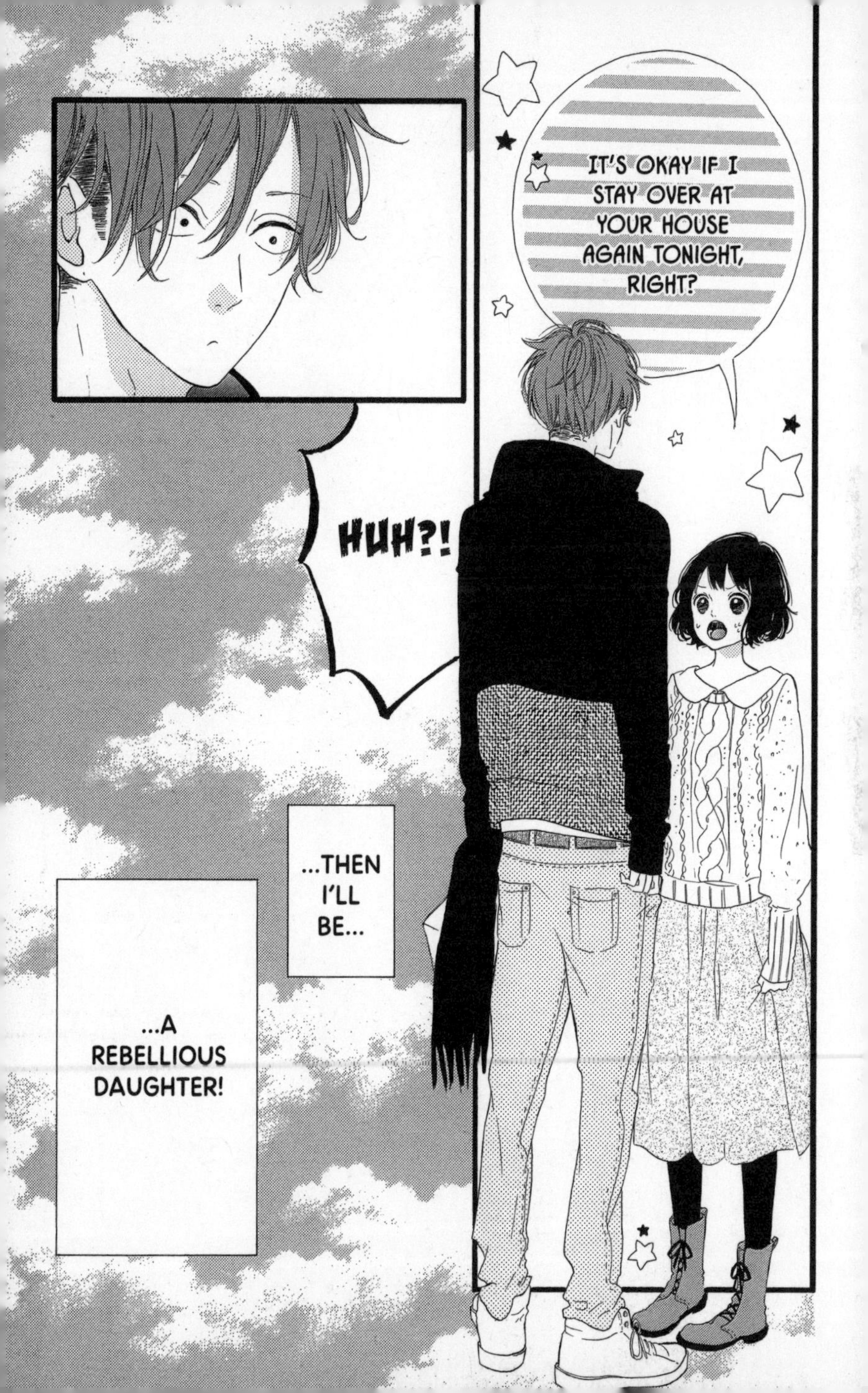
IT'S OKAY IF I STAY OVER AT YOUR HOUSE AGAIN TONIGHT, RIGHT?
HUH?!
...THEN I'LL BE...
...A REBELLIOUS DAUGHTER!

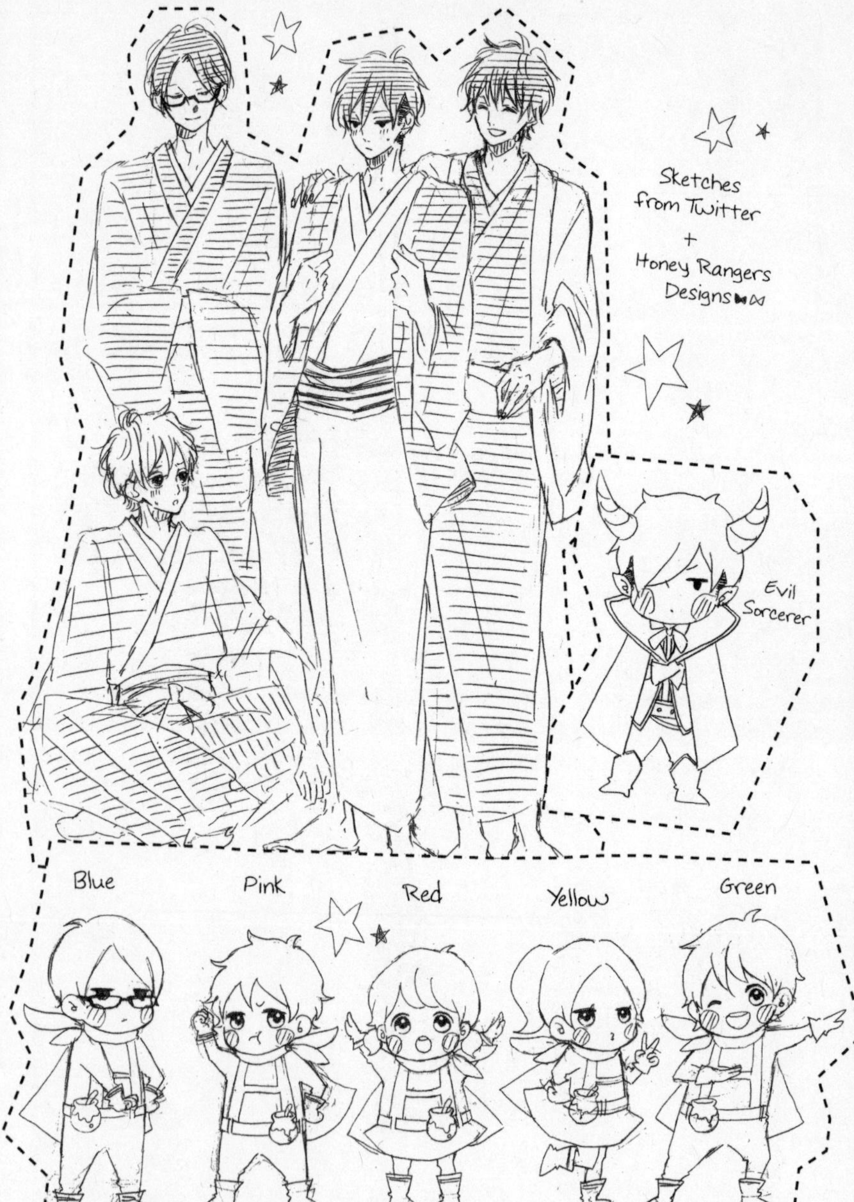
Sketches from Twitter + Honey Rangers Designs
Evil Sorcerer
Blue
Pink
Red
Yellow
Green

#24

Welcome Home

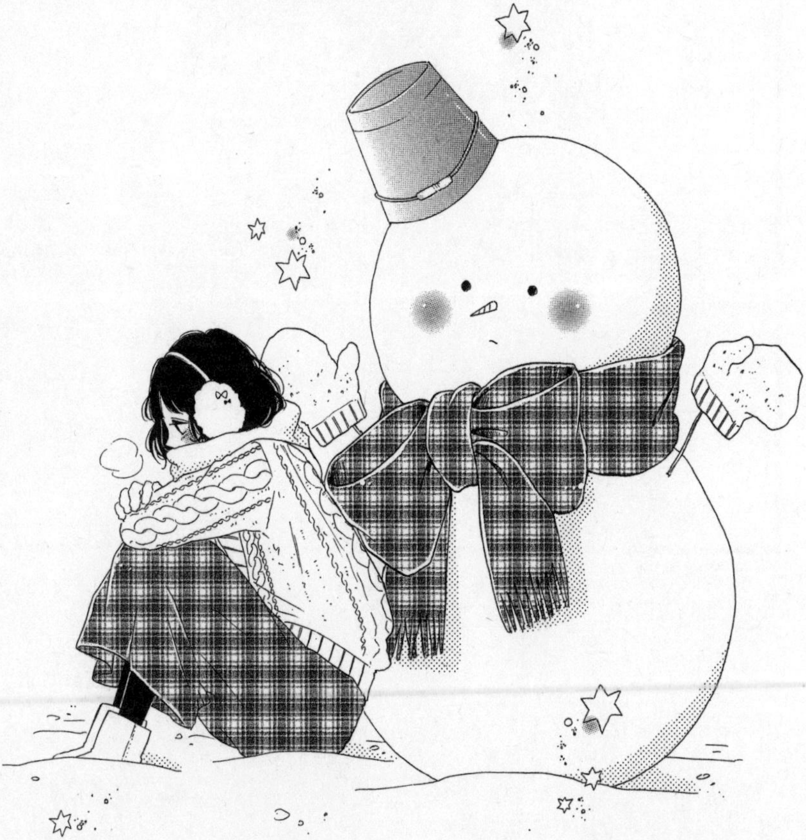

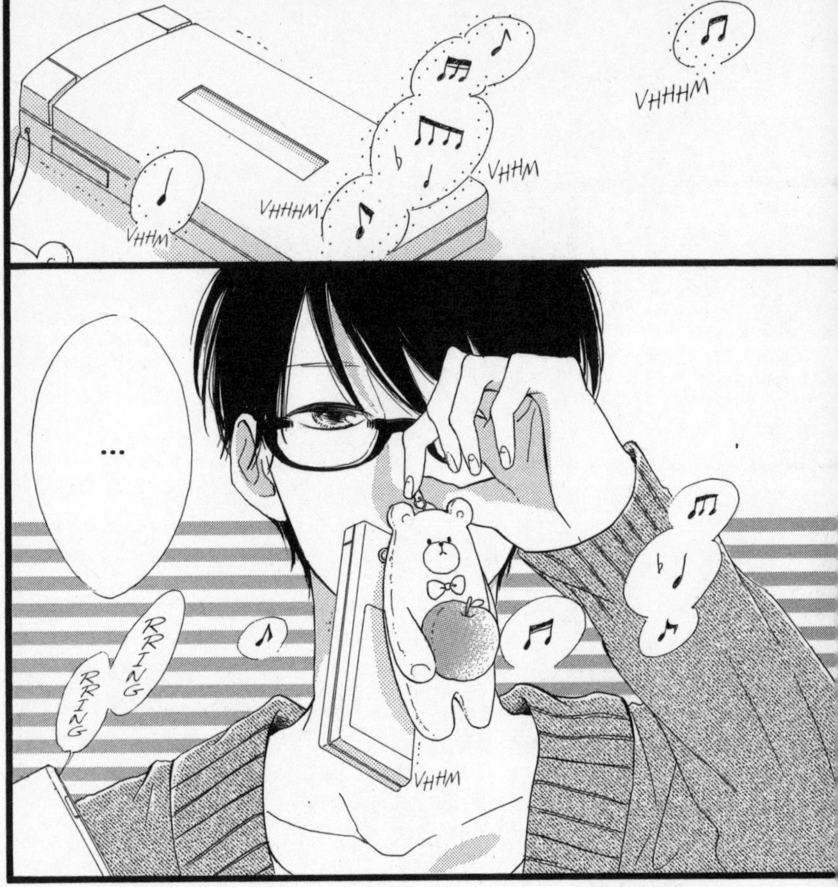
VHHHM
VHHM
VHHHM
VHHM
...
RRING
RRING
VHHM
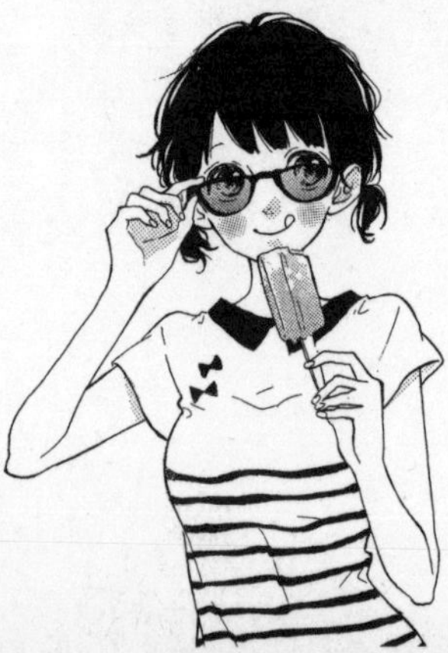

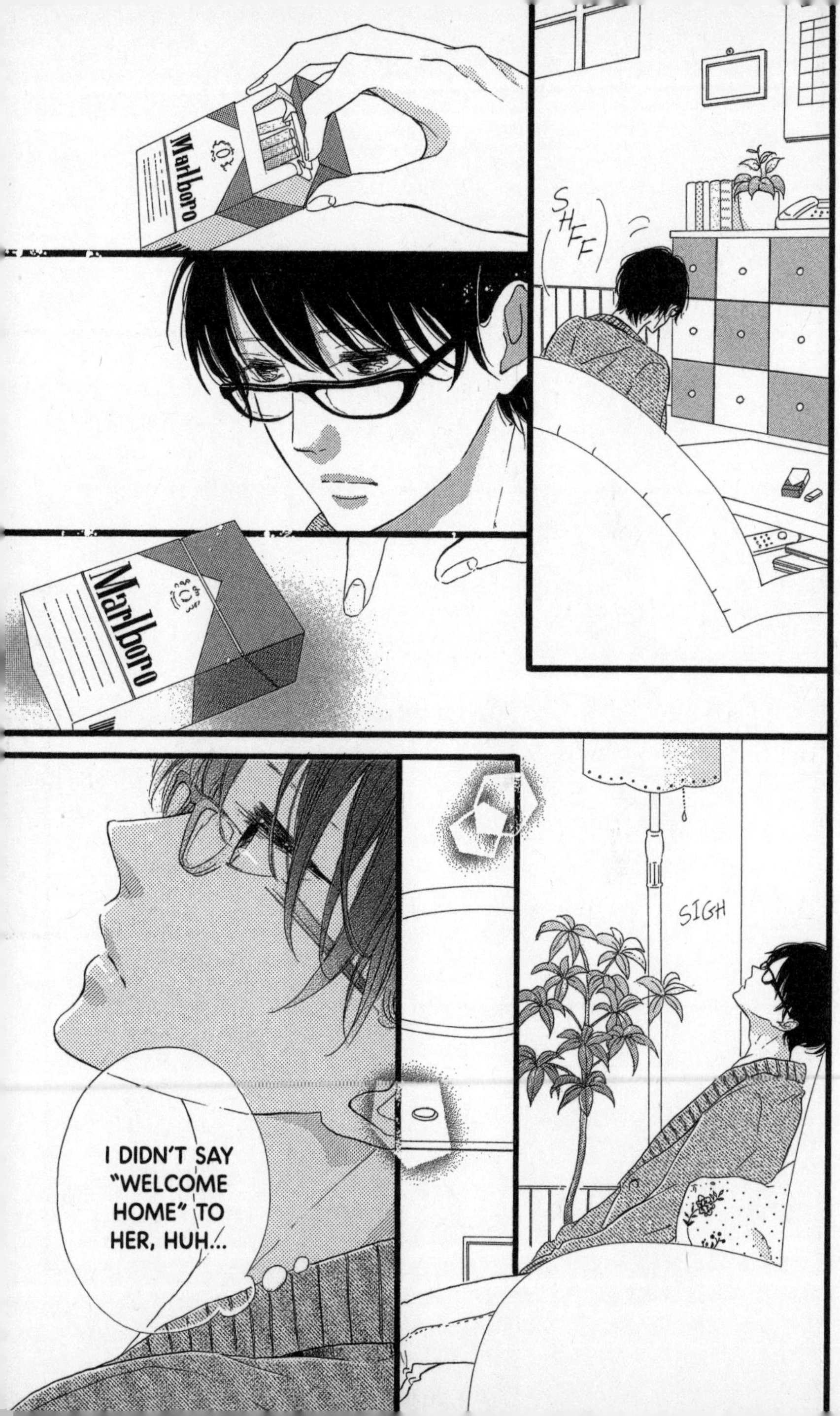
SHFF
Marlboro
Marlboro
SIGH
I DIDN'T SAY "WELCOME HOME" TO HER, HUH...

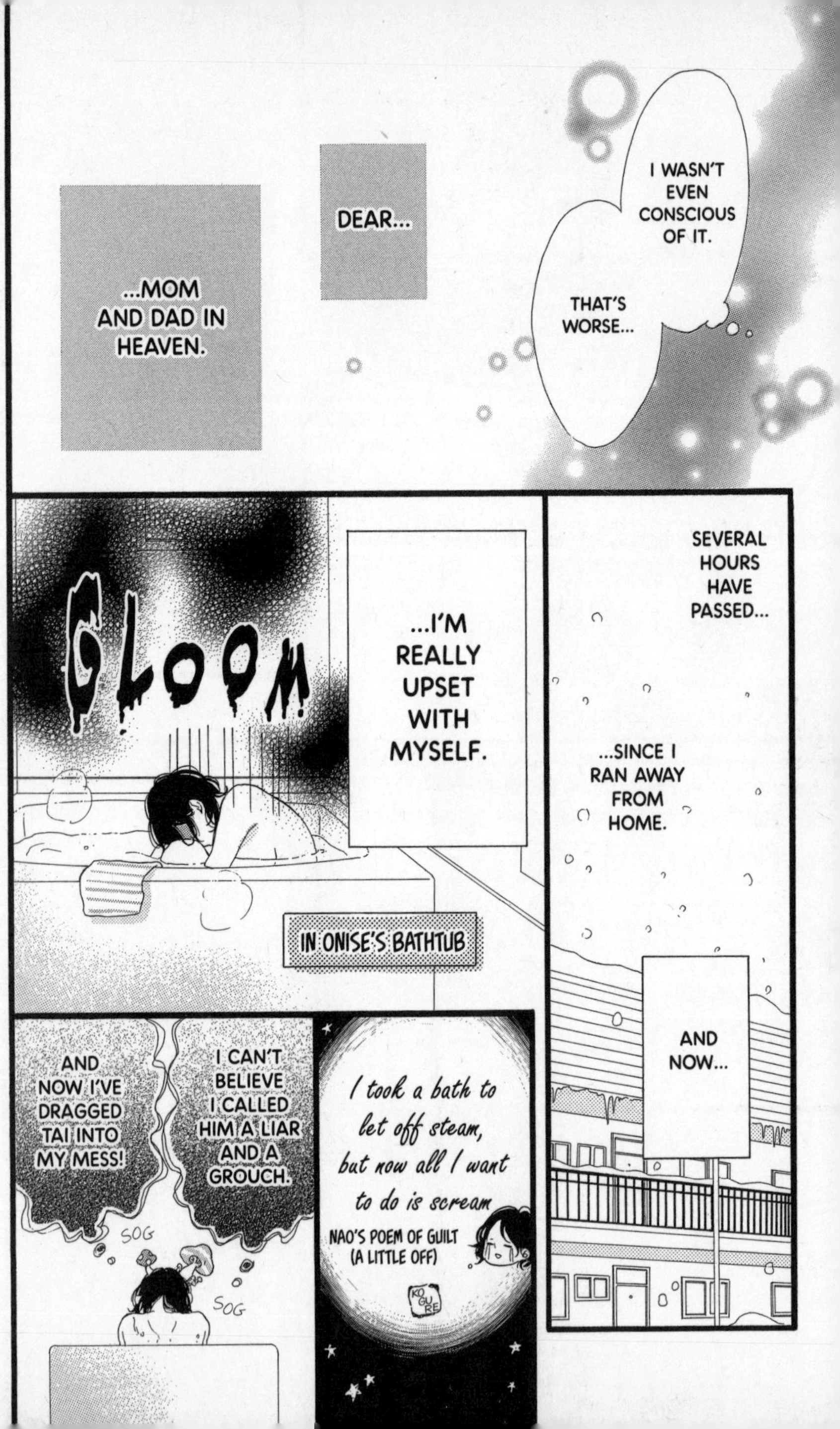
I WASN'T EVEN CONSCIOUS OF IT.
THAT'S WORSE...
DEAR...
...MOM AND DAD IN HEAVEN.
SEVERAL HOURS HAVE PASSED...
...SINCE I RAN AWAY FROM HOME.
AND NOW...
...I'M REALLY UPSET WITH MYSELF.
GLOOM
IN ONISE'S BATHTUB
I took a bath to let off steam, but now all I want to do is scream
NAO'S POEM OF GUILT (A LITTLE OFF)
I CAN'T BELIEVE I CALLED HIM A LIAR AND A GROUCH.
AND NOW I'VE DRAGGED TAI INTO MY MESS!
SOG
SOG

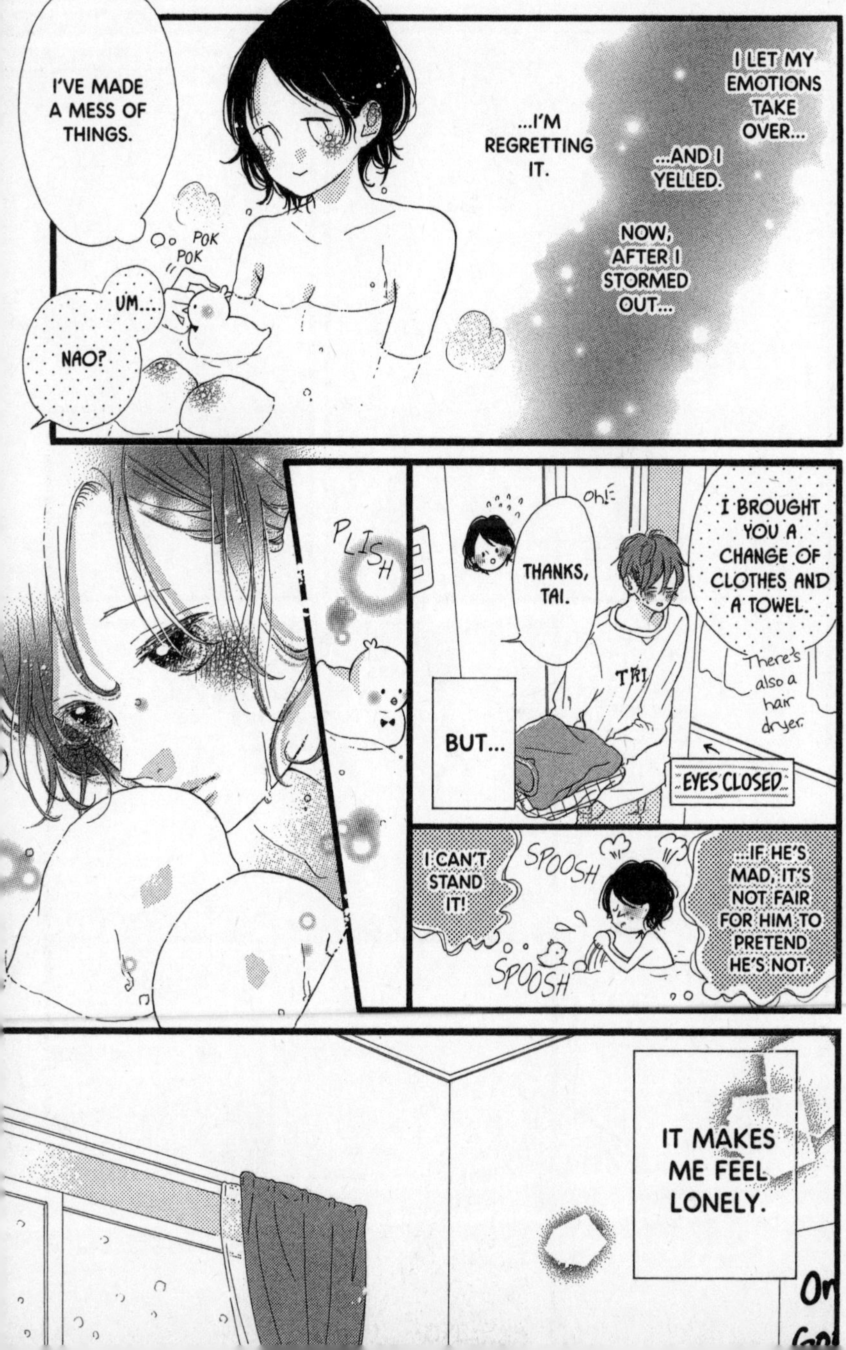
I LET MY EMOTIONS TAKE OVER...
...AND I YELLED.
NOW, AFTER I STORMED OUT...
...I'M REGRETTING IT.
I'VE MADE A MESS OF THINGS.
POK POK
UM... NAO?
I BROUGHT YOU A CHANGE OF CLOTHES AND A TOWEL.
There's also a hair dryer.
EYES CLOSED
Oh!
THANKS, TAI.
BUT...
...IF HE'S MAD, IT'S NOT FAIR FOR HIM TO PRETEND HE'S NOT.
SPOOSH
SPOOSH
I CAN'T STAND IT!
PLISH
IT MAKES ME FEEL LONELY.

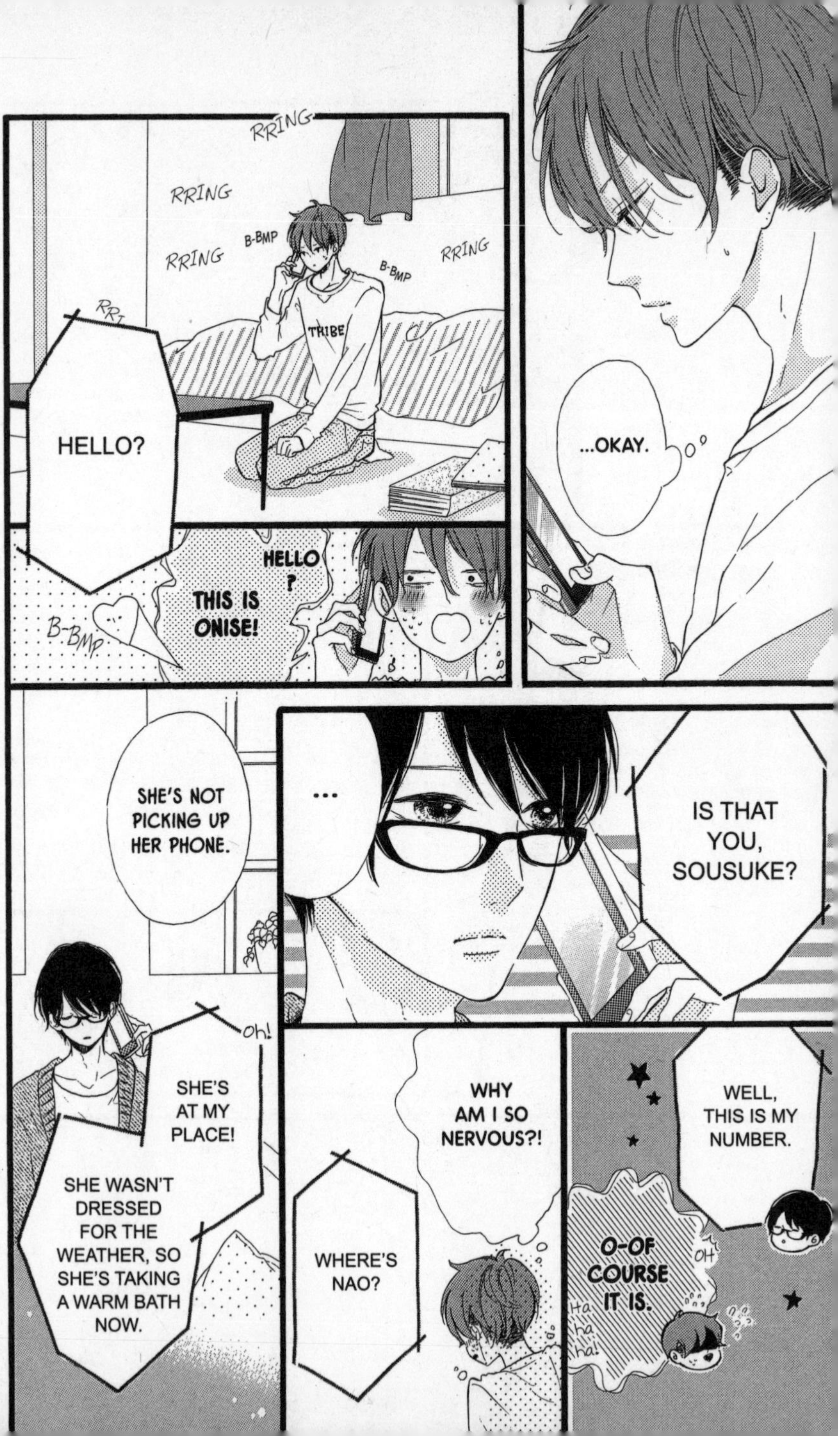
...OKAY.
RRING
RRING
RRING
B-BMP
RRING
B-BMP
RRI
TRIBE
HELLO?
HELLO?
THIS IS ONISE!
B-BMP
...
IS THAT YOU, SOUSUKE?
WELL, THIS IS MY NUMBER.
OH
O-OF COURSE IT IS.
Ha ha ha!
WHY AM I SO NERVOUS?!
WHERE'S NAO?
SHE'S NOT PICKING UP HER PHONE.
Oh!
SHE'S AT MY PLACE!
SHE WASN'T DRESSED FOR THE WEATHER, SO SHE'S TAKING A WARM BATH NOW.

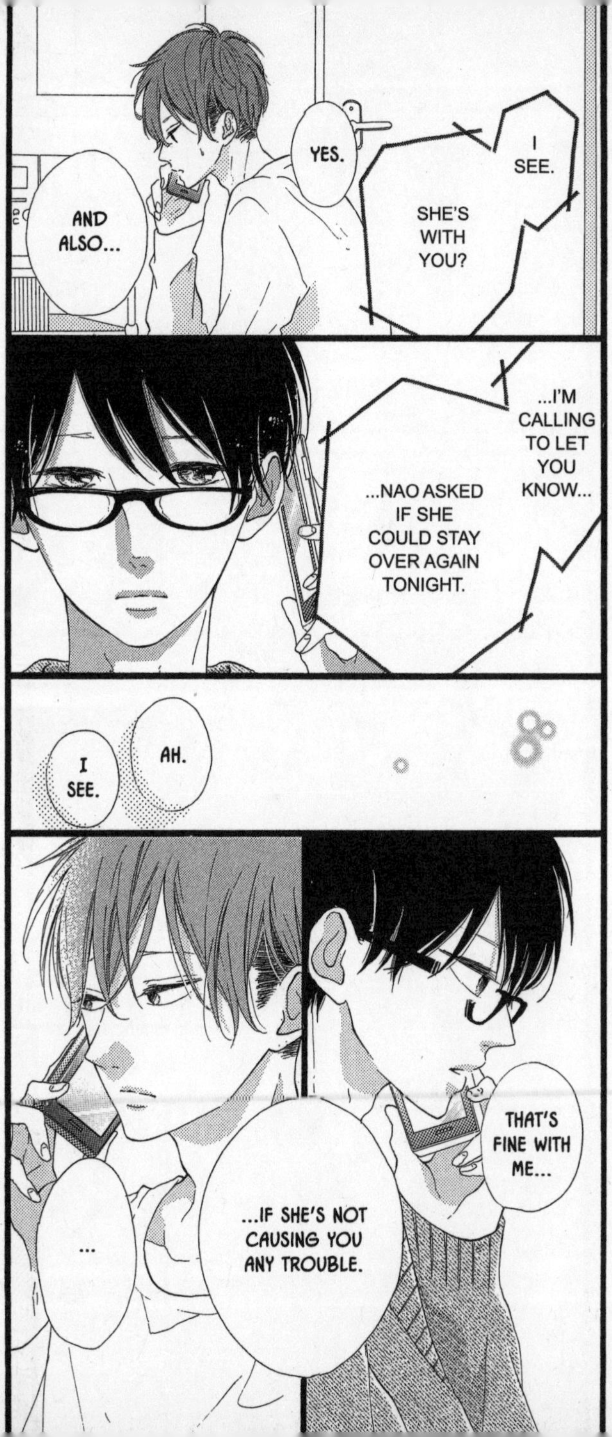
I SEE.
SHE'S WITH YOU?
YES.
AND ALSO...
...I'M CALLING TO LET YOU KNOW...
...NAO ASKED IF SHE COULD STAY OVER AGAIN TONIGHT.
AH.
I SEE.
...THAT'S FINE WITH ME...
...IF SHE'S NOT CAUSING YOU ANY TROUBLE.
...

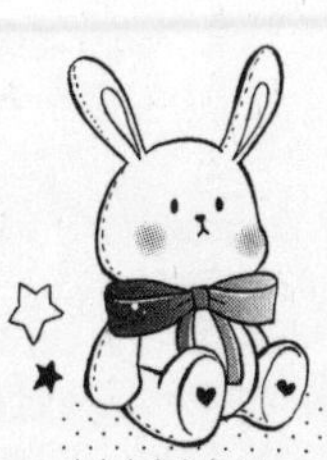

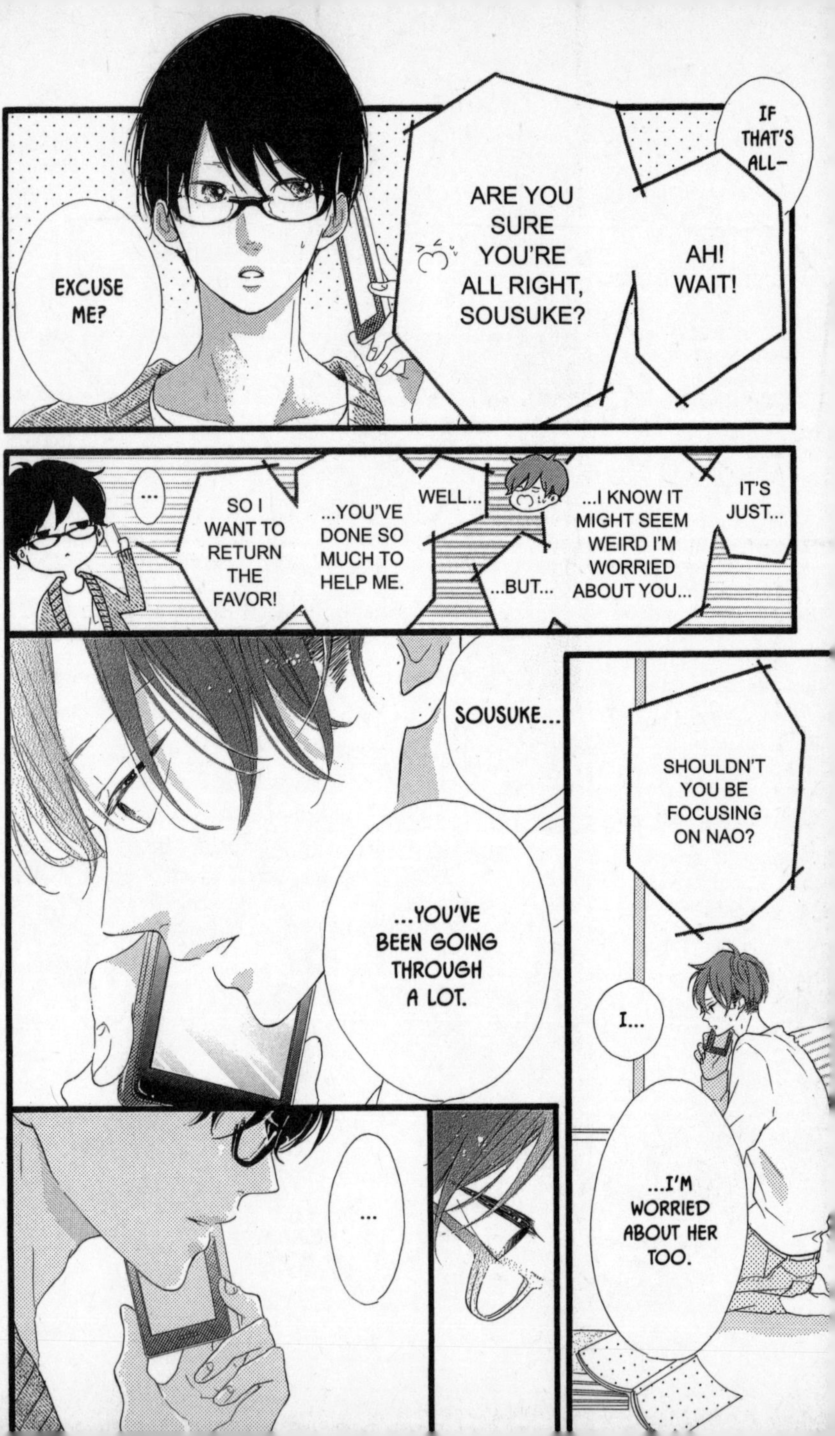
IF THAT'S ALL—
AH! WAIT!
ARE YOU SURE YOU'RE ALL RIGHT, SOUSUKE?
EXCUSE ME?
IT'S JUST...
...I KNOW IT MIGHT SEEM WEIRD I'M WORRIED ABOUT YOU...
...BUT...
WELL...
...YOU'VE DONE SO MUCH TO HELP ME.
SO I WANT TO RETURN THE FAVOR!
...
SOUSUKE...
SHOULDN'T YOU BE FOCUSING ON NAO?
I...
...I'M WORRIED ABOUT HER TOO.
...YOU'VE BEEN GOING THROUGH A LOT.
...

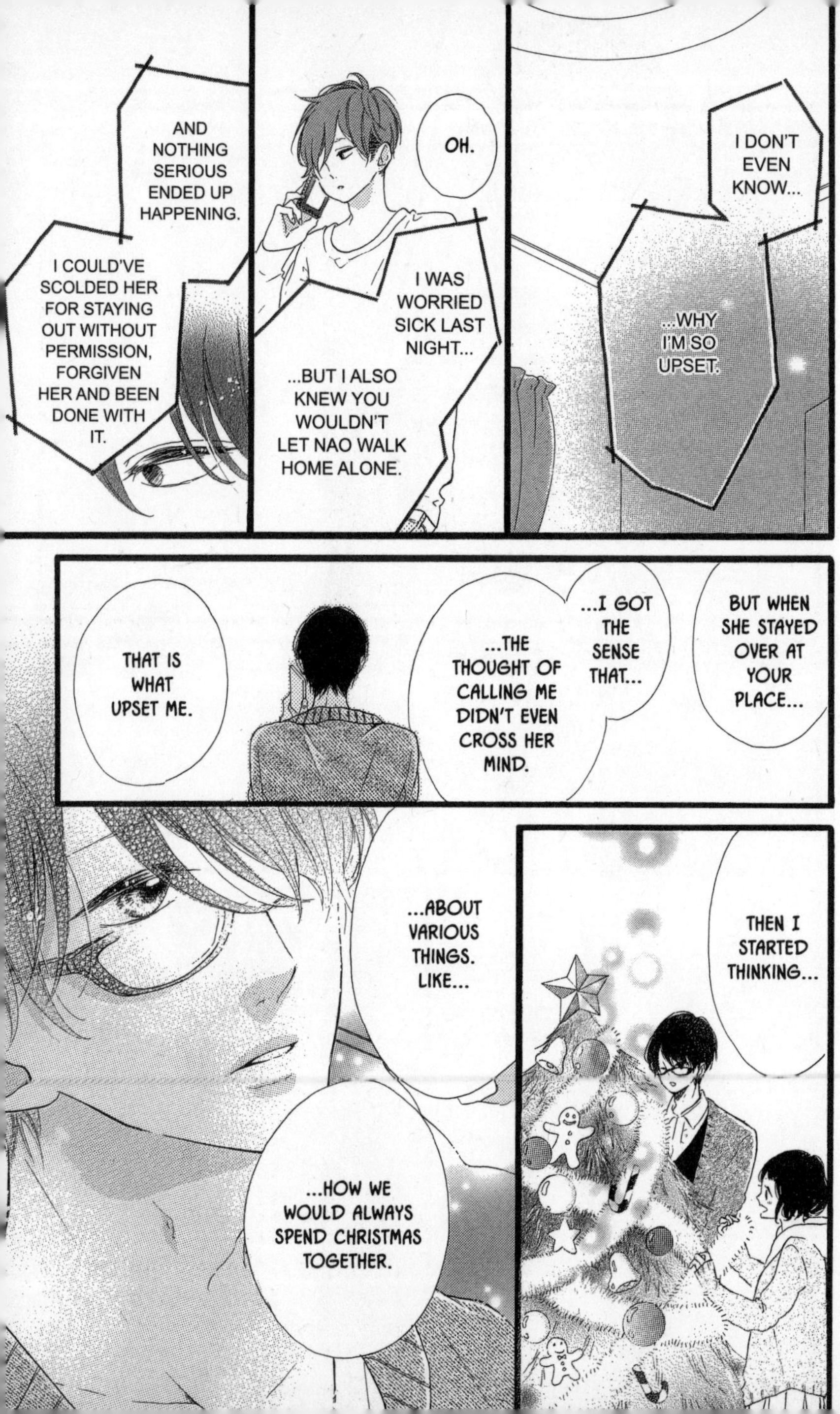
I DON'T EVEN KNOW...
...WHY I'M SO UPSET.
OH.
I WAS WORRIED SICK LAST NIGHT...
...BUT I ALSO KNEW YOU WOULDN'T LET NAO WALK HOME ALONE.
AND NOTHING SERIOUS ENDED UP HAPPENING.
I COULD'VE SCOLDED HER FOR STAYING OUT WITHOUT PERMISSION, FORGIVEN HER AND BEEN DONE WITH IT.
BUT WHEN SHE STAYED OVER AT YOUR PLACE...
...I GOT THE SENSE THAT...
...THE THOUGHT OF CALLING ME DIDN'T EVEN CROSS HER MIND.
THAT IS WHAT UPSET ME.
THEN I STARTED THINKING...
...ABOUT VARIOUS THINGS. LIKE...
...HOW WE WOULD ALWAYS SPEND CHRISTMAS TOGETHER.

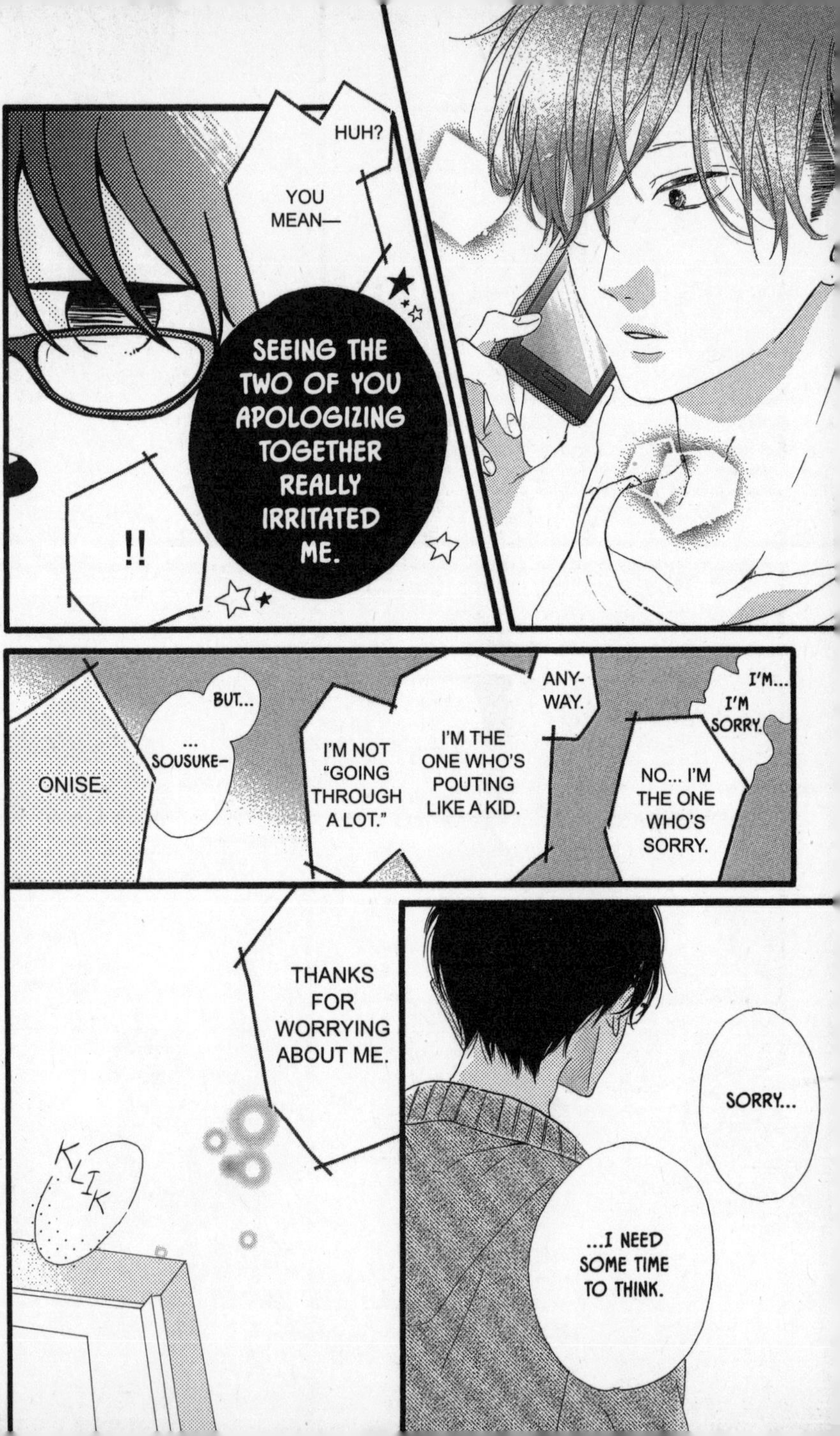
HUH?
YOU MEAN—
SEEING THE TWO OF YOU APOLOGIZING TOGETHER REALLY IRRITATED ME.
!!
I'M... I'M SORRY.
NO... I'M THE ONE WHO'S SORRY.
ANY-WAY.
I'M THE ONE WHO'S POUTING LIKE A KID.
I'M NOT "GOING THROUGH A LOT."
BUT...
...SOUSUKE-
ONISE.
SORRY...
...I NEED SOME TIME TO THINK.
THANKS FOR WORRYING ABOUT ME.
KLIK

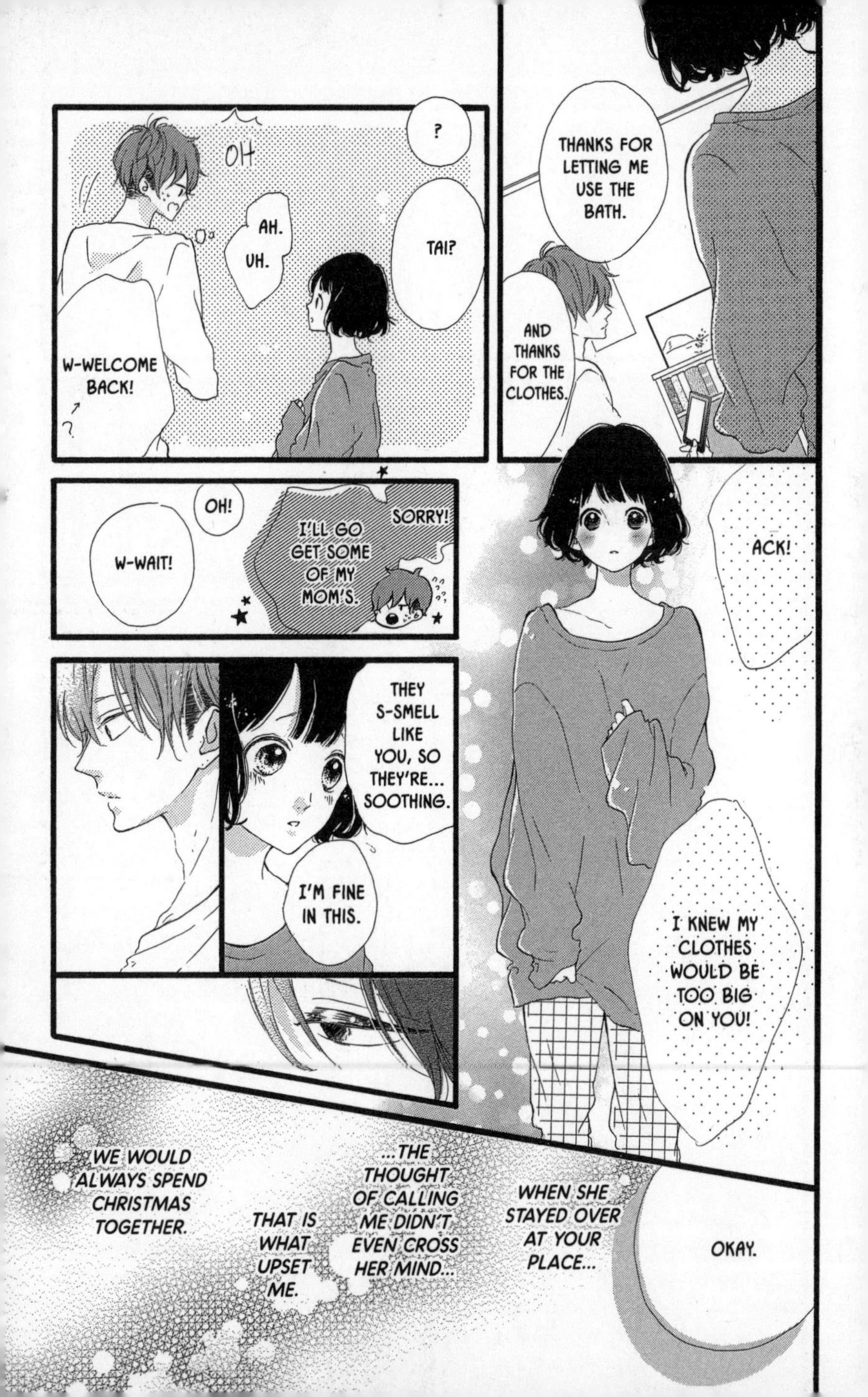
THANKS FOR LETTING ME USE THE BATH.
AND THANKS FOR THE CLOTHES.
?
TAI?
OH
AH.
UH.
W-WELCOME BACK!
ACK!
I KNEW MY CLOTHES WOULD BE TOO BIG ON YOU!
SORRY!
I'LL GO GET SOME OF MY MOM'S.
OH!
W-WAIT!
THEY S-SMELL LIKE YOU, SO THEY'RE... SOOTHING.
I'M FINE IN THIS.
OKAY.
WHEN SHE STAYED OVER AT YOUR PLACE...
...THE THOUGHT OF CALLING ME DIDN'T EVEN CROSS HER MIND...
THAT IS WHAT UPSET ME.
WE WOULD ALWAYS SPEND CHRISTMAS TOGETHER.

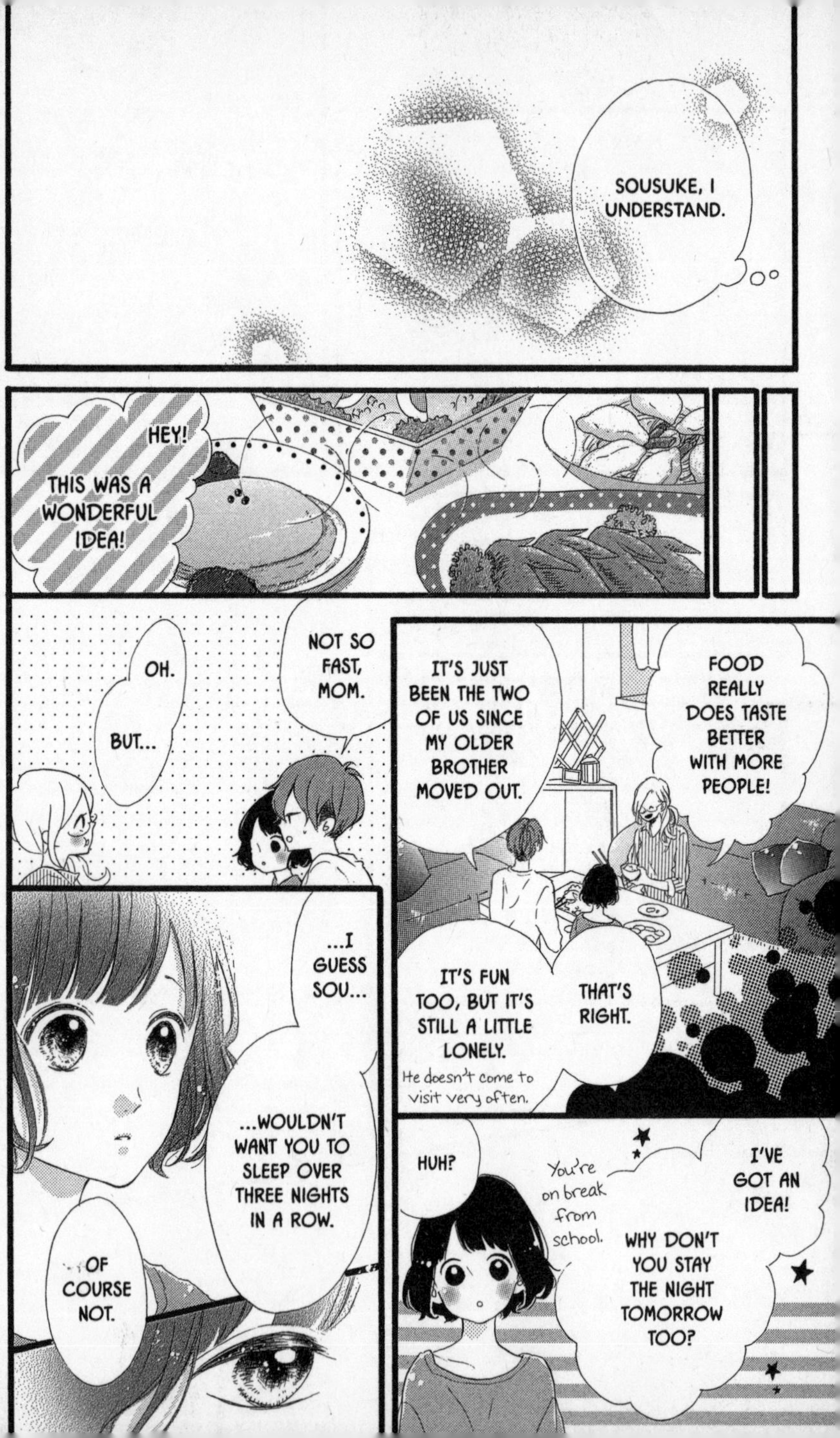
SOUSUKE, I UNDERSTAND.
HEY!
THIS WAS A WONDERFUL IDEA!
FOOD REALLY DOES TASTE BETTER WITH MORE PEOPLE!
IT'S JUST BEEN THE TWO OF US SINCE MY OLDER BROTHER MOVED OUT.
THAT'S RIGHT.
IT'S FUN TOO, BUT IT'S STILL A LITTLE LONELY.
He doesn't come to visit very often.
I'VE GOT AN IDEA!
WHY DON'T YOU STAY THE NIGHT TOMORROW TOO?
You're on break from school.
HUH?
NOT SO FAST, MOM.
OH.
BUT...
...I GUESS SOU...
...WOULDN'T WANT YOU TO SLEEP OVER THREE NIGHTS IN A ROW.
OF COURSE NOT.

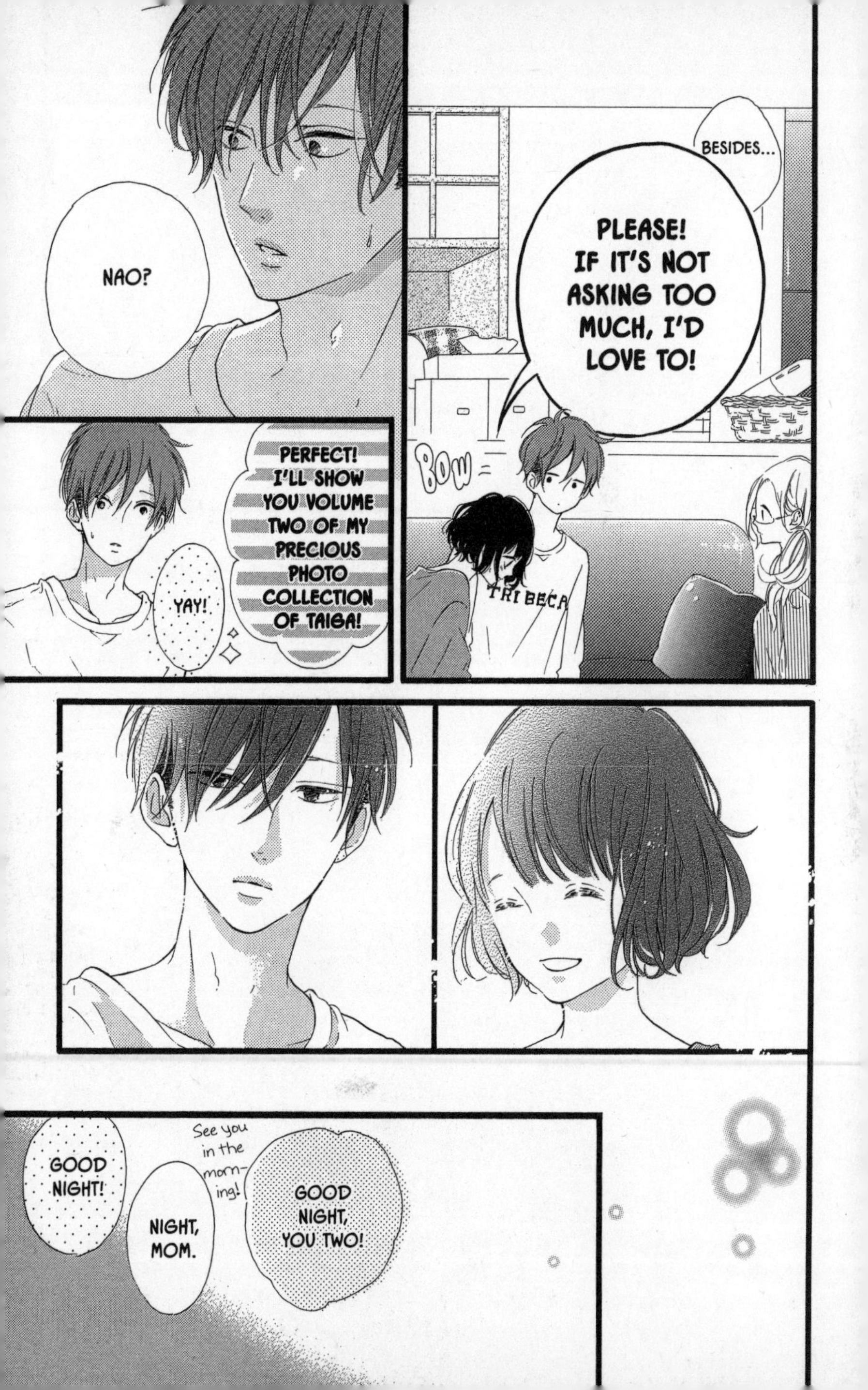

BESIDES...
PLEASE! IF IT'S NOT ASKING TOO MUCH, I'D LOVE TO!
BOW
NAO?
PERFECT! I'LL SHOW YOU VOLUME TWO OF MY PRECIOUS PHOTO COLLECTION OF TAIGA!
YAY!
TRIBECA
GOOD NIGHT, YOU TWO!
See you in the morning!
NIGHT, MOM.
GOOD NIGHT!

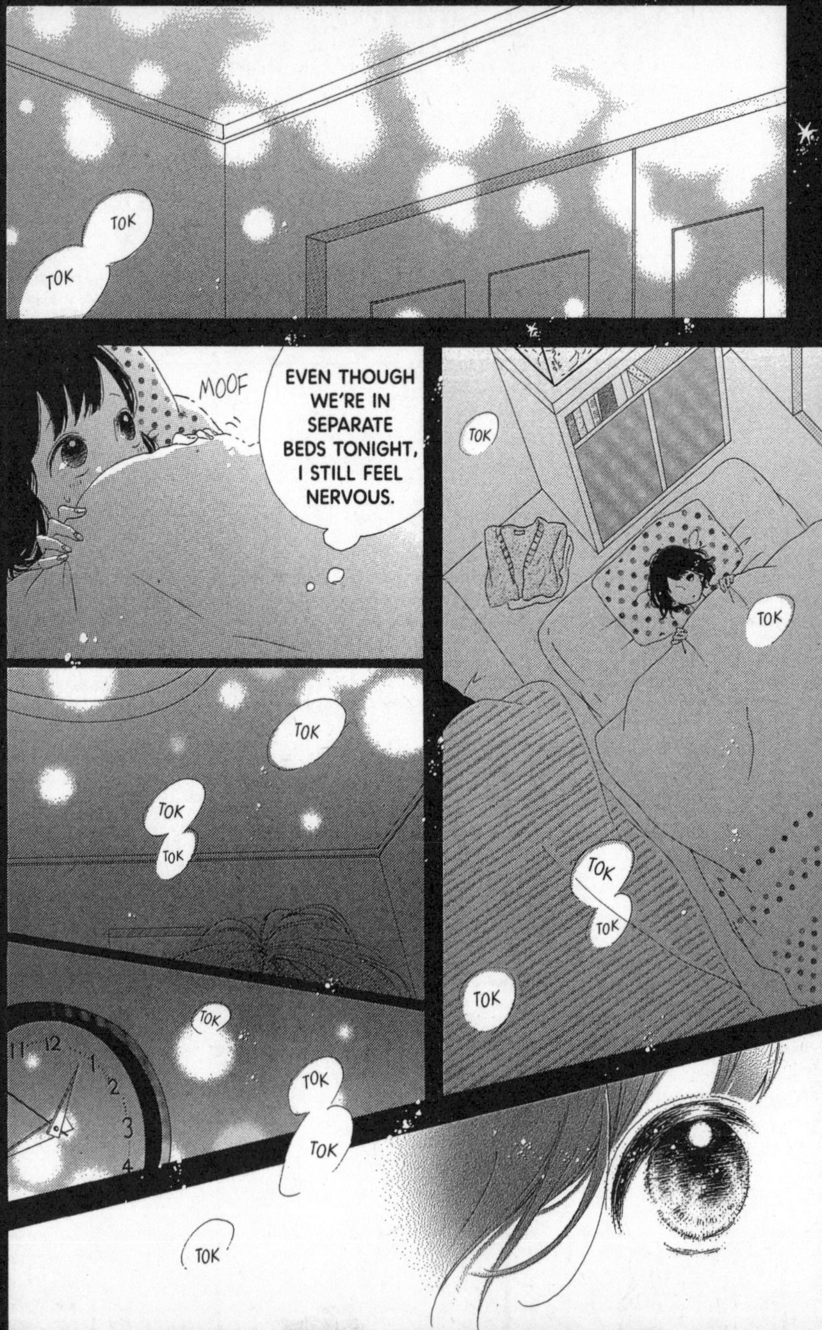
TOK
TOK
TOK
TOK
TOK
TOK
TOK
EVEN THOUGH WE'RE IN SEPARATE BEDS TONIGHT, I STILL FEEL NERVOUS.
MOOF
TOK
TOK
TOK
TOK
TOK
TOK
TOK

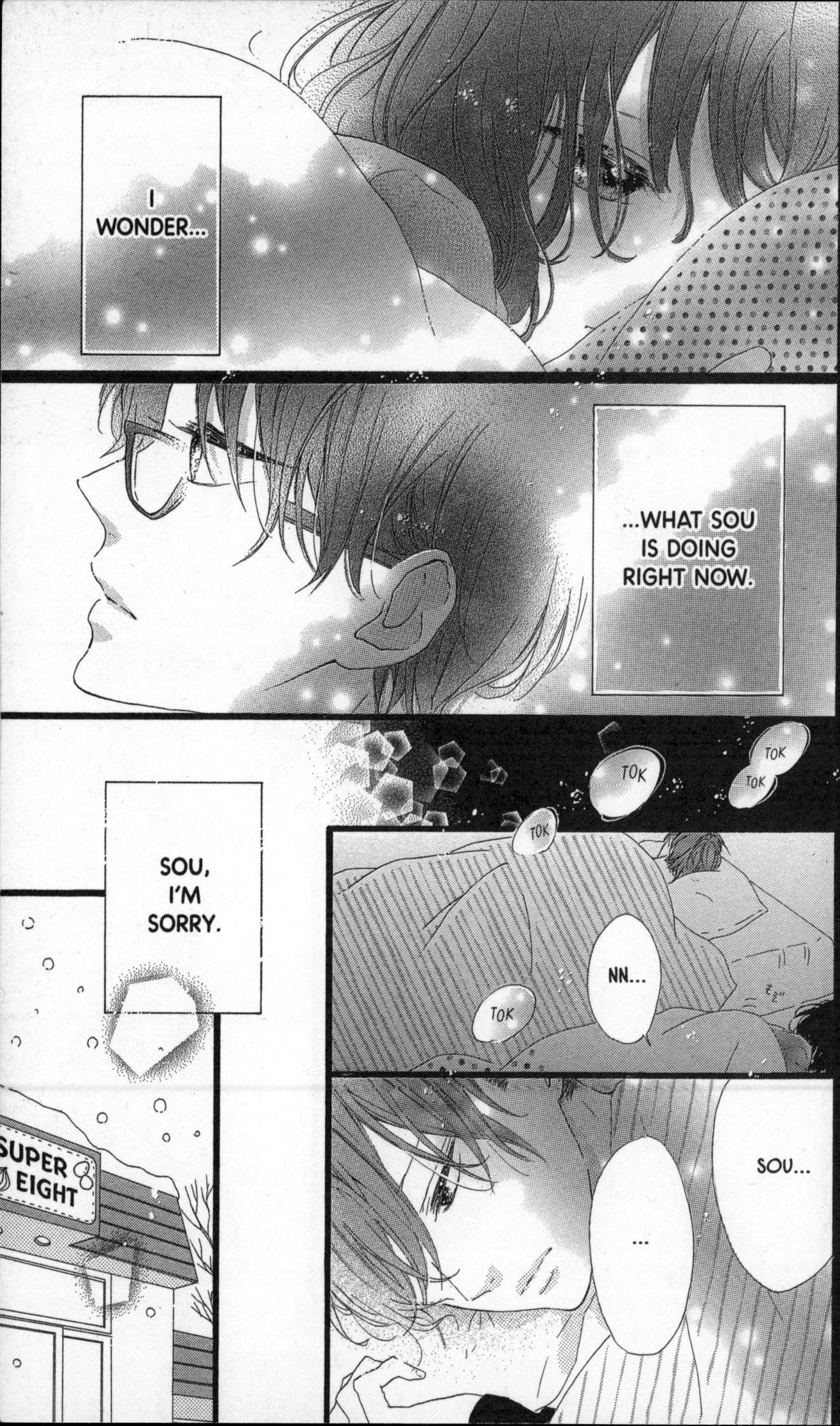
I WONDER...
...WHAT SOU IS DOING RIGHT NOW.
TOK
TOK
TOK
TOK
NN...
TOK
SOU...
...
SOU, I'M SORRY.
SUPER EIGHT

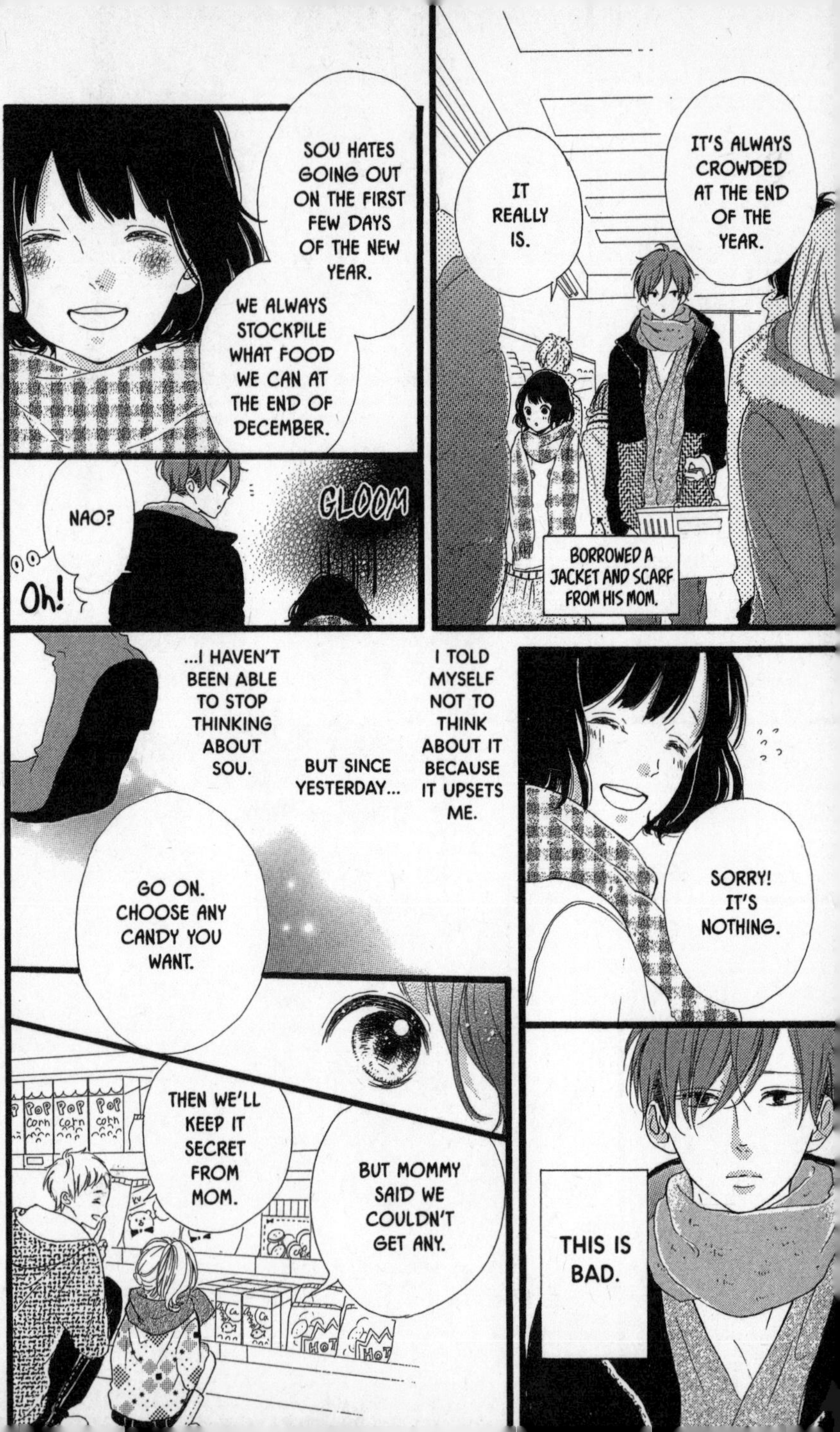
IT'S ALWAYS CROWDED AT THE END OF THE YEAR.
IT REALLY IS.
BORROWED A JACKET AND SCARF FROM HIS MOM.
SOU HATES GOING OUT ON THE FIRST FEW DAYS OF THE NEW YEAR.
WE ALWAYS STOCKPILE WHAT FOOD WE CAN AT THE END OF DECEMBER.
GLOOM
NAO?
Oh!
SORRY! IT'S NOTHING.
I TOLD MYSELF NOT TO THINK ABOUT IT BECAUSE IT UPSETS ME.
BUT SINCE YESTERDAY...
...I HAVEN'T BEEN ABLE TO STOP THINKING ABOUT SOU.
GO ON. CHOOSE ANY CANDY YOU WANT.
THIS IS BAD.
BUT MOMMY SAID WE COULDN'T GET ANY.
THEN WE'LL KEEP IT SECRET FROM MOM.

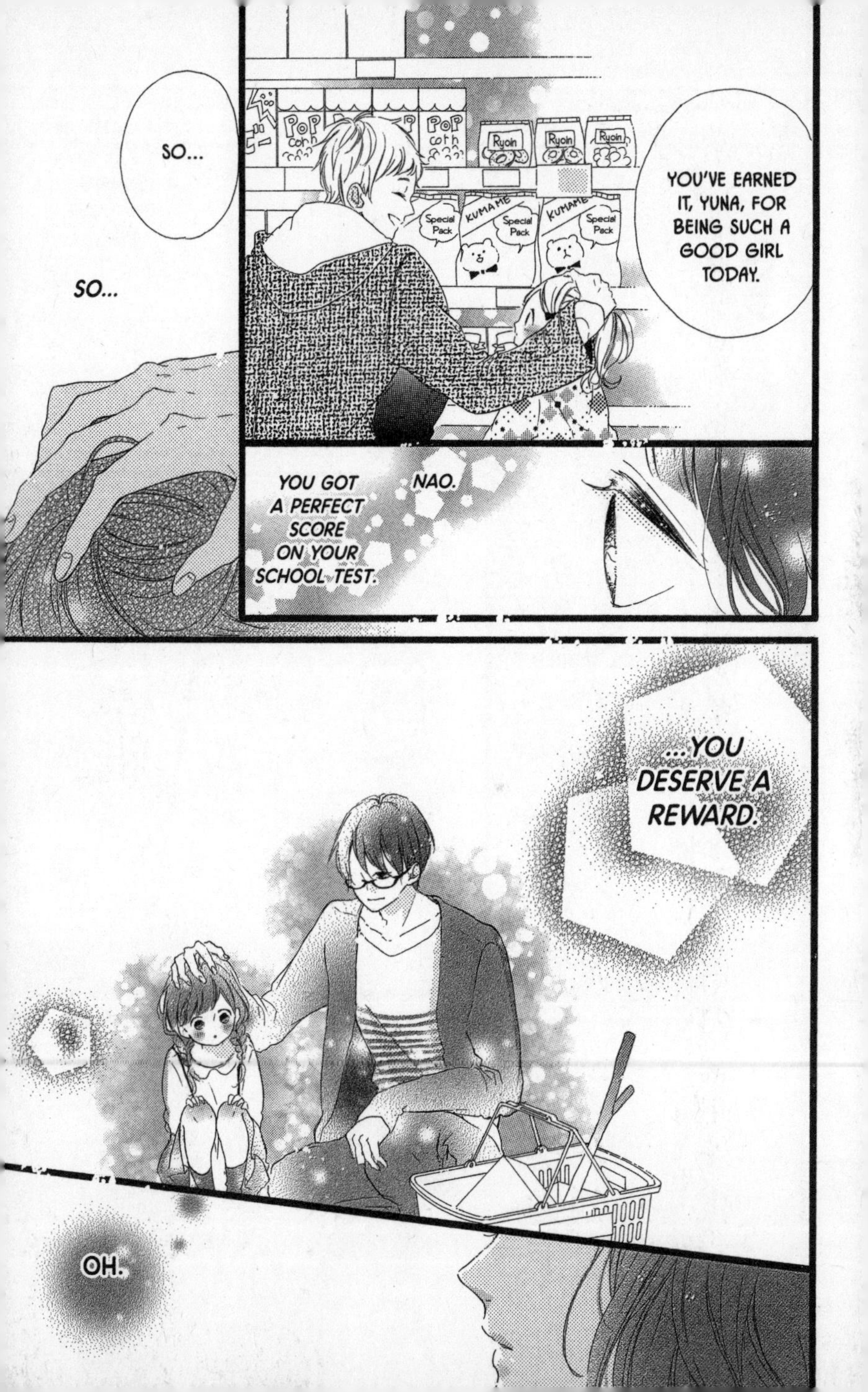

YOU'VE EARNED IT, YUNA, FOR BEING SUCH A GOOD GIRL TODAY.
POP corn
POP corn
Ryoin
Ryoin
Ryoin
KUMAME
KUMAME
Special Pack
Special Pack
Special Pack
SO...
SO...
NAO.
YOU GOT A PERFECT SCORE ON YOUR SCHOOL TEST.
...YOU DESERVE A REWARD.
OH.

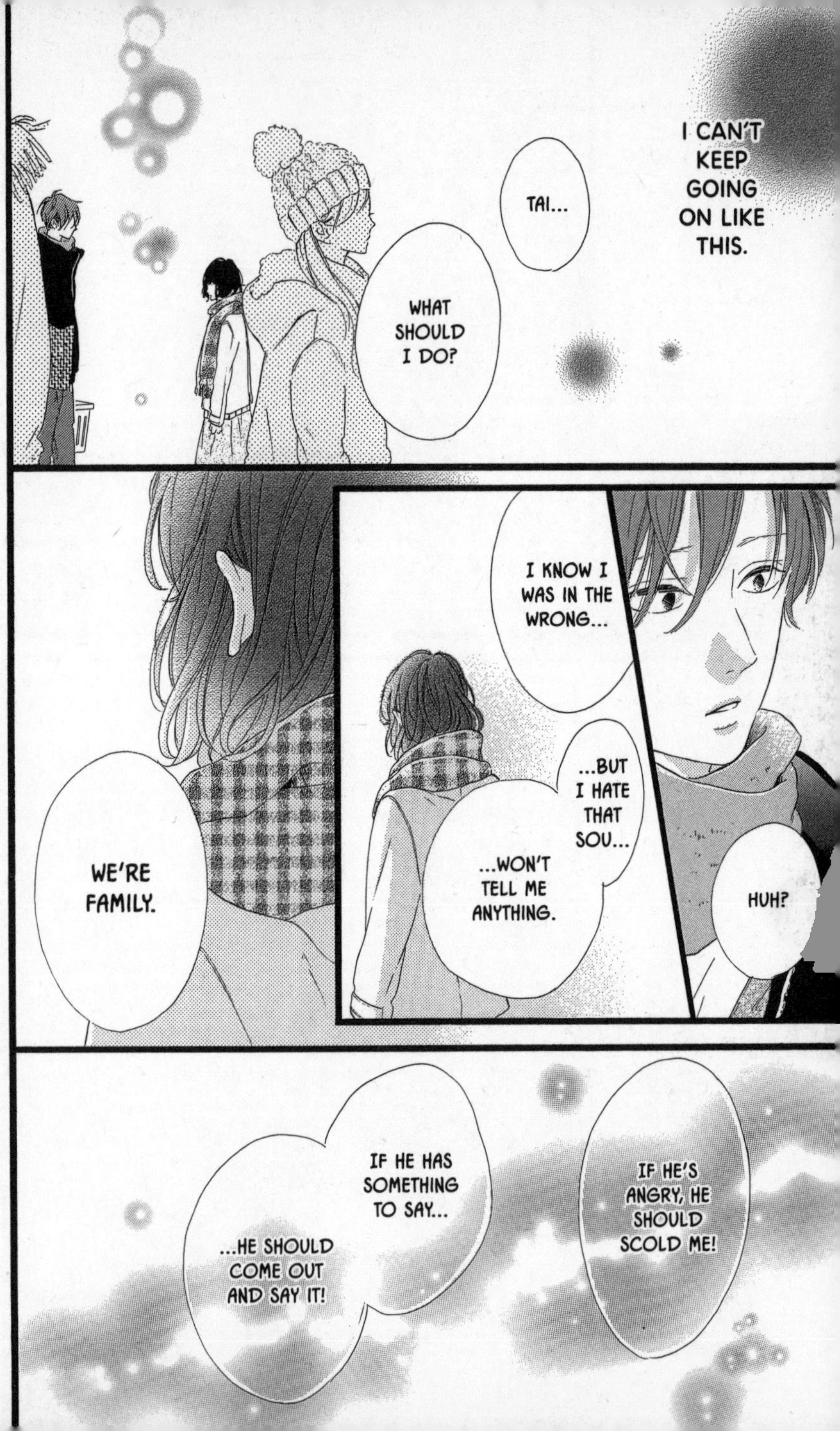
I CAN'T KEEP GOING ON LIKE THIS.
TAI...
WHAT SHOULD I DO?
I KNOW I WAS IN THE WRONG...
...BUT I HATE THAT SOU...
...WON'T TELL ME ANYTHING.
HUH?
WE'RE FAMILY.
IF HE'S ANGRY, HE SHOULD SCOLD ME!
IF HE HAS SOMETHING TO SAY...
...HE SHOULD COME OUT AND SAY IT!

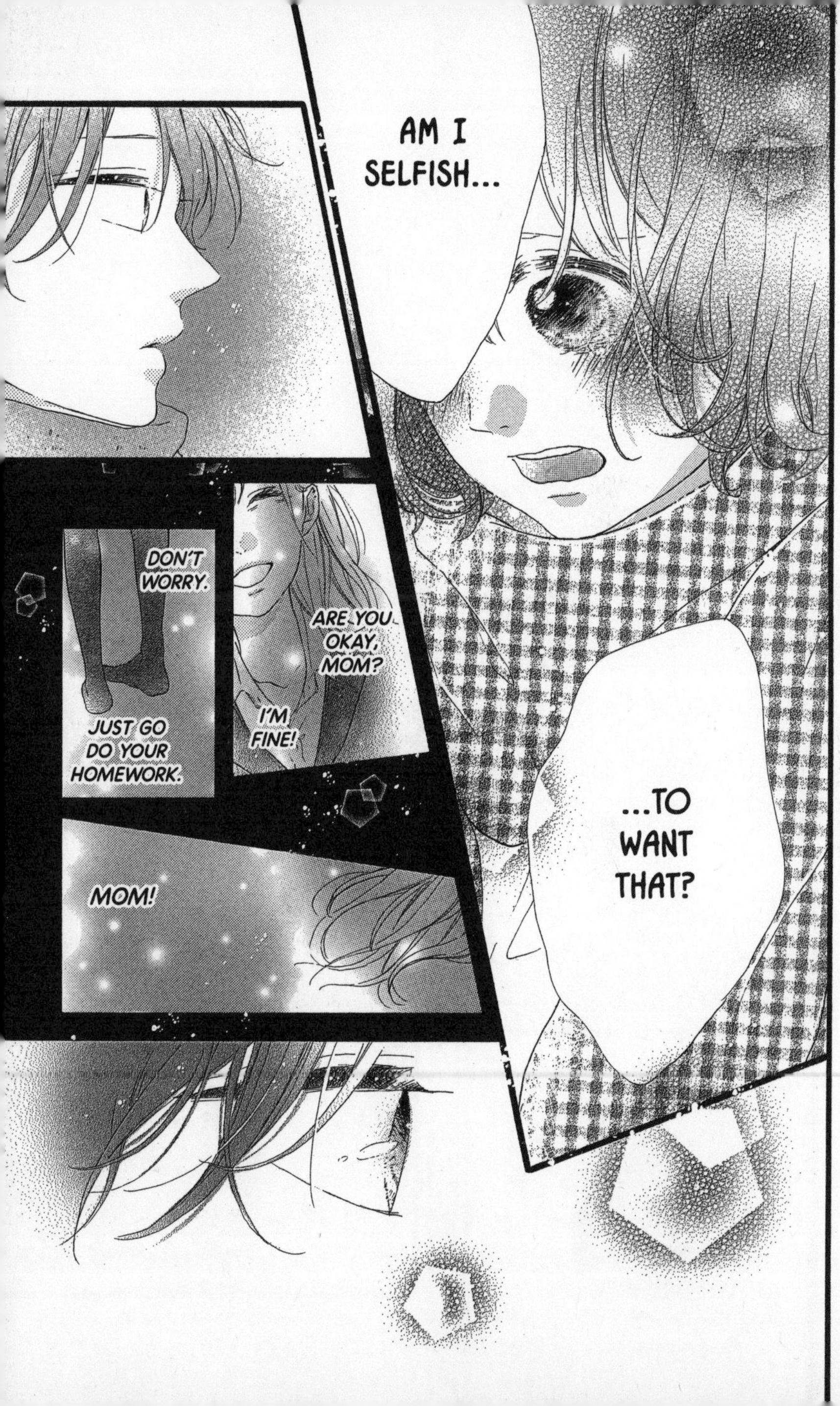
AM I SELFISH...
...TO WANT THAT?
ARE YOU OKAY, MOM?
I'M FINE!
DON'T WORRY.
JUST GO DO YOUR HOMEWORK.
MOM!

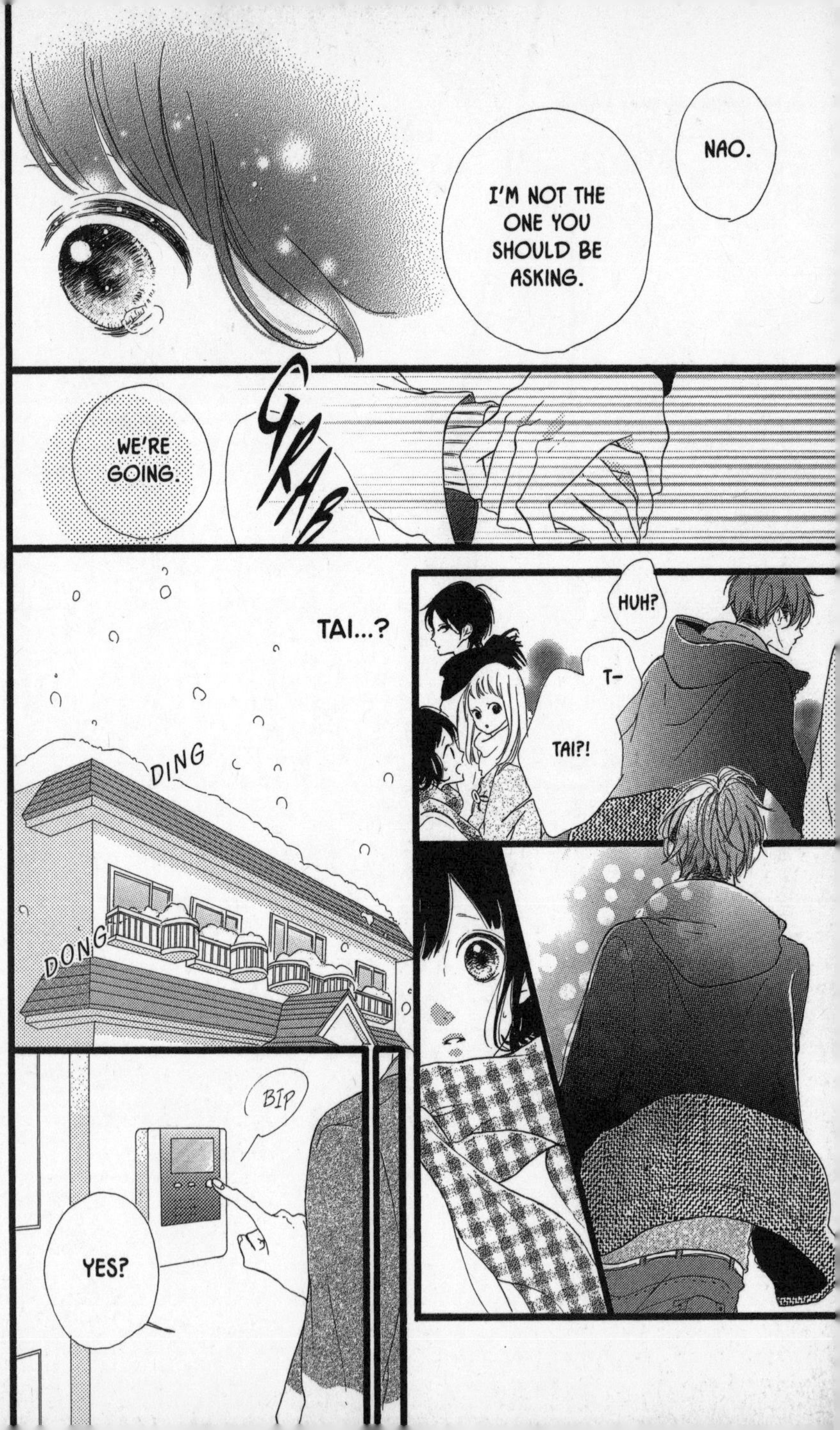
NAO.
I'M NOT THE ONE YOU SHOULD BE ASKING.
GRAB
WE'RE GOING.
HUH?
T-
TAI?!
TAI...?
DING
DONG
BIP
YES?

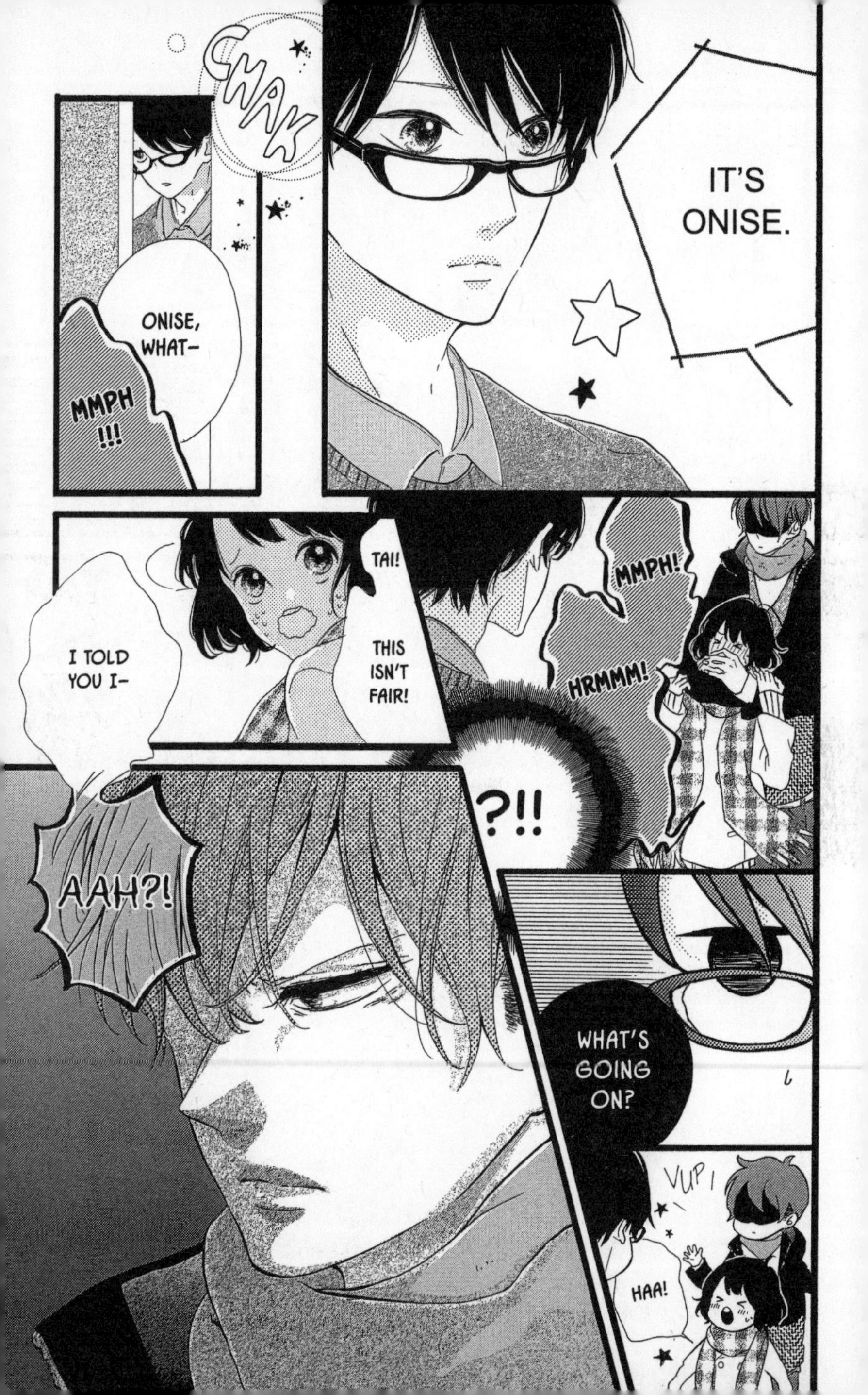
IT'S ONISE.
CHAK
ONISE, WHAT–
MMPH !!!
MMPH!
HRMMM!
TAI!
THIS ISN'T FAIR!
I TOLD YOU I–
?!!
WHAT'S GOING ON?
VUP!
HAA!
AAH?!

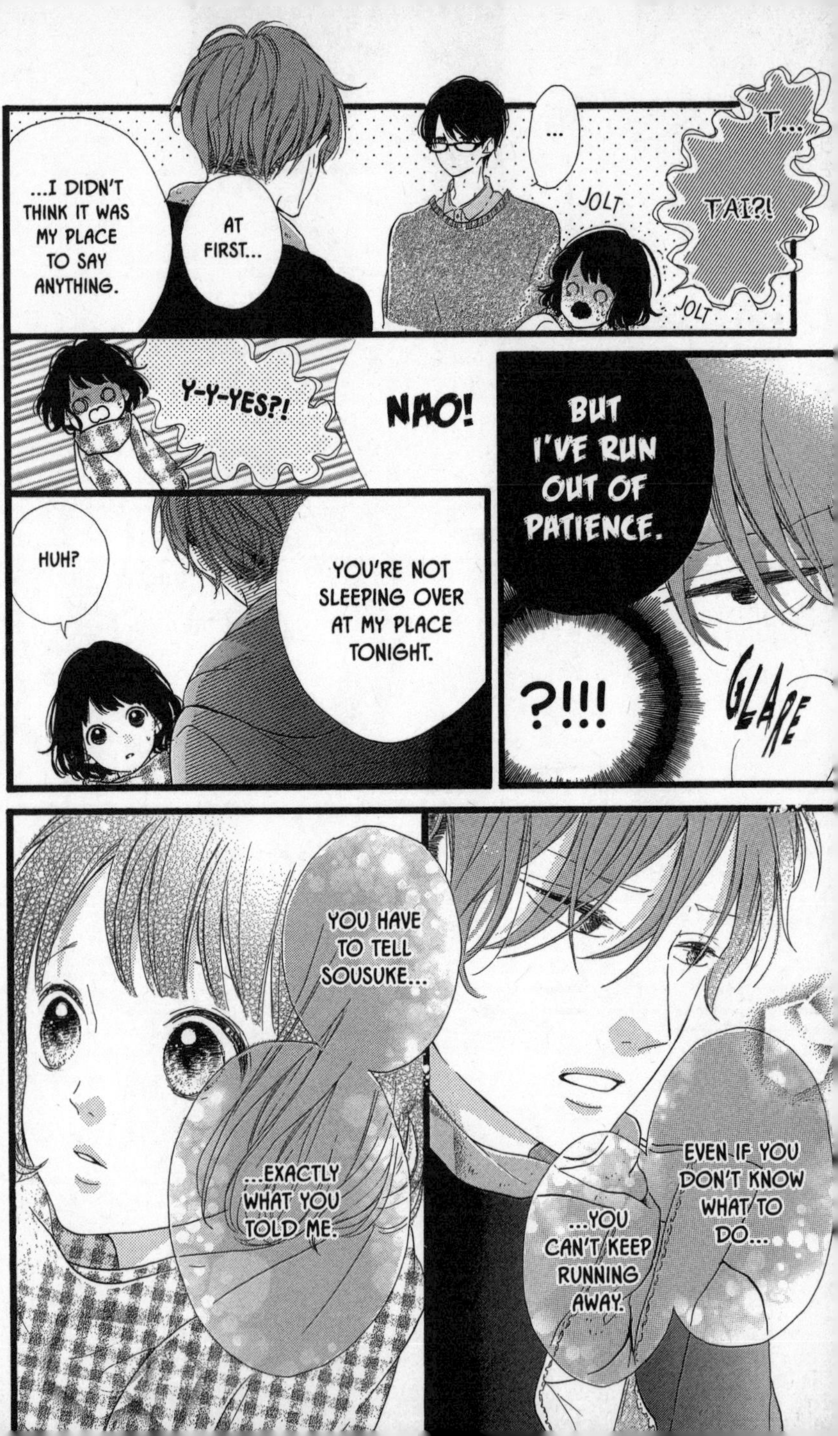
T... TAI?!
JOLT
JOLT
...
AT FIRST...
...I DIDN'T THINK IT WAS MY PLACE TO SAY ANYTHING.
BUT I'VE RUN OUT OF PATIENCE.
GLARE
?!!!
NAO!
Y-Y-YES?!
YOU'RE NOT SLEEPING OVER AT MY PLACE TONIGHT.
HUH?
EVEN IF YOU DON'T KNOW WHAT TO DO...
...YOU CAN'T KEEP RUNNING AWAY.
YOU HAVE TO TELL SOUSUKE...
...EXACTLY WHAT YOU TOLD ME.

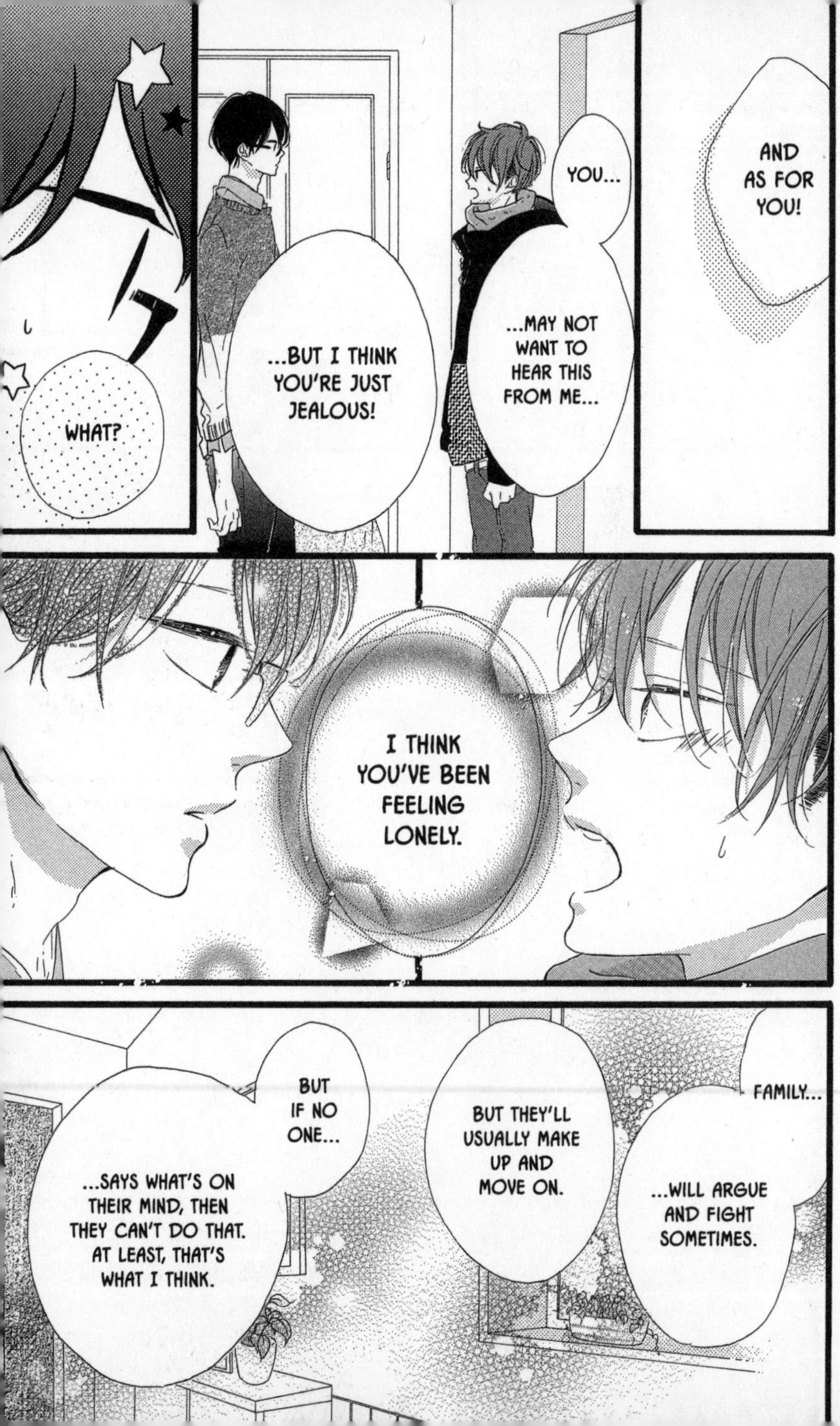
AND AS FOR YOU!
YOU...
...MAY NOT WANT TO HEAR THIS FROM ME...
...BUT I THINK YOU'RE JUST JEALOUS!
WHAT?
I THINK YOU'VE BEEN FEELING LONELY.
FAMILY...
...WILL ARGUE AND FIGHT SOMETIMES.
BUT THEY'LL USUALLY MAKE UP AND MOVE ON.
BUT IF NO ONE...
...SAYS WHAT'S ON THEIR MIND, THEN THEY CAN'T DO THAT. AT LEAST, THAT'S WHAT I THINK.

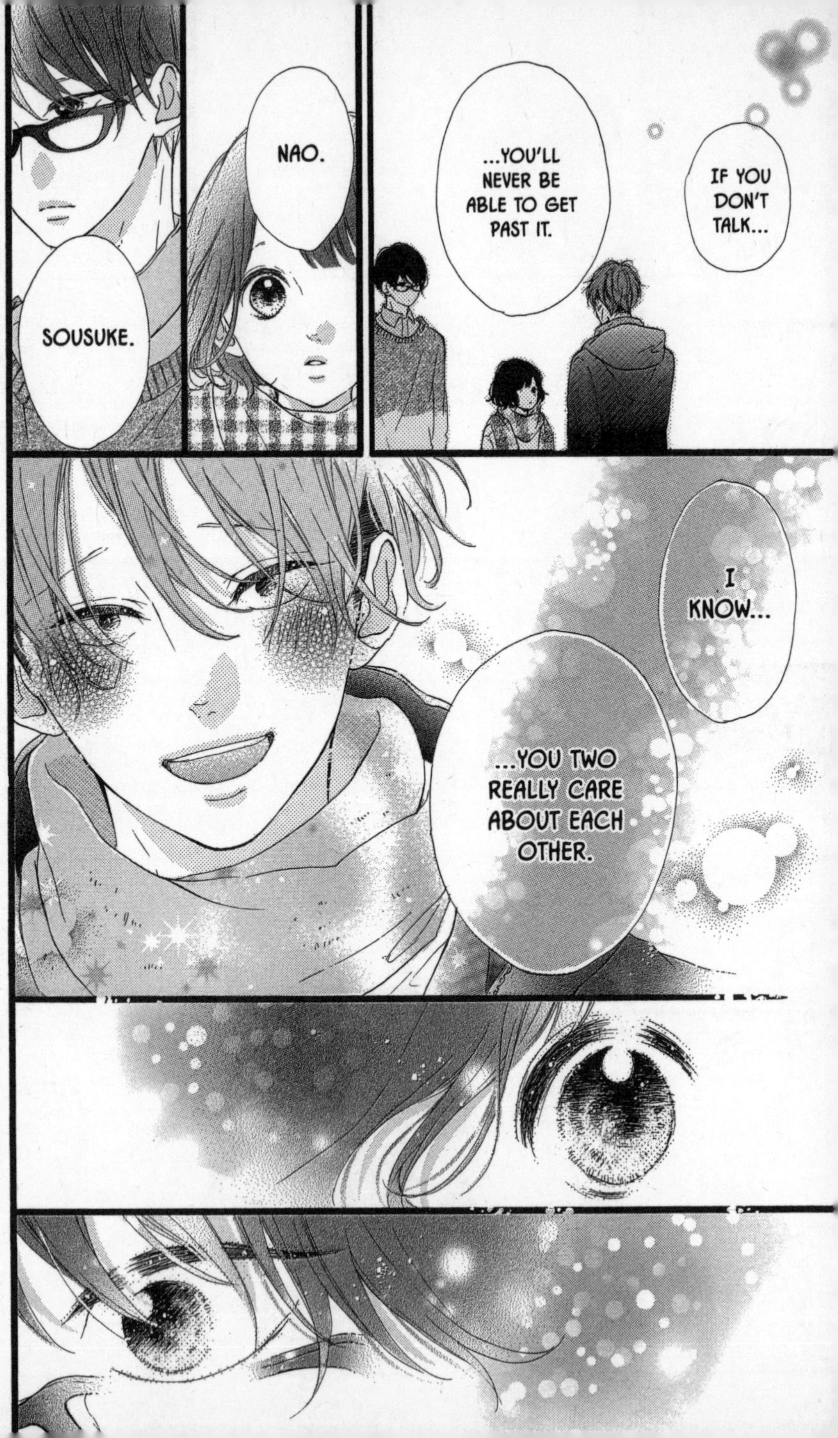
IF YOU DON'T TALK...
...YOU'LL NEVER BE ABLE TO GET PAST IT.
NAO.
SOUSUKE.
I KNOW...
...YOU TWO REALLY CARE ABOUT EACH OTHER.

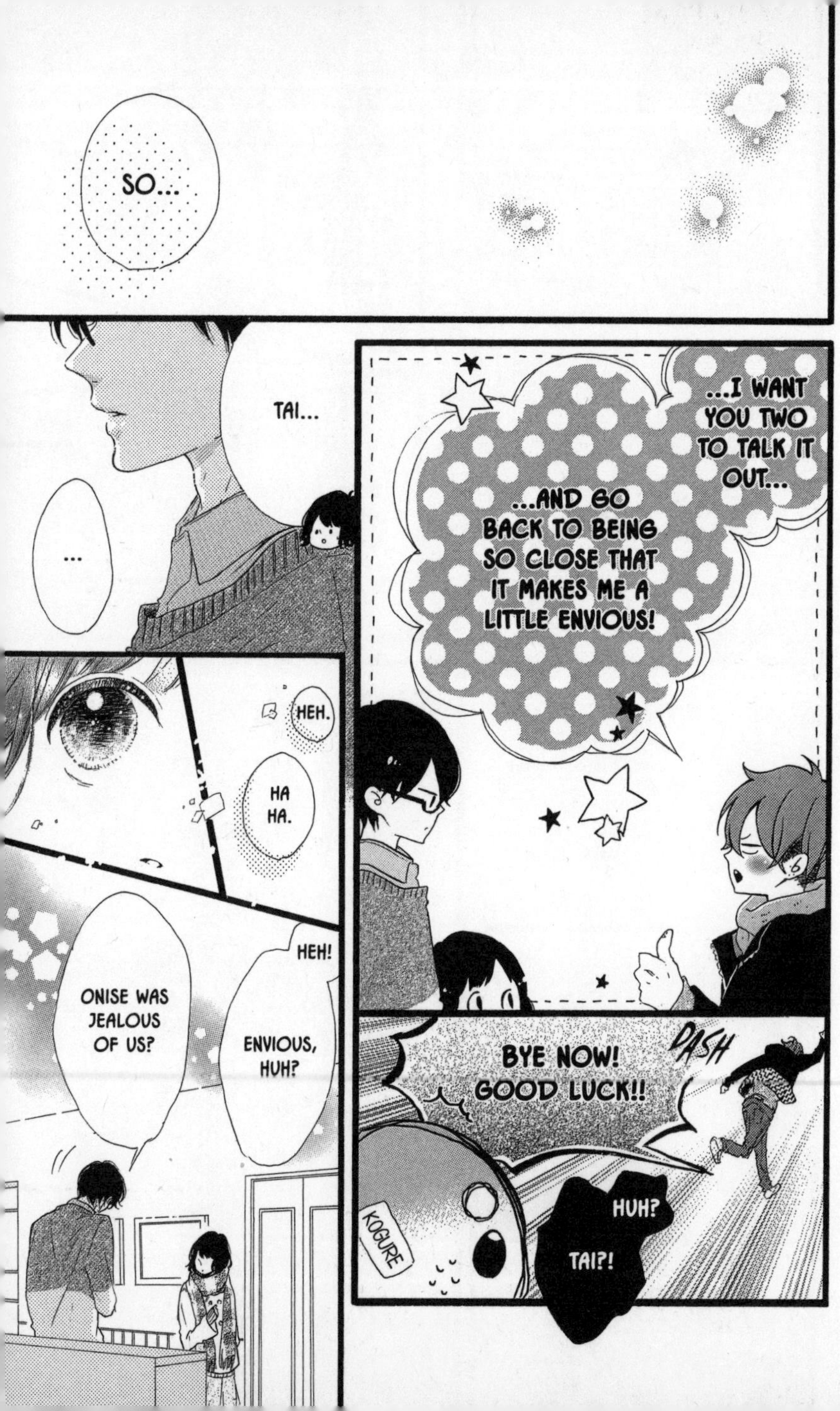
SO...
...I WANT YOU TWO TO TALK IT OUT...
...AND GO BACK TO BEING SO CLOSE THAT IT MAKES ME A LITTLE ENVIOUS!
BYE NOW! GOOD LUCK!!
DASH
KOGURE
HUH?
TAI?!
TAI...
...
HEH.
HA HA.
HEH!
ENVIOUS, HUH?
ONISE WAS JEALOUS OF US?

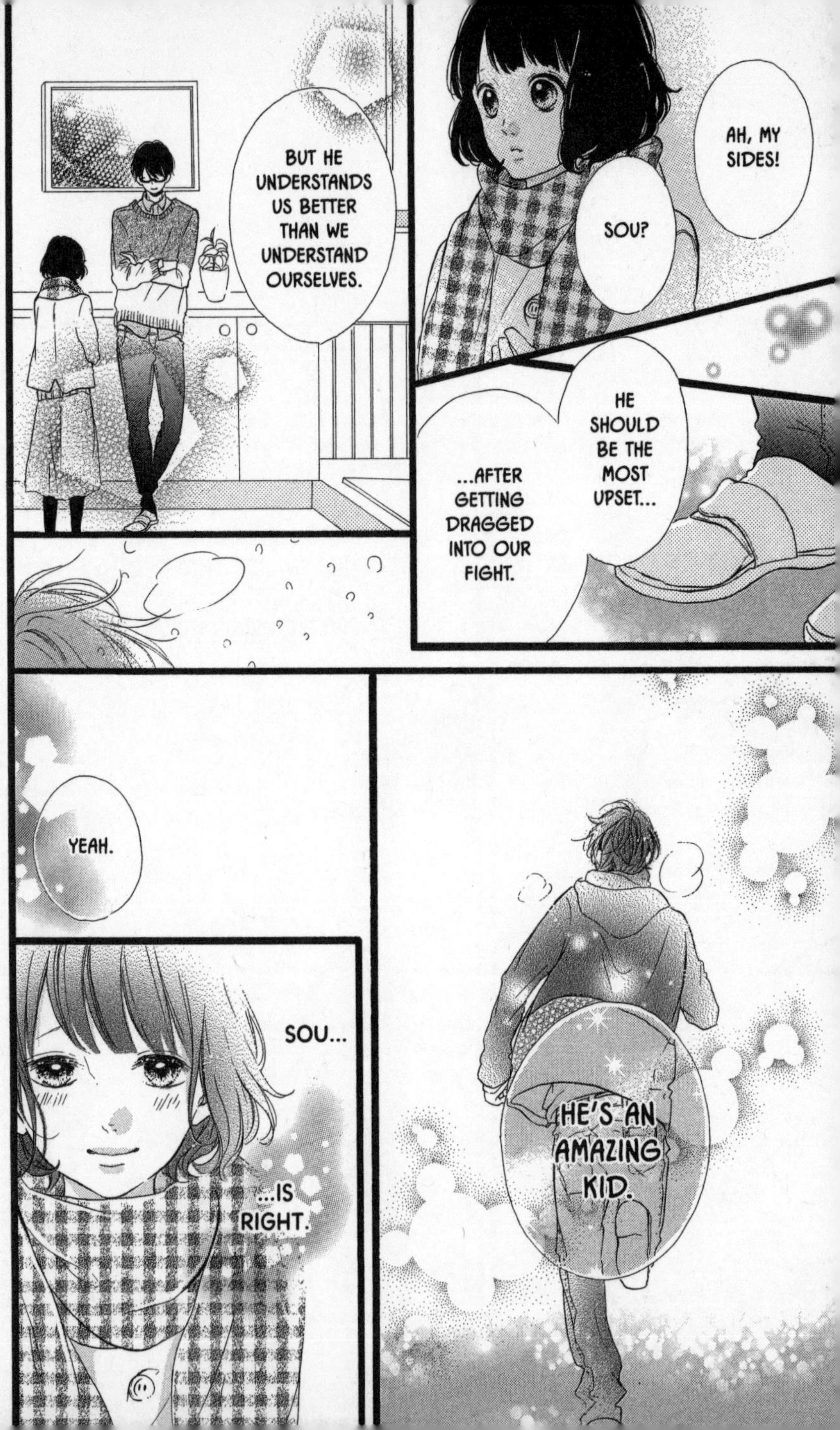
AH, MY SIDES!
SOU?
HE SHOULD BE THE MOST UPSET...
...AFTER GETTING DRAGGED INTO OUR FIGHT.
BUT HE UNDERSTANDS US BETTER THAN WE UNDERSTAND OURSELVES.
HE'S AN AMAZING KID.
YEAH.
SOU...
...IS RIGHT.

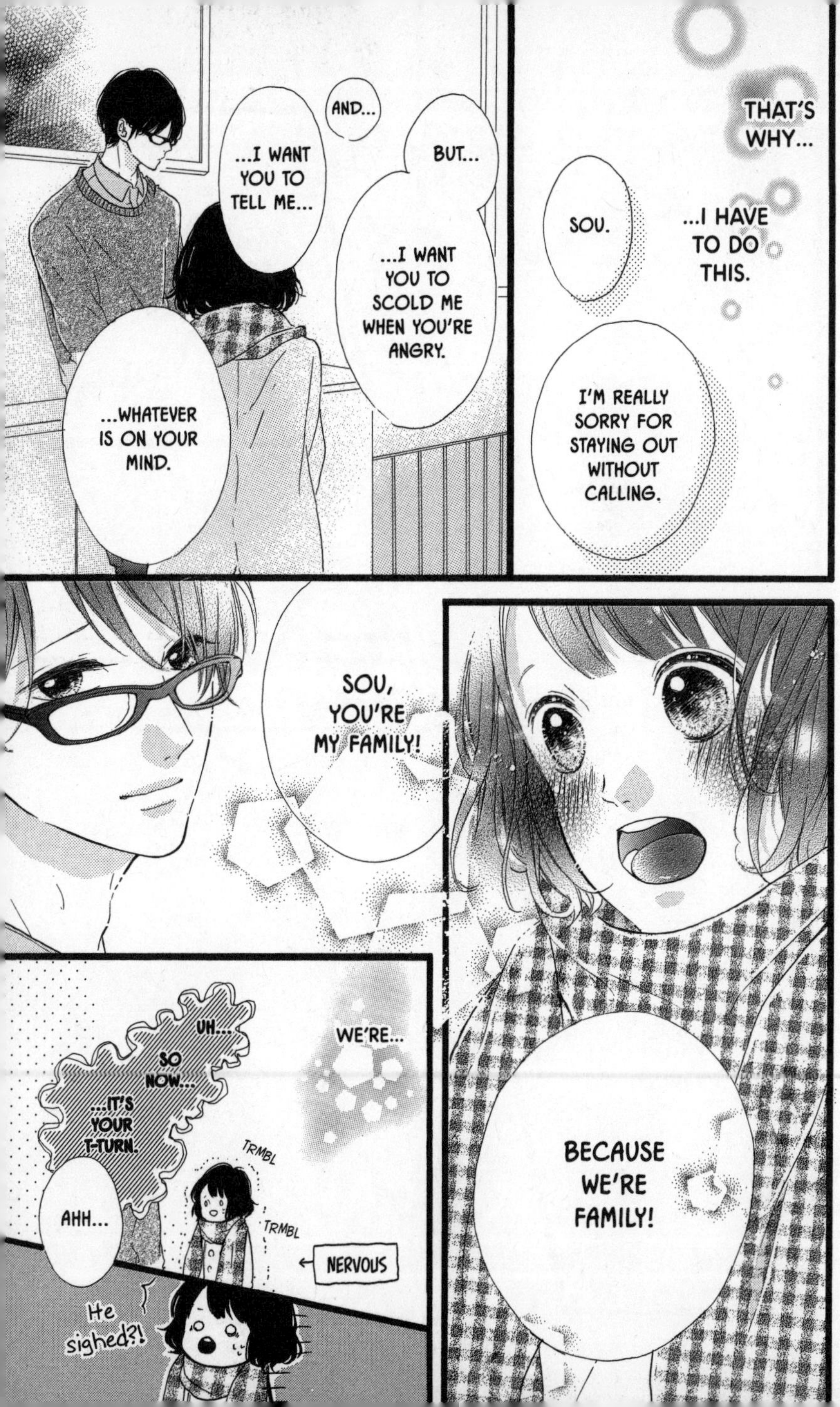
THAT'S WHY...
...I HAVE TO DO THIS.
SOU.
I'M REALLY SORRY FOR STAYING OUT WITHOUT CALLING.
BUT...
...I WANT YOU TO SCOLD ME WHEN YOU'RE ANGRY.
AND...
...I WANT YOU TO TELL ME...
...WHATEVER IS ON YOUR MIND.
SOU, YOU'RE MY FAMILY!
BECAUSE WE'RE FAMILY!
WE'RE...
UH...
SO NOW...
...IT'S YOUR T-TURN.
TRMBL
TRMBL
NERVOUS
AHH...
He sighed?!

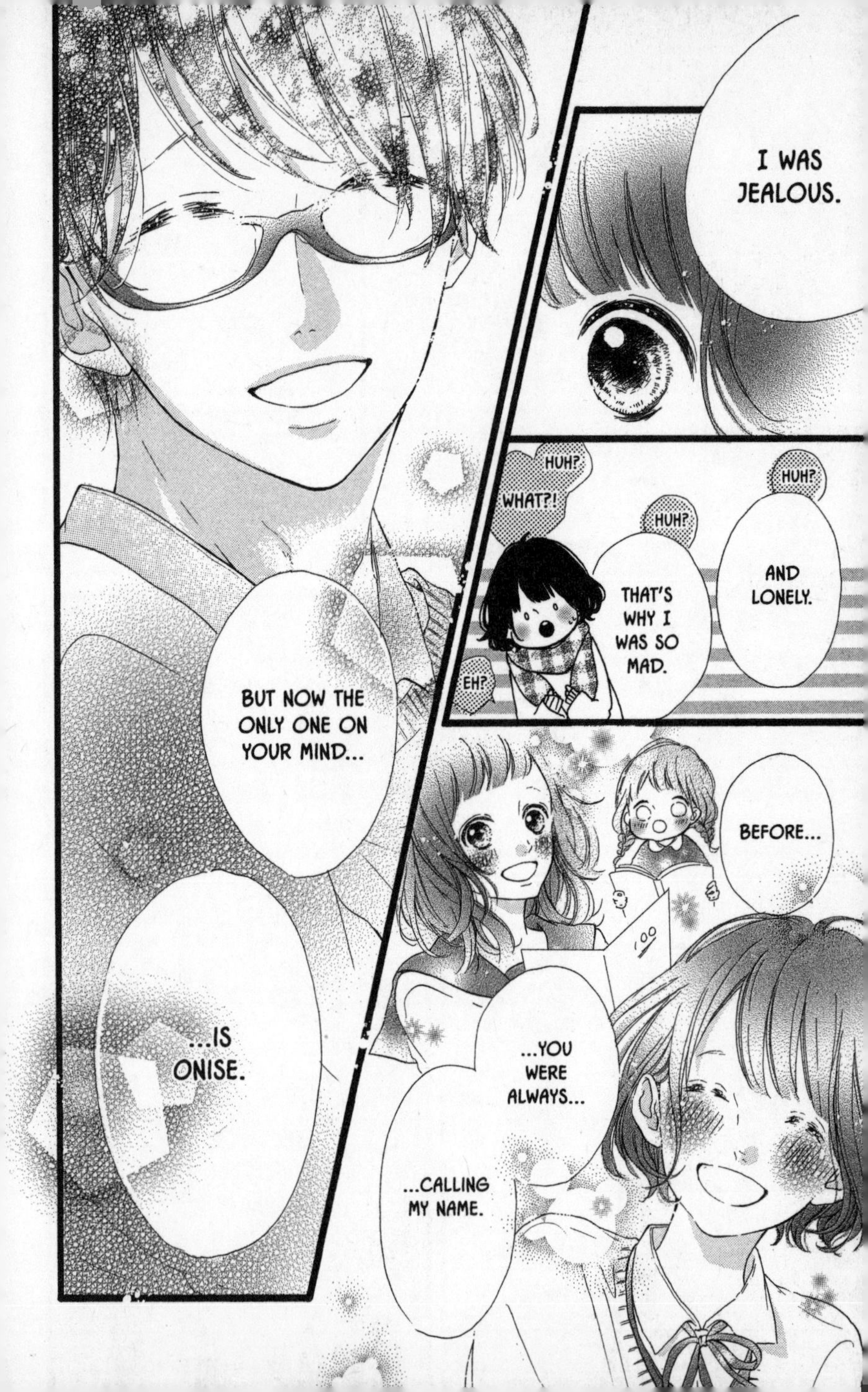
I WAS JEALOUS.
HUH?
HUH?
AND LONELY.
HUH?
WHAT?!
THAT'S WHY I WAS SO MAD.
EH?
BUT NOW THE ONLY ONE ON YOUR MIND...
...IS ONISE.
BEFORE...
...YOU WERE ALWAYS...
...CALLING MY NAME.

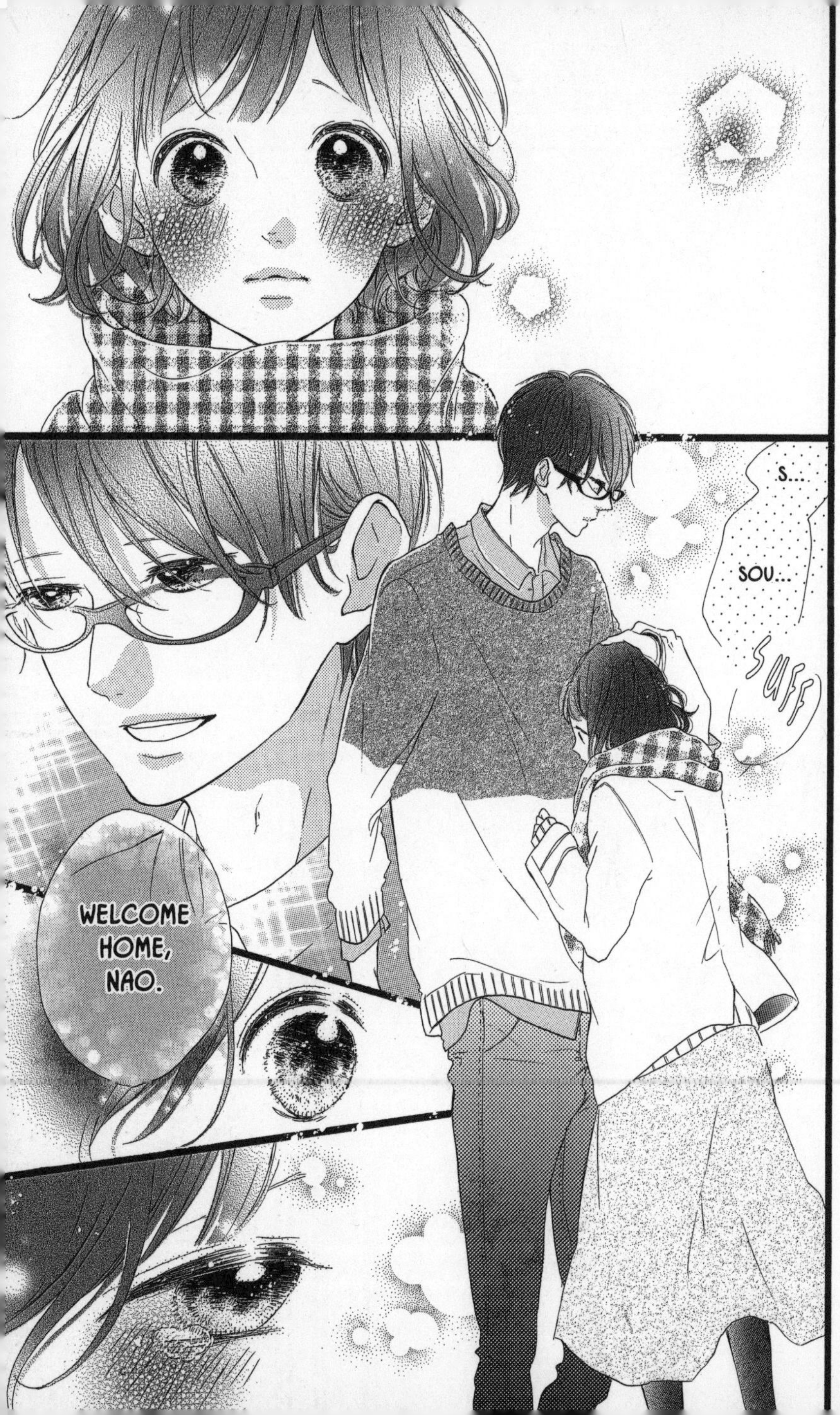
S...
SOU...
SUFF
WELCOME HOME, NAO.

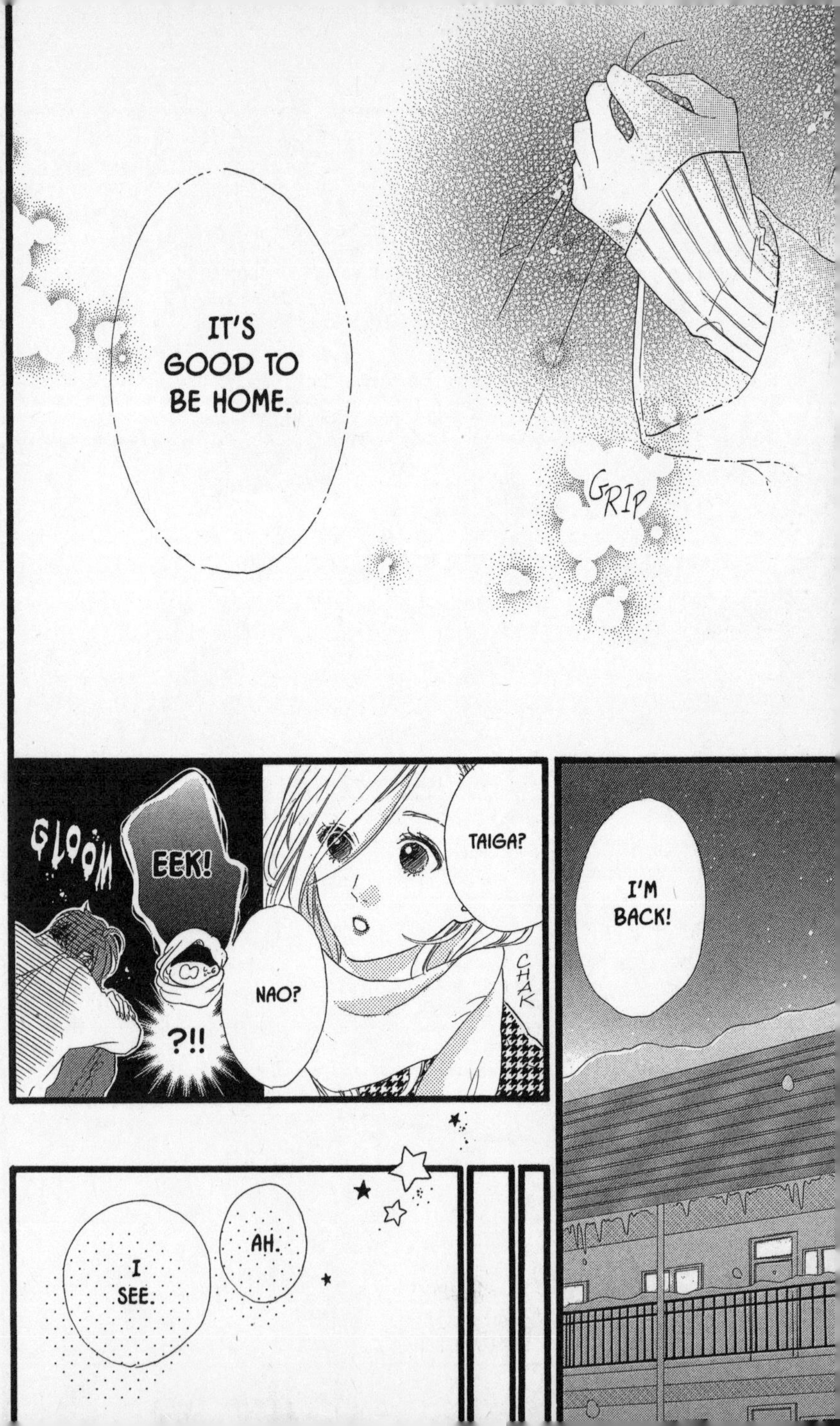
IT'S GOOD TO BE HOME.
GRIP
I'M BACK!
TAIGA?
CHAK
NAO?
EEK!
GLOOM
?!!
AH.
I SEE.

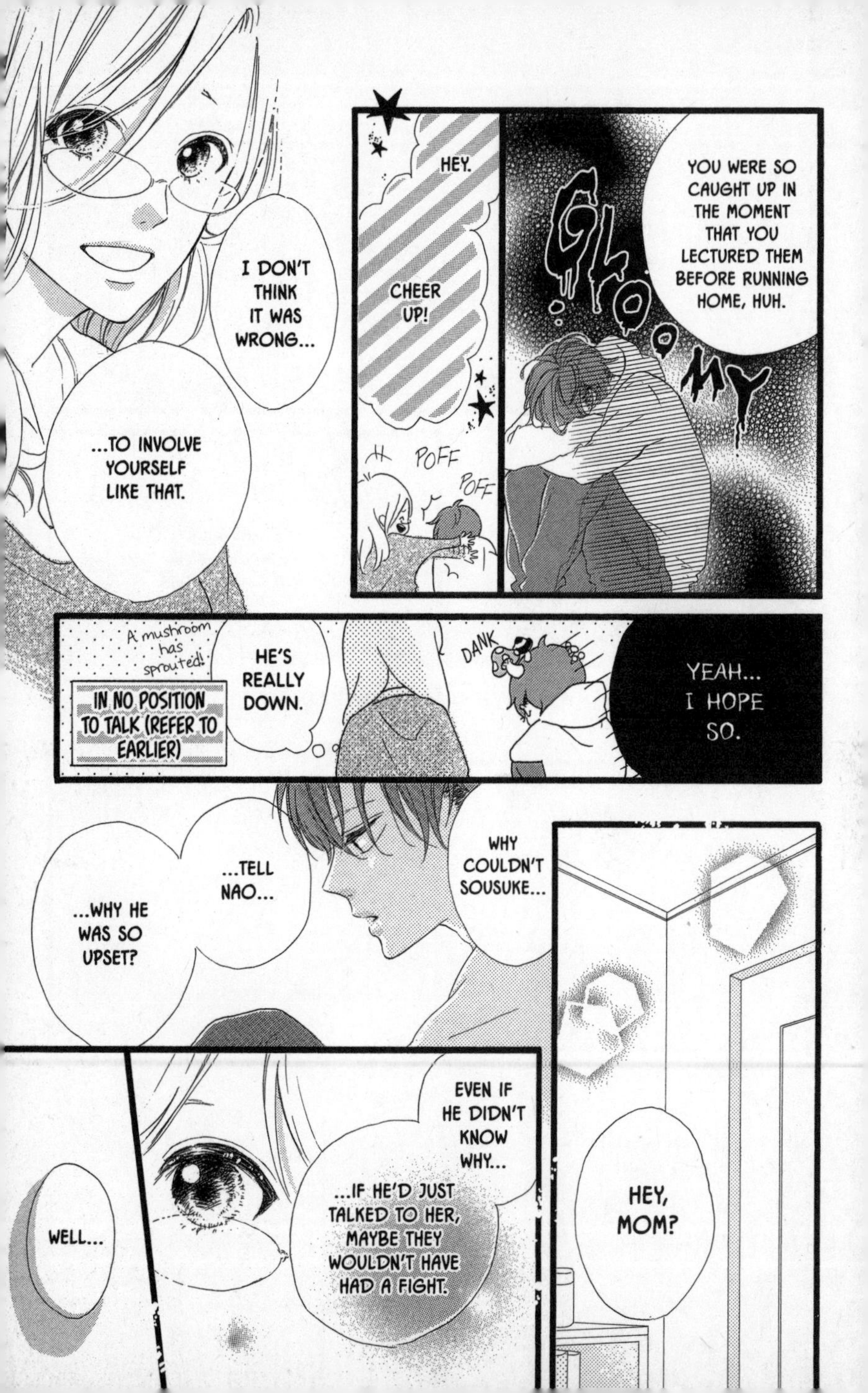
YOU WERE SO CAUGHT UP IN THE MOMENT THAT YOU LECTURED THEM BEFORE RUNNING HOME, HUH.
GLOOMY
HEY.
CHEER UP!
POFF
POFF
I DON'T THINK IT WAS WRONG...
...TO INVOLVE YOURSELF LIKE THAT.
YEAH... I HOPE SO.
DANK
HE'S REALLY DOWN.
A mushroom has sprouted!
IN NO POSITION TO TALK (REFER TO EARLIER)
HEY, MOM?
WHY COULDN'T SOUSUKE...
...TELL NAO...
...WHY HE WAS SO UPSET?
EVEN IF HE DIDN'T KNOW WHY...
...IF HE'D JUST TALKED TO HER, MAYBE THEY WOULDN'T HAVE HAD A FIGHT.
WELL...

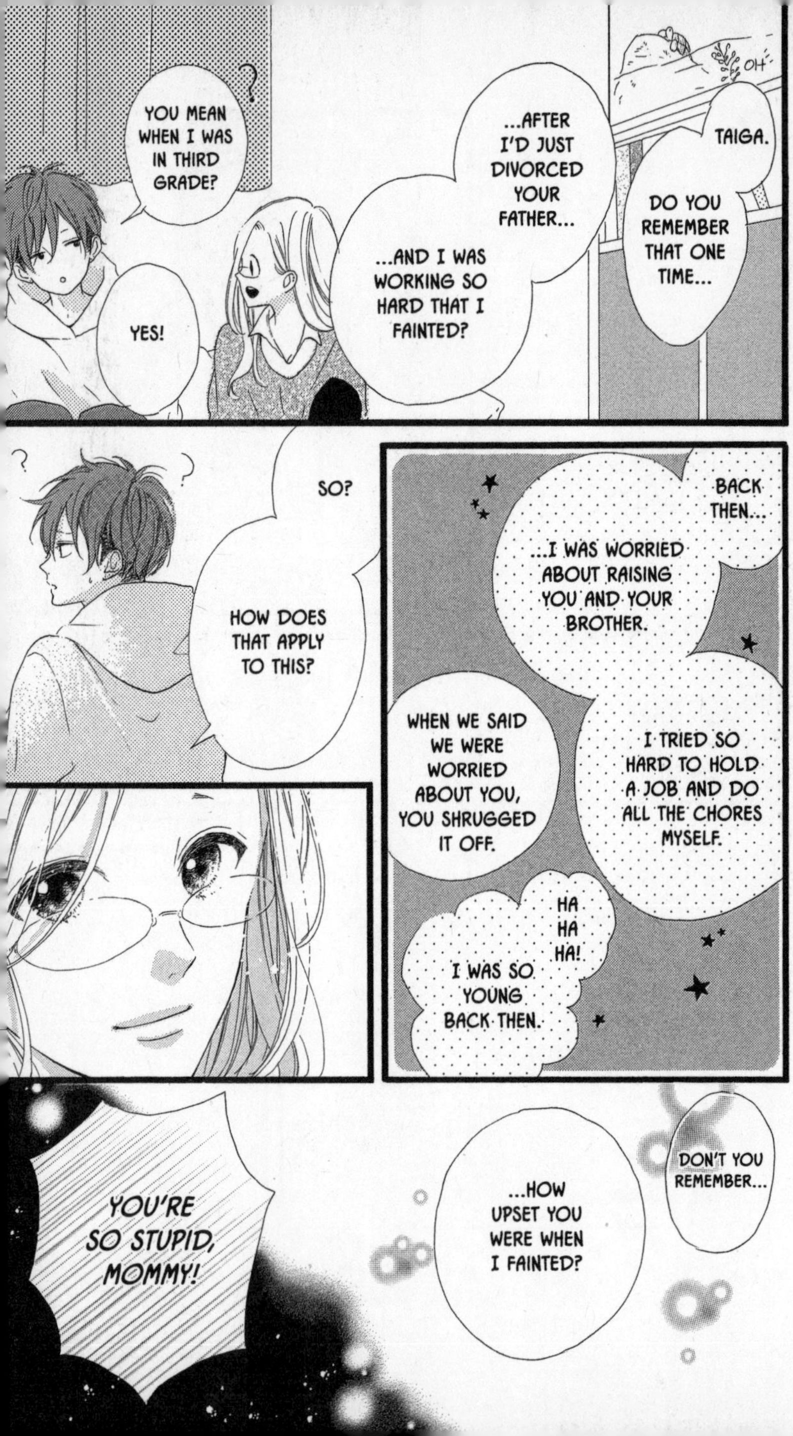
OH
TAIGA.
DO YOU REMEMBER THAT ONE TIME...
...AFTER I'D JUST DIVORCED YOUR FATHER...
...AND I WAS WORKING SO HARD THAT I FAINTED?
YOU MEAN WHEN I WAS IN THIRD GRADE?
YES!
BACK THEN...
...I WAS WORRIED ABOUT RAISING YOU AND YOUR BROTHER.
I TRIED SO HARD TO HOLD A JOB AND DO ALL THE CHORES MYSELF.
WHEN WE SAID WE WERE WORRIED ABOUT YOU, YOU SHRUGGED IT OFF.
HA HA HA!
I WAS SO YOUNG BACK THEN.
SO?
HOW DOES THAT APPLY TO THIS?
DON'T YOU REMEMBER...
...HOW UPSET YOU WERE WHEN I FAINTED?
YOU'RE SO STUPID, MOMMY!

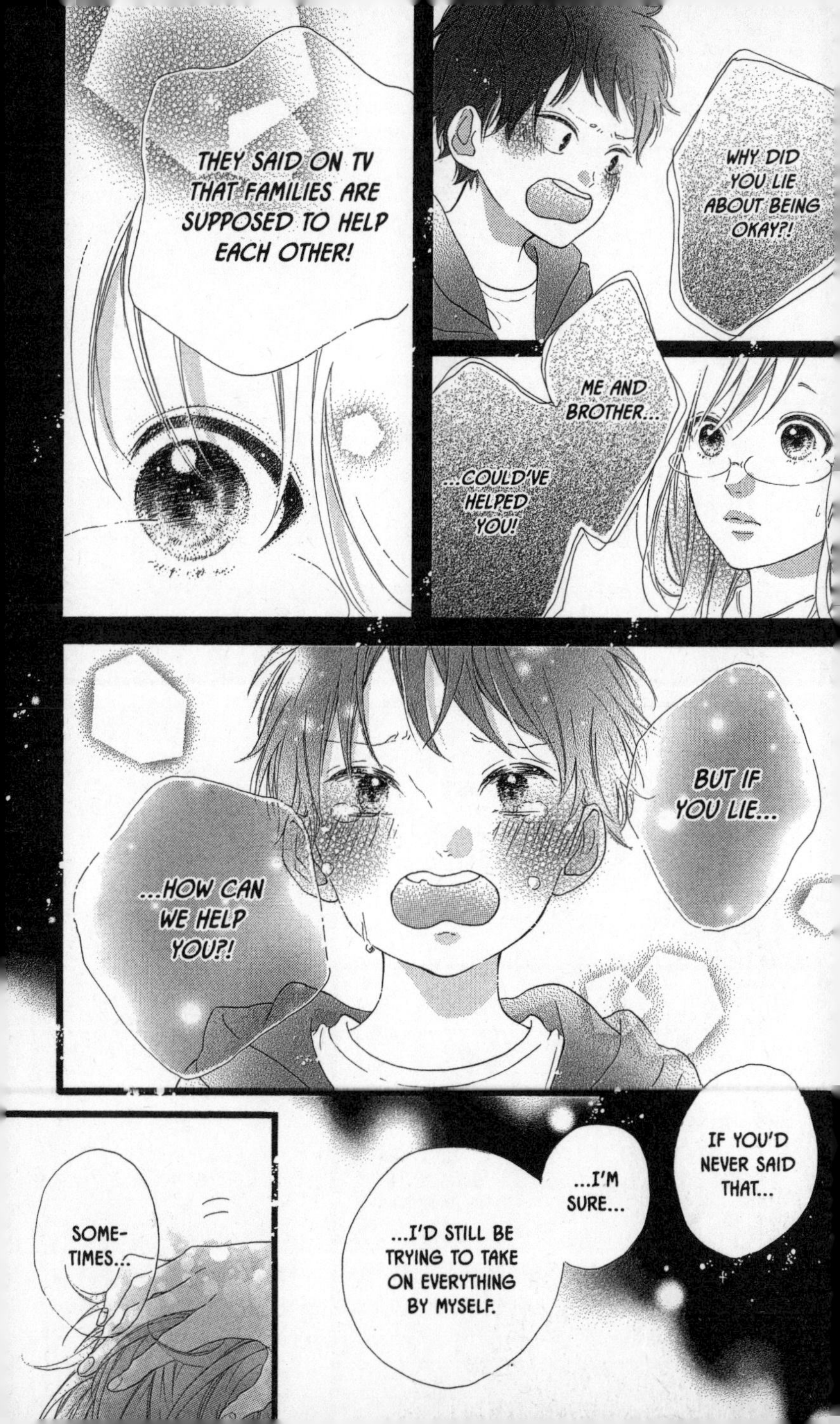
WHY DID YOU LIE ABOUT BEING OKAY?!
ME AND BROTHER...
...COULD'VE HELPED YOU!
THEY SAID ON TV THAT FAMILIES ARE SUPPOSED TO HELP EACH OTHER!
BUT IF YOU LIE...
...HOW CAN WE HELP YOU?!
IF YOU'D NEVER SAID THAT...
...I'M SURE...
...I'D STILL BE TRYING TO TAKE ON EVERYTHING BY MYSELF.
SOME-TIMES...

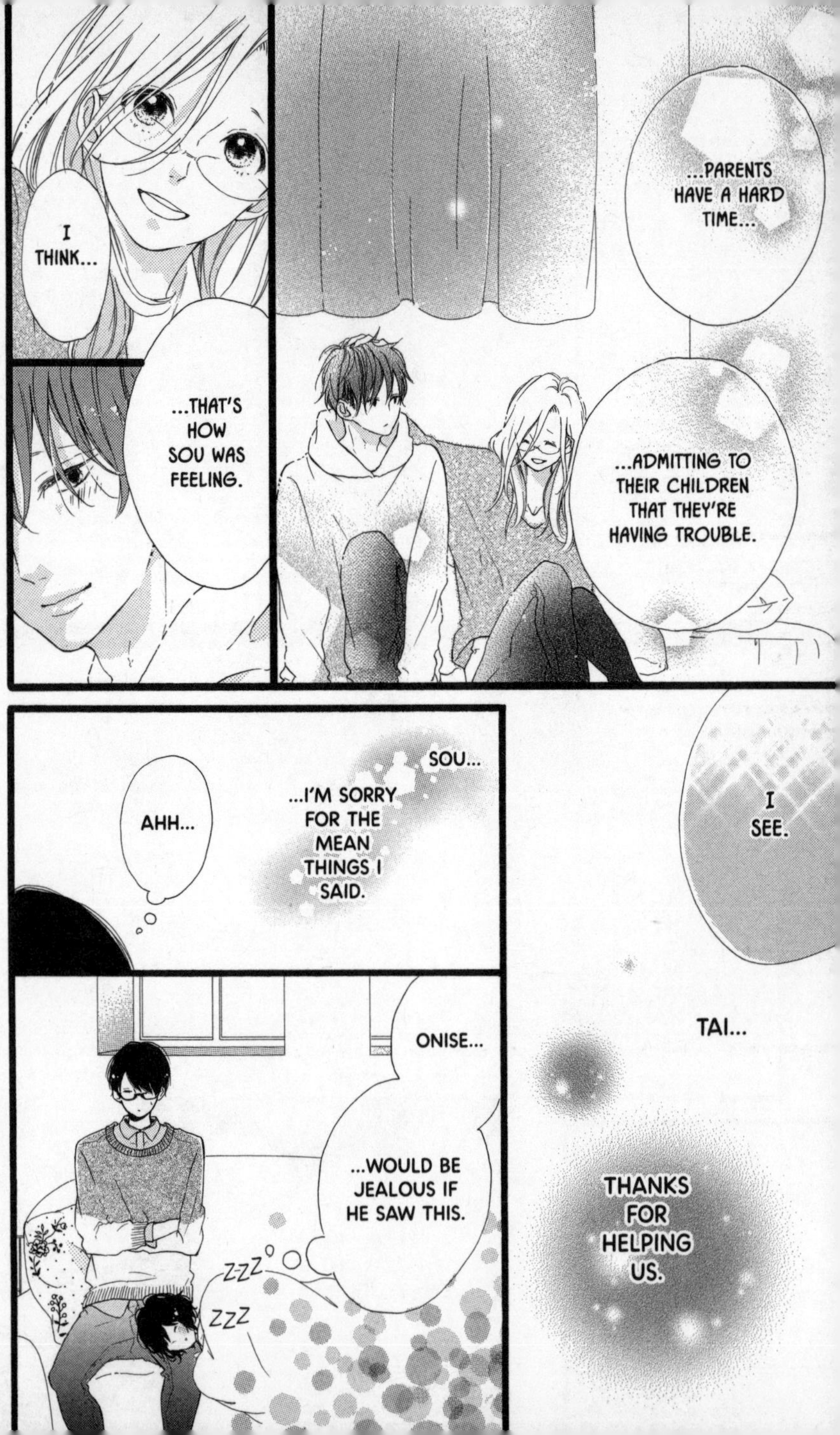
...PARENTS HAVE A HARD TIME...
...ADMITTING TO THEIR CHILDREN THAT THEY'RE HAVING TROUBLE.
I THINK...
...THAT'S HOW SOU WAS FEELING.
I SEE.
TAI...
THANKS FOR HELPING US.
SOU...
...I'M SORRY FOR THE MEAN THINGS I SAID.
AHH...
ONISE...
...WOULD BE JEALOUS IF HE SAW THIS.
Z-ZZ
ZZZ

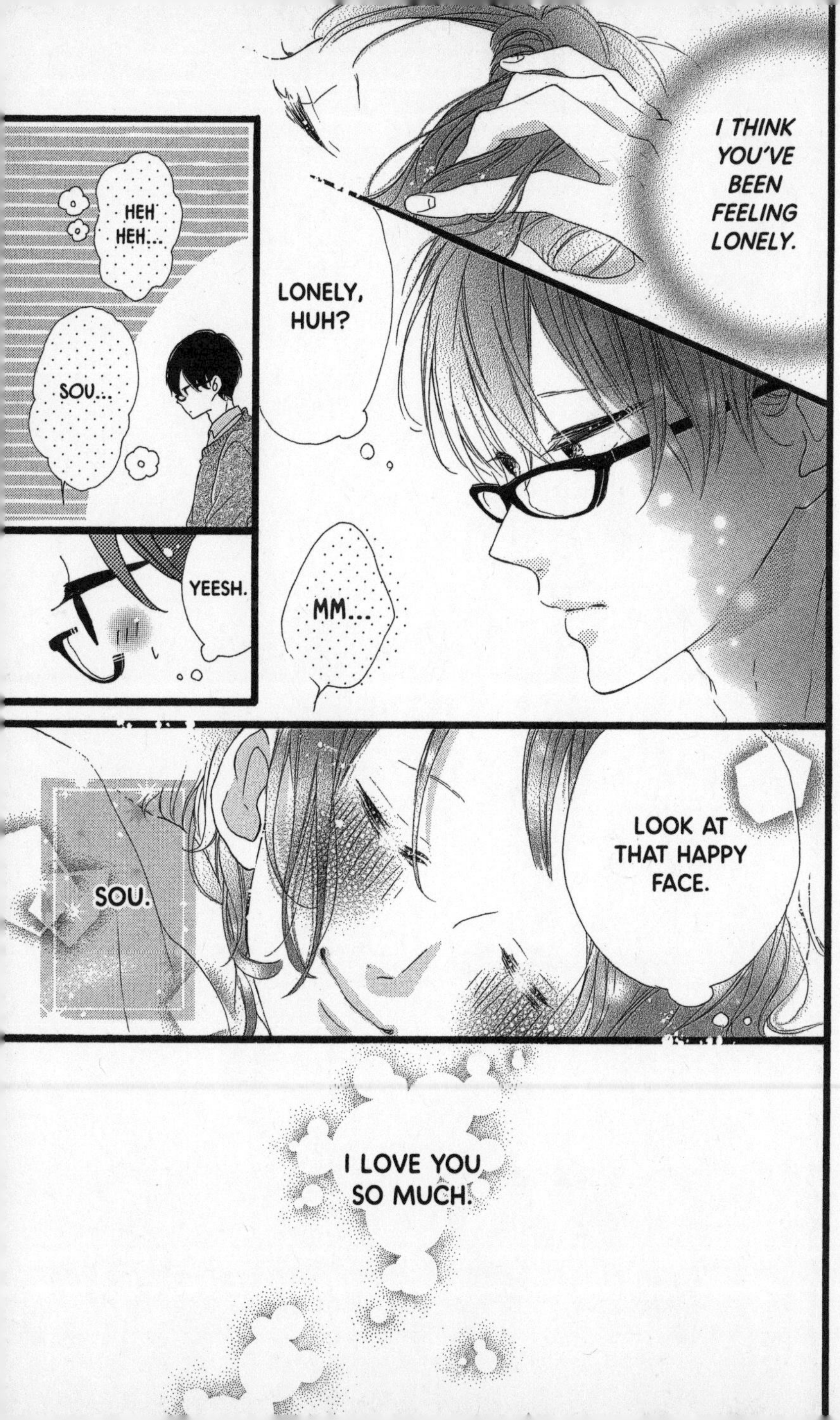
I THINK YOU'VE BEEN FEELING LONELY.
LONELY, HUH?
MM...
HEH HEH...
SOU...
YEESH.
LOOK AT THAT HAPPY FACE.
SOU.
I LOVE YOU SO MUCH.

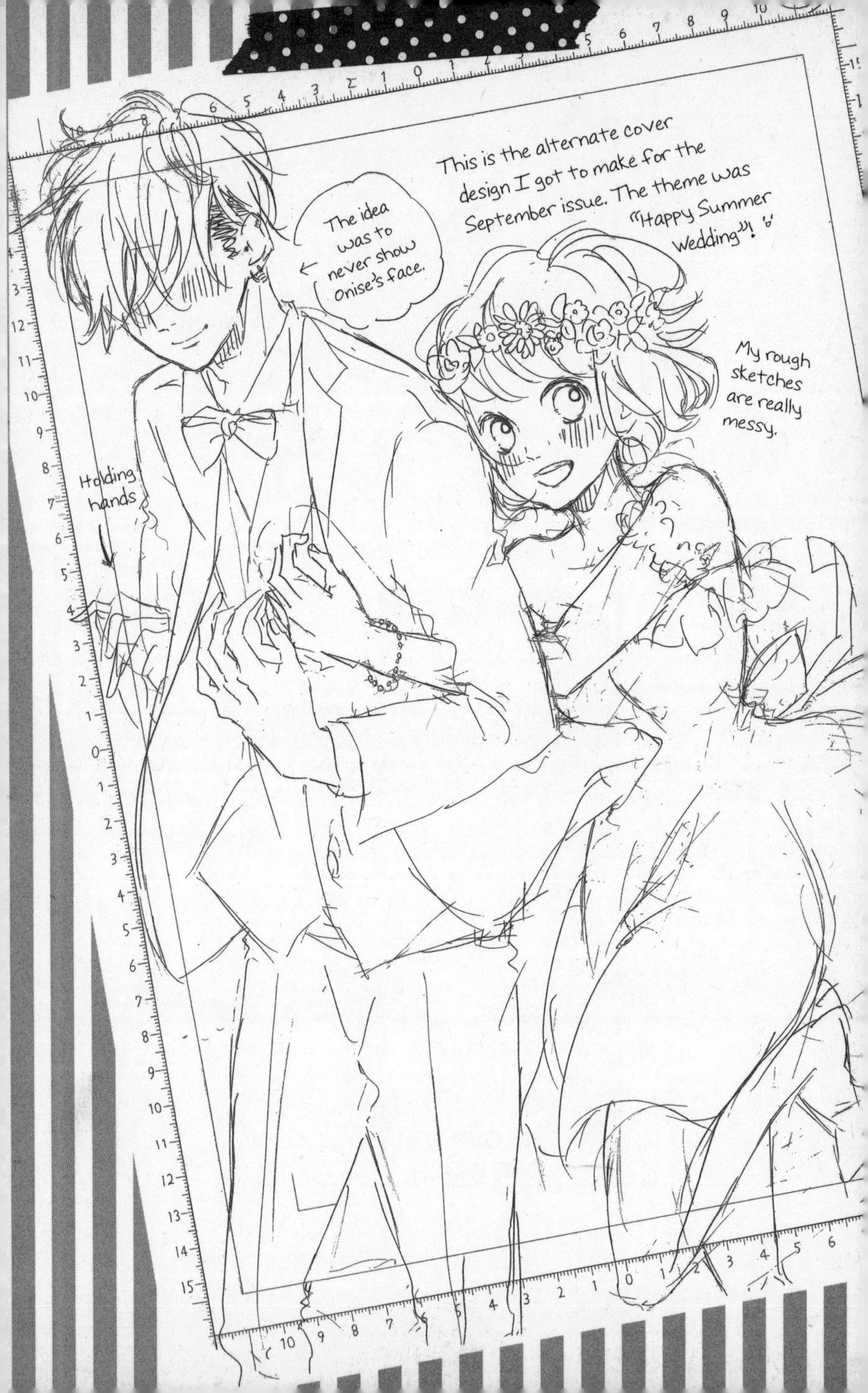
This is the alternate cover design I got to make for the September issue. The theme was "Happy Summer Wedding"! ♡
The idea was to never show Onise's face.
My rough sketches are really messy.
Holding hands

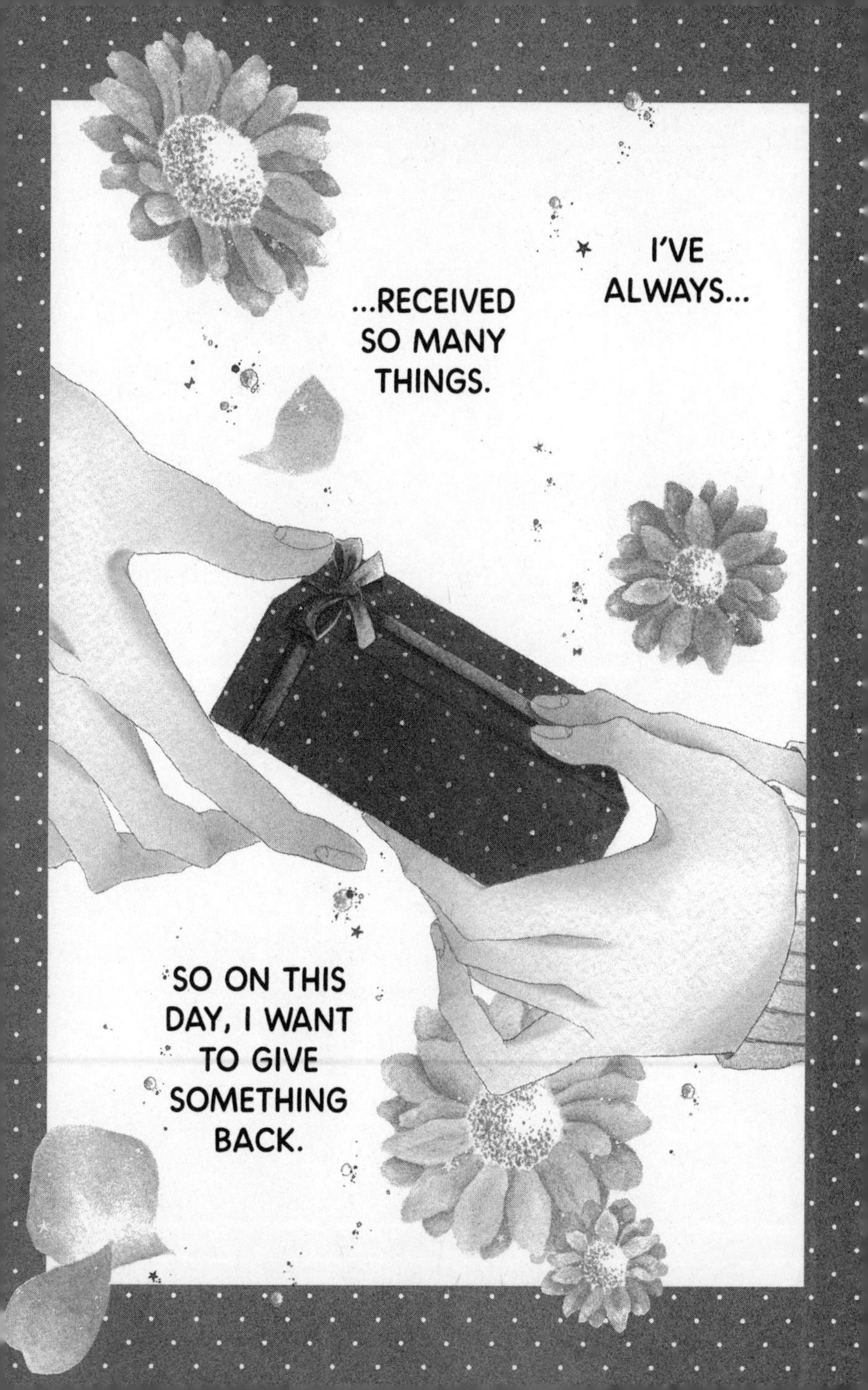
I'VE ALWAYS...
...RECEIVED SO MANY THINGS.
SO ON THIS DAY, I WANT TO GIVE SOMETHING BACK.

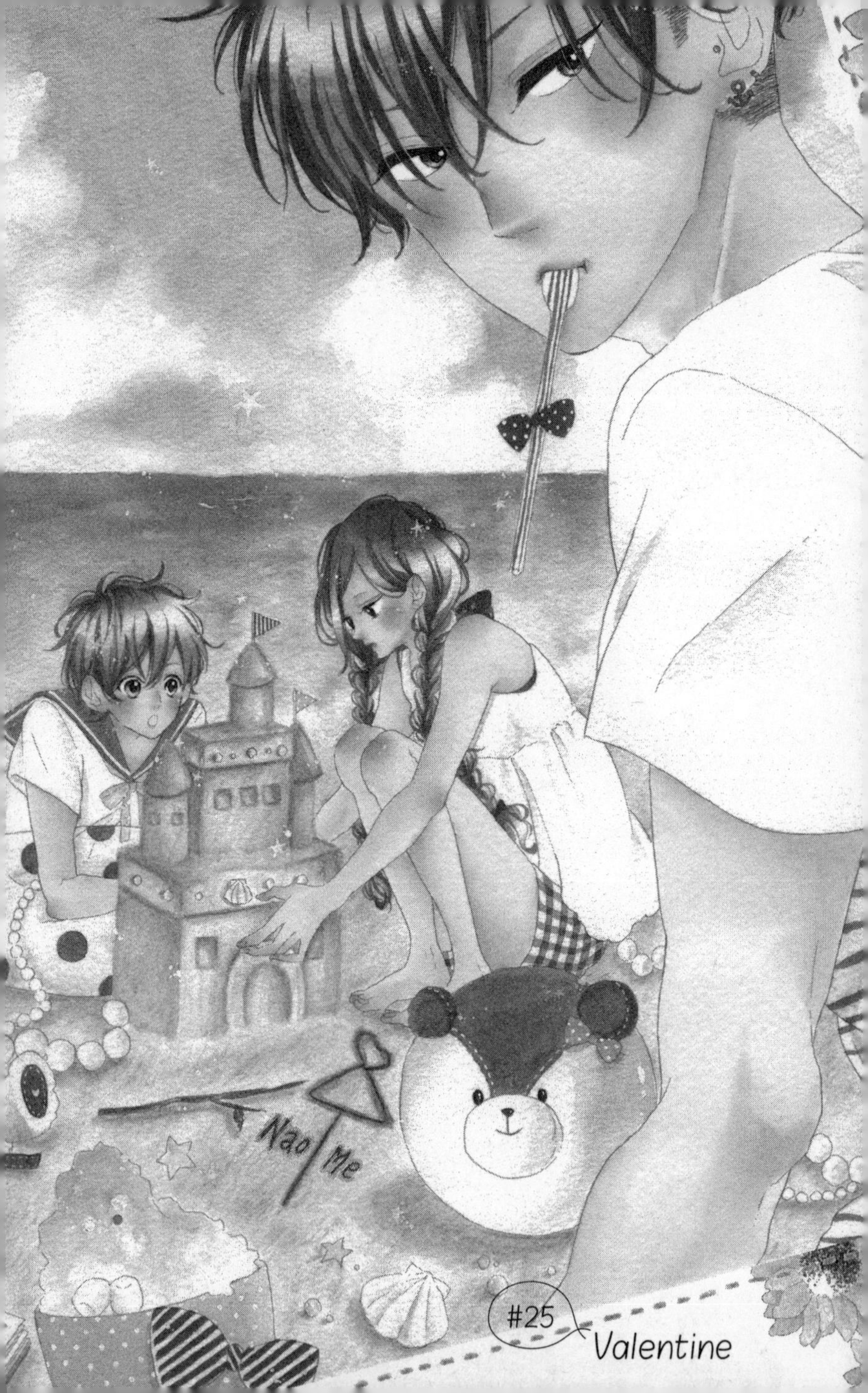
Nao
Me
#25
Valentine

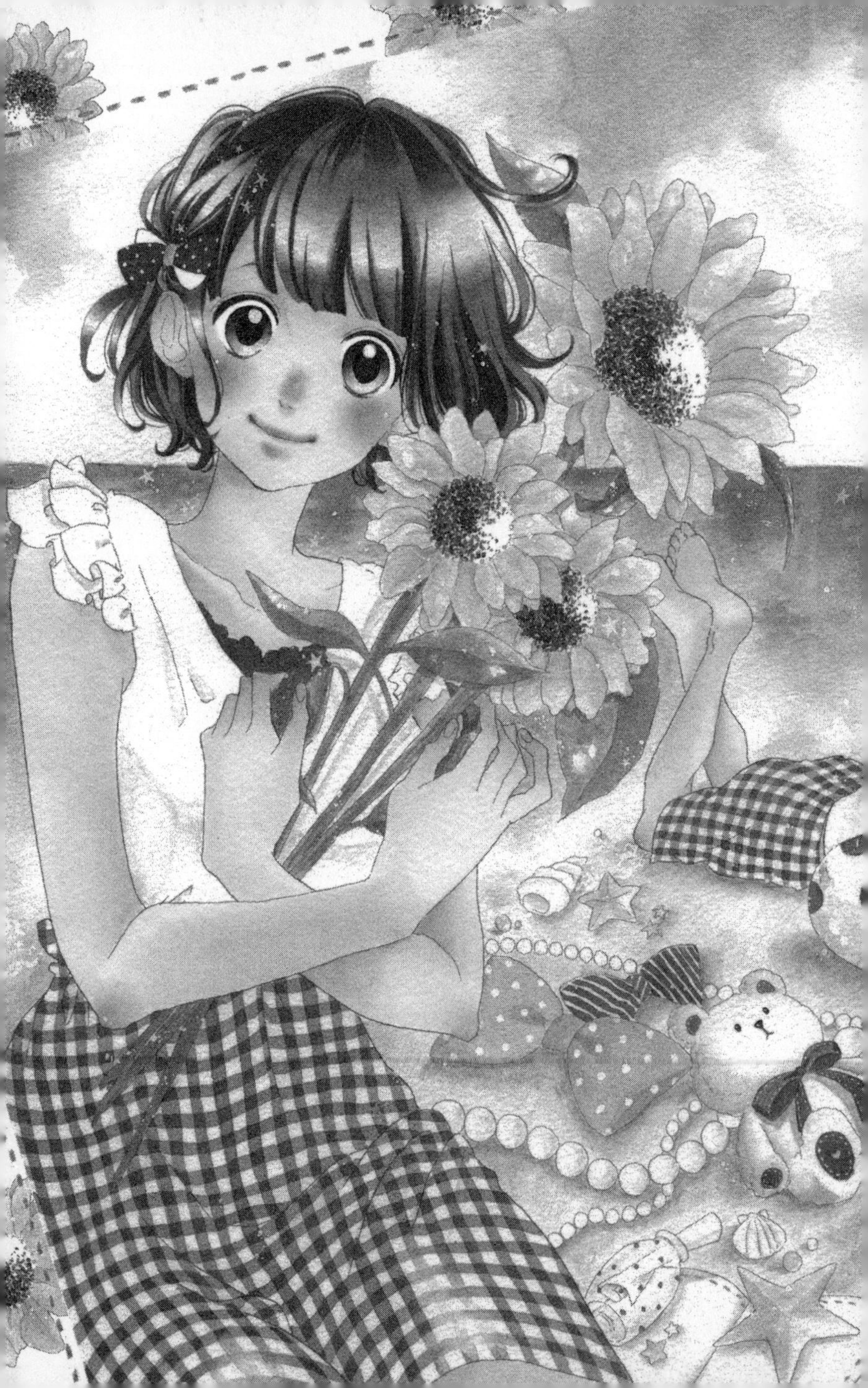

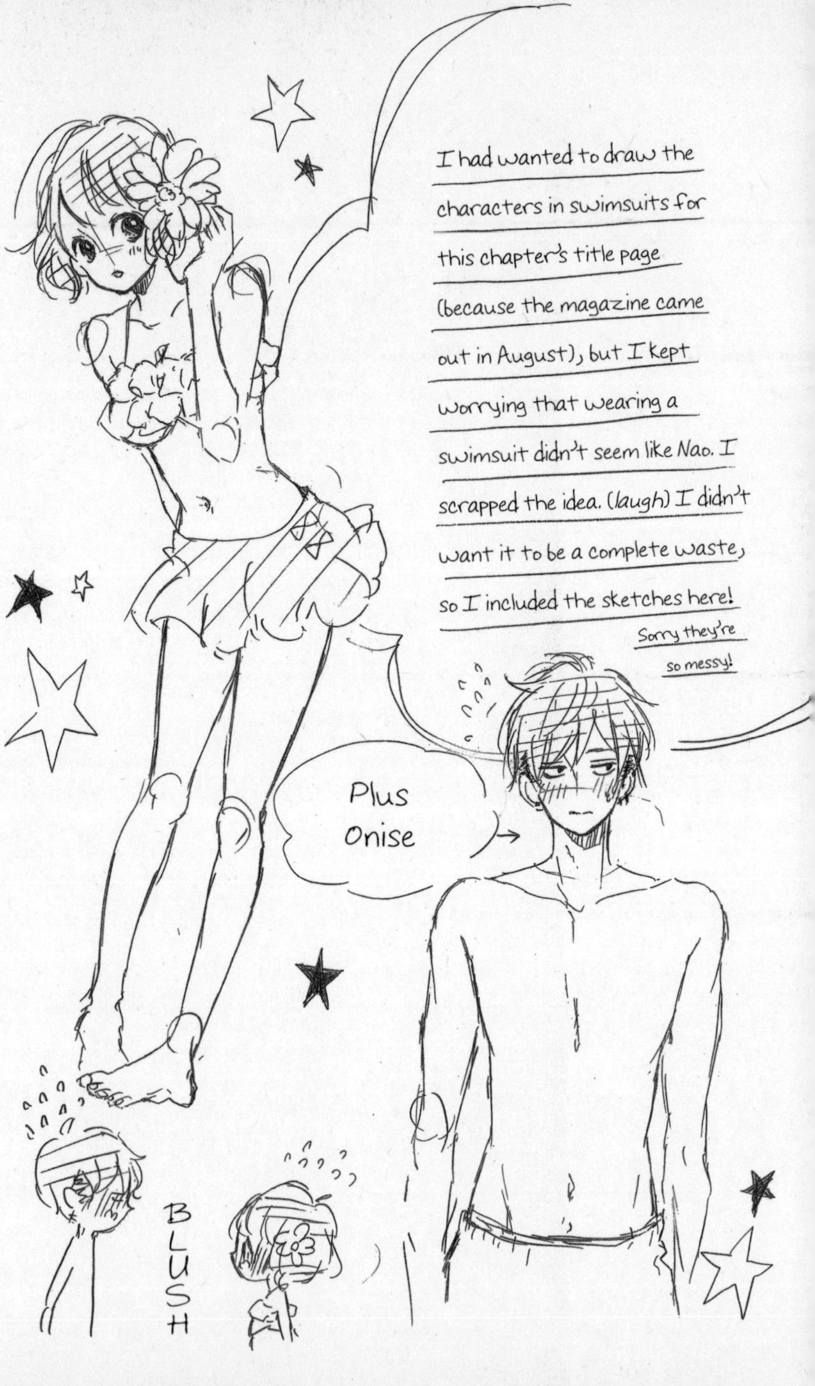

I had wanted to draw the characters in swimsuits for this chapter's title page (because the magazine came out in August), but I kept worrying that wearing a swimsuit didn't seem like Nao. I scrapped the idea. (laugh) I didn't want it to be a complete waste, so I included the sketches here!
Sorry they're so messy!
Plus Onise
BLUSH

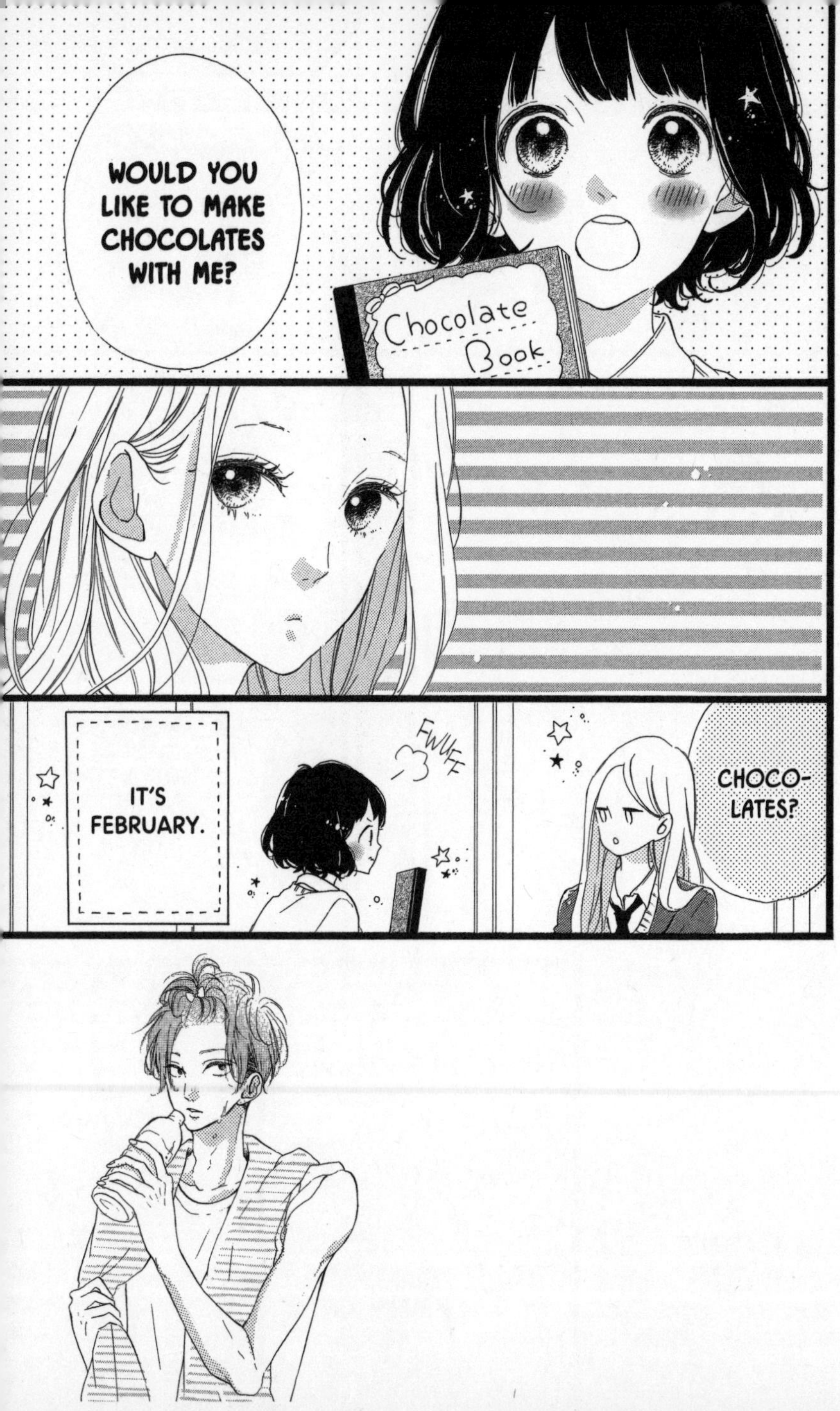
WOULD YOU LIKE TO MAKE CHOCOLATES WITH ME?
Chocolate Book
CHOCO-LATES?
FWUFF
IT'S FEBRUARY.

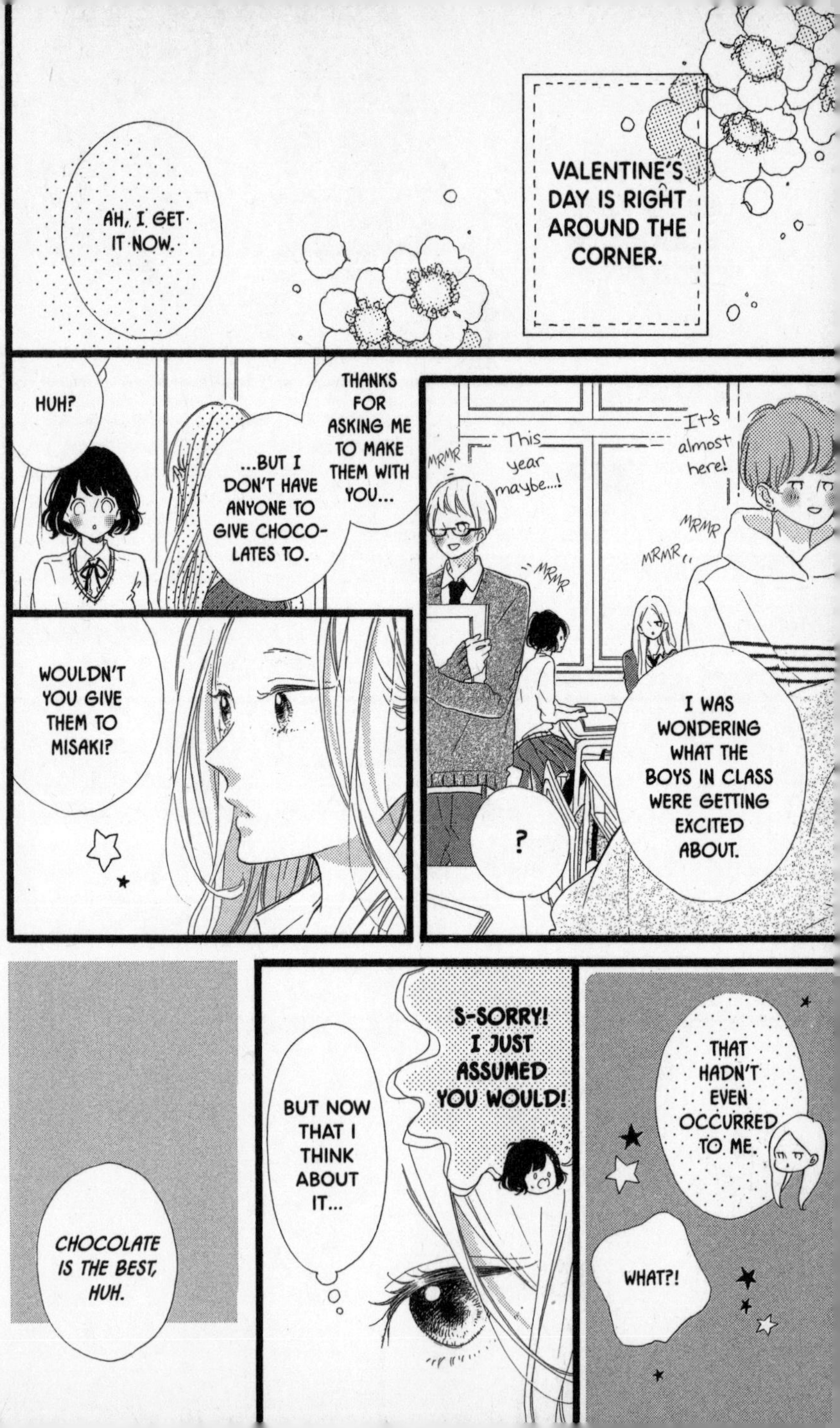
VALENTINE'S DAY IS RIGHT AROUND THE CORNER.
AH, I GET IT NOW.
It's almost here!
MRMR
This year maybe...!
MRMR
MRMR
MRMR
I WAS WONDERING WHAT THE BOYS IN CLASS WERE GETTING EXCITED ABOUT.
?
THANKS FOR ASKING ME TO MAKE THEM WITH YOU...
...BUT I DON'T HAVE ANYONE TO GIVE CHOCOLATES TO.
HUH?
WOULDN'T YOU GIVE THEM TO MISAKI?
THAT HADN'T EVEN OCCURRED TO ME.
WHAT?!
S-SORRY! I JUST ASSUMED YOU WOULD!
BUT NOW THAT I THINK ABOUT IT...
CHOCOLATE IS THE BEST, HUH.

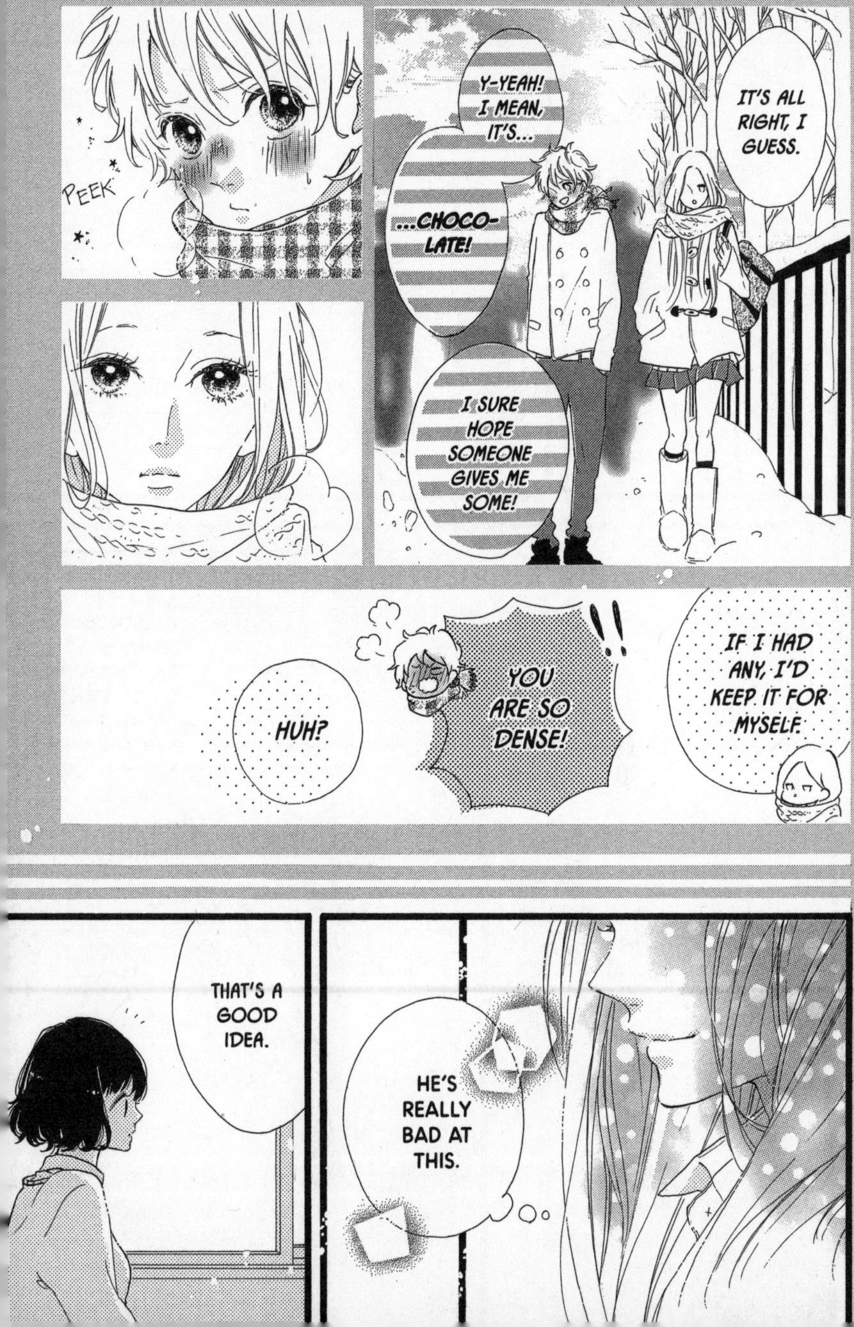
IT'S ALL RIGHT, I GUESS.
Y-YEAH! I MEAN, IT'S...
...CHOCO-LATE!
I SURE HOPE SOMEONE GIVES ME SOME!
PEEK
IF I HAD ANY, I'D KEEP IT FOR MYSELF.
!!
YOU ARE SO DENSE!
HUH?
HE'S REALLY BAD AT THIS.
THAT'S A GOOD IDEA.

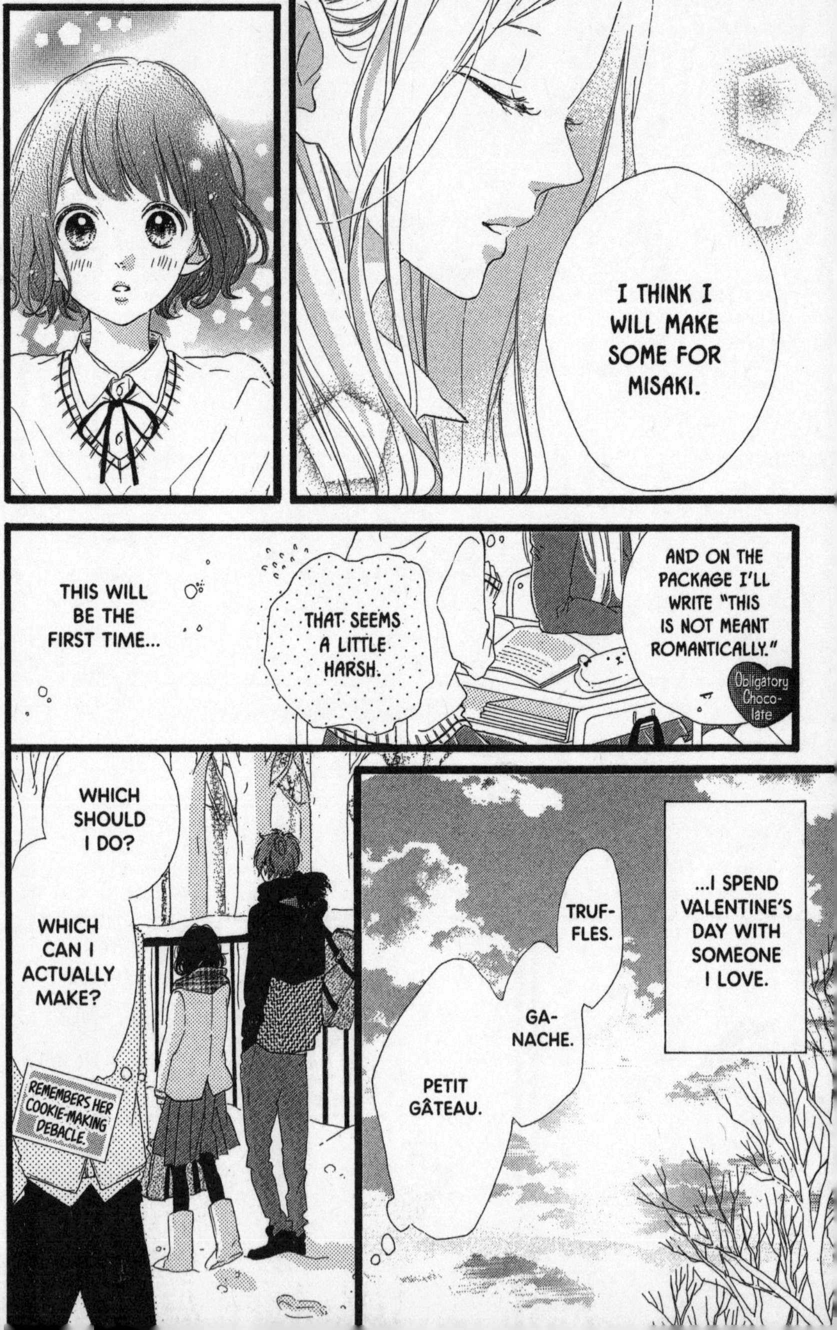
I THINK I WILL MAKE SOME FOR MISAKI.
AND ON THE PACKAGE I'LL WRITE "THIS IS NOT MEANT ROMANTICALLY."
Obligatory Choco-late
THAT SEEMS A LITTLE HARSH.
THIS WILL BE THE FIRST TIME...
...I SPEND VALENTINE'S DAY WITH SOMEONE I LOVE.
TRUF-FLES.
GA-NACHE.
PETIT GÂTEAU.
WHICH SHOULD I DO?
WHICH CAN I ACTUALLY MAKE?
REMEMBERS HER COOKIE-MAKING DEBACLE.

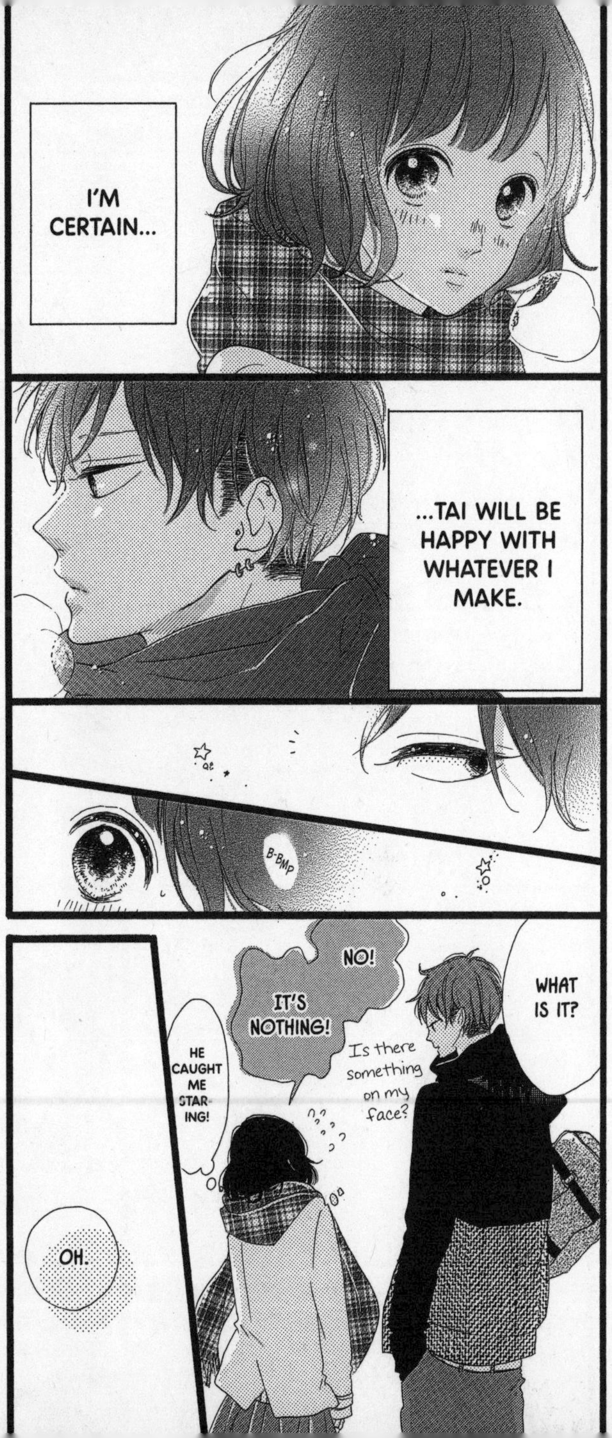
I'M CERTAIN...
...TAI WILL BE HAPPY WITH WHATEVER I MAKE.
B-BMP
WHAT IS IT?
Is there something on my face?
NO! IT'S NOTHING!
HE CAUGHT ME STAR-ING!
OH.
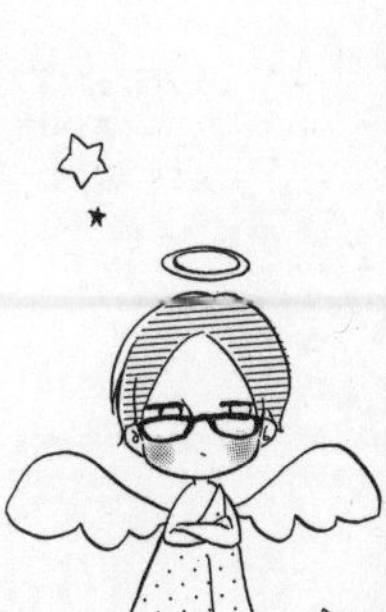

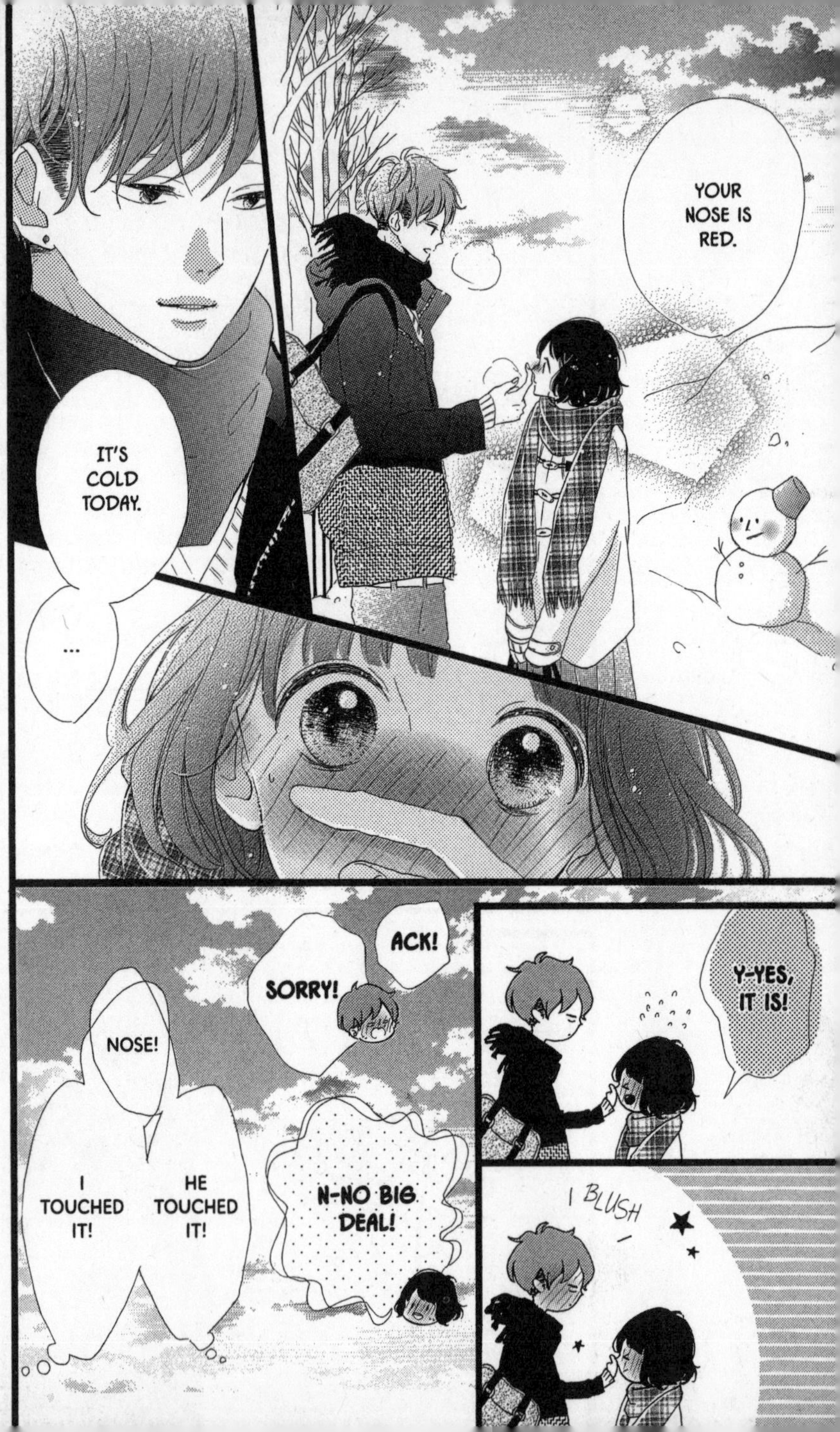
YOUR NOSE IS RED.
IT'S COLD TODAY.
...
Y-YES, IT IS!
BLUSH
ACK!
SORRY!
NOSE!
HE TOUCHED IT!
N-NO BIG DEAL!
I TOUCHED IT!

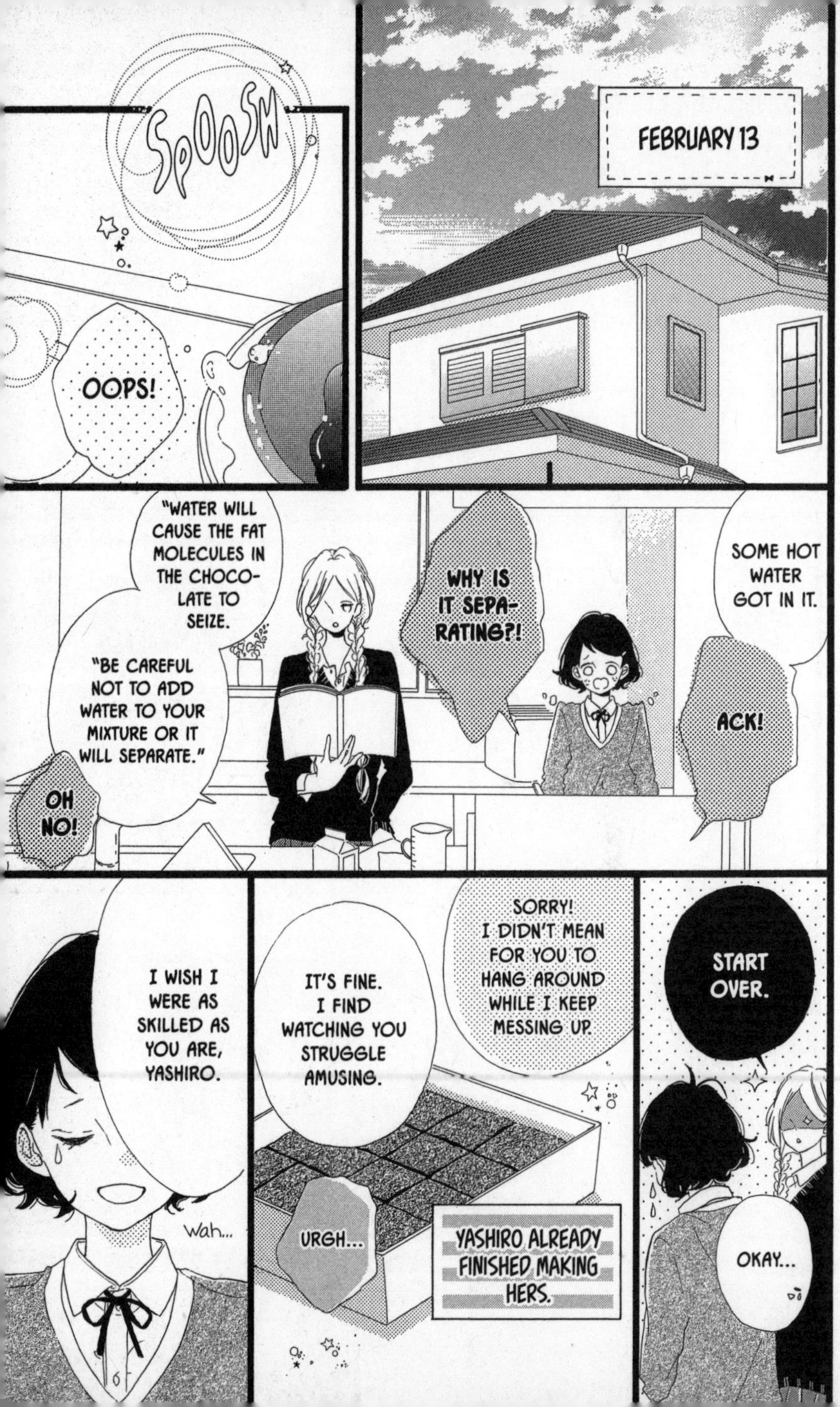
FEBRUARY 13
SPOOSH
OOPS!
SOME HOT WATER GOT IN IT.
ACK!
WHY IS IT SEPA-RATING?!
"WATER WILL CAUSE THE FAT MOLECULES IN THE CHOCO-LATE TO SEIZE.
"BE CAREFUL NOT TO ADD WATER TO YOUR MIXTURE OR IT WILL SEPARATE."
OH NO!
START OVER.
OKAY...
SORRY! I DIDN'T MEAN FOR YOU TO HANG AROUND WHILE I KEEP MESSING UP.
IT'S FINE. I FIND WATCHING YOU STRUGGLE AMUSING.
URGH...
YASHIRO ALREADY FINISHED MAKING HERS.
I WISH I WERE AS SKILLED AS YOU ARE, YASHIRO.
Wah...

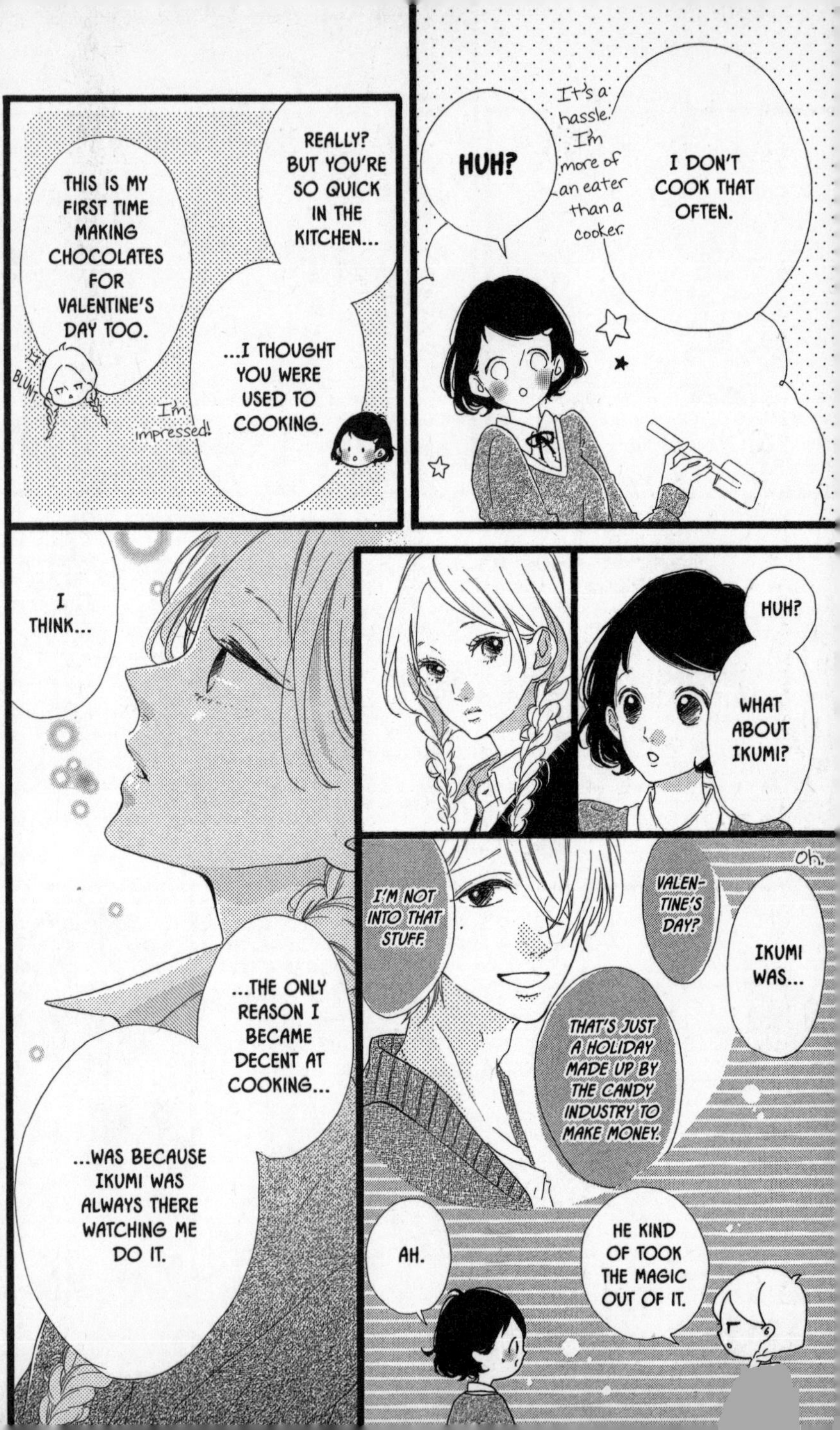
I DON'T COOK THAT OFTEN.
It's a hassle. I'm more of an eater than a cooker.
HUH?
REALLY? BUT YOU'RE SO QUICK IN THE KITCHEN...
...I THOUGHT YOU WERE USED TO COOKING.
I'm impressed!
THIS IS MY FIRST TIME MAKING CHOCOLATES FOR VALENTINE'S DAY TOO.
BLUNT
HUH?
WHAT ABOUT IKUMI?
Oh.
IKUMI WAS...
VALEN-TINE'S DAY?
I'M NOT INTO THAT STUFF.
THAT'S JUST A HOLIDAY MADE UP BY THE CANDY INDUSTRY TO MAKE MONEY.
HE KIND OF TOOK THE MAGIC OUT OF IT.
AH.
I THINK...
...THE ONLY REASON I BECAME DECENT AT COOKING...
...WAS BECAUSE IKUMI WAS ALWAYS THERE WATCHING ME DO IT.

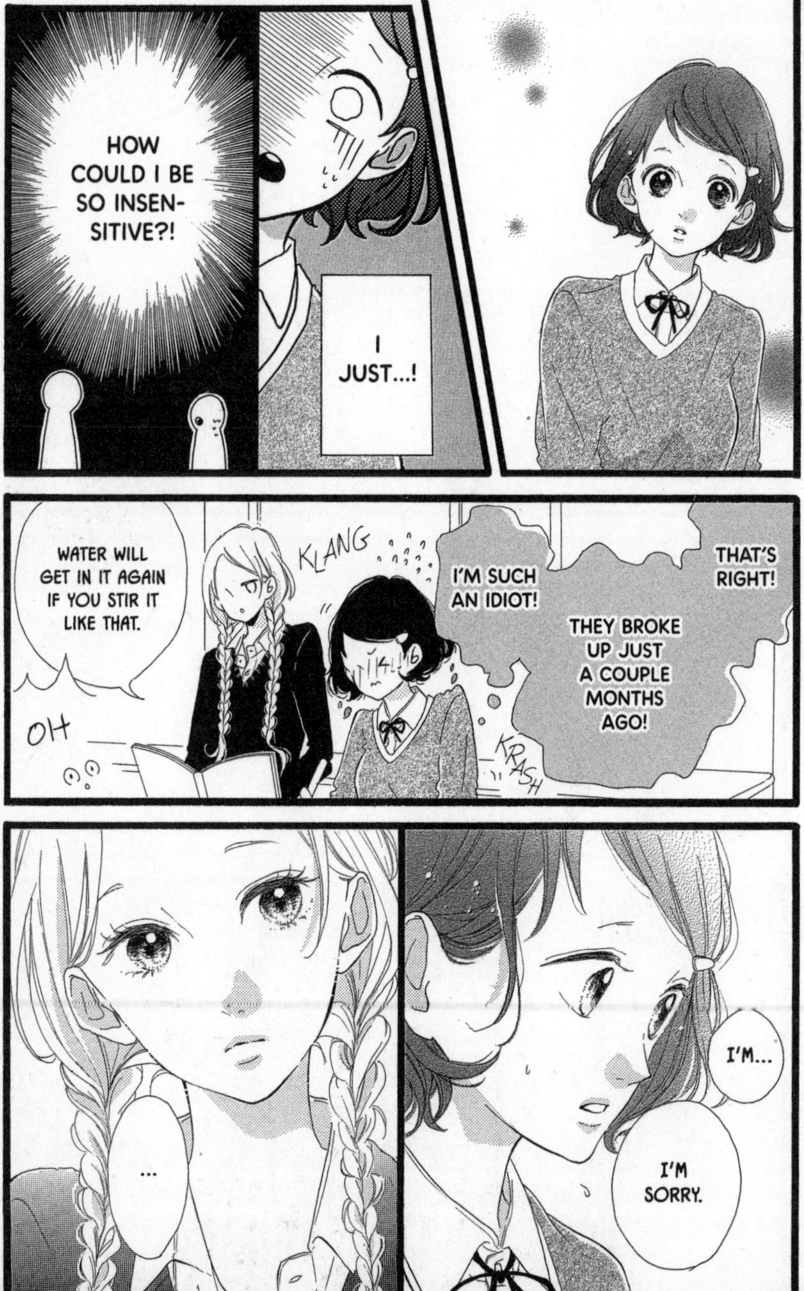
I JUST...!
HOW COULD I BE SO INSENSITIVE?!
THAT'S RIGHT!
THEY BROKE UP JUST A COUPLE MONTHS AGO!
I'M SUCH AN IDIOT!
KRASH
KLANG
WATER WILL GET IN IT AGAIN IF YOU STIR IT LIKE THAT.
OH
I'M...
I'M SORRY.
...

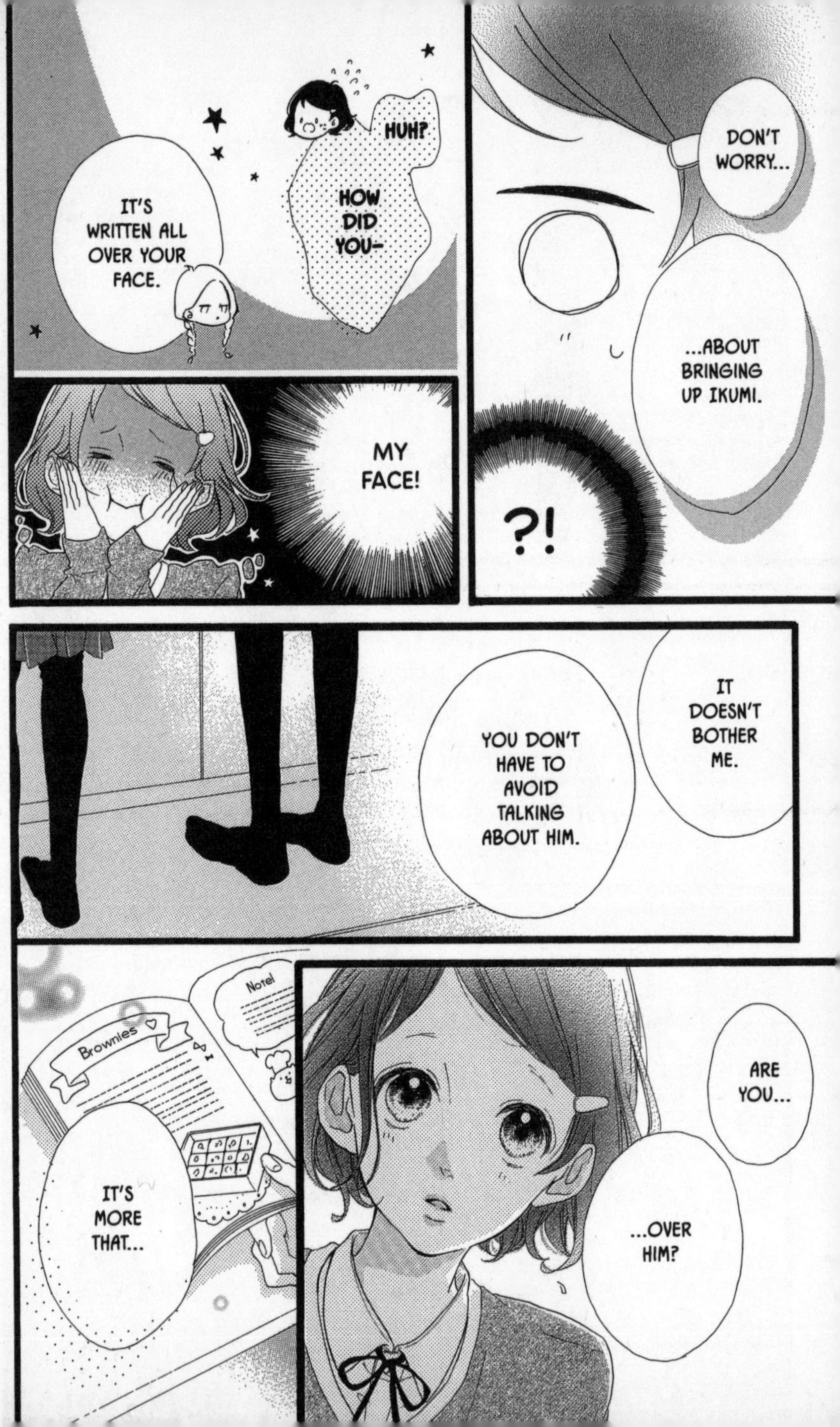
DON'T WORRY...
...ABOUT BRINGING UP IKUMI.
?!
HUH?
HOW DID YOU-
IT'S WRITTEN ALL OVER YOUR FACE.
MY FACE!
IT DOESN'T BOTHER ME.
YOU DON'T HAVE TO AVOID TALKING ABOUT HIM.
ARE YOU...
...OVER HIM?
Note!
Brownies
IT'S MORE THAT...

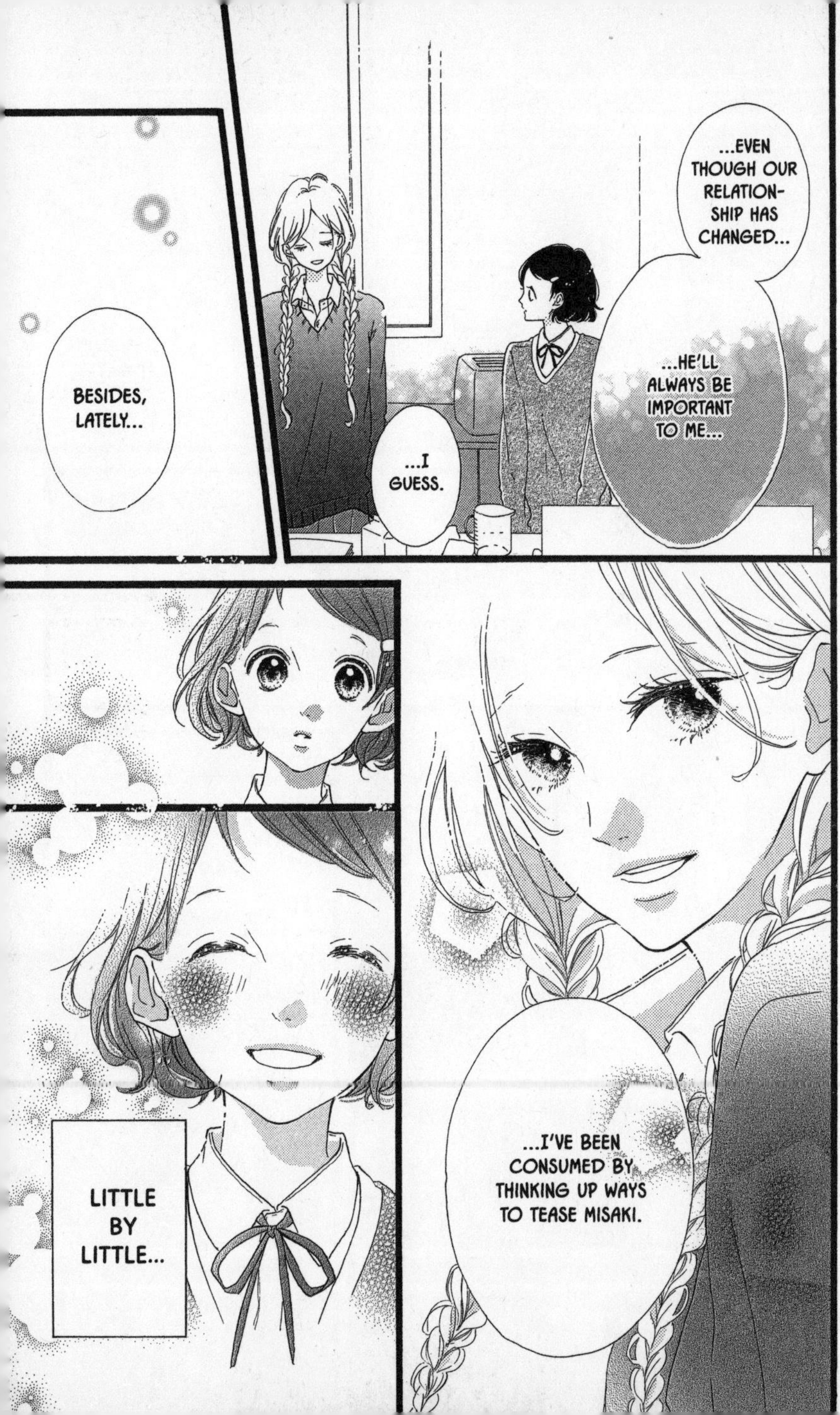
...EVEN THOUGH OUR RELATION-SHIP HAS CHANGED...
...HE'LL ALWAYS BE IMPORTANT TO ME...
...I GUESS.
BESIDES, LATELY...
...I'VE BEEN CONSUMED BY THINKING UP WAYS TO TEASE MISAKI.
LITTLE BY LITTLE...

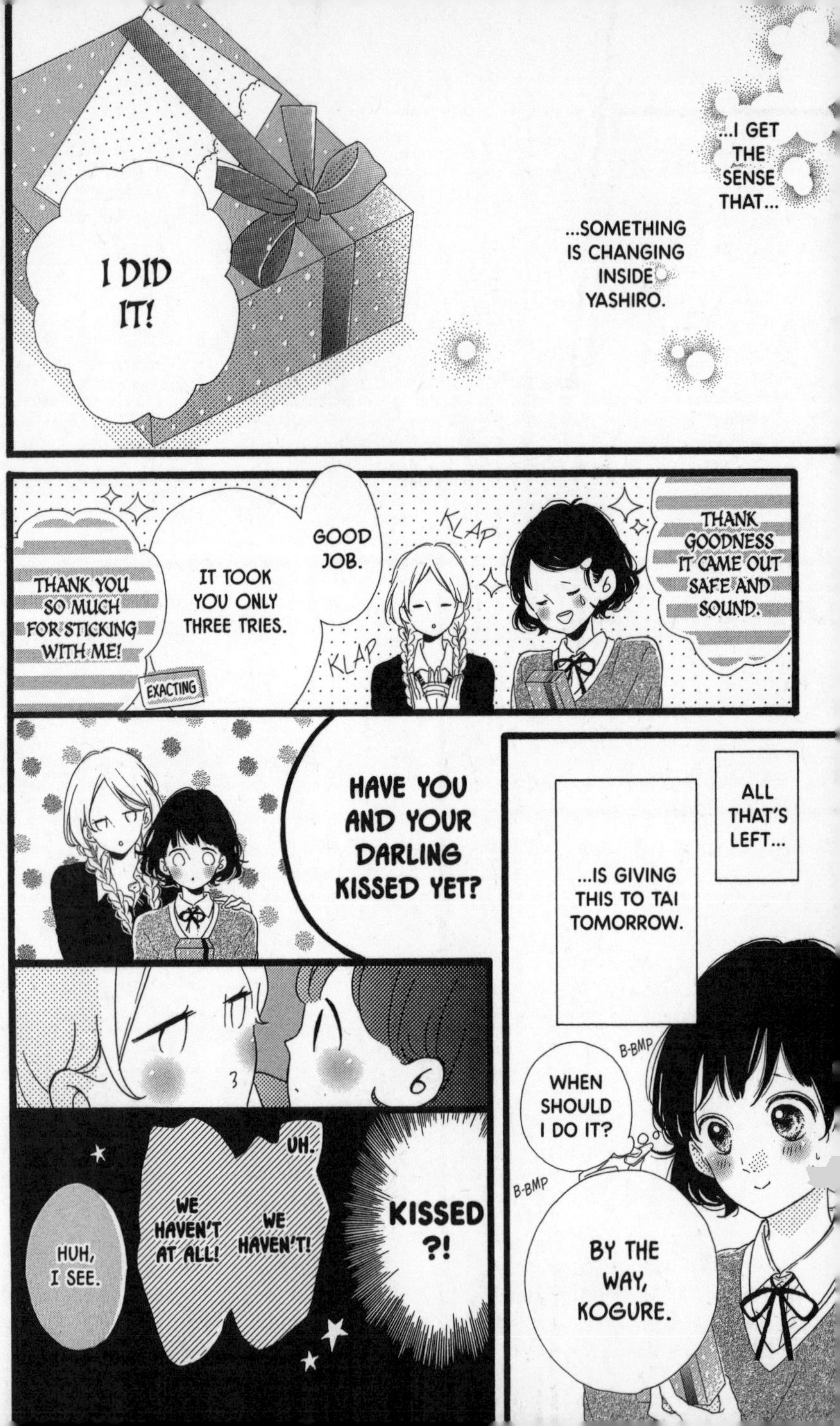
...I GET THE SENSE THAT...
...SOMETHING IS CHANGING INSIDE YASHIRO.
I DID IT!
THANK GOODNESS IT CAME OUT SAFE AND SOUND.
KLAP
KLAP
GOOD JOB.
IT TOOK YOU ONLY THREE TRIES.
THANK YOU SO MUCH FOR STICKING WITH ME!
EXACTING
ALL THAT'S LEFT...
...IS GIVING THIS TO TAI TOMORROW.
B-BMP
WHEN SHOULD I DO IT?
B-BMP
BY THE WAY, KOGURE.
HAVE YOU AND YOUR DARLING KISSED YET?
KISSED ?!
UH.
WE HAVEN'T!
WE HAVEN'T AT ALL!
HUH, I SEE.

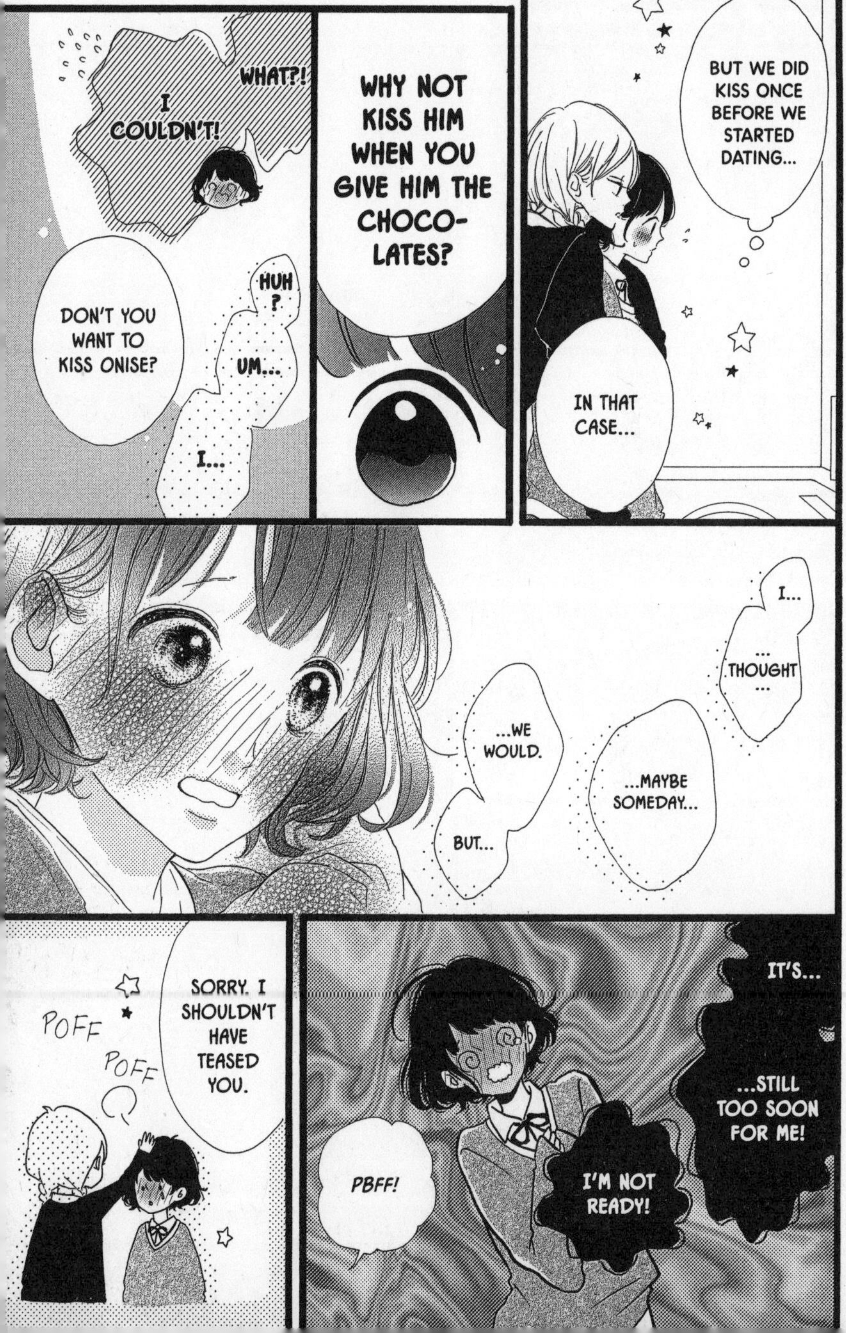
BUT WE DID KISS ONCE BEFORE WE STARTED DATING...
IN THAT CASE...
WHY NOT KISS HIM WHEN YOU GIVE HIM THE CHOCO-LATES?
WHAT?!
I COULDN'T!
HUH?
DON'T YOU WANT TO KISS ONISE?
UM...
I...
I...
...THOUGHT...
...MAYBE SOMEDAY...
...WE WOULD.
BUT...
IT'S...
...STILL TOO SOON FOR ME!
I'M NOT READY!
PBFF!
SORRY. I SHOULDN'T HAVE TEASED YOU.
POFF
POFF

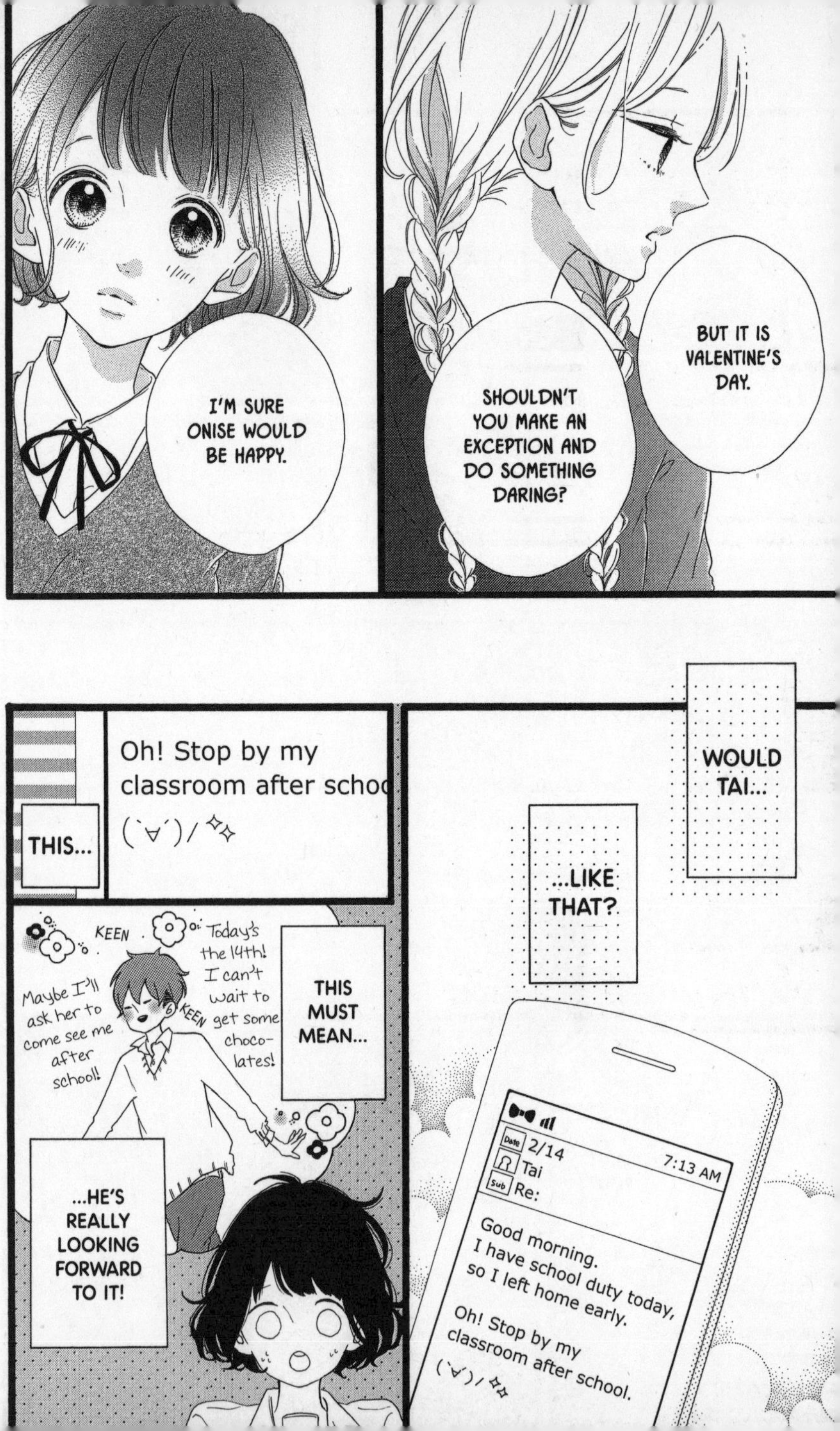
BUT IT IS VALENTINE'S DAY.
SHOULDN'T YOU MAKE AN EXCEPTION AND DO SOMETHING DARING?
I'M SURE ONISE WOULD BE HAPPY.
WOULD TAI...
...LIKE THAT?
2/14
7:13 AM
Tai
Re:
Good morning.
I have school duty today, so I left home early.
Oh! Stop by my classroom after school.
(´∀`)/ ✧✧
Oh! Stop by my classroom after schoo
(´∀`)/ ✧✧
THIS...
THIS MUST MEAN...
Today's the 14th! I can't wait to get some chocolates!
KEEN
Maybe I'll ask her to come see me after school!
KEEN
...HE'S REALLY LOOKING FORWARD TO IT!

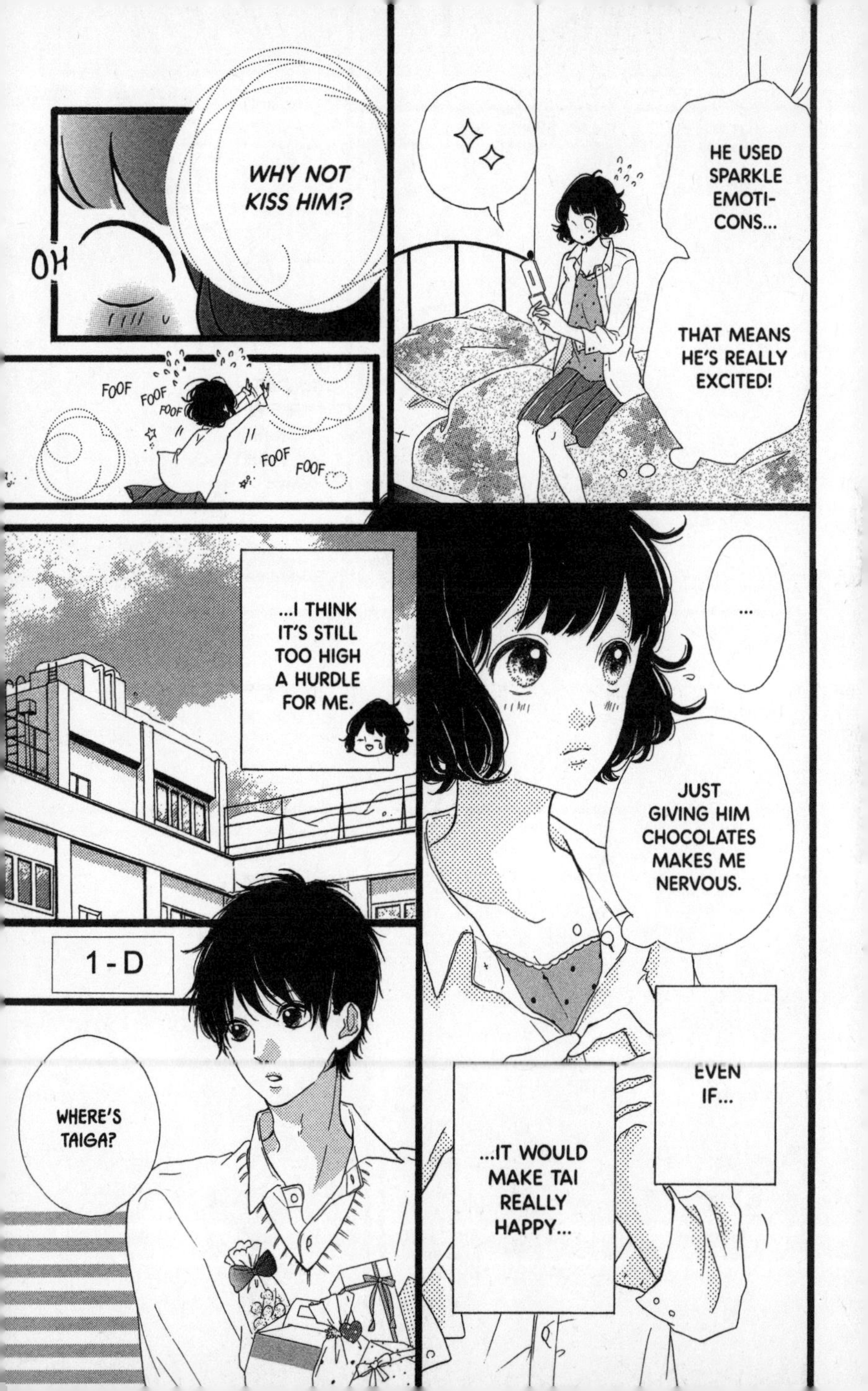
HE USED SPARKLE EMOTI-CONS...
THAT MEANS HE'S REALLY EXCITED!
WHY NOT KISS HIM?
OH
FOOF
FOOF
FOOF
FOOF
FOOF
...
JUST GIVING HIM CHOCOLATES MAKES ME NERVOUS.
EVEN IF...
...IT WOULD MAKE TAI REALLY HAPPY...
...I THINK IT'S STILL TOO HIGH A HURDLE FOR ME.
1 - D
WHERE'S TAIGA?

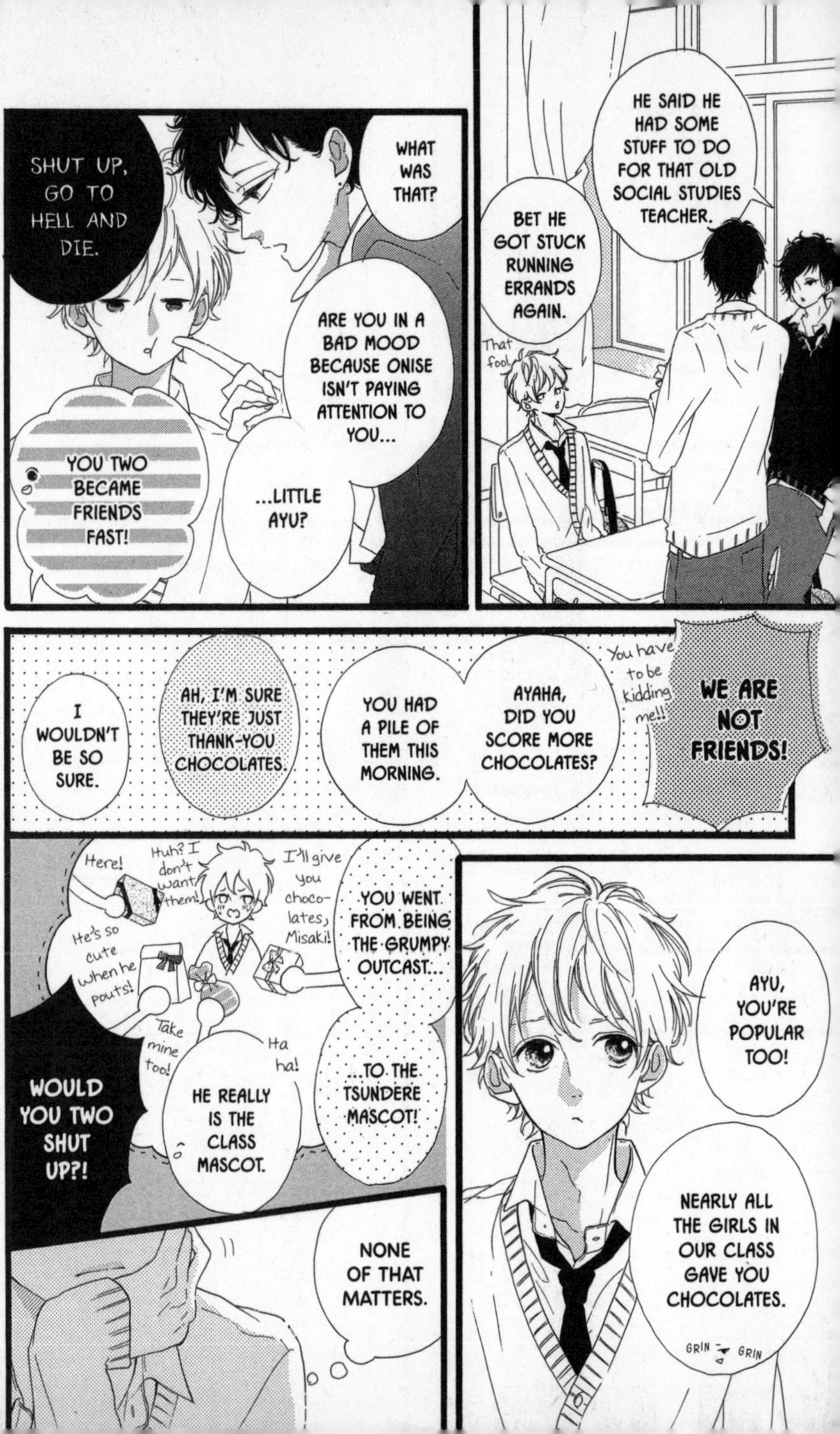
HE SAID HE HAD SOME STUFF TO DO FOR THAT OLD SOCIAL STUDIES TEACHER.
BET HE GOT STUCK RUNNING ERRANDS AGAIN.
That fool.
ARE YOU IN A BAD MOOD BECAUSE ONISE ISN'T PAYING ATTENTION TO YOU...
...LITTLE AYU?
SHUT UP, GO TO HELL AND DIE.
WHAT WAS THAT?
YOU TWO BECAME FRIENDS FAST!
WE ARE NOT FRIENDS!
You have to be kidding me!!
AYAHA, DID YOU SCORE MORE CHOCOLATES?
YOU HAD A PILE OF THEM THIS MORNING.
AH, I'M SURE THEY'RE JUST THANK-YOU CHOCOLATES.
I WOULDN'T BE SO SURE.
AYU, YOU'RE POPULAR TOO!
NEARLY ALL THE GIRLS IN OUR CLASS GAVE YOU CHOCOLATES.
GRIN GRIN
YOU WENT FROM BEING THE GRUMPY OUTCAST...
I'll give you chocolates, Misaki!
Huh? I don't want them!
Here!
He's so cute when he pouts!
Take mine too!
Ha ha!
...TO THE TSUNDERE MASCOT!
HE REALLY IS THE CLASS MASCOT.
WOULD YOU TWO SHUT UP?!
NONE OF THAT MATTERS.

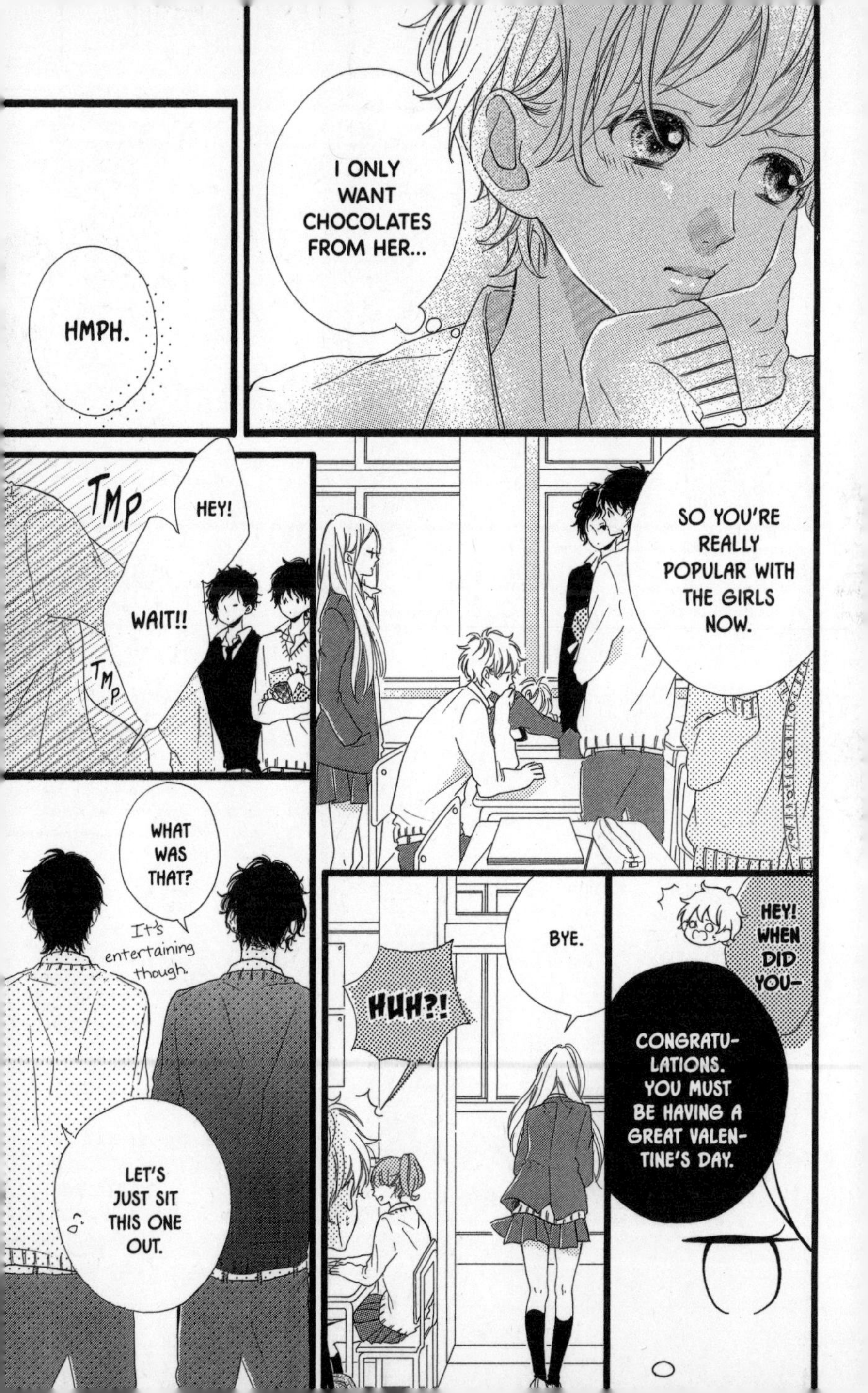
I ONLY WANT CHOCOLATES FROM HER...
HMPH.
SO YOU'RE REALLY POPULAR WITH THE GIRLS NOW.
TMP
HEY!
WAIT!!
TMP
HEY! WHEN DID YOU-
CONGRATULATIONS. YOU MUST BE HAVING A GREAT VALENTINE'S DAY.
BYE.
HUH?!
WHAT WAS THAT?
It's entertaining though.
LET'S JUST SIT THIS ONE OUT.

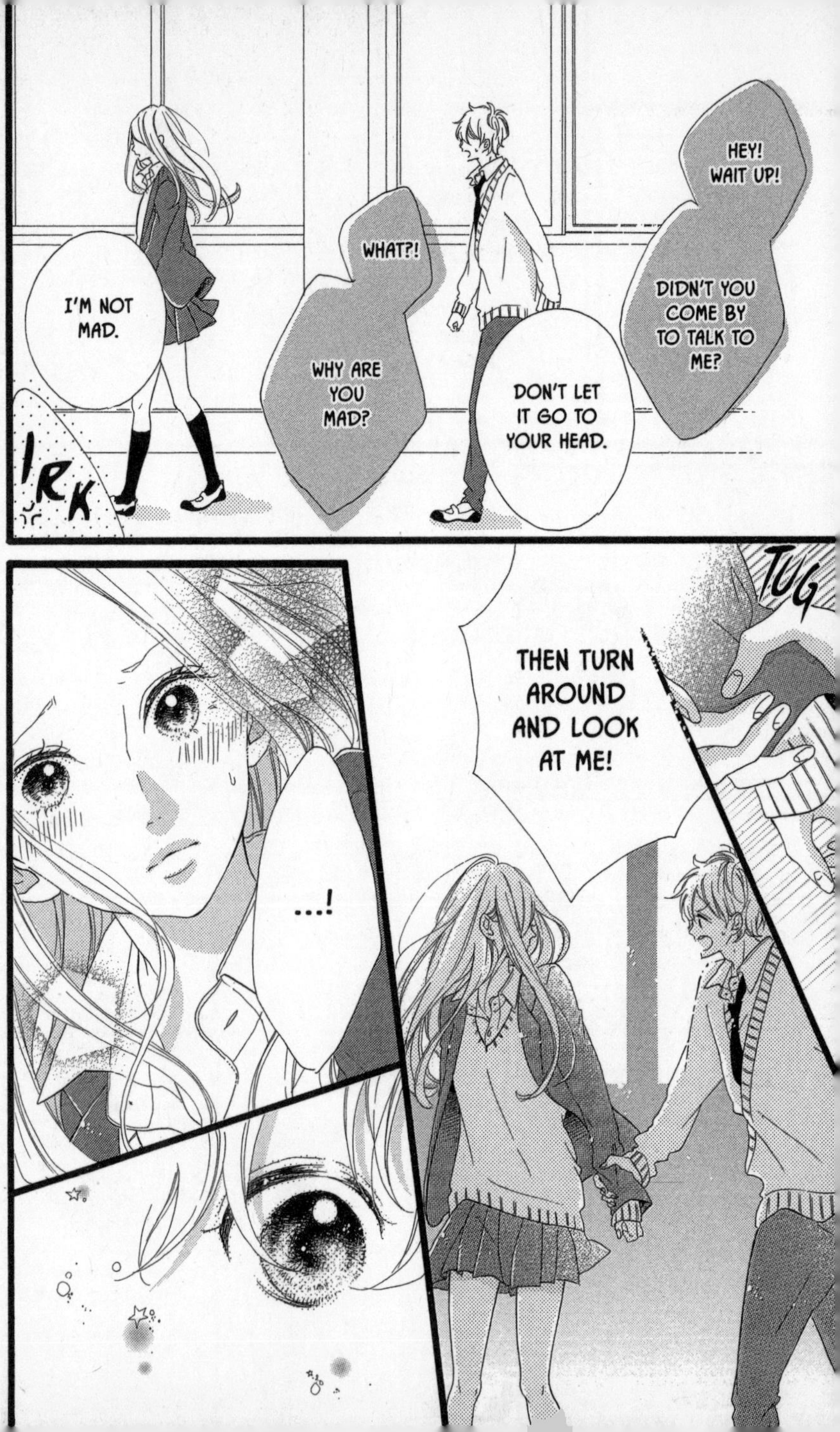
HEY! WAIT UP!
DIDN'T YOU COME BY TO TALK TO ME?
DON'T LET IT GO TO YOUR HEAD.
WHAT?!
WHY ARE YOU MAD?
I'M NOT MAD.
IRK
TUG
THEN TURN AROUND AND LOOK AT ME!
...!

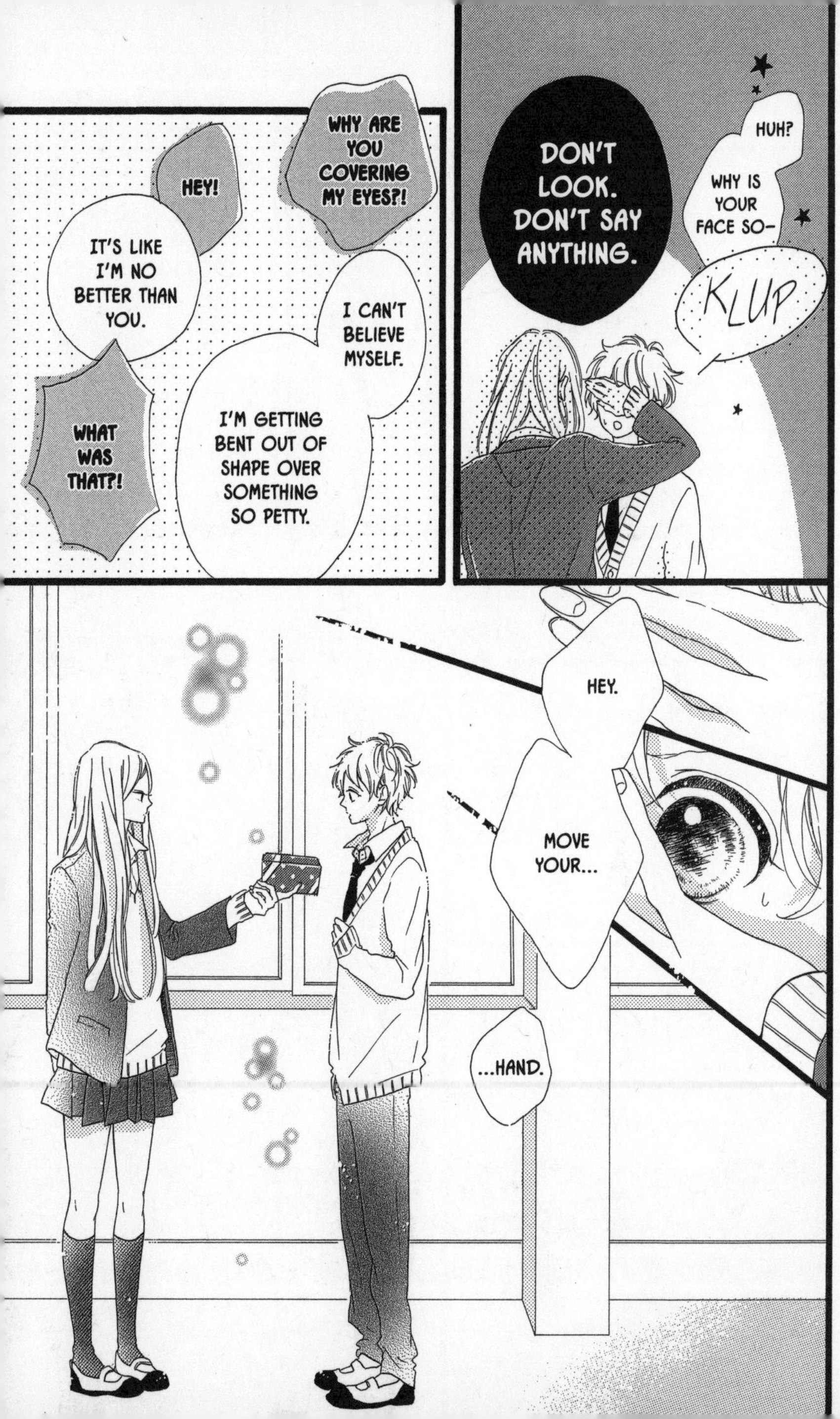
HUH?
WHY IS YOUR FACE SO-
KLUP
DON'T LOOK. DON'T SAY ANYTHING.
WHY ARE YOU COVERING MY EYES?!
HEY!
I CAN'T BELIEVE MYSELF.
IT'S LIKE I'M NO BETTER THAN YOU.
I'M GETTING BENT OUT OF SHAPE OVER SOMETHING SO PETTY.
WHAT WAS THAT?!
HEY.
MOVE YOUR...
...HAND.

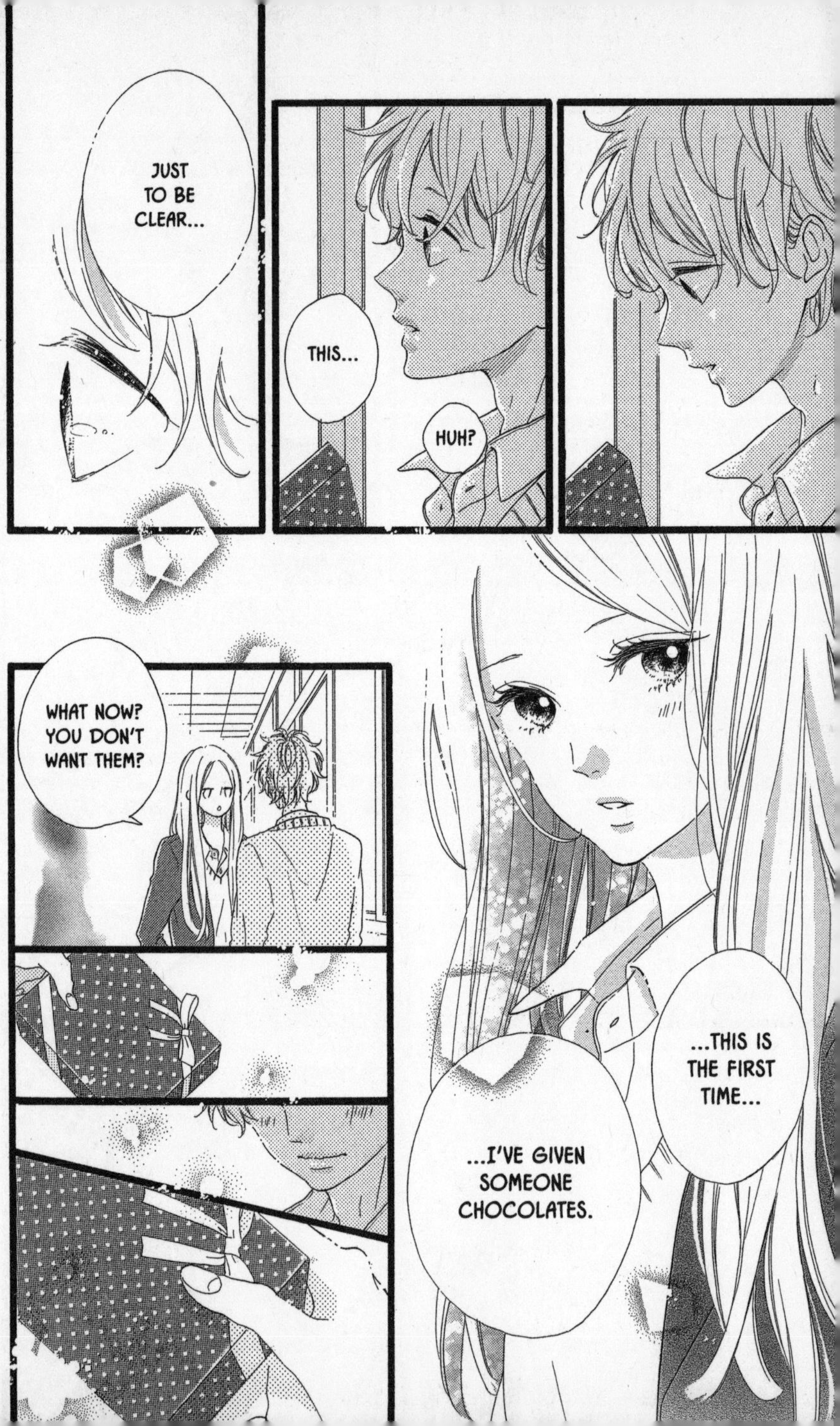
THIS...
HUH?
JUST TO BE CLEAR...
...THIS IS THE FIRST TIME...
...I'VE GIVEN SOMEONE CHOCOLATES.
WHAT NOW? YOU DON'T WANT THEM?

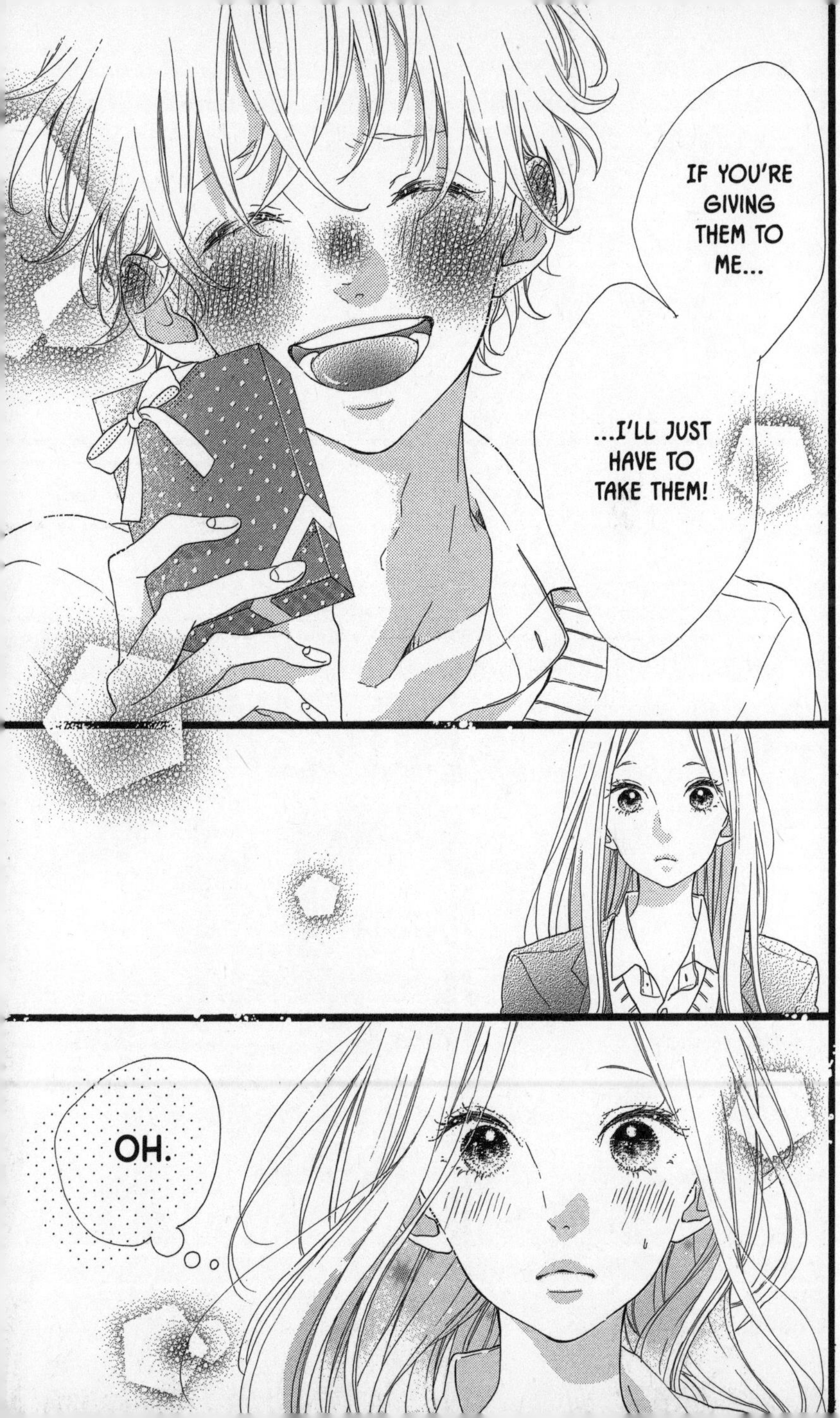
IF YOU'RE GIVING THEM TO ME...
...I'LL JUST HAVE TO TAKE THEM!
OH.

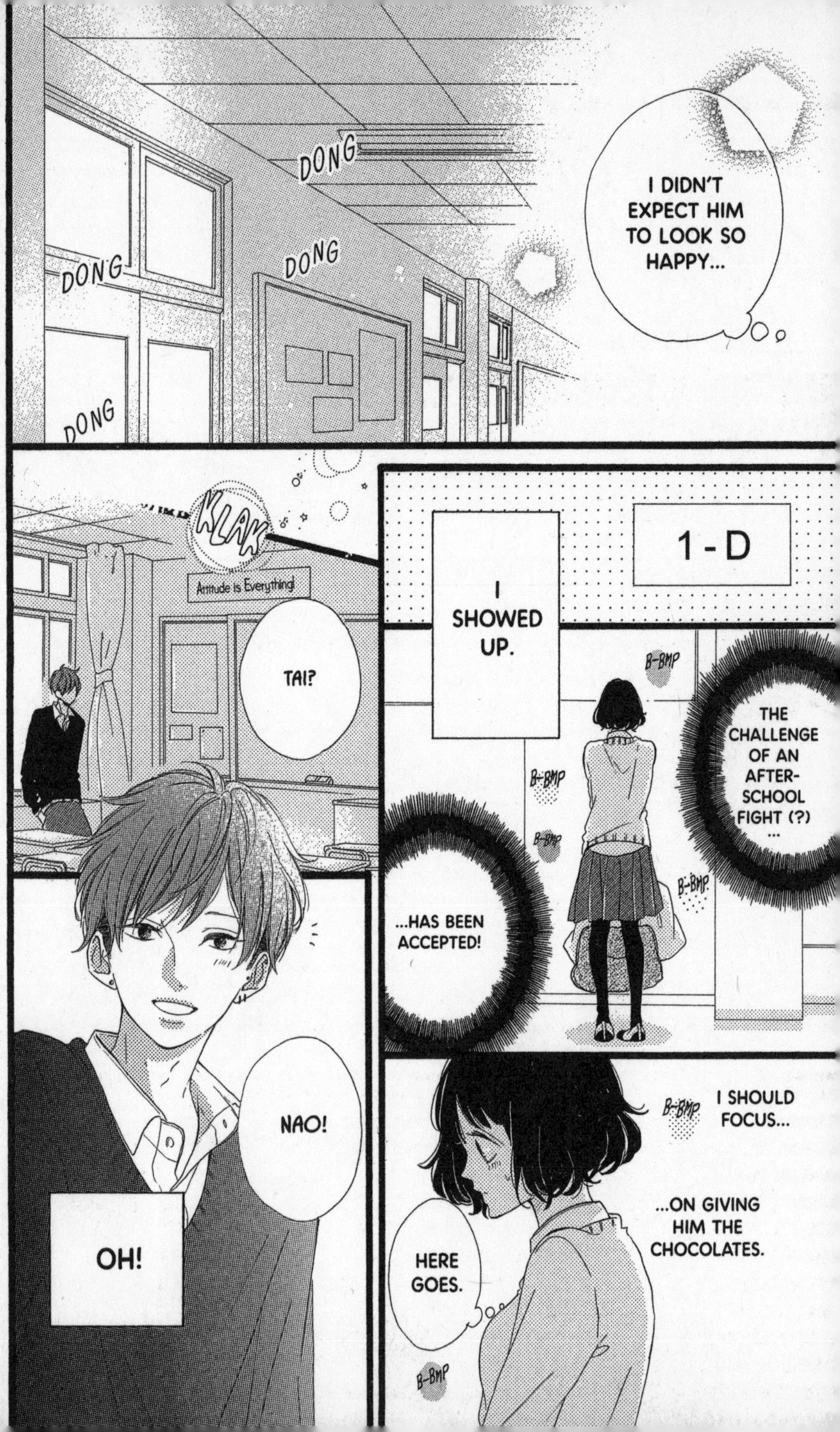
I DIDN'T EXPECT HIM TO LOOK SO HAPPY...
DONG
DONG
DONG
DONG
1 - D
I SHOWED UP.
B-BMP
B-BMP
B-BMP
B-BMP
THE CHALLENGE OF AN AFTER-SCHOOL FIGHT (?) ...
...HAS BEEN ACCEPTED!
B-BMP
I SHOULD FOCUS...
...ON GIVING HIM THE CHOCOLATES.
HERE GOES.
B-BMP
KLAK
Attitude is Everything!
TAI?
NAO!
OH!

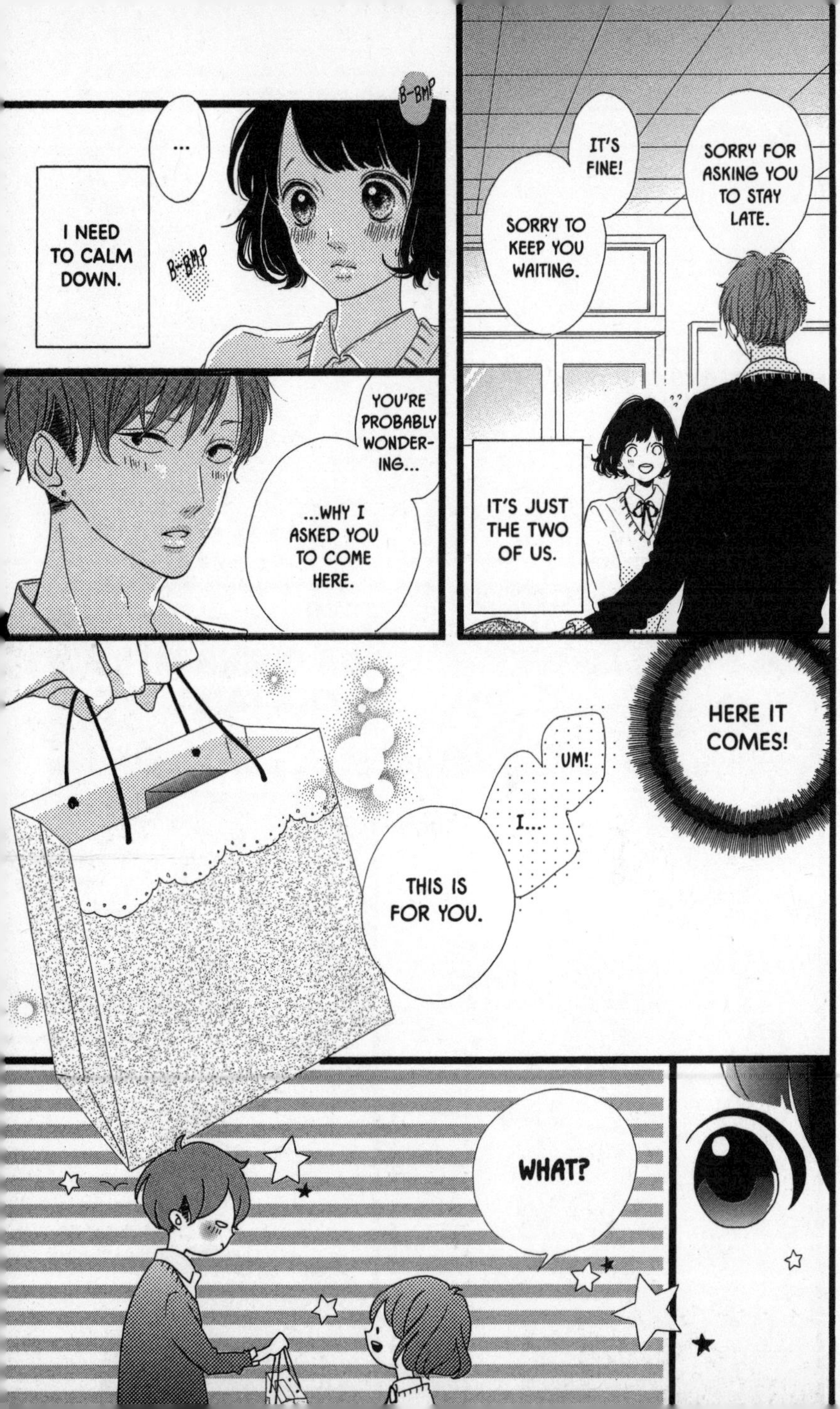
SORRY FOR ASKING YOU TO STAY LATE.
IT'S FINE!
SORRY TO KEEP YOU WAITING.
IT'S JUST THE TWO OF US.
B-BMP
...
I NEED TO CALM DOWN.
B-BMP
YOU'RE PROBABLY WONDER-ING...
...WHY I ASKED YOU TO COME HERE.
HERE IT COMES!
UM!
I...
THIS IS FOR YOU.
WHAT?

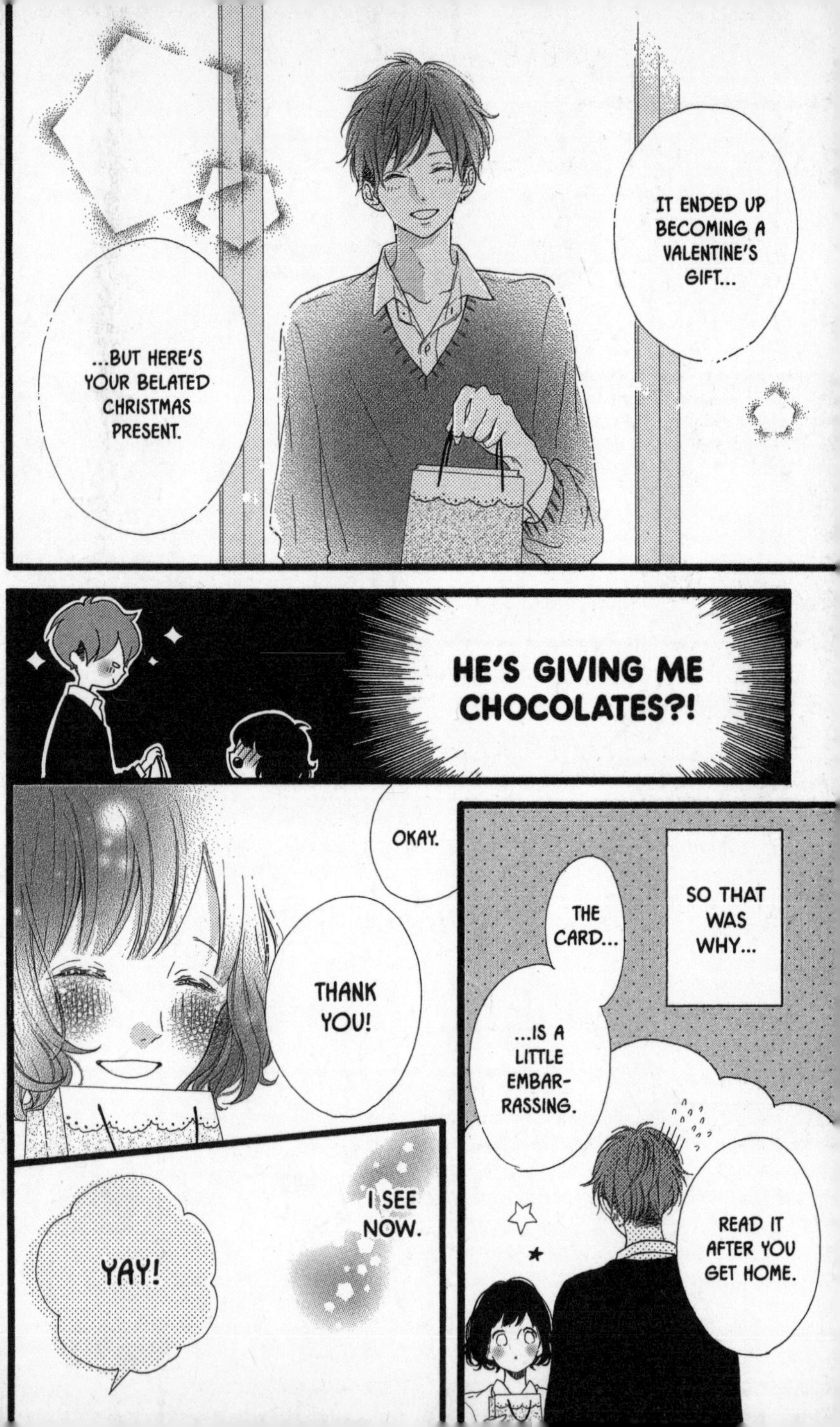
IT ENDED UP BECOMING A VALENTINE'S GIFT...
...BUT HERE'S YOUR BELATED CHRISTMAS PRESENT.
HE'S GIVING ME CHOCOLATES?!
SO THAT WAS WHY...
THE CARD...
...IS A LITTLE EMBAR-RASSING.
READ IT AFTER YOU GET HOME.
OKAY.
THANK YOU!
I SEE NOW.
YAY!

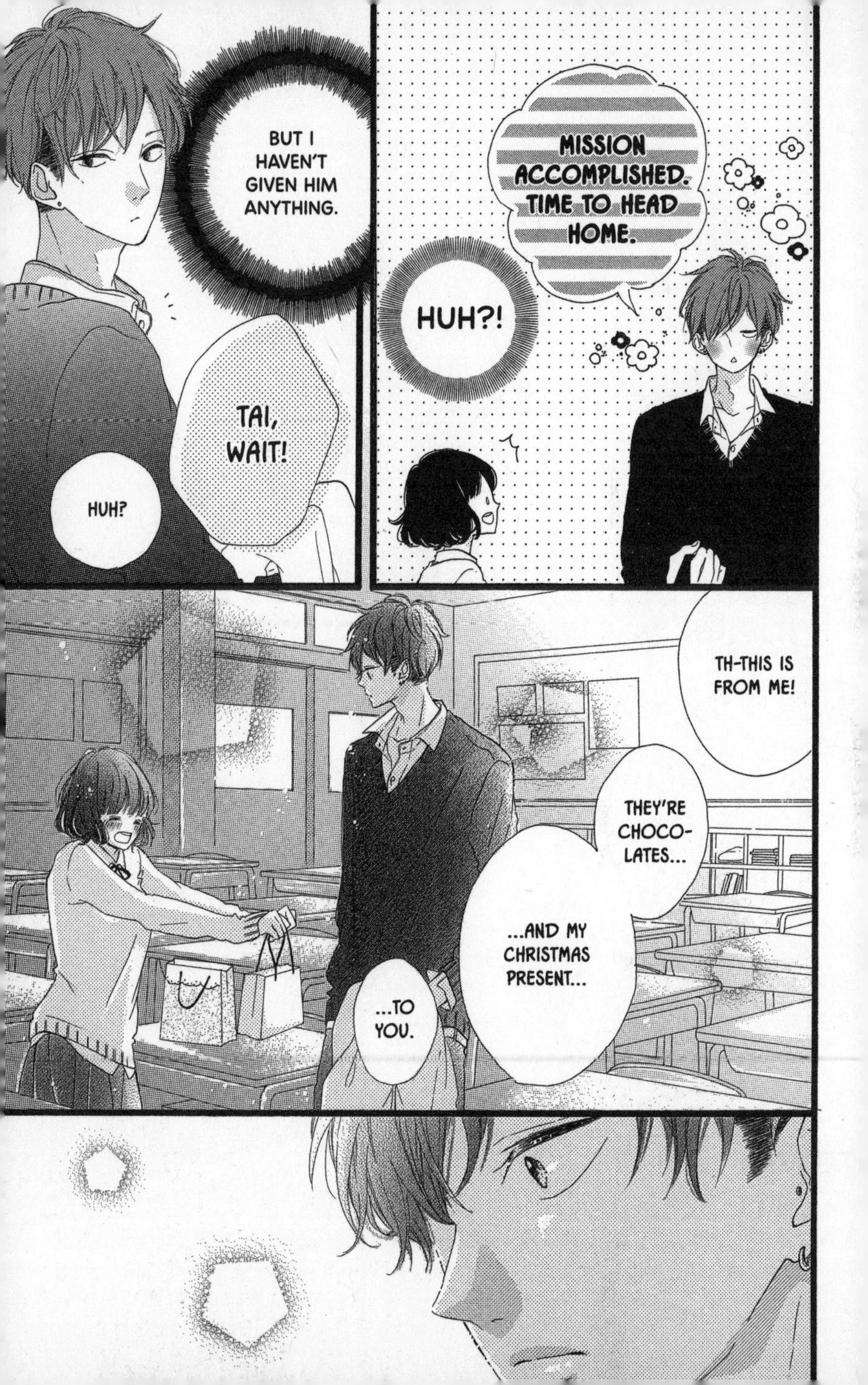
MISSION ACCOMPLISHED. TIME TO HEAD HOME.
HUH?!
BUT I HAVEN'T GIVEN HIM ANYTHING.
TAI, WAIT!
HUH?
TH-THIS IS FROM ME!
THEY'RE CHOCO-LATES...
...AND MY CHRISTMAS PRESENT...
...TO YOU.

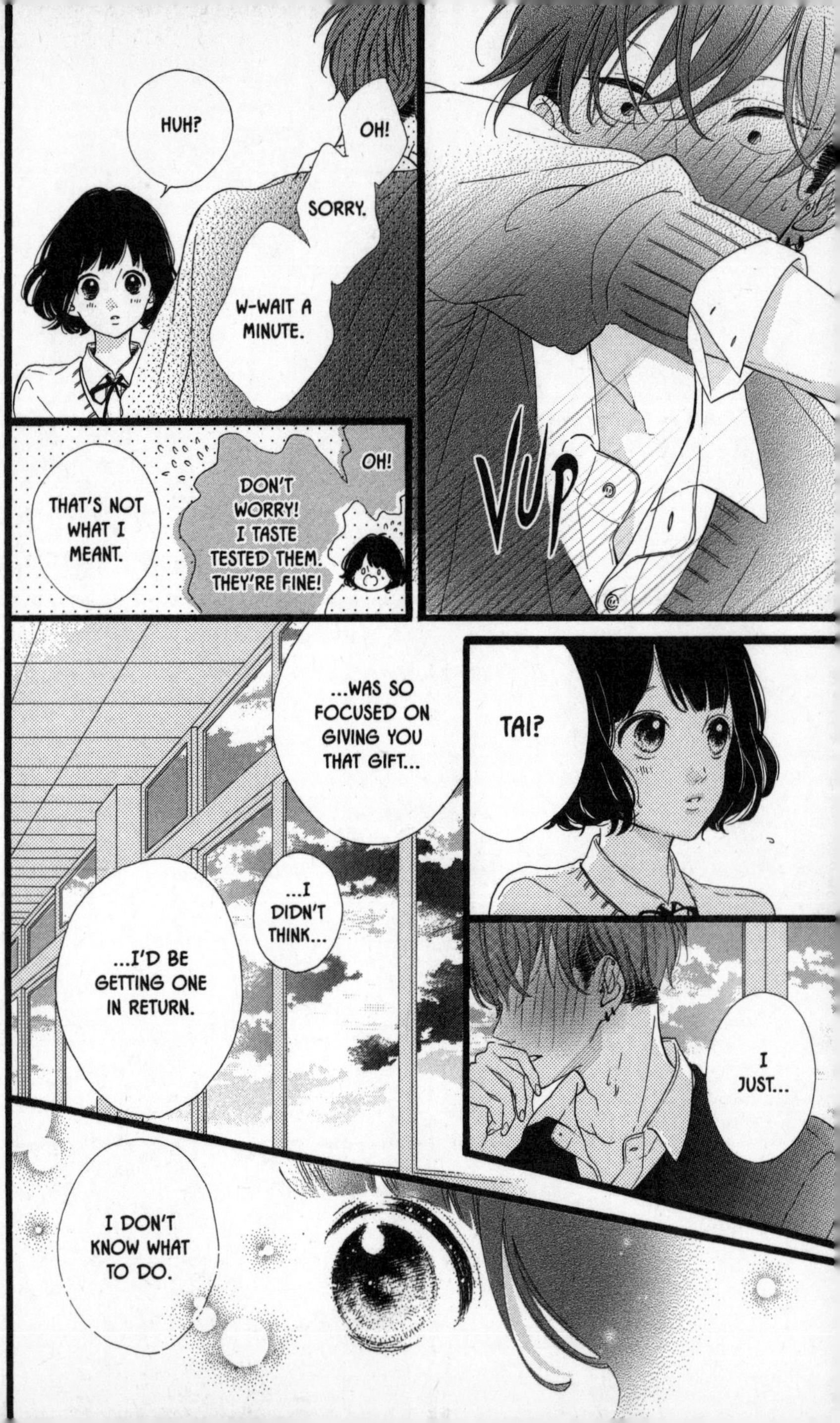
VUP
HUH?
OH!
SORRY.
W-WAIT A MINUTE.
OH!
DON'T WORRY! I TASTE TESTED THEM. THEY'RE FINE!
THAT'S NOT WHAT I MEANT.
TAI?
I JUST...
...WAS SO FOCUSED ON GIVING YOU THAT GIFT...
...I DIDN'T THINK...
...I'D BE GETTING ONE IN RETURN.
I DON'T KNOW WHAT TO DO.

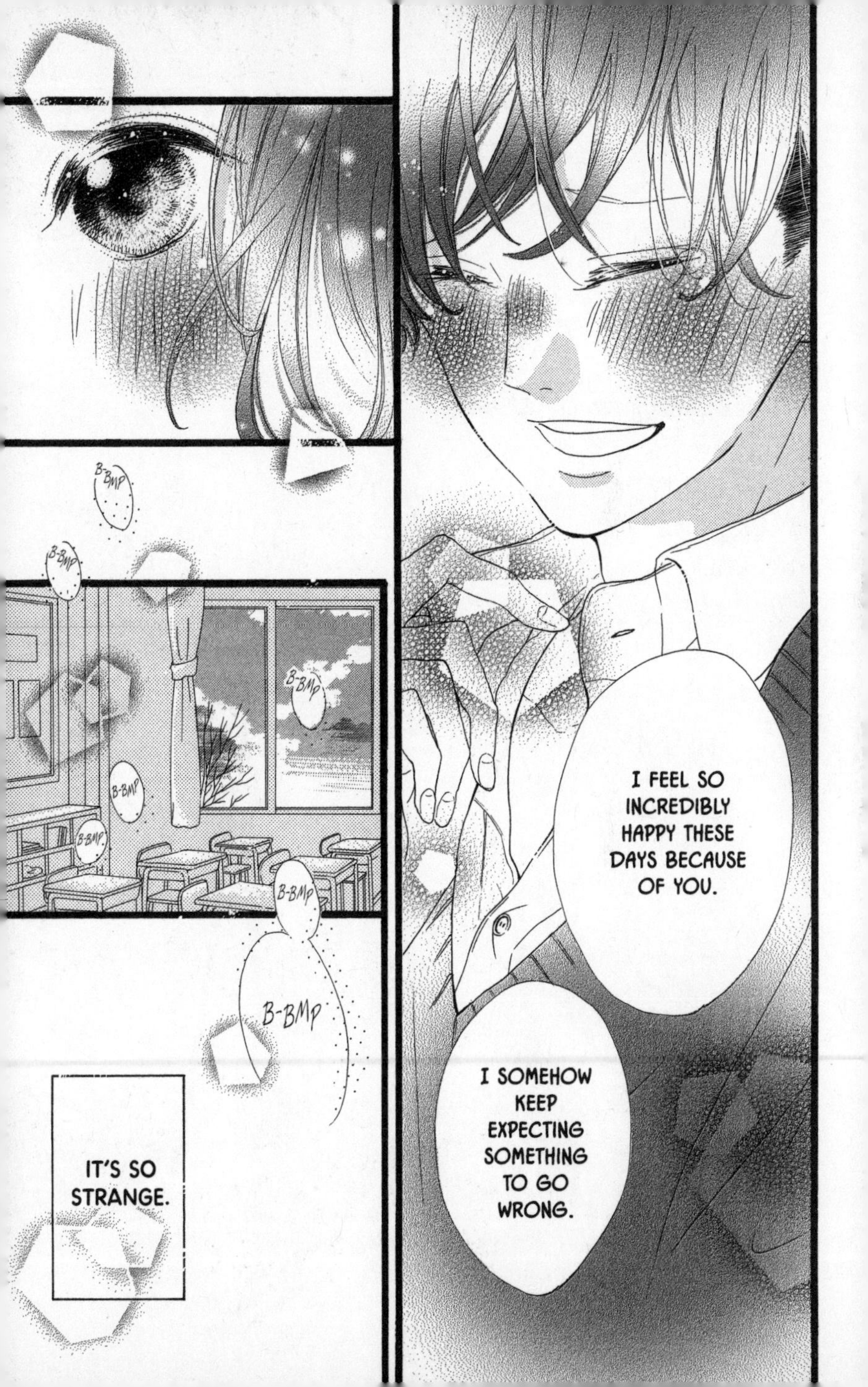
I FEEL SO INCREDIBLY HAPPY THESE DAYS BECAUSE OF YOU.
I SOMEHOW KEEP EXPECTING SOMETHING TO GO WRONG.
B-BMP
B-BMP
B-BMP
B-BMP
B-BMP
B-BMP
B-BMP
IT'S SO STRANGE.

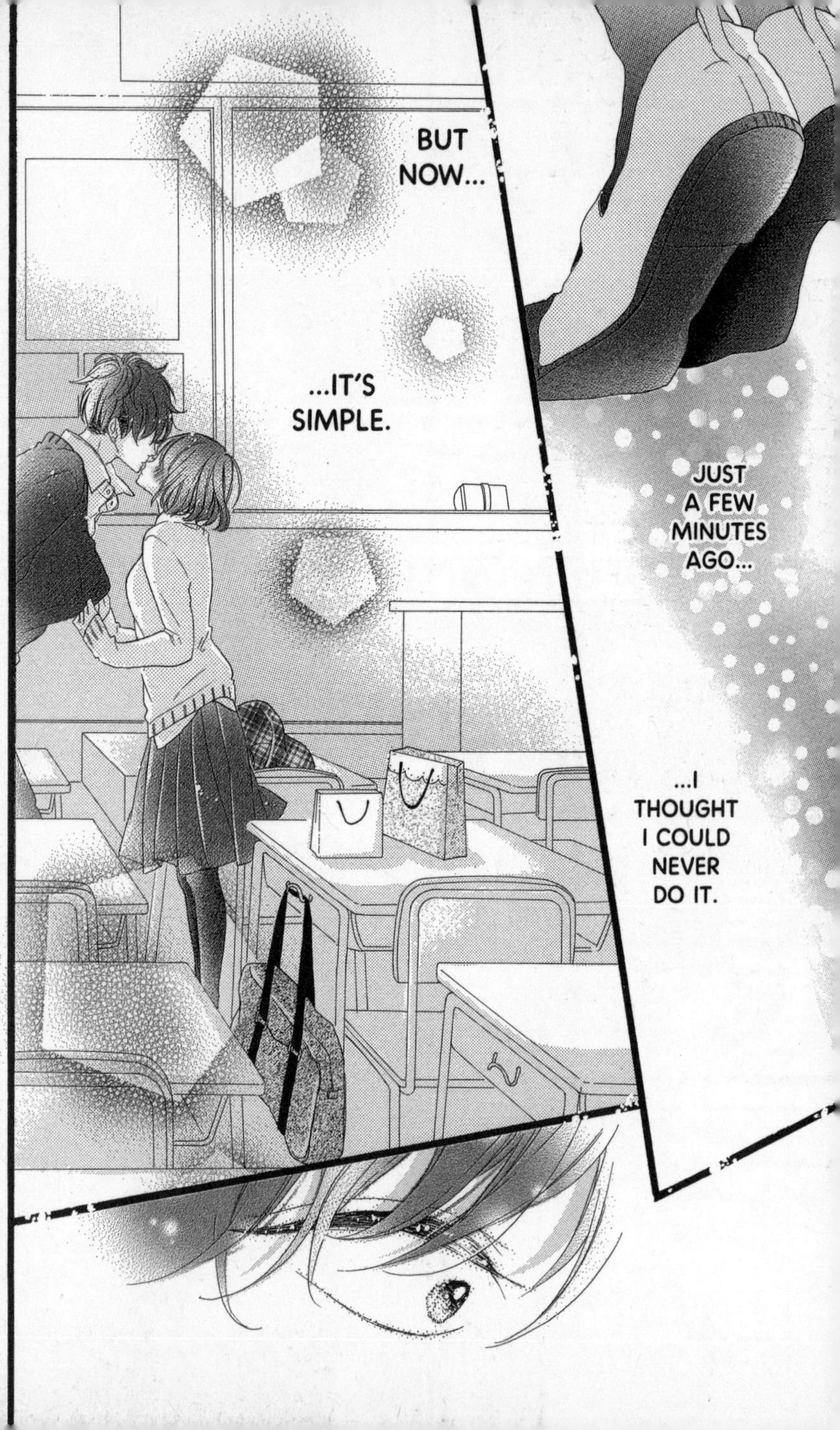
JUST A FEW MINUTES AGO...
...I THOUGHT I COULD NEVER DO IT.
BUT NOW...
...IT'S SIMPLE.

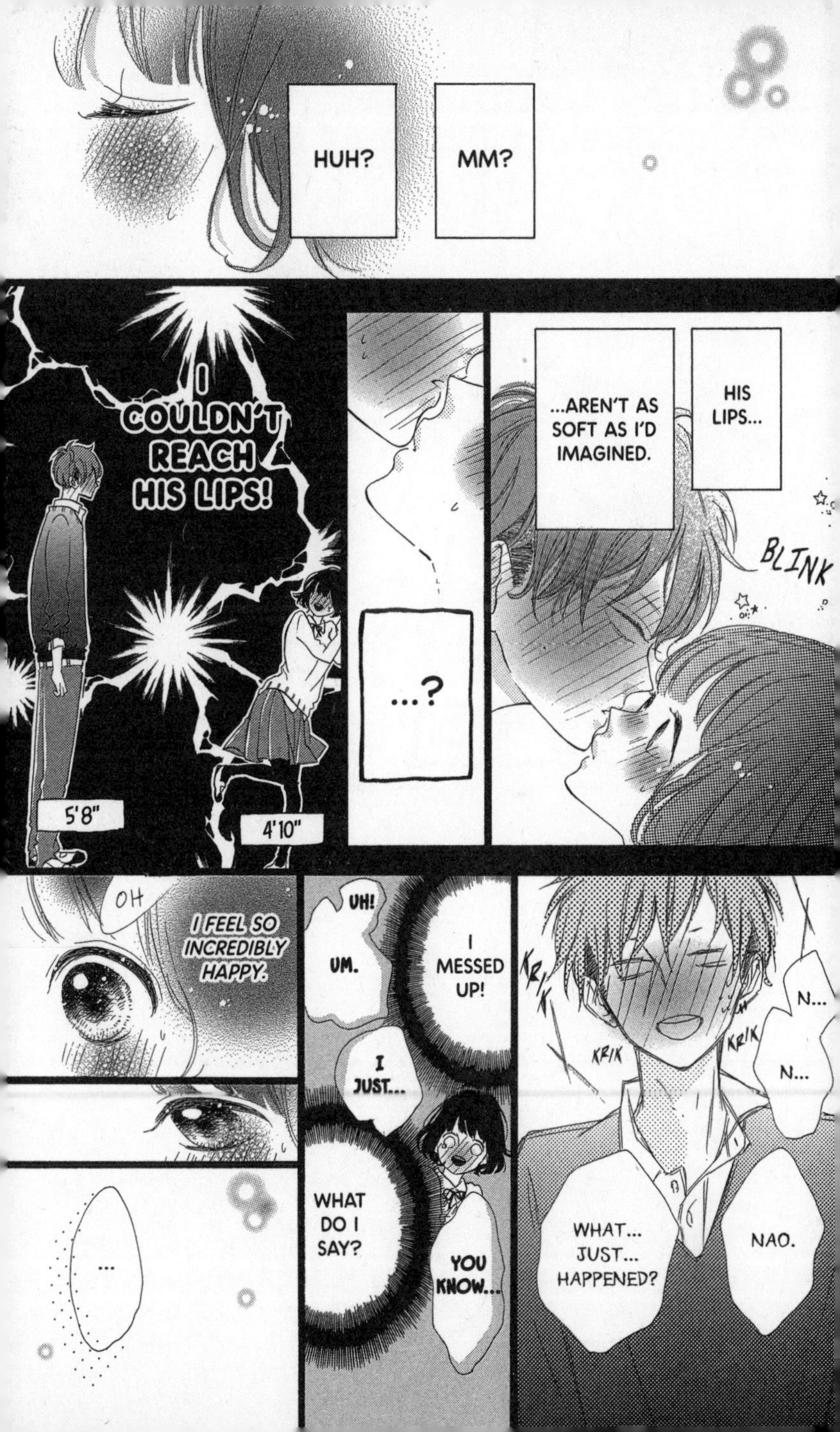
MM?
HUH?
HIS LIPS...
...AREN'T AS SOFT AS I'D IMAGINED.
BLINK
...?
I COULDN'T REACH HIS LIPS!
5'8"
4'10"
N...
N...
KRIK
KRIK
KRIK
NAO.
WHAT... JUST... HAPPENED?
I MESSED UP!
UH!
UM.
I JUST...
WHAT DO I SAY?
YOU KNOW...
OH
I FEEL SO INCREDIBLY HAPPY.
...

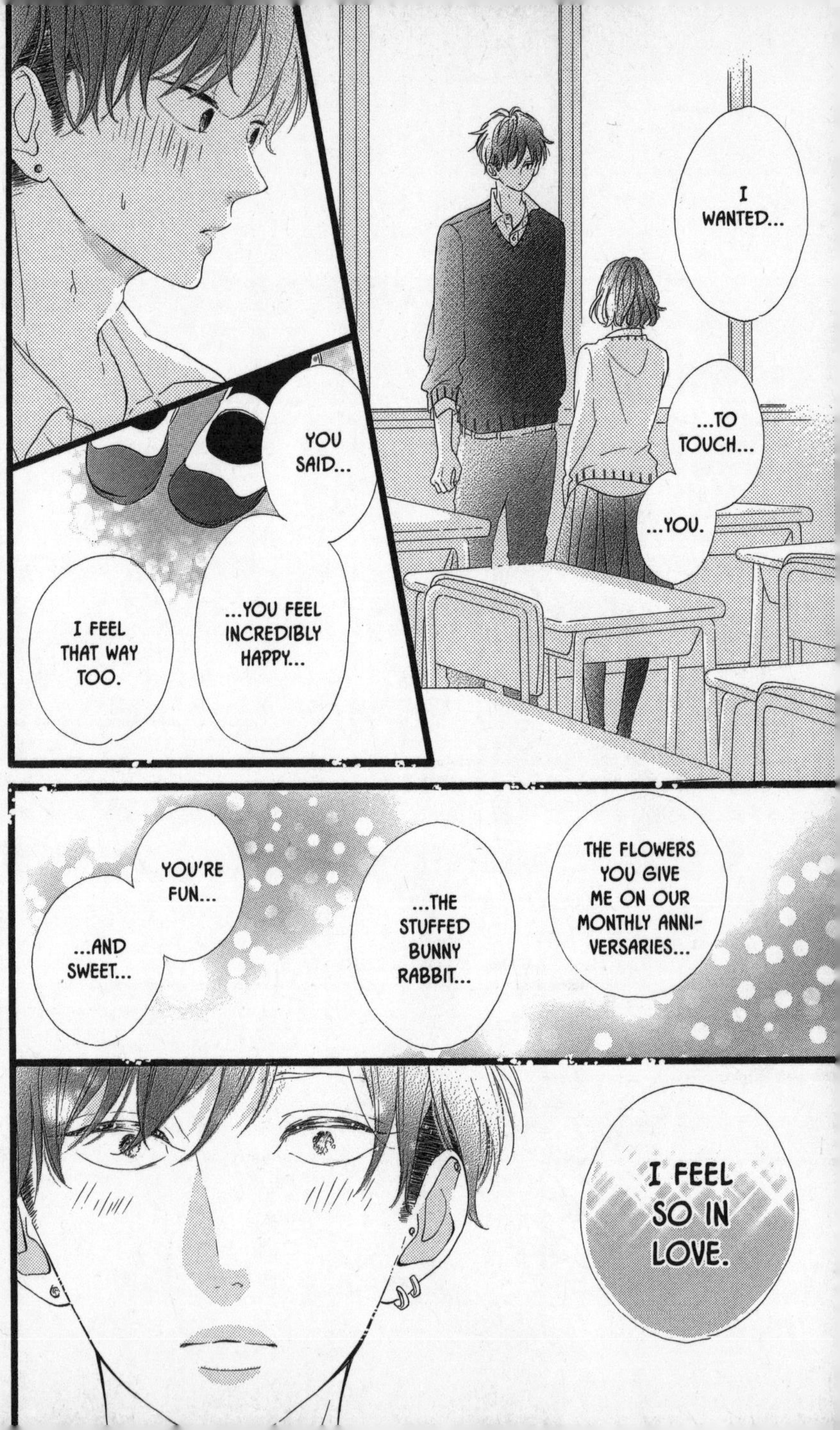
I WANTED...
...TO TOUCH...
...YOU.
YOU SAID...
...YOU FEEL INCREDIBLY HAPPY...
I FEEL THAT WAY TOO.
THE FLOWERS YOU GIVE ME ON OUR MONTHLY ANNI-VERSARIES...
...THE STUFFED BUNNY RABBIT...
YOU'RE FUN...
...AND SWEET...
I FEEL SO IN LOVE.

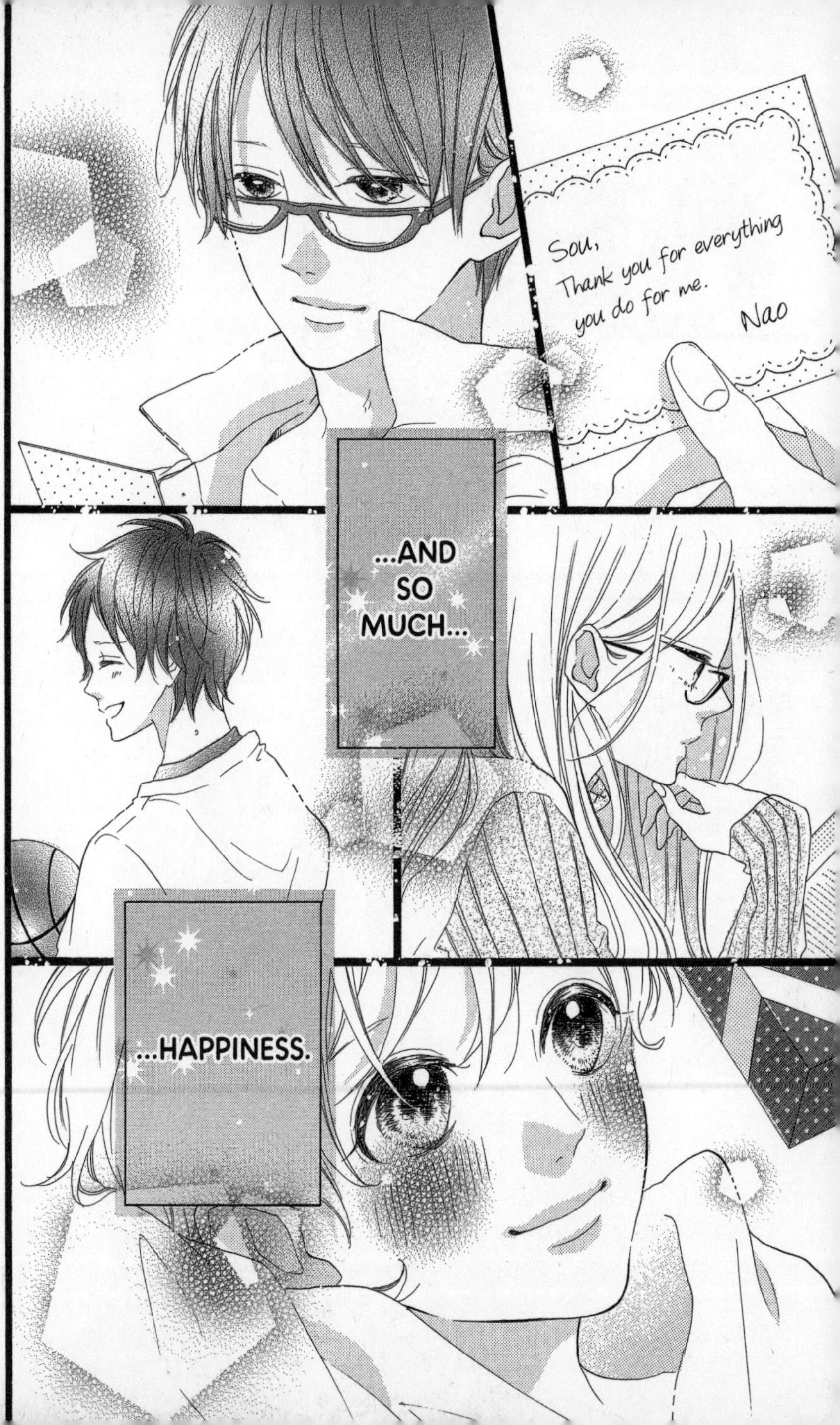
Sou,
Thank you for everything you do for me.
Nao
...AND SO MUCH...
...HAPPINESS.

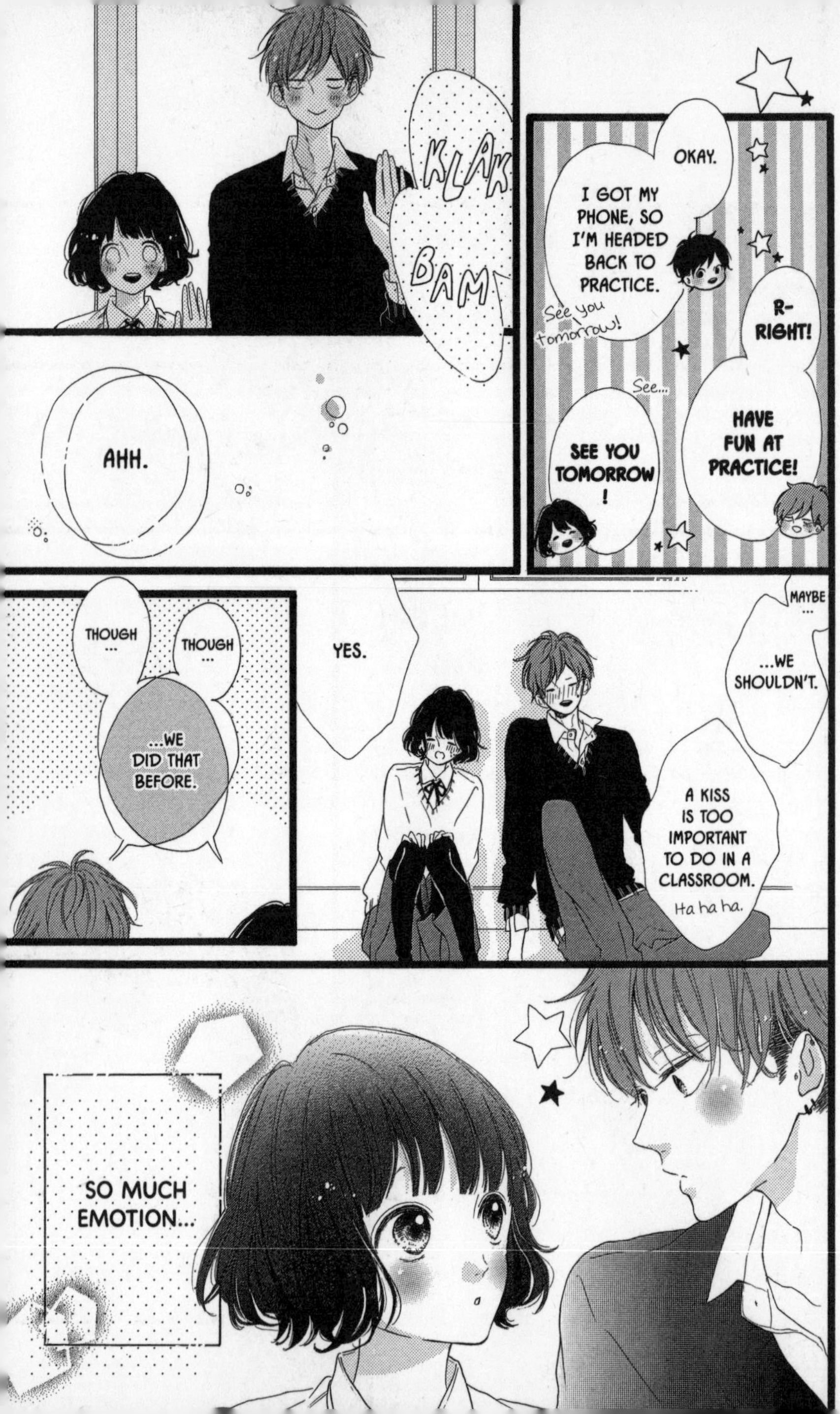
OKAY.
I GOT MY PHONE, SO I'M HEADED BACK TO PRACTICE.
See you tomorrow!
R-RIGHT!
HAVE FUN AT PRACTICE!
See...
SEE YOU TOMORROW!
KLAK
BAM
AHH.
MAYBE...
...WE SHOULDN'T.
A KISS IS TOO IMPORTANT TO DO IN A CLASSROOM.
Ha ha ha.
YES.
THOUGH...
THOUGH...
...WE DID THAT BEFORE.
SO MUCH EMOTION...

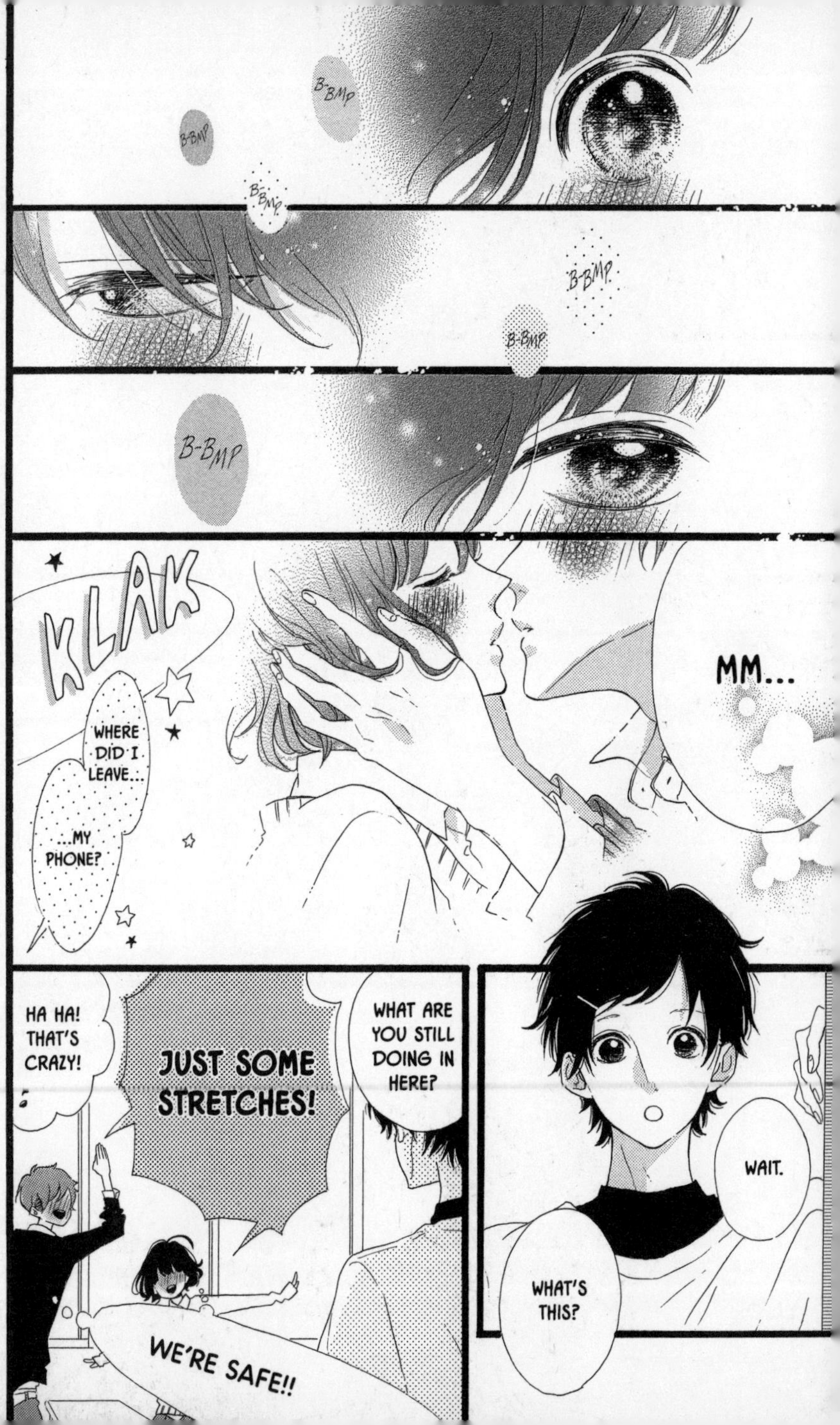
B-BMP
B-BMP
B-BMP
B-BMP
B-BMP
B-BMP
MM...
KLAK
WHERE DID I LEAVE...
...MY PHONE?
WAIT.
WHAT'S THIS?
WHAT ARE YOU STILL DOING IN HERE?
JUST SOME STRETCHES!
HA HA! THAT'S CRAZY!
WE'RE SAFE!!

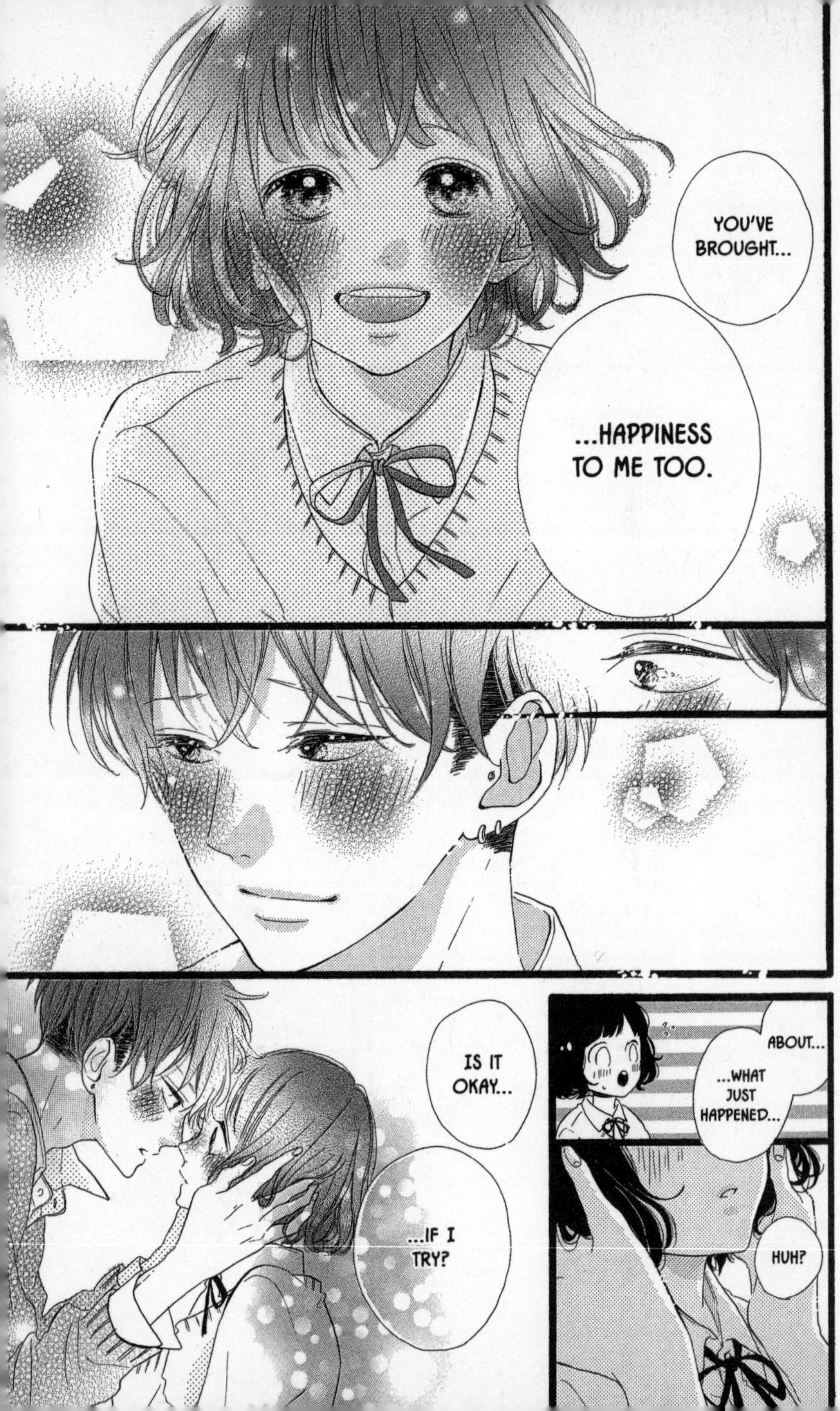
YOU'VE BROUGHT...
...HAPPINESS TO ME TOO.
ABOUT...
...WHAT JUST HAPPENED...
HUH?
IS IT OKAY...
...IF I TRY?

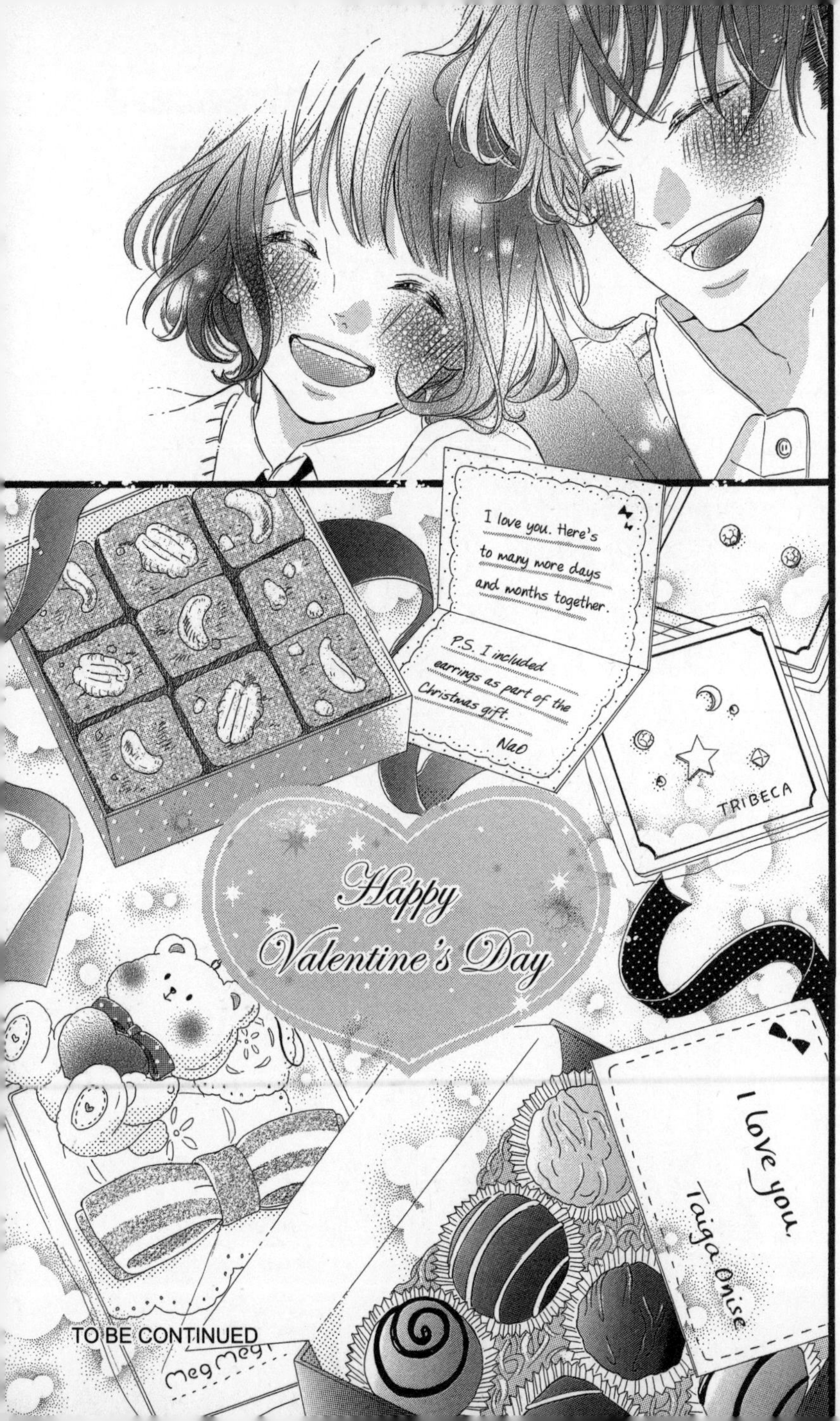
I love you. Here's to many more days and months together.
P.S. I included earrings as part of the Christmas gift.
NaO
TRIBECA
Happy Valentine's Day
I love you.
Taiga Onise
MegMeg
TO BE CONTINUED

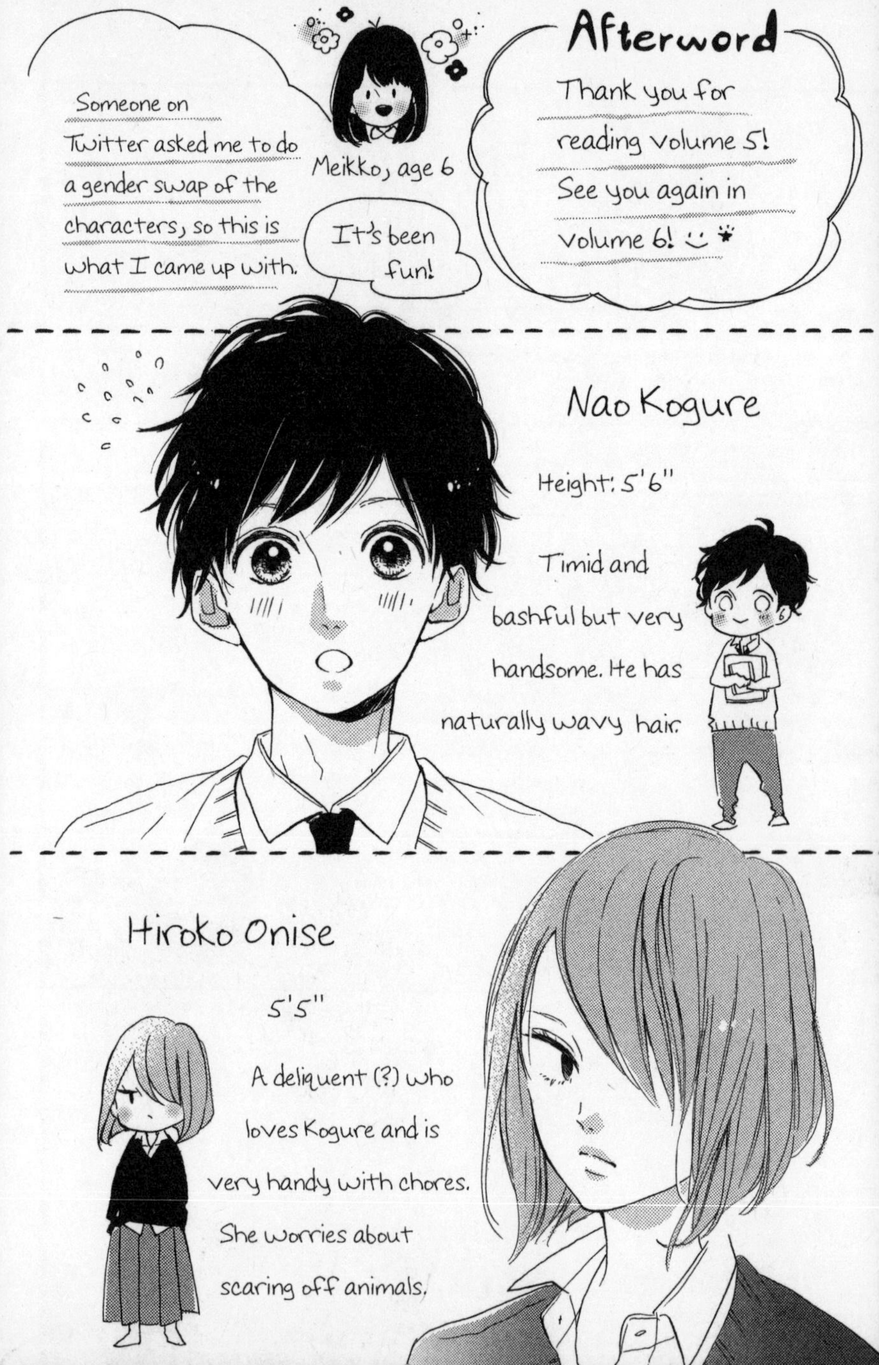
Afterword
Thank you for reading volume 5! See you again in volume 6!
It's been fun!
Meikko, age 6
Someone on Twitter asked me to do a gender swap of the characters, so this is what I came up with.
Nao Kogure
Height: 5'6"
Timid and bashful but very handsome. He has naturally wavy hair.
Hiroko Onise
5'5"
A deliquent (?) who loves Kogure and is very handy with chores. She worries about scaring off animals.

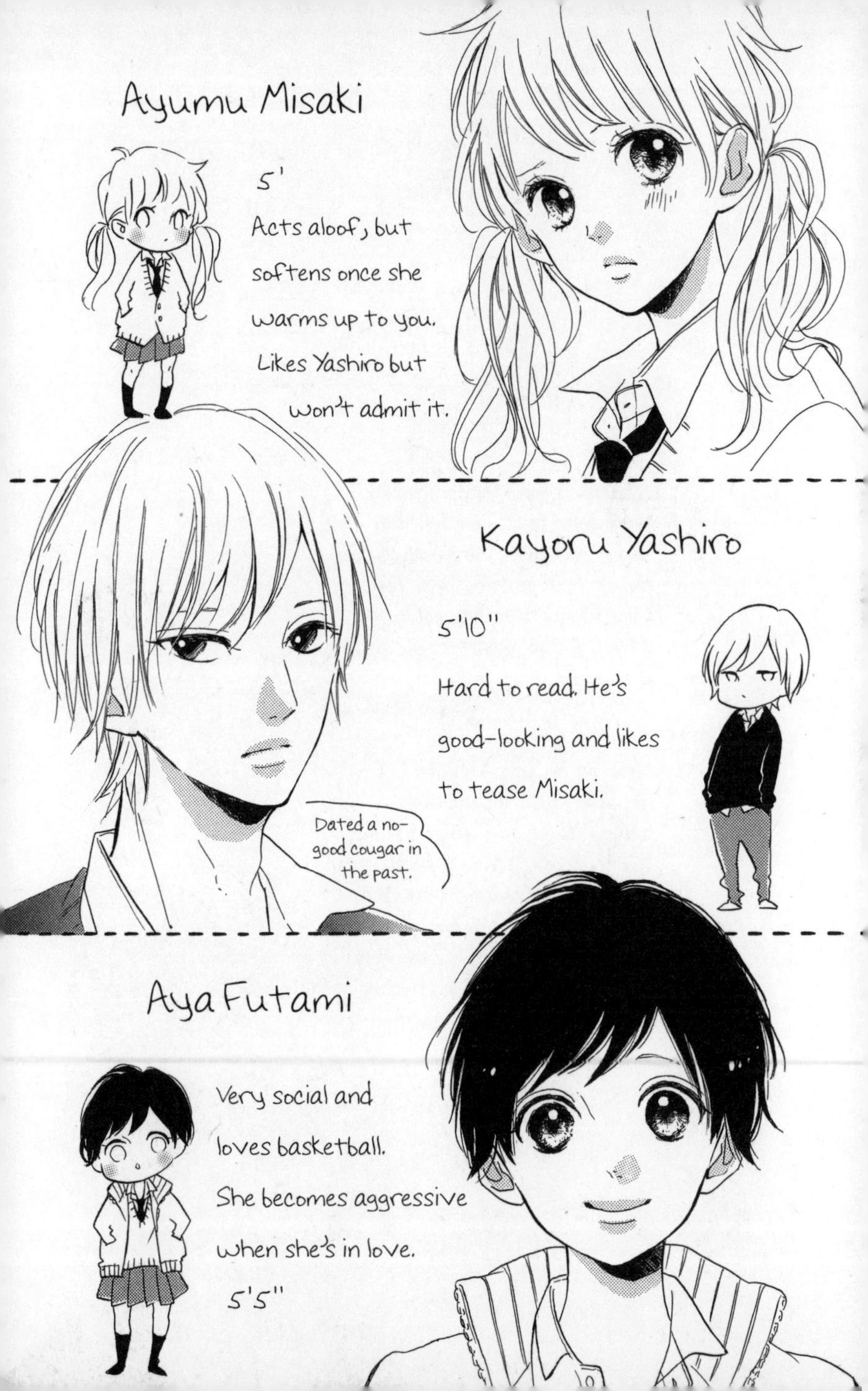
Ayumu Misaki
5'
Acts aloof, but softens once she warms up to you. Likes Yashiro but won't admit it.
Kayoru Yashiro
5'10"
Hard to read. He's good-looking and likes to tease Misaki.
Dated a no-good cougar in the past.
Aya Futami
Very social and loves basketball. She becomes aggressive when she's in love.
5'5"

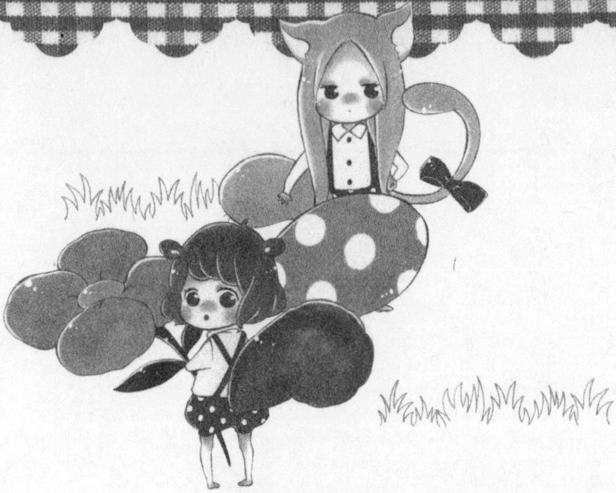

It's already been four and a half years since I first debuted, and two years since I started *Honey So Sweet.* Time is flying by so fast, I feel like I can't keep up! (*laugh*) Thank you so much for reading this!

—Amu Meguro

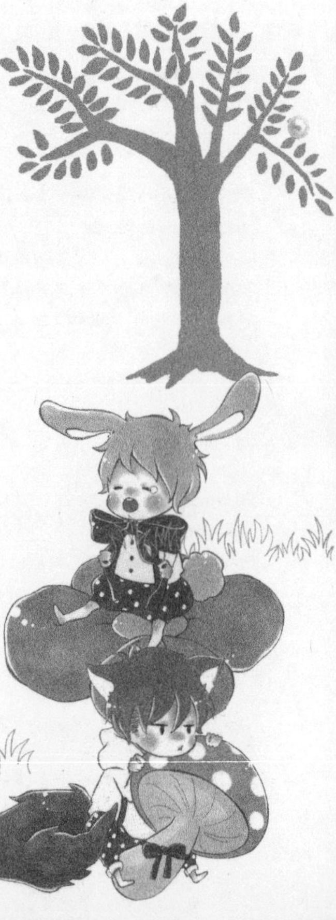

Newcomer Amu Meguro debuted with the one-shot manga *Makka na Ringo ni Kuchizuke O* (A Kiss for a Bright Red Apple). Born in Hokkaido, her hobbies are playing with her niece and eating. *Honey So Sweet* is her current series in *Bessatsu Margaret* magazine.

Honey
So Sweet

Shojo Beat Edition

Volume 5

STORY AND ART BY
Amu Meguro

Translation/Katherine Schilling
Touch-Up Art & Lettering/Inori Fukuda Trant
Design/Izumi Evers
Editor/Nancy Thistlethwaite

HONEY © 2012 by Amu Meguro
All rights reserved.
First published in Japan in 2012 by SHUEISHA Inc., Tokyo.
English translation rights arranged by SHUEISHA Inc.

Printed in the U.S.A.

Published by VIZ Media, LLC
P.O. Box 77010
San Francisco, CA 94107

10 9 8 7 6 5 4 3 2 1
First printing, January 2017

www.viz.com   www.shojobeat.com

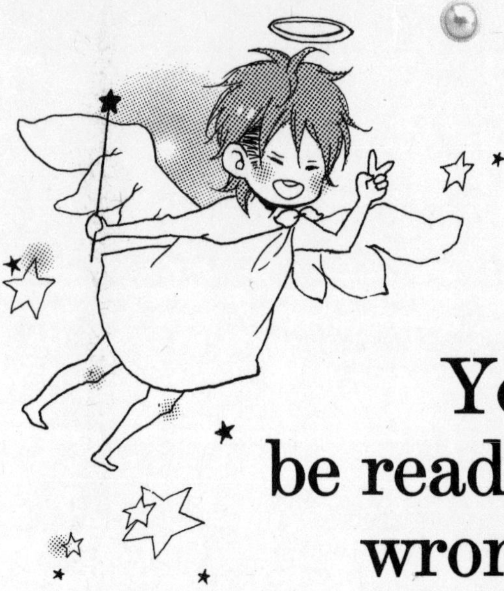

You may be reading the wrong way!

This book reads right to left to maintain the original presentation and art of the Japanese edition, so action, sound effects and word balloons are reversed. This diagram shows how to follow the panels. Turn to the other side of the book to begin.

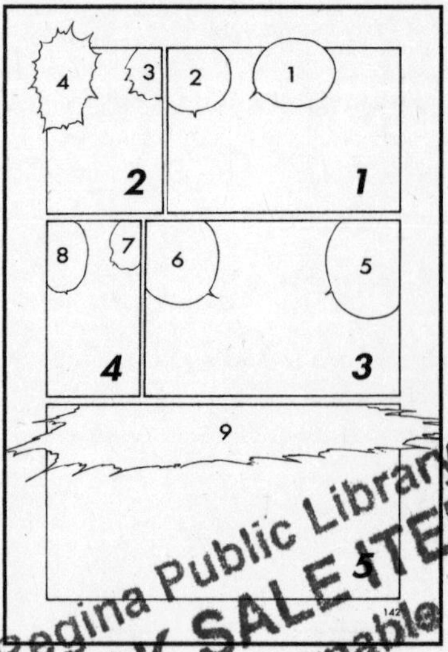
1
2
1
3
4
2
5
6
3
7
8
4
9
5
142